DANGEROUS NEIGHBORS
Page 143

WORKS
of
JULES VERNE

EDITED BY

CHARLES F. HORNE, Ph.D.

Professor of English, College of the City of New York;
Author of "The Technique of the Novel," etc.

WILDSIDE PRESS

CONTENTS

VOLUME TWO

ILLUSTRATIONS

Volume Two

INTRODUCTION TO VOLUME TWO

AVING won the attention of the public with " Five Weeks in a Balloon," Jules Verne wrote in rapid succession several truly masterly tales. Of these remarkable inventions of the human mind, " A Journey to the Center of the Earth " was the first to be completed in its present form. It was published in 1864, in a series of books by Verne, denominated " Voyages Extraordinaires." This series, started in that year by the publisher Hetzel, has been continued to the present time.

This particular " Voyage " has sometimes been declared our author's masterpiece. In it he for the first time gives free rein to that bold yet scientifically exact imagination whereby he has constructed for us in fancy the entire universe. There is nothing in all the daring visions of this tale which even to-day our scientists would declare impossible. The interior of the earth is still unknown; and there may well be rifts, passages, descending from extinct volcanoes and penetrating far within. There may well be huge cavities, bubbles left in the cooling mass, vast enough to harbor inland seas, and shelter many of the ancient forms of life now extinct upon earth's surface.

The main scientific objection to this, as indeed to most of the more fanciful of Verne's tales, lies in the extravagant means he employs to bring his explorers home again from their reckless ventures. But, as romance obviously demands their return somehow, science discreetly accepts in silence the astonishing accidents and coincidences whereby they escape the doom they have invited.

The other narrative included in the present volume, the first book of " The Adventures of Captain Hatteras," was also published by Hetzel in 1864, being begun even before the "*Journey to the Center of the Earth.*" This *vigorous Arctic tale was used to found and introduce a "Magazine of Adventure," which has been continued somewhat irregularly ever since. After the adventures, trials and triumphs of Captain Hatteras had been completed in another tale, the two were revised and republished; and they are here given in their later form.*

The first book, "The English at the North Pole," contains an accurate picture of Arctic life and of the Arctic geography known to the world of 1864. The account of the Franklin expedition and of the persistent and heroic search for its relief is carefully studied and complete, only it necessarily fails to include the later investigations of the American expedition under Lieutenant Schwatka. These finally settled the last details of the historic tragedy.

In " The English at the North Pole " as in " Five Weeks in a Balloon," Verne invents little. Here, despite the misleading title, the characters do not penetrate beyond known bounds; and their experiences are just such as our author had read in his careful study of the books of the polar explorers. But these adventures are here made intense and living, and are woven by the born story-teller into a thrilling tale.

A Trip to the Center of the Earth

CHAPTER I
MY UNCLE MAKES A GREAT DISCOVERY

OOKING back to all that has occurred to me since that eventful day, I am scarcely able to believe in the reality of my adventures. They were truly so wonderful that even now I am bewildered when I think of them.

My uncle was a German, though I am English, he having married my mother's sister. Being very much attached to his fatherless nephew, he invited me to study under him in his home in the fatherland. This home was in a large town, and my uncle a professor of philosophy, chemistry, geology, mineralogy, and many other ologies.

One day, after passing some hours in the laboratory—my uncle being absent at the time—I suddenly felt the necessity of renovating the tissues—*i. e.*, I was hungry, and was about to rouse up our old French cook, when my uncle, Professor Von Hardwigg, suddenly opened the street door, and came rushing upstairs.

Now, Professor Hardwigg, my worthy uncle, is by no means a bad sort of man; he is, however, choleric and original. To hear with him means to obey; and scarcely had his heavy feet resounded within our joint domicile than he shouted for me to attend upon him. " Harry—Harry—Harry——"

I hastened to obey, but before I could reach his room, jumping three steps at a time, he was stamping his right foot upon the landing. " Harry! " he cried, in a frantic tone, " are you coming up? "

To tell the truth, at that moment I was far more interested in the question as to what was to constitute our dinner than in any problem of science; to me soup was

3

more interesting than soda, an omelette more tempting than arithmetic, and an artichoke of ten times more value than any amount of asbestos. But my uncle was not a man to be kept waiting; so adjourning all minor questions, I presented myself before him.

He was a very learned man. Now, most persons in this category supply themselves with information, as peddlers do with goods, for the benefit of others, and lay up stores in order to diffuse them abroad for the benefit of society in general. Not so my excellent uncle, Professor Hardwigg; he studied, he consumed the midnight oil, he pored over heavy tomes, and digested huge quartos and folios, in order to keep the knowledge acquired to himself. There was a reason, and it may be regarded as a good one, why my uncle objected to display his learning more than was absolutely necessary; he stammered, and when intent upon explaining the phenomena of the heavens, was apt to find himself at fault, and allude in such a vague way to sun, moon, and stars, that few were able to comprehend his meaning. To tell the honest truth, when the right word would not come, it was generally replaced by a very powerful adjective.

In connection with the sciences there are many almost unpronounceable names—names very much resembling those of Welsh villages; and my uncle being very fond of using them, his habit of stammering was not thereby improved. In fact, there were periods in his discourse when he would finally give up and swallow his discomfiture—in a glass of water.

As I said, my uncle, Professor Hardwigg, was a very learned man; and I now add a most kind relative. I was bound to him by the double ties of affection and interest. I took deep interest in all his doings, and hoped some day to be almost as learned myself. It was a rare thing for me to be absent from his lectures. Like him, I preferred mineralogy to all the other sciences. My anxiety was to gain *real knowledge of the earth.* Geology and mineralogy were to us the sole objects of life, and in connection with these studies many a fair specimen of stone, chalk, or metal did we break with our hammers.

But before I state the subject on which my uncle wished to confer with me, I must say a word about his personal appearance. Alas! my readers will see a very different portrait of him at a future time, after he has gone through the fearful adventures yet to be related.

My uncle was fifty years old; tall, thin, and wiry. Large spectacles hid, to a certain extent, his vast, round and goggle eyes, while his nose was irreverently compared to a thin file. So much indeed did it resemble that useful article, that a compass was said in his presence to have made considerable deviation. The truth being told, however, the only article really attracted to my uncle's nose was tobacco.

Another peculiarity of his was, that he always stepped a yard at a time, clenched his fists as if he were going to hit you, and was, when in one of his peculiar humors, very far from a pleasant companion.

It is further necessary to observe, that he lived in a very nice house, in that very nice street, the Königstrasse at Hamburg. Though lying in the center of a town, it was perfectly rural in its aspect—half wood, half bricks, with old-fashioned gables—one of the few old houses spared by the great fire of 1842. When I say a nice house, I mean a handsome house—old, tottering, and not exactly comfortable to English notions: a house a little off the perpendicular and inclined to fall into the neighboring canal; exactly the house for a wandering artist to depict; all the more that you could scarcely see it for ivy and a magnificent old tree which grew over the door.

My uncle was rich; his house was his own property, and he had a considerable private income. To my notion the best part of his possessions was his god-daughter, Gretchen, who unfortunately was away upon a visit on that momentous day. The old cook, the young lady, the Professor and I were the sole inmates of his home.

I loved mineralogy, I loved geology. To me there was nothing like pebbles—and if my uncle had been in a little less of a fury, we should have been the happiest of families. To prove the excellent Hardwigg's impatience, I solemnly declare that when the flowers in the drawing-room pots began to grow, he rose every morning at four o'clock to make them grow quicker by pulling the leaves!

Having described my uncle, I will now give an account of our interview. He received me in his study; a perfect museum, containing every natural curiosity that can well be imagined—minerals, however, predominating. Every one was familiar to me, having been catalogued by my own hand. My uncle, apparently oblivious of the fact that he had summoned me to his presence, was absorbed in a book. He was particularly fond of early editions, tall copies, and unique works.

"Wonderful!" he cried, tapping his forehead. "Wonderful—wonderful!" It was one of those yellow-leaved volumes now rarely found on stalls, and to me it appeared to possess but little value. My uncle, however, was in raptures. He admired its binding, the clearness of its characters, the ease with which it opened in his hand, and repeated aloud, half-a-dozen times, that it was very, very old.

To my fancy he was making a great fuss about nothing, but it was not my province to say so. On the contrary, I professed considerable interest in the subject, and asked him what it was about.

"It is the Heims-Kringla of Snorre Tarleson," he said, "the celebrated Icelandic author of the tweifth century—it is a true and correct account of the Norwegian princes who reigned in Iceland."

My next question related to the language in which it was written. I hoped at all events it was translated into German. My uncle was indignant at the very thought, and declared he wouldn't give a penny for a translation. His delight was to have found the original work in the Icelandic tongue, which he declared to be one of the most magnificent and yet simple idioms in the world—while at the same time its grammatical combinations were the most varied known to students.

"About as easy as German?" was my insidious remark.

My uncle shrugged his shoulders.

"The letters at all events," I said, "are rather difficult of comprehension."

"It is a Runic manuscript, the language of the original population of Iceland, invented by Odin himself," cried my uncle, angry at my ignorance.

I was about to venture upon some misplaced joke on the subject, when a small scrap of parchment fell out of the leaves. Like a hungry man snatching at a morsel of bread the Professor seized it. It was about five inches by three and was scrawled over in the most extraordinary fashion.

The lines opening the next chapter are an exact fac-simile of what was written on the venerable piece of parch-ment—and have wonderful importance, as they induced my uncle to undertake the most wonderful series of adventures which ever fell to the lot of human beings.

My uncle looked keenly at the document for some mo-ments and then declared that it was Runic. The letters were similar to those in the book, but then what did they mean? This was exactly what I wanted to know.

Now, as I had a strong conviction that the Runic alpha-bet and dialect were simply an invention to mystify poor human nature, I was delighted to find that my uncle knew as much about the matter as I did—which was nothing. At all events, the tremulous motion of his fingers made me think so.

" And yet," he muttered to himself, " it is old Icelandic, I am sure of it."

My uncle ought to have known, for he was a perfect polyglot dictionary in himself. He did not pretend, like a certain learned pundit, to speak the two thousand lan-guages and four thousand idioms made use of in different parts of the globe, but he did know all the more important ones.

It is a matter of great doubt to me now, to what violent measures my uncle's impetuosity might have led him, had not the clock struck two, and our old French cook called out to let us know that dinner was on the table.

" Bother the dinner! " cried my uncle. But I was hun-gry, I sallied forth to the dining-room, where I took up my usual quarters. Out of politeness I waited three minutes, but no sign of my uncle, the Professor. I was surprised. He was not usually so blind to the pleasure of a good din-ner. It was the acme of German luxury—parsley soup, a ham omelette with sorrel trimmings, an oyster of veal stewed with prunes, delicious fruit, and sparkling Moselle. For the sake of poring over that musty old piece of parchment, my uncle forbore to share our meal. To satisfy my con-science, I ate for both.

The old cook and housekeeper was nearly out of her mind. After taking so much trouble, to find her master not appear at dinner was to her a sad disappointment—which, as she watched the havoc I was making on the viands, became also alarm.   If my uncle were to come to table after all?

Suddenly, just as I had consumed the last apple and drank the last glass of wine, a terrible voice was heard at no great distance.   It was my uncle roaring for me to come to him. I made very nearly one leap of it—so loud, so fierce was his tone.

CHAPTER II
THE MYSTERIOUS PARCHMENT

```
ᛪ.ᛆᛘᛔᛘ    ᛏ�429ᛏᚨᛏ    ᛘᛏᛏᛁᛒᚨ
ᛘᛍᛏᛘᛘᚤᚠ  ᚤᛆᛏᛏᛁᛏᚠ    ᛘᛁᛏᛒᛆᛍᛏ
ᛎᛏ.ᛘ9ᛏᛘ  9ᛏᚴ9ᛏᛏᛘ    ᛘᚴ ᛒᛒᛆᛆᛘ
ᛏᚤᛏᛘ9ᛏ   ᛘᚴ9ᛏᚤᛏ      ᚴᚴᛁᛘᛘ9
9ᛏᚢ99ᚴ    .ᛘᛘᚤᛆᚤ      ᛁᛏ99ᛒᛘ
ᚤᚤᛒᛆᚤᛁ    ᛏᛏᚢ ᛏᚢᚤ    ᚠᛆ9ᛆᛏᚢ
ᛒᛏ,ᛁ9ᚤ    ᛘᛘᛏᛁᛒᚨ      ᚤᛏᛒᛁᛁᛁ
```

" I DECLARE," cried my uncle, striking the table fiercely with his fist, " I declare to you it is Runic—and contains some wonderful secret, which I must get at, at any price."

I was about to reply when he stopped me.   " Sit down," he said, quite fiercely, " and write to my dictation."

I obeyed.   " I will substitute," he said, " a letter of our alphabet for that of the Runic: we will then see what that will produce.   Now, begin and make no mistakes."

The dictation commenced with the following incomprehensible result :—

m.rnlls	esruel	seecJde
sgtssmf	unteief	niedrke
kt,samn	atrateS	Saodrrn
emtnael	nuaect	rrilSa
Atvaar	.nscrc	ieaabs
ccdrmi	eeutul	frantu
dt,iac	oscibo	KediiI

Scarcely giving me time to finish, my uncle snatched the document from my hands and examined it with the most rapt and deep attention.

" I should like to know what it means," he said, after a long period.

I certainly could not tell him, nor did he expect me to— his conversation being uniformly answered by himself.

" I declare it puts me in mind of a cryptograph," he cried, " unless, indeed, the letters have been written without any real meaning; and yet why take so much trouble? Who knows but I may be on the verge of some great discovery? "

My candid opinion was that it was all rubbish! But this opinion I kept carefully to myself, as my uncle's choler was not pleasant to bear. All this time he was comparing the book with the parchment.

" The manuscript volume and the smaller document are written in different hands," he said, " the cryptograph is of much later date than the book; there is an undoubted proof of the correctness of my surmise. The first letter is a double M, which was only added to the Icelandic language in the twelfth century—this makes the parchment two hundred years posterior to the volume."

The circumstance appeared very probable and very logical, but it was all surmise to me.

" To me it appears probable that this sentence was written by some owner of the book. Now who was the owner, is the next important question. Perhaps by great good luck it may be written somewhere in the volume."

With these words Professor Hardwigg took off his spectacles, and, taking a powerful magnifying glass, examined the book carefully. On the fly leaf was what appeared to be a blot of ink, but on examination proved to be a line of writing almost effaced by time. This was what he sought and, after some considerable time, he made out these letters:

ᛏᛉᚾᛏ ᛋᛁᚱᚴᚾᛋᛋᛏᚷ

" Ärne Saknussemm!" he cried in a joyous and triumphant tone, " that is not only an Icelandic name, but of a learned professor of the sixteenth century, a celebrated alchemist."

I bowed as a sign of respect.

" These alchemists," he continued, " Avicena, Bacon, Lully, Paracelsus, were the true, the only learned men of the day. They made surprising discoveries. May not this Saknussemm, nephew mine, have hidden on this bit of parchment some astounding invention? I believe the cryptograph to have a profound meaning—which I must make out."

My uncle walked about the room in a state of excitement almost impossible to describe.

"It may be so, sir," I timidly observed, "but why conceal it from posterity, if it be a useful, a worthy discovery?"

".Why—how should I know? Did not Galileo make a secret of his discoveries in connection with Saturn? But we shall see. Until I discover the meaning of this sentence I will neither eat nor sleep."

"My dear uncle——" I began.

"Nor you either," he added. It was lucky I had taken double allowance that day.

"In the first place," he continued, "there must be a clue to the meaning. If we could find that, the rest would be easy enough."

I began seriously to reflect. The prospect of going without food and sleep was not a promising one, so I determined to do my best to solve the mystery. My uncle, meanwhile, went on with his soliloquy.

"The way to discover it is easy enough. In this document there are one hundred and thirty-two letters, giving seventy-nine consonants to fifty-three vowels. This is about the proportion found in most southern languages, the idioms of the north being much more rich in consonants. We may confidently predict, therefore, that we have to deal with a southern dialect."

Nothing could be more logical.

"Now," said Professor Hardwigg, "to trace the particular language."

"As Shakespeare says, 'that is the question,'" was my rather satirical reply.

"This man Saknussemm," he continued, "was a very learned man: now as he did not write in the language of his birth-place, he probably, like most learned men of the sixteenth century, wrote in Latin. If, however, I prove wrong in this guess, we must try Spanish, French, Italian, Greek, and even Hebrew. My own opinion, though, is decidedly in favor of Latin."

This proposition startled me. Latin was my favorite study, and it seemed sacrilege to believe this gibberish to belong to the country of Virgil.

"Barbarous Latin, in all probability," continued my uncle, "but still Latin."

"Very probably," I replied, not to contradict him.

"Let us see into the matter," continued my uncle; "here

you see we have a series of one hundred and thirty-two letters, apparently thrown pell-mell upon paper, without method or organization.   There are words which are composed wholly of consonants, such as *m.rnlls,* others which are nearly all vowels, the fifth, for instance, which is *unteief,* and one of the last *oseibo.*   This appears an extraordinary combination.   Probably we shall find that the phrase is arranged according to some mathematical plan.   No doubt a certain sentence has been written out and then jumbled up —some plan to which some figure is the clue.   Now, Harry, to show your English wit—what is that figure?"

I could give him no hint.   My thoughts were indeed far away.   While he was speaking I had caught sight of the portrait of my cousin Gretchen, and was wondering when she would return.   We were affianced, and loved one another very sincerely.   But my uncle, who never thought of such sublunary matters, knew nothing of this.   Without noticing my abstraction, the Professor began reading the puzzling cryptograph all sorts of ways, according to some theory of his own.   Presently, rousing my wandering attention, he dictated one precious attempt to me.

I mildly handed it over to him.   It read as follows:—

*messunkaSenrA.icefdoK.segnittamurtn
ecertserrette,rotaivsadua,ednecsedsadne
lacartniiiluJsiratracSarbmutabiledmek
meretarcsilucoIsleffenSnI.*

I could scarcely keep from laughing, while my uncle, on the contrary, got in a towering passion, struck the table with his fist, darted out of the room, out of the house, and then taking to his heels was presently lost to sight.

CHAPTER III
AN ASTOUNDING DISCOVERY

"WHAT is the matter?" cried the cook, entering the room; "when will master have his dinner?"

"Never."

"And, his supper?"

"I don't know.   He says he will eat no more, neither shall I.   My uncle has determined to fast and make me fast until he reads this abominable inscription," I replied.

"You will be starved to death," she said.

I was very much of the same opinion, but not liking to say so, sent her away, and began some of my usual work of classification. But busy as I made myself, nothing could keep me from thinking alternately of the stupid manuscript and of the pretty Gretchen.

Several times I was tempted to go out, but my uncle would have been angry at my absence. At the end of an hour, my allotted task was done. How to pass the time? I began by lighting my pipe. Like all other students, I delighted in tobacco; and, seating myself in the great armchair, I began to meditate.

Where was my uncle? I could easily imagine him tearing along some solitary road, gesticulating, talking to himself, cutting the air with his cane, and still thinking of the absurd bit of hieroglyphics. Would he hit upon some clue? Would he come home in better humor? While these thoughts were passing through my brain, I mechanically took up the execrable puzzle and tried every imaginable way of grouping the letters. I put them together by twos, by threes, fours, and fives—in vain. Nothing intelligible came out, except that the fourteenth, fifteenth and sixteenth made *ice* in English; the eighty-fourth, eighty-fifth and eighty-sixth, the word *sir;* then at last I seemed to find the Latin words *rota, mutabile, ira, nec, atra.*

"Ha! there seems to be some truth in my uncle's notion," thought I.

Then again I seemed to find the word *luco,* which means sacred wood. Then in the third line I appeared to make out *labiled,* a perfect Hebrew word, and at the last the syllables *mère, are, mer,* which were French. It was enough to drive one mad. Four different idioms in this absurd phrase. What connection could there be between ice, sir, anger, cruel, sacred wood, changing, mother, are and sea? The first and the last might, in a sentence connected with Iceland, mean sea of ice. But what of the rest of this monstrous cryptograph?

I was, in fact, fighting against an insurmountable difficulty; my brain was almost on fire; my eyes were strained with staring at the parchment; the whole absurd collection of letters appeared to dance before my vision in a number of black little groups. My mind was possessed with temporary hallucination—I was stifling. I wanted air. Mechanically I fanned myself with the document, of which now I saw the back and then the front.

Imagine my surprise when glancing at the back of the wearisome puzzle, the ink having gone through, I clearly made out Latin words, and among others *craterem* and *terrestre*.

I had discovered the secret! It came upon me like a flash of lightning. I had got the clue. All you had to do to understand the document was to read it backwards. All the ingenious ideas of the Professor were realized; he had dictated it rightly to me; by a mere accident I had discovered what he so much desired.

My delight, my emotion may be imagined, my eyes were dazzled and I trembled so that at first I could make nothing of it. One look, however, would tell me all I wished to know.

"Let me read," I said to myself, after drawing a long breath. I spread it before me on the table, I passed my finger over each letter, I spelt it through; in my excitement I read it out.

What horror and stupefaction took possession of my soul. I was like a man who had received a knock-down blow. Was it possible that I really read the terrible secret, and it had really been accomplished! A man had dared to do—what?

No living being should ever know "Never!" cried I, jumping up; "Never shall my uncle be made aware of the dread secret. He would be quite capable of undertaking the terrible journey. Nothing would check him, nothing stop him. Worse, he would compel me to accompany him, and we should be lost forever. But no; such folly and madness cannot be allowed."

I was almost beside myself with rage and fury. "My worthy uncle is already nearly mad," I cried aloud. "This would finish him. By some accident he may make the discovery; in which case, we are both lost. Perish the fearful secret—let the flames forever bury it in oblivion."

I snatched up book and parchment, and was about to cast them into the fire, when the door opened and my uncle entered. I had scarcely time to put down the wretched documents before my uncle was by my side. He was profoundly absorbed. His thoughts were evidently bent on the terrible parchment. Some new combination had probably struck him while taking his walk. He seated himself in his arm-chair, and with a pen began to make an algebraical calculation. I watched him with anxious eyes. My flesh crawled as it became probable that he would discover *the* secret. His combinations I knew were useless, I having discovered the one only clue. For three mortal hours he continued without speaking a word, without raising his head, scratching, re-writing, calculating over and over again. I knew that in time he must hit upon the right phrase. The letters of every alphabet have only a certain number of combinations. But then years might elapse before he would arrive at the correct solution.

Still time went on; night came, the sounds in the streets ceased—and still my uncle went on, not even answering our worthy cook when she called us to supper. I did not dare to leave him, so waved her away, and at last fell asleep on the sofa.

When I awoke my uncle was still at work. His red eyes, his pallid countenance, his matted hair, his feverish hands, his hecticly flushed cheeks, showed how terrible had been his struggle with the impossible, and what fearful fatigue he had undergone during that long sleepless night. It made me quite ill to look at him. Though he was rather severe with me, I loved him, and my heart ached at his sufferings. He was so overcome by one idea that he could not even get in a passion! All his energies were focussed on one point. And I knew that by speaking one little word all this suffering would cease. I could not speak it.

My heart was, nevertheless, inclining towards him. Why, then, did I remain silent? In the interest of my uncle himself. "Nothing shall make me speak," I muttered. "He will want to follow in the footsteps of the other! I know him well. His imagination is a perfect volcano, and to make discoveries in the interests of geology he would sacrifice his life. I will therefore be silent and strictly keep the secret I have discovered. To reveal it would be suicidal. He would not only rush, himself, to destruction, but drag me with him." I crossed my arms, looked another way and smoked—resolved never to speak.

When our cook wanted to go out to market, or on any other errand, she found the front door locked and the key taken away. Was this done purposely or not? Surely Professor Hardwigg did not intend the old woman and myself to become martyrs to his obstinate will. Were we to be starved to death? A frightful recollection came to my mind. Once we had fed on bits and scraps for a week while he sorted some curiosities. It gave me the cramp even to think of it!

I wanted my breakfast, and I saw no way of getting it. Still my resolution held good. I would starve rather than yield. But the cook began to take me seriously to task. What was to be done? She could not go out; and I dared not.

My uncle continued counting and writing; his imagination seemed to have translated him to the skies. He neither thought of eating nor drinking. In this way twelve o'clock came round. I was hungry, and there was nothing in the house. The cook had eaten the last bit of bread. This could not go on. It did, however, until two, when my sensations were terrible. After all, I began to think the document very absurd. Perhaps it might only be a gigantic hoax. Besides, some means would surely be found to keep my uncle back from attempting any such absurd expedition. On the other hand, if he did attempt anything so Quixotic, I should not be compelled to accompany him. Another line of reasoning partially decided me. Very likely he would make the discovery himself when I should have suffered starvation for nothing. Under the influence of hunger this reasoning appeared admirable. I determined to tell all.

The question now arose as to how it was to be done. I was still dwelling on the thought, when he rose and put on his hat. What! go out and lock us in? Never!

" Uncle," I began.

He did not appear even to hear me.

" Professor Hardwigg," I cried.

" What," he retorted, " did you speak? "

" How about the key? "

" What key—the key of the door? "

" No—of these horrible hieroglyphics? "

He looked at me from under his spectacles, and started

at the odd expression of my face. Rushing forward, he clutched me by the arm and keenly examined my countenance. His very look was an interrogation. I simply nodded.

With an incredulous shrug of the shoulders, he turned upon his heel. Undoubtedly he thought I had gone mad.

"I have made a very important discovery."

His eyes flashed with excitement. His hand was lifted in a menacing attitude. For a moment neither of us spoke. It is hard to say which was most excited.

"You don't mean to say that you have any idea of the meaning of the scrawl?"

"I do," was my desperate reply. "Look at the sentence as dictated by you.

"Well, but it means nothing," was the angry answer.

"Nothing if you read from left to right, but mark, if from right to left——"

"Backwards!" cried my uncle, in wild amazement. "Oh most cunning Saknussemm; and I to be such a blockhead." He snatched up the document, gazed at it with haggard eye, and read it out as I had done. It read as follows:—

In Sneffels yoculis craterem kem delebat
Umbra Scartaris Julii intra calendas descende.
Audas viator, et terrestre centrum attinges.
Kod feci. Arne Saknussemm.

Which dog-Latin being translated, reads as follows: "Descend into the crater of Yocul of Sneffels, which the shade of Scartaris caresses, before the kalends of July, audacious traveler, and you will reach the center of the earth. I did it.   ARNE SAKNUSSEMM."

My uncle leaped three feet from the ground with joy. He looked radiant and handsome. He rushed about the room wild with delight and satisfaction. He knocked over tables and chairs. He threw his books about until at last utterly exhausted, he fell into his arm-chair. "What's o'clock?" he asked.

"About three."

"My dinner does not seem to have done me much good," he observed, "Let me have something to eat. We can then start at once. Get my portmanteau ready."

"What for?"

"And your own," he continued. "We start at once."

My horror may be conceived. I resolved however to show no fear. Scientific reasons were the only ones likely to influence my uncle. Now, there were many against this terrible journey. The very idea of going down to the center of the earth was simply absurd. I determined therefore to argue the point after dinner.

My uncle's rage was now directed against the cook for having no dinner ready. My explanation however satisfied him, and giving her the key she soon contrived to get sufficient to satisfy our voracious appetites.

During the repast my uncle was rather gay than otherwise. He made some of those peculiar jokes which belong exclusively to the learned. As soon however as dessert was over, he called me to his study. We each took a chair on opposite sides of the table.

"Henry," he said, in a soft and winning voice; "I have always believed you ingenious, and you have rendered me a service never to be forgotten. Without you, this great, this wondrous discovery would never have been made. It is my duty, therefore, to insist on your sharing the glory."

"He is in a good humor," thought I; "I'll soon let him know my opinion of glory."

"In the first place," he continued, "you must keep the whole affair a profound secret. There is no more envious race of men than scientific discoverers. Many would start on the same journey. At all events, we will be the first in the field."

"I doubt your having many competitors," was my reply.

"A man of real scientific acquirements would be delighted at the chance. We should find a perfect stream of pilgrims on the traces of Arne Saknussemm, if this document were once made public."

"But my dear sir, is not this paper very likely to be a hoax?" I urged.

"The book in which we find it is sufficient proof of its authenticity," he replied.

"I thoroughly allow that the celebrated Professor wrote the lines, but only, I believe, as a kind of mystification," was my answer.

Scarcely were the words out of my mouth, when I was

sorry I had uttered them. My uncle looked at me with a dark and gloomy scowl, and I began to be alarmed for the results of our conversation. His mood soon changed, however, and a smile took the place of a frown. "We shall see," he remarked, with decisive emphasis.

"But see, what is all this about Yocul, and Sneffels, and this Scartaris? I have never heard anything about them."

"The very point to which I am coming. I lately received from my friend, Augustus Peterman, of Leipzig, a map. Take down the third atlas from the second shelf, series Z, plate 4."

I rose, went to the shelf, and presently returned with the volume indicated.

"This," said my uncle, "is one of the best maps of Iceland. I believe it will settle all your doubts, difficulties and objections."

With a grim hope to the contrary, I stooped over the map.

CHAPTER IV
WE START ON THE JOURNEY

"You see, the whole island is made up of volcanoes," said the Professor, "and note that they all bear the name of Yokul. The word is Icelandic, and means a glacier. In most of the lofty mountains of that region the volcanic eruptions come forth from ice-bound caverns. Hence the name applied to every volcano on this extraordinary island."

"But what does this word Sneffels mean?"

To this question I expected no rational answer. I was mistaken. "Follow my finger to the western coast of Iceland, there you see Reykjawik, its capital. Follow the direction of one of its innumerable fjords or arms of the sea, and what do you see below the sixty-fifth degree of latitude?"

"'A' peninsula—very like a thigh-bone in shape."

"And in the center of it——?"

"'A' mountain."

"Well, that's Sneffels."

I had nothing to say.

"That is Sneffels—a mountain about five thousand feet in height, one of the most remarkable in the whole island, and certainly doomed to be the most celebrated in the world, for through its crater we shall reach the Center of the Earth."

"Impossible!" cried I, startled and shocked at the thought.

"Why impossible?" said Professor Hardwigg in his severest tones.

"Because its crater is choked with lava, by burning rocks —by infinite dangers."

"But if it be extinct?"

"That would make a difference."

"Of course it would. There are about three hundred volcanoes on the whole surface of the globe—but the greater number are extinct. Of these Sneffels is one. No eruption has occurred since 1219—in fact it has ceased to be a volcano at all."

After this what more could I say? Yes—I thought of another objection. "But what is all this about Scartaris and the kalends of July——?"

My uncle reflected deeply. Presently he gave forth the result of his reflections in a sententious tone. "What appears obscure to you, to me is light. This very phrase shows how particular Saknussemm is in his directions. The Sneffels' mountain has many craters. He is careful therefore to point the exact one which is the highway into the Interior of the Earth. He lets us know, for this purpose, that about the end of the month of June, the shadow of Mount Scartaris falls upon the one crater. There can be no doubt about the matter."

My uncle had an answer for everything. "I accept all your explanations," I said, "and Saknussemm is right. He found out the entrance to the bowels of the earth, he has indicated correctly, but that he or anyone else ever followed up the discovery, is madness to suppose."

"Why so, young man?"

"All scientific teaching, theoretical and practical, shows it to be impossible."

"I care nothing for theories," retorted my uncle.

"But is it not well-known that heat increases one degree for every seventy feet you descend into the earth? which gives a fine idea of the central heat. All the matters which compose the globe are in a state of incandescence; even gold, platinum, and the hardest rocks are in a state of fusion. What would become of us?"

"Don't be alarmed at the heat, my boy."

"How so?"

"Neither you nor anybody else knows anything about the real state of the earth's interior. All modern experiments tend to explode the older theories. Were any such heat to exist, the upper crust of the earth would be shattered to atoms, and the world would be at an end."

A long, learned and not uninteresting discussion followed, which ended in this: "I do not believe in the dangers and difficulties which you, Henry, seem to multiply; and the only way to learn, is like Arne Saknussemm, to go and see."

"Well," cried I, overcome at last, "let us go and see. Though how we can do that in the dark is another mystery."

"Fear nothing. We shall overcome these, and many other difficulties. Besides, as we approach the Center, I expect to find it luminous——"

"Nothing is impossible."

"And now that we have come to a thorough understanding, not a word to any living soul. Our success depends on secrecy and despatch."

Thus ended our memorable conference, which roused a perfect fever in me. Leaving my uncle, I went forth like one possessed. Reaching the banks of the Elbe, I began to think. Was all I had heard really and truly possible? Was my uncle in his sober senses, and could the interior of the earth be reached? Was I the victim of a madman, or was he a discoverer of rare courage and grandeur of conception?

To a certain extent I was anxious to be off. I was afraid my enthusiasm would cool. I determined to pack up at once. At the end of an hour, however, on my way home, I found that my feelings had very much changed. "I'm all abroad," I cried; "'tis a nightmare—I must have dreamed it."

At this moment I came face to face with Gretchen, whom I warmly embraced. "So you have come to meet me," she said; "how good of you. But what is the matter?"

Well, it was no use mincing the matter, I told her all. She listened with awe, and for some minutes she could not speak. "Well?" I at last asked, rather anxiously.

"What a magnificent journey. If I were only a man! A journey worthy of the nephew of Professor Hardwigg. I should look upon it as an honor to accompany him."

"My dear Gretchen, I thought you would be the first to cry out against this mad enterprise."

"No; on the contrary, I glory in it. It is magnificent, splendid—an idea worthy of my father. Henry Lawson, I envy you."

This was, as it were, conclusive. The final blow of all.

When we entered the house we found my uncle surrounded by workmen and porters, who were packing up. He was pulling and hauling at a bell. "Where have you been wasting your time? Your portmanteau is not packed —my papers are not in order—the precious tailor has not brought my clothes, nor my gaiters—the key of my carpet bag is gone!"

I looked at him stupefied. And still he tugged away at the bell. "We are really off, then?" I said.

"Yes—of course, and yet you go out for a stroll, unfortunate boy!"

"And when do we go?"

"The day after to-morrow, at daybreak."

I heard no more; but darted off to my little bedchamber and locked myself in. There was no doubt about it now. My uncle had been hard at work all the afternoon. The garden was full of ropes, rope-ladders, torches, gourds, iron clamps, crow-bars, alpenstocks, and pickaxes—enough to load ten men.

I passed a terrible night. I was called early the next day to learn that the resolution of my uncle was unchanged and irrevocable. I also found my cousin and affianced wife as warm on the subject as was her father.

Next day, at five o'clock in the morning, the post-chaise was at the door. Gretchen and the old cook received the keys of the house; and, scarcely pausing to wish anyone good-bye, we started on our adventurous journey into the Center of the Earth.

CHAPTER V
FIRST LESSONS IN CLIMBING

At Altona, a suburb of Hamburg, is the Chief Station of the Kiel railway, which was to take us to the shores of the Belt; and exactly at seven o'clock we were seated opposite each other in a first-class railway carriage. My uncle said nothing. He was too busy examining his papers, among which of course was the famous parchment, and some letters of introduction from the Danish consul, which were to pave the way to an introduction to the Governor of Iceland. In three hours we reached Kiel, and our baggage was at once transferred to the steamer.

We had now a day before us, a delay of about ten hours. Which fact put my uncle in a towering passion. We had nothing to do but to walk about the pretty town and bay. At length, however, we went on board, and at half past ten were steaming down the Great Belt. The next morning we reached Copenhagen, where, scarcely taking time for refreshment, my uncle hurried out to present one of his letters of introduction. It was to the director of the Museum of Antiquities, who having been informed that we were tourists bound for Iceland, did all he could to assist us. One wretched hope sustained me now. Perhaps no vessel was bound for such distant parts.

Alas! a little Danish schooner, the *Valkyrie,* was to sail on the second of June for Reykjawik. The captain, M. Bjarne, was on board, and was rather surprised at the energy and cordiality with which his future passenger shook him by the hand. To him a voyage to Iceland was merely a matter of course. My uncle, on the other hand, considered the event of sublime importance. The honest sailor took advantage of the Professor's enthusiasm to double the fare.

" On Tuesday morning at seven o'clock be on board," said M. Bjarne, handing us our receipts.

" Excellent! Capital! Glorious! " remarked my uncle as we sat down to a late breakfast; " refresh yourself, my boy, and we will take a run through the town."

Our meal concluded, we went to the Kongens-Nye-Torw; to the king's magnificent palace; to the beautiful bridge over the canal near the Museum; to the immense cenotaph of Thorwaldsen with its hideous naval groups; to the castle of Rosenberg; and to all the other lions of the place,—none of which my uncle even saw, so absorbed was he in his anticipated triumphs.

But one thing struck his fancy, and that was a certain singular church steeple situated on the Island of Amak, which is the south-east quarter of the city of Copenhagen. My uncle at once ordered me to turn my steps that way. This church exhibited nothing remarkable in itself; in fact, the worthy Professor had only been attracted to it by one circumstance, which was, that its rather elevated steeple started from a circular platform, after which there was an exterior staircase, which wound round to the very summit.

"Let us ascend," said my uncle.

"But I never could climb church towers," I cried, "I am subject to dizziness in my head."

"The very reason why you should go up. I want to cure you of a bad habit."

"But my good sir——"

"I tell you to come. What is the use of wasting so much valuable time?"

It was impossible to dispute the dictatorial commands of my uncle. I yielded with a groan. On payment of a fee, a verger gave us the key. He, for one, was not partial to the ascent. My uncle at once showed me the way, running up the steps like a school-boy. I followed as well as I could, though no sooner was I outside the tower, than my head began to swim. There was nothing of the eagle about me. The earth was enough for me, and no ambitious desire to soar ever entered my mind. Still things did not go badly until I had ascended 150 steps, and was near the platform, when I began to feel the rush of cold air. I could scarcely stand, when clutching the railings, I looked upwards. The railing was frail enough, but nothing to those which skirted the terrible winding staircase, that appeared, from where I stood, to ascend to the skies.

"Now then, Henry."

"I can't do it!" I cried, in accents of despair.

"Are you, after all, a coward, sir?" said my uncle in a pitiless tone. "Go up, I say!"

To this there was no reply possible. And yet the keen air acted violently on my nervous system; sky, earth, all seemed to swim round; while the steeple rocked like a ship.

My legs gave way like those of a drunken man.   I crawled upon my hands and knees; I hauled myself up slowly, crawling like a snake.   Presently I closed my eyes, and allowed myself to be dragged upwards.

"Look around you," said my uncle, in a stern voice, "heaven knows what profound abysses you may have to look down.   This is excellent practice."

Slowly, and shivering all the while with cold, I opened my eyes.   What then did I see?   My first glance was upwards at the cold fleecy clouds, which as by some optical delusion appeared to stand still, while the steeple, the weathercock, and our two selves were carried swiftly along. Far away on one side could be seen the grassy plain, while on the other lay the sea bathed in translucent light.   The Sund, or Sound as we call it, could be discovered beyond the point of Elsinore, crowded with white sails, which, at that distance, looked like the wings of sea-gulls; while to the east could be made out the far-off coast of Sweden. The whole appeared a magic panorama.

Faint and bewildered as I was, there was no remedy for it.   Rise and stand up I must.   Despite my protestations my first lesson lasted quite an hour.   When, nearly two hours later, I reached the bosom of mother earth, I was like a rheumatic old man bent double with pain. "Enough for one day," said my uncle, rubbing his hands, "we will begin again to-morrow."

There was no remedy.   My lessons lasted five days, and at the end of that period, I ascended blithely enough, and found myself able to look down into the depths below without even winking, and with some degree of pleasure.

CHAPTER VI
OUR VOYAGE TO ICELAND

THE hour of departure came at last.   The night before, the worthy Mr. Thompson brought us the most cordial letters of introduction for Count Trampe, Governor of Iceland, for M. Pictursson, coadjutor to the bishop, and for M. Finsen, mayor of the town of Reykjawik.   In return, my uncle nearly crushed his hands, so warmly did he shake them.

On the second of the month, at two in the morning, our precious cargo of luggage was taken on board the good ship *Valkyrie*. We followed, and were very politely introduced by the captain to a small cabin with two standing bed places, neither very well ventilated nor very comfortable. But in the cause of science men are expected to suffer.

"Well, and have we a fair wind?" cried my uncle, in his most mellifluous accents.

"An excellent wind!" replied Captain Bjarne; "we shall leave the Sound, going free with all sails set." A few minutes afterwards, the schooner started before the wind, under all the canvas she could carry, and entered the channel. An hour later, the capital of Denmark seemed to sink into the waves, and we were at no great distance from the coast of Elsinore. My uncle was delighted; for myself, moody and dissatisfied, I appeared almost to expect a glimpse of the ghost of Hamlet.

"Sublime madman," thought I, "you doubtless, would approve our proceedings. You might perhaps even follow us to the center of the earth, there to resolve your eternal doubts."

"How long will the voyage last?" asked my uncle.

"Well, I should think about ten days," replied the skipper, "unless, indeed, we meet with some north-east gales among the Faroe Islands."

"At all events, there will be no very considerable delay," cried the impatient Professor.

"No, Mr. Hardwigg," said the captain, "no fear of that. At all events, we shall get there some day."

The voyage offered no incident worthy of record. I bore it very well, but my uncle to his great annoyance, and even shame, was remarkably sea-sick! This *mal de mer* troubled him the more, that it prevented him from questioning Captain Bjarne as to the subject of Sneffels, as to the means of communication, and the facilities of transport. All these explanations he had to adjourn to the period of his arrival. His time meanwhile, was spent lying in bed groaning, and dwelling anxiously on the hoped-for termination of the voyage. I did not pity him.

On the eleventh day we sighted Cape Portland, over which towered Mount Myrdals Yokul, which, the weather being clear, we made out very readily.   The cape itself is nothing but a huge mount of granite standing naked and alone to meet the Atlantic waves.   The *Valkyrie* kept off the coast, steering to the westward.   On all sides were to be seen whole "schools" of whales and sharks.   After some hours we came in sight of a solitary rock in the ocean, forming a mighty vault, through which the foaming waves poured with intense fury.   The islets of Westman appeared to leap from the ocean, being so low in the water as scarcely to be seen, until you were right upon them.   From that moment the schooner was steered to the westward in order to round Cape Reykjaness, the western point of Iceland.

My uncle, to his great disgust, was unable even to crawl on deck, so heavy a sea was on, and thus lost the first view of the Land of Promise.   Forty-eight hours later, after a storm which drove us far to sea under bare poles, we came once more in sight of land, and were boarded by a pilot, who, after three hours of dangerous navigation, brought the schooner safely to an anchor in the bay of Faxa before Reykjawik.

My uncle came out of his cabin pale, haggard, thin, but full of enthusiasm, his eyes dilated with pleasure and satisfaction.   Nearly the whole population of the town was on foot to see us land.   The fact was, that scarcely any one of them but expected some goods by the periodical vessel.

Professor Hardwigg was in haste to leave his prison, or rather as he called it, his hospital; but before he attempted to do so, he caught hold of my hand, led me to the quarter-deck of the schooner, took my arm with his left hand, and pointed inland with his right, over the northern part of the bay, to where rose a high two-peaked mountain—a double cone covered with eternal snow.   "Behold," he whispered in an awe-stricken voice, "behold—Mount Sneffels!"

Without further remark, he put his finger to his lips, frowned darkly, and descended into the small boat which awaited us.   I followed, and in a few minutes we stood upon the soil of mysterious Iceland!

Scarcely were we fairly on shore when there appeared before us a man of excellent appearance, wearing the costume of a military officer.   He was, however, but a civil

servant, a magistrate, the governor of the island—Baron
Trampe. The Professor knew whom he had to deal with.
He therefore handed him the letters from Copenhagen, and
a brief conversation in Danish followed, to which I of
course was a stranger, and for a very good reason, for I
did not know the language in which they conversed. I afterwards heard, however, that Baron Trampe placed himself entirely at the beck and call of Professor Hardwigg.

My uncle was also most graciously received by M. Finsen, the mayor, who as far as costume went, was quite as
military as the governor, but also from character and occupation quite as pacific. As for his coadjutor, M. Pictursson, he was absent on an episcopal visit to the northern portion of the diocese. We were therefore compelled to defer
the pleasure of being presented to him. His absence was,
however, compensated by the presence of M. Fridriksson,
Professor of natural science in the college of Reykjawik,
a man of invaluable ability. This modest scholar spoke
no languages save Icelandic and Latin. When, therefore,
he addressed himself to me in the language of Horace, we
at once came to undertsand one another. He was, in fact,
the only person that I did thoroughly understand during
the whole period of my residence in this benighted island.

Out of three rooms of which his house was composed,
two were placed at our service, and in a few hours we were
installed with all our baggage, the amount of which rather
astonished the simple inhabitants of Reykjawik.

"Now, Harry," said my uncle, rubbing his hands, "all
goes well, the worst difficulty is now over."

"How the worst difficulty over?" I cried in fresh amazement.

"Doubtless. Here we are in Iceland. Nothing more
remains but to descend into the bowels of the earth."

"Well, sir, to a certain extent you are right. We have
only to go down—but, as far as   am concerned, that is
not the question. I want to know how we are to get up
again."

"That is the least part of the business, and does not in
any way trouble me. In the meantime, there is not an
hour to lose. I am about to visit the public library. Very
likely I may find there some manuscripts from the hand
of Saknussemm. I shall be glad to consult them."

"In the meanwhile," I replied, "I will take a walk through the town. Will you not likewise do so?"

"I feel no interest in the subject," said my uncle. "What for me is curious in this island, is not what is above the surface, but what is below."

I bowed by way of reply, put on my hat and furred cloak, and went out.

It was not an easy matter to lose oneself in the two streets of Reykjawik; I had therefore no need to ask my way. The town lies on a flat and marshy plain, between two hills. A vast field of lava skirts it on one side, falling away in terraces towards the sea. On the other hand is the large bay of Faxa, bordered on the north by the enormous glacier of Sneffels. In the bay the *Valkyrie* was then the only vessel at anchor. Generally there were one or two English or French gunboats, to watch and protect the fisheries in the offing. They were now, however, absent on duty.

In three hours my tour was complete. The general impression upon my mind was sadness. No trees, no vegetation, so to speak—on all sides volcanic peaks—the huts of turf and earth—more like roofs than houses. Thanks to the heat of these residences, grass grows on the roof, which grass is carefully cut for hay. I saw but few inhabitants during my excursion, but I met a crowd on the beach, drying, salting and loading cod-fish, the principal article of exportation. The men appeared robust but heavy; fair-haired like Germans, but of pensive mien—exiles of a higher scale in the ladder of humanity than the Esquimaux, but, I thought, much more unhappy, since with superior perceptions they are compelled to live within the limits of the Polar Circle.

CHAPTER VII
CONVERSATION AND DISCOVERY

WHEN I returned, dinner was ready. This meal was devoured by my worthy relative with avidity and voracity. His shipboard diet had turned his interior into a perfect gulf. The repast, which was more Danish than Icelandic, was in itself nothing, but the excessive hospitality of our host made us enjoy it doubly. The conversation turned upon scientific matters, and M. Fridriksson asked my uncle what he thought of the public library.

"Library, sir?" cried my uncle; "it appears to me a col-lection of useless odd volumes, and a beggarly amount of empty shelves."

"What!" cried M. Fridriksson; "why, we have eight thousand volumes of most rare and valuable works—some in the Scandinavian language, besides all the new publications from Copenhagen."

"Eight thousand volumes, my dear sir—why, where are they?" cried my uncle.

"Scattered over the country, Professor Hardwigg. We are very studious, my dear sir, though we do live in Iceland. Every farmer, every laborer, every fisherman can both read and write—and we think that books instead of being locked up in cupboards, far from the sight of students, should be distributed as widely as possible. The books of our library are, therefore, passed from hand to hand without returning to the library shelves perhaps for years."

"Then when foreigners visit you, there is nothing for them to see?"

"Well, sir, foreigners have their own libraries, and our first consideration is, that our humbler classes should be highly educated. Fortunately, the love of study is innate in the Icelandic people. In 1816 we founded a Literary Society and Mechanics' Institute; many foreign scholars of eminence are honorary members; we publish books destined to educate our people, and these books have rendered valuable services to our country. Allow me to have the honor, Professor Hardwigg, to enrol you as an honorary member?"

My uncle, who already belonged to nearly every literary and scientific institution in Europe, immediately yielded to the amiable wishes of good M. Fridriksson. "And now," said the latter after many expressions of gratitude and good-will, "if you will tell me what books you expected to find, perhaps I may be of some assistance to you."

I watched my uncle keenly. For a minute or two he hesitated, as if unwilling to speak; to speak openly was, perhaps, to unveil his projects. Nevertheless, after some reflection, he made up his mind. "Well, M. Fridriksson," he said in any easy, unconcerned kind of way, "I was desirous of ascertaining, if among other valuable works, you had any by the learned Arne Saknussemm."

"Arne Saknussemm!" cried the Professor of Reykja-wik; "you speak of one of the most distinguished scholars of the sixteenth century, of the great naturalist, the great alchemist, the great traveler."

"Exactly so."

"One of the most distinguished men connected with Ice-landic science and literature."

"As you say, sir——"

"A man illustrious above all."

"Yes, sir, all this is true, but his works?"

"We have none of them."

"Not in Iceland?"

"There are none in Iceland or elsewhere," answered the other, sadly.

"Why so?"

"Because Arne Saknussemm was persecuted for heresy, and in 1573 his works were publicly burnt at Copenhagen by the hands of the common hangman."

"Very good! capital!" murmured my uncle, to the great astonishment of the worthy Icelander.

"You said, sir——"

"Yes, yes, all is clear, I see the link in the chain; every-thing is explained, and I now understand why Arne Sak-nussemm, put out of court, forced to hide his magnificent discoveries, was compelled to conceal beneath the veil of an incomprehensible cryptograph, the secret——"

"What secret?"

"A secret—which," stammered my uncle.

"Have you discovered some wonderful manuscript?"

"No, no, I was carried away by my enthusiasm. A mere supposition."

"Very good, sir. But, really, to turn to another sub-ject, I hope you will not leave our island without examin-ing into its mineralogical riches."

"Well, the fact is, I am rather late. So many learned men have been here before me."

"Yes, yes, but there is still much to be done," cried M. Fridriksson.

"You think so," said my uncle, his eyes twinkling with hidden satisfaction.

"Yes, you have no idea how many unknown mountains, glaciers, volcanoes there are which remain to be studied. Without moving from where we sit, I can show you one. Yonder on the edge of the horizon, you see Sneffels."

"Oh yes, Sneffels," said my uncle.

"One of the most curious volcanoes in existence, the crater of which has been rarely visited."

"Extinct?"

"Extinct, any time these five hundred years," was the ready reply.

"Well," said my uncle, who dug his nails into his flesh, and pressed his knees tightly together to prevent himself leaping up with joy. "I have a great mind to begin my studies with an examination of the geological mysteries of this Mount Seffel—Feisel—what do you call it?"

"Sneffels, my dear sir."

This portion of the conversation took place in Latin, and I therefore understood all that had been said. I could scarcely keep my countenance when I found my uncle so cunningly concealing his delight and satisfaction. I must confess that his artful grimaces, put on to conceal his happiness, made him look like a new Mephistopheles. "Yes, yes," he continued, "your proposition delights me. I will endeavor to climb to the summit of Sneffels, and, if possible, will descend into its crater."

"I very much regret," continued M. Fridriksson "that my occupation will entirely preclude the possibility of my accompanying you. It would have been both pleasurable and profitable if I could have spared the time."

"No, no, a thousand times no," cried my uncle. "I do not wish to disturb the serenity of any man. I thank you, however, with all my heart. The presence of one so learned as yourself, would no doubt have been most useful, but the duties of your office and profession before everything."

In the innocence of his simple heart, our host did not perceive the irony of these remarks. "I entirely approve your project," he continued after some further remarks. "It is a good idea to begin by examining this volcano. You will make a harvest of curious observations. In the first place, how do you propose to get to Sneffels?"

"By sea. I shall cross the bay. Of course that is the most rapid route."

" Of course. But still it cannot be done."

" Why ? "

" We have not an available boat in all Reykjawik," replied the other.

" What is to be done ? "

" You must go by land along the coast. It is longer, but much more interesting."

" Then I must have a guide."

" Of course ; and I have your very man."

" Somebody on whom I can depend ? "

" Yes, an inhabitant of the peninsula on which Sneffels is situated. He is a very shrewd and worthy man, with whom you will be pleased. He speaks Danish like a Dane."

" When can I see him—to-day ? "

" No, to-morrow; he will not be here before."

" To-morrow be it," replied my uncle, with a deep sigh.

The conversation ended by compliments on both sides. During the dinner my uncle had learned much as to the history of Arne Saknussemm, the reasons for his mysterious and hieroglyphical document. He also became aware that his host would not accompany him on his adventurous expedition, and that next day we should have a guide.

CHAPTER VIII
THE EIDER-DOWN HUNTER—OFF AT LAST

That evening I took a brief walk on the shore near Reykjawik, after which I returned to an early sleep on my bed of coarse planks, where I slept the sleep of the just. When I awoke I heard my uncle speaking loudly in the next room. I rose hastily and joined him. He was talking in Danish with a man of tall stature, and of perfectly Herculean build. This man appeared to be possessed of very great strength. His eyes, which started rather prominently from a very large head, the face belonging to which was simple and naive, appeared very quick and intelligent. Very long hair, which even in England would have been accounted exceedingly red, fell over his athletic shoulders. This native of Iceland was active and supple in appearance, though he scarcely moved his arms, being in fact one of those men who despise the habit of gesticulation common to southern people.

Everything in this man's manner revealed a calm and phlegmatic temperament. There was nothing indolent about him, but his appearance spoke of tranquility. He was one of those who never seemed to expect anything from anybody, who liked to work when he thought proper, and whose philosophy nothing could astonish or trouble.

I began to comprehend his character, simply from the way in which he listened to the wild and impassioned verbiage of my worthy uncle. While the excellent Professor spoke sentence after sentence, he stood with folded arms, utterly still, motionless to all my uncle's gesticulations. When he wanted to say No he moved his head from left to right; when he acquiesced he nodded, so slightly that you could scarcely see the undulation of his head. This economy of motion was carried to the length of avarice.

Judging from his appearance I should have been a long time before I had suspected him to be what he was, a mighty hunter. Certainly his manner was not likely to frighten the game. How, then, did he contrive to get at his prey? My surprise was slightly modified when I knew that this tranquil and solemn personage, was only a hunter of the eider-duck, the down of which is, after all, the greatest source of the Icelanders' wealth.

This grave, sententious, silent person, as phlegmatic as an Englishman on the French stage, was named Hans Bjelke. He had called upon us in consequence of the recommendation of M. Fridriksson. He was, in fact, our future guide. It struck me that had I sought the world over, I could not have found a greater contradiction to my impulsive uncle. They, however, readily understood one another. Neither of them had any thought about money; one was ready to take all that was offered him, the other ready to offer anything that was asked. It may readily be conceived, then, that an understanding was soon come to between them.

The understanding was, that he was to take us to the village of Stapi, situated on the southern slope of the peninsula. of Sneffels, at the very foot of the volcano. Hans, the guide, told us the distance was about twenty-two miles, a journey which my uncle supposed would take about two days. But when my uncle came to understand that they

were Danish miles, of eight thousand yards each, he was
obliged to be more moderate in his ideas, and, considering
the horrible roads we had to follow, to allow eight or ten
days for the journey.   Four horses were prepared for us,
two to carry the baggage, and two to bear the important
weight of myself and uncle.   Hans declared that nothing
ever would make him climb on the back of any animal.   He
knew every inch of that part of the coast, and promised to
take us the very shortest way.

His engagement with my uncle was by no means to cease
with our arrival at Stapi; he was further to remain in his
service during the whole time required for the completion
of his scientific investigations, at the fixed salary of three
rix-dollars a week, being exactly fourteen shillings and two-
pence, minus one farthing, English currency.   One stipula-
tion, however, was made by the guide—the money was to
be paid to him every Saturday night, failing which, his engagement was at an end.

The day of our departure was fixed.   My uncle wished
to hand the eider-down hunter an advance, but he refused
in one emphatic word—" *Efter.*"

Which being translated from Icelandic into plain English
means—After.

The treaty concluded, our worthy guide retired without
another word.   " A splendid fellow," said my uncle; " only
he little suspects the marvelous part he is about to play in
the history of the world."

" You mean, then," I cried in amazement, " that he should
accompany us? "

" To the Interior of the Earth, yes; " replied my uncle.
" Why not? "

There were yet forty-eight hours to elapse before we
made our final start.   Our whole time was taken up in
making preparations for our journey.   All our industry and
ability were devoted to packing every object in the most ad-
vantageous manner—the instruments on one side, the arms
on the other, the tools here and the provisions there.   There
were, in fact, four distinct groups.

The instruments were of course of the best manufacture:—

1. A centigrade thermometer of Eizel, counting up to
150 degrees, which to me did not appear half enough—or

too much. Too hot by half, if the degree of heat was to ascend so high—in which case we should certainly be cooked —not enough, if we wanted to ascertain the exact temperature of springs or metal in a state of fusion.

2. A *manometer* worked by compressed air, an instrument used to ascertain the upper atmospheric pressure on the level of the ocean. Perhaps a common barometer would not have done as well, the atmospheric pressure being likely to increase in proportion as we descended below the surface of the earth.

3. A first-class chronometer made by Boissonnas, of Geneva, set at the meridian of Hamburg, from which Germans calculated as the English do from Greenwich.

4. Two compasses, one for horizontal guidance, the other to ascertain the dip.

5. A night glass.

6. Two Ruhmkorff's coils, which, by means of a current of electricity, would ensure us a very excellent, easily carried, and certain means of obtaining light.

7. A voltaic battery on the newest principle.

Our arms consisted of two rifles, with two revolving six-shooters. Why these arms were provided it was impossible for me to say. I had every reason to believe that we had neither wild beasts nor savage natives to fear. My uncle, on the other hand, was quite as devoted to his arsenal as to his collection of instruments, and above all was very careful with his provision of fulminating or gun cotton, warranted to keep in any climate, and of which the expansive force was known to be greater than that of ordinary gunpowder.

Our tools consisted of two pickaxes, two crowbars, a silken ladder, three iron-shod Alpine poles, a hatchet, a hammer, a dozen wedges, some pointed pieces of iron, and a quantity of strong rope. You may conceive that the whole made a tolerable parcel, especially when I mention that the ladder itself was three hundred feet long!

Then there came the important question of provisions. The hamper was not very large but tolerably satisfactory, for I knew that in concentrated essence of meat and biscuit there was enough to last six months. The only liquid provided by my uncle was scheidam. Of water, not a drop. We had, however, an ample supply of gourds, and my uncle counted on finding water, and enough to fill them, as soon as we commenced our downward journey.

My remarks as to the temperature and quality of such water, and even as to the possibility of none being found, remained wholly without effect.

To make up the exact list of our traveling gear—for the guidance of future travelers—I will add, that we carried a medicine and surgical chest with all apparatus necessary for wounds, fractures and blows; lint, scissors, lancets—in fact, a perfect collèction of horrible-looking instruments; a number of phials containing ammonia, alcohol, ether, goulard water, aromatic vinegar, in fact, every possible and impossible drug—finally, all the materials for working the Ruhmkorff coil!

My uncle had also been careful to lay in a goodly supply of tobacco, several flasks of very fine gunpowder, boxes of tinder, besides a large belt crammed full of notes and gold. Good boots rendered water-tight were to be found to the number of six in the tool-box. "My boy, with such clothing, with such boots, and such general equipments," said my uncle, in a state of rapturous delight; "we may hope to travel far."

It took a whole day to put all these matters in order. In the evening we dined with Baron Trampe, in company with the Mayor of Reykjawik, and Doctor Hyaltalin, the great medical man of Iceland. M. Fridriksson was not present. Unfortunately, the consequence was, that I did not understand a word that was said at dinner—a kind of semi-official reception. One thing I can say, my uncle never left off speaking.

The next day our labor came to an end. Our worthy host delighted my uncle, Professor Hardwigg, by giving him a good map of Iceland, a most important and precious document for a mineralogist. Our last evening was spent in a long conversation with M. Fridriksson, whom I liked very much—the more that I never expected to see him or any one else again. After this agreeable way of spending an hour or so, I tried to sleep. In vain; with the exception of a few dozes, my night was miserable.

At five o'clock in the morning I was awakened from the only real half hour's sleep of the night, by the loud neighing of horses under my window. I hastily dressed myself and went down into the street. Hans was engaged in putting the finishing stroke to our baggage, which he did in a silent, quiet way that won my admiration, and yet he did it admirably well. My uncle wasted a great deal of breath in giving him directions, but worthy Hans took not the slightest notice of his words.

At six o'clock all our preparations were completed, and M. Fridriksson shook hands heartily with us. My uncle thanked him warmly, in the Icelandic language, for his kind hospitality, speaking truly from the heart. As for myself I put together a few of my best Latin phrases and paid him the highest compliments I could. This fraternal and friendly duty performed, we sallied forth and mounted our horses.

As soon as we were quite ready, M. Fridriksson advanced, and by way of farewell, called after me in the words of Virgil—words which appeared to have been made for us, travelers starting for an uncertain destination.

"*Et quacunque viam dederit fortuna sequamur.*"

("And whichsoever way thou goest, may fortune follow!")

CHAPTER IX
OUR START—WE MEET WITH ADVENTURES BY THE WAY

THE weather was overcast but settled, when we commenced our adventurous and perilous journey. We had neither to fear fatiguing heat nor drenching rain. It was, in fact, real tourist weather. As there is nothing I like better than horse exercise, the pleasure of riding through an unknown country, caused the early part of our enterprise to be particularly agreeable to me. I began to enjoy the exhilarating delight of traveling, a life of desire, gratification and liberty. The truth is, that my spirits rose so rapidly that I began to be indifferent to what had once appeared to be a terrible journey.

"After all," I said to myself, "what do I risk? Simply to take a journey through a curious country, to climb a remarkable mountain, and if the worst comes to the worst, to descend into the crater of an extinct volcano." There could be no doubt that this was all this terrible Saknussemm had done. As to the existence of a gallery or of subterraneous passages leading into the interior of the earth, the idea was simply absurd, the hallucination of a distempered imagination. All, then, that may be required of me I will do cheerfully, and will create no difficulty.

It was just before we left Reykjawik that I came to this decision. Hans, our extraordinary guide, went first, walking with a steady, rapid, and unvarying step. Our two horses with the luggage followed of their own accord, without requiring whip or spur. My uncle and I came behind, cutting a very tolerable figure upon our small but vigorous animals. Hans, on taking his departure from Reykjawik, had followed the line of the sea. We took our way through poor and sparse meadows, which made a desperate effort every year to show a little green. They very rarely succeed in a good show of yellow. Every now and then a spur of rock came down through the arid ground, leaving us scarcely room to pass. Our horses, however, appeared not only well acquainted with the country, but by a kind of instinct, knew which was the best road. My uncle had not even the satisfaction of urging forward his steed by whip, spur, or voice. It was utterly useless to show any signs of impatience. I could not help smiling to see him look so big on his little horse; his long legs now and then touching the ground made him look like a six-footed centaur.

"Good beast, good beast," he would cry. "I assure you, Henry, that I begin to think no animal is more intelligent than an Icelandic horse. Snow, tempest, impracticable roads, rocks, icebergs—nothing stops him. He is brave; he is sober; he is safe; he never makes a false step; never glides or slips from his path. I dare to say that if any river, any ford has to be crossed—and I have no doubt there will be many—you will see him enter the water without hesitation like an amphibious animal, and reach the opposite side in safety. We must not, however, attempt to hurry him; we must allow him to have his own way, and I will undertake to say that between us we shall do our ten leagues a day."

"We may do so," was my reply, "but what about our worthy guide?"

"I have not the slightest anxiety about him; that sort of people go ahead without knowing even what they are about. Look at Hans. He moves so little that it is impossible for him to become fatigued. Besides, if he were to complain of weariness, he could have the loan of my horse. I should have a violent attack of the cramp if I were not to have some sort of exercise. My arms are right—but my legs are getting a little stiff."

All this while we were advancing at a rapid pace. The country we had reached was already nearly a desert. Here and there could be seen an isolated farm, some solitary boër, or Icelandic house, built of wood, earth, fragments of lava —looking like beggars on the highway of life. These wretched and miserable huts excited in us such pity that we felt half disposed to leave alms at every door. In this country there are no roads, paths are nearly unknown, and vegetation, poor as it was, slowly as it reached perfection, soon obliterated all traces of the few travelers who passed from place to place.

A few stray cows and sheep were only seen occasionally. What, then, must we expect when we come to the up-heaved regions—to the districts broken and roughened from volcanic eruptions and subterraneous commotions?

We were to learn this all in good time. I saw, however, on consulting the map, that we avoided a good deal of this rough country, by following the winding and desolate shores of the sea. In reality, the great volcanic movement of the island, and all its attendant phenomena, is concentrated in the interior of the island; there, horizontal layers or strata of rocks, piled one upon the other, eruptions of basaltic origin, and streams of lava, have given this country a kind of supernatural reputation.

Little did I expect, however, the spectacle which awaited us when we reached the peninsula of Sneffels, where agglomerations of nature's ruins form a kind of terrible chaos.

Some two hours or more after we had left the city of Reykjawik, we reached the little town called Aoalkirkja, or the principal church. It consists simply of a few houses —not what in England or Germany we should call a hamlet. Hans stopped here one-half hour. He shared our frugal breakfast, answered *yes* and *no* to my uncle's questions as to the nature of the road, and at last when asked where we were to pass the night was as laconic as usual. "Gardar!" was his one-worded reply.

I took occasion to consult the map, to see where Gardar was to be found. After looking keenly I found a small town of that name on the borders of the Hvalfjord, about four miles from Reykjawik. I pointed this out to my uncle, who made a very energetic grimace.

"Only four miles out of twenty-two? Why it is only a little walk."

He was about to make some energetic observation to the guide, but Hans, without taking the slightest notice of him, went in front of the horses, and walked ahead with the same imperturbable phlegm he had always exhibited.

Still traveling over those apparently interminable and sandy prairies, we were compelled to go round the Kollafjord, then following a narrow strip of shore between high rocks and the sea, we came to the "aoalkirkja" of Brantar, and after another mile to "Saurboer Annexia," a chapel of ease, situated on the southern bank of the Hvalfjord. It was four o'clock in the evening and we had traveled four Danish miles, about equal to twenty English.

The fjord was in this place about half-a-mile in width. The sweeping and broken waves came rolling in upon the pointed rocks; the gulf was surrounded by rocky walls—a mighty cliff, three thousand feet in height, remarkable for its brown strata, separated here and there by beds of tufa of a reddish hue. Now, whatever may have been the intelligence of our horses, I had not the slightest reliance upon them, as a means of crossing a stormy arm of the sea. To ride over salt water upon the back of a little horse seemed to me absurd.

"If they are really intelligent," I said to myself, "they will certainly not make the attempt. In any case, I shall trust rather to my own intelligence than theirs."

But my uncle was in no humor to wait. He dug his heels into the sides of his steed, and made for the shore. His horse went to the very edge of the water, sniffed at the approaching wave and retreated.

My uncle, who was, sooth to say, quite as obstinate as the beast he bestrode, insisted on his making the desired advance. This attempt was followed by a new refusal on the part of the horse which quietly shook his head. This demonstration of rebellion was followed by a volley of words and a stout application of whipcord; also followed by kicks on the part of the horse, which threw its head and heels upwards and tried to throw his rider. At length the sturdy little pony, spreading out his legs, in a stiff and ludicrous attitude, got from under the professor's legs, and left him standing, with both feet on a separate stone, like the Colossus of Rhodes.

"Wretched animal!" cried my uncle, suddenly transformed into a foot passenger—and as angry and ashamed as a dismounted cavalry officer on the field of battle.

"*Farja,*" said the guide, tapping him familiarly on the shoulder.

"What, a ferry boat!"

"*Der,*" answered Hans, pointing to where lay the boat in question—"there."

"Well," I cried, much relieved by the information; "so it is."

"Why did you not say so before," cried my uncle; "why not start at once?"

"*Tidvatten,*" said the guide.

"What does he say?" I asked, considerably puzzled by the delay and the dialogue.

"He says tide," replied my uncle, translating the Danish word for my information.

"Of course, I understand—we must wait till the tide serves."

"*For bida?*" asked my uncle.

"*Ja,*" replied Hans.

My uncle frowned, stamped his feet and then followed the horses to where the boat lay. I thoroughly understood and appreciated the necessity for waiting, before crossing the fjord, for that moment when the sea at its highest point is in a state of slack water. As neither the ebb nor flow can then be felt, the ferry boat was in no danger of being carried out to sea, or dashed upon the rocky coast.

The favorable moment did not come until six o'clock in the evening. Then my uncle, myself, and guide, two boatmen and the four horses got into a very awkward flat-bottom boat. Accustomed as I had been to the steam ferryboats of the Elbe, I found the long oars of the boatmen but sorry means of locomotion. We were more than an hour in crossing the fjord; but at length the passage was concluded without accident. Half-an-hour later we reached Gardar.

CHAPTER X
TRAVELING IN ICELAND

It ought, one would have thought, to have been night, even in the sixty-fifth parallel of latitude; but still the nocturnal illumination did not surprise me. For in Iceland, during the months of June and July, the sun never sets. The temperature, however, was very much lower than I expected. I was cold, but even that did not affect me so much as ravenous hunger. Welcome indeed, therefore, was the hut which hospitably opened its doors to us.

It was merely the house of a peasant, but in the matter of hospitality, it was worthy of being the palace of a king. As we alighted at the door the master of the house came forward, held out his hand, and without any further ceremony, signaled to us to follow him. We followed him, for to accompany him was impossible. A long, narrow, gloomy passage led into the interior of this habitation, made from beams roughly squared by the ax. This passage gave ingress to every room. The chambers were four in number— the kitchen, the work-shop, where the weaving was carried on, the general sleeping-chamber of the family, and the best room, to which strangers were especially invited. My uncle, whose lofty stature had not been taken into consideration when the house was built, contrived to knock his head against the beams of the roof.

As soon as we had freed ourselves from our heavy traveling costume, the voice of our host was heard calling to us to come into the kitchen, the only room in which the Icelanders ever make any fire, no matter how cold it may be. My uncle, nothing loth, hastened to obey this hospitable and friendly invitation. I followed.

On our entrance, our worthy host, as if he had not seen us before, advanced ceremoniously, uttered a word which means " be happy," and then kissed both of us on the cheek. His wife followed, pronounced the same word, with the same ceremonial, then the husband and wife, placing their right hands upon their hearts, bowed profoundly.

This excellent Icelandic woman was the mother of nineteen children, who, little and big, rolled, crawled, and walked about in the midst of volumes of smoke arising from the angular fire-place in the middle of the room. Every now and then I could see a fresh white head, and a slightly melancholy expression of countenance, peering at me through the vapor. Both my uncle and myself, however, were very friendly with the whole party, and before we were aware of it, there were three or four of these little ones on our shoulders, as many on our boxes, and the rest hanging about our legs. Those who could speak kept crying out *saellvertu* in every possible and impossible key. Those who did not speak only made all the more noise.

This concert was interrupted by the announcement of supper. At this moment our worthy guide, the eider-duck hunter, came in after seeing to the feeding and stabling of the horses—which consisted in letting them loose to browse on the stunted green of the Icelandic prairies. There was little for them to eat, but moss and some very dry and innutritious grass; next day they were ready before the door, some time before we were.

"Welcome," said Hans. Then tranquilly, with the air of an automaton, without any more expression in one kiss than another, he embraced the host and hostess and their nineteen children.

This ceremony concluded to the satisfaction of all parties, we all sat down to table, that is twenty-four of us, somewhat crowded. Those who were best off had only two juveniles on their knees. As soon, however, as the inevitable soup was placed on the table, natural taciturnity common even to Icelandic babies, prevailed over all else. Our host filled our plates with a portion of *Lichen* soup of Iceland moss, of by no means disagreeable flavor, an enormous lump of fish floating in sour butter. After that there came some " skyr," a kind of curds and whey, served with biscuits and juniper-berry juice. To drink, we had blanda, skimmed milk with water. I was hungry, so hungry, that by way of dessert I finished up with a basin of thick oaten porridge.

As soon as the meal was over, the children disappeared, whilst the grown people sat around the fire-place, on which was placed turf, heather, cow dung and dried fish-bones. As soon as everybody was sufficiently warm, a general dispersion took place, all retiring to their respective couches.

Our hostess offered to pull off our stockings and trousers, according to the custom of the country, but as we graciously declined to be so honored, she left us to our bed of dry fodder.

Next day, at five in the morning, we took our leave of these hospitable peasants. My uncle had great difficulty in making them accept a sufficient and proper remuneration. That evening, after fording the Alfa and the Heta, two rivers rich in trout and pike, we were compelled to pass the night in a deserted house, worthy of being haunted by all the fays of Scandinavian mythology. The King of Cold had taken up his residence there, and made us feel his presence all night.

The two following days were remarkable by their lack of any particular incidents. Always the same damp and swampy soil; the same dreary uniformity; the same sad and monotonous aspect of scenery. I confess that fatigue began to tell severely upon me; but my uncle was as firm and as hard as he had been on the first day. I could not help admiring both the excellent Professor and the worthy guide; for they appeared to regard this rugged expedition as a mere walk!

On Saturday, the 20th of June, at six o'clock in the evening, we reached Budir, a small town picturesquely situated on the shore of the ocean; and here the guide asked for his money. My uncle settled with him immediately. It was now the family of Hans himself, that is to say, his uncles, his cousins-german, who offered us hospitality. We were exceedingly well received, and without taking too much advantage of the goodness of these worthy people, I should have liked very much to have rested with them after the fatigues of the journey. But my uncle, who did not require rest, had no idea of anything of the kind; and despite the fact that next day was Sunday, I was compelled once more to mount my steed.

The soil was again affected by the neighborhood of the mountains, whose granite peered out of the ground like tops of an old oak. We were skirting the enormous base of the mighty volcano. My uncle never took his eyes from off it; he could not keep from gesticulating, and looking at it with a kind of sullen defiance as much as to say " That is the giant I have made up my mind to conquer."

After four hours of steady traveling, the horses stopped of themselves before the door of the presbytery of Stapi. We had reached the foot of the volcano.

CHAPTER XI
WE REACH MOUNT SNEFFELS—THE " REYKIR "

STAPI is a town consisting of thirty huts, built on a large plain of lava, exposed to the rays of the sun, reflected from the volcano. It stretches its humble tenements along the end of a little fjord, surrounded by a basaltic wall of the most singular character. Here we found Nature proceeding geometrically, and working quite after a human fashion, as if she had employed the plummet line, the compass and the rule. If elsewhere she produces grand artistic effects by piling up huge masses without order or connection—if elsewhere we see truncated cones, imperfect pyramids, with an odd succession of lines; here, as if wishing to give a lesson in regularity, and preceding the architects of the early ages, she has erected a severe order of architecture, which neither the splendors of Babylon nor the marvels of Greece ever surpassed. The walls of the fjord, like nearly the whole of the peninsula, consisted of a series of vertical columns, in height about thirty feet. These upright pillars of stone, of the finest proportions, supported an archivault of horizontal columns which formed a kind of half-vaulted roof above the sea. At certain intervals, and below this natural basin, the eye was pleased and surprised by the sight of oval openings through which the outward waves came thundering in volleys of foam. Some banks of basalt, torn from their fastenings by the fury of the waves, lay scattered on the ground like the ruins of an ancient temple—ruins eternally young, over which the storms of ages swept without producing any perceptible effect!

This was the last stage of our journey. Hans had brought us along with fidelity and intelligence, and I began to feel somewhat more comfortable when I reflected that he was to accompany us still farther on our way.

When we halted before the house of the Rector, a small and incommodious cabin, neither handsome nor more comfortable than those of his neighbors, I saw a man in the act of shoeing a horse, a hammer in his hand, and a leathern apron tied around his waist.

" Be happy," said the eider-down hunter, using his national salutation in his own language.

" *Good-dag*—good-day! " replied the former, in excellent Danish.

" Kyrkoherde," cried Hans, turning round and introducing him to my uncle.

" The Rector," repeated the worthy Professor; " it appears, my dear Harry, that this worthy man is the Rector, and is not above doing his own work."

During the speaking of these few words the guide intimated to the Kyrkoherde what was the true state of the case. The good man, ceasing from his occupation, gave a kind of halloo, upon which a tall woman, almost a giantess, came out of the hut. She was at least six feet high, which in that region is something considerable. My first impression was one of horror. I thought she had come to give us the Icelandic kiss. I had, however, nothing to fear, for she did not even show much inclination to receive us into her house.

The room devoted to strangers appeared to me to be by far the worst in the presbytery; it was narrow, dirty and offensive. There was, however, no choice about the matter. The Rector had no notion of practicing the usual cordial and antique hospitality. My uncle soon became aware of the kind of man he had to deal with. Instead of a worthy and learned scholar, he found a dull, ill-mannered peasant. He therefore resolved to start on his great expedition as soon as possible. He did not care about fatigue, and resolved to spend a few days in the mountains.

The preparations for our departure were made the very next day after our arrival at Stapi; Hans now hired three Icelanders to take the place of the horses—which could no longer carry our luggage. When, however, these worthy islanders had reached the bottom of the crater, they were to go back and leave us to ourselves. This point was settled before they would agree to start. On this occasion, my uncle partially confided in Hans, the eider-duck hunter, and gave him to understand that it was his intention to continue his exploration of the volcano to the last possible limits.

Hans listened calmly, and then nodded his head. To go there, or elsewhere, to bury himself in the bowels of the earth, or to travel over its summit, was all the same to him! As for me, amused and occupied by the incidents of travel, I had begun to forget the inevitable future; but now I was once more destined to realize the actual state of affairs. What was to be done? Run away? But if I really had intended to leave Professor Hardwigg to his fate, it should have been at Hamburg and not at the foot of Sneffels.

One idea above all others, began to trouble me: a very terrible idea, and one calculated to shake the nerves of a man even less sensitive than myself. "Let us consider the matter," I said to myself; "we are going to ascend the Sneffels mountain. Well and good. We are about to pay a visit to the very bottom of the crater. Good, still. Others have done it and did not perish from that course.

"That, however, is not the whole matter to be considered. If a road does really present itself by which to descend into the dark and subterraneous bowels of Mother Earth, if this thrice unhappy Saknussemm has really told the truth, we shall be most certainly lost in the midst of the labyrinth of subterraneous galleries of the volcano. Now, we have no evidence to prove that Sneffels is really extinct. What proof have we that an eruption is not shortly about to take place? Because the monster has slept soundly since 1229, does it follow that he is never to wake? If he does wake what is to become of us?"

These were questions worth thinking about, and upon them I reflected long and deeply. I could not lie down in search of sleep without dreaming of eruptions. The more I thought, the more I objected to be reduced to the state of dross and ashes. I could stand it no longer; so I determined at last to submit the whole case to my uncle, in the most adroit manner possible, and under the form of some totally irreconcilable hypothesis.

I sought him. I laid before him my fears, and then drew back in order to let him get his passion over at his ease.

"I have been thinking about the matter," he said, in the quietest tone in the world.

What did he mean? Was he at last about to listen to the voice of reason? Did he think of suspending his projects?

It was almost too much happiness to be true. I however made no remark. In fact, I was only too anxious not to interrupt him, and allowed him to reflect at his leisure. After some moments he spoke out.

"I have been thinking about the matter," he resumed. "Ever since we have been at Stapi, my mind has been almost solely occupied with the grave question which has been submitted to me by yourself—for nothing would be unwiser and more inconsistent than to act with imprudence."

"I heartily agree with you, my dear uncle," was my somewhat hopeful rejoinder.

"It is now six hundred years since Sneffels has spoken, but though now reduced to a state of utter silence, he may speak again. New volcanic eruptions are always preceded by perfectly well-known phenomena. I have closely examined the inhabitants of this region; I have carefully studied the soil, and I beg to tell you emphatically, my dear Harry, there will be no eruption at present."

As I listened to his positive affirmations, I was stupefied and could say nothing.

"I see you doubt my word," said my uncle; "follow me."

I obeyed mechanically. Leaving the presbytery, the Professor took a road through an opening in the basaltic rock, which led far away from the sea. We were soon in open country, if we could give such a name to a place all covered with volcanic deposits. The whole land seemed crushed under the weight of enormous stones—of trap, of basalt, of granite, of lava, and of all other volcanic substances.

I could see many spouts of steam rising in the air. These white vapors, called in the Icelandic language "reykir," come·from hot water fountains, and indicate by their violence the volcanic activity of the soil. Now the sight of these appeared to justify my apprehension. I was, therefore, all the more surprised and mortified when my uncle thus addressed me. "You see all this smoke, Harry, my boy?"

"Yes, sir."

"Well, as long as you see them thus, you have nothing to fear from the volcano."

"How can that be?"

"Be careful to remember this," continued the Professor.

"At the approach of an eruption these spouts of vapor redouble their activity—to disappear altogether during the period of volcanic eruption; for the elastic fluids, no longer having the necessary tension, seek refuge in the interior of the crater, instead of escaping through the fissures of the earth. If, then, the steam remains in its normal or habitual state, if their energy does not increase, and if you add to this, the remark, that the wind is not replaced by heavy atmospheric pressure and dead calm, you may be quite sure that there is no fear of any immediate eruption."

"But——"

"Enough, my boy. When science has sent forth her fiat—it is only to hear and obey."

I came back to the house quite downcast and disappointed. My uncle had completely defeated me with his scientific arguments. Nevertheless, I had still one hope, and that was, when once we were at the bottom of the crater, that it would be impossible in default of a gallery or tunnel, to descend any deeper; and this, despite all the learned Saknussemms in the world.

I passed the whole of the following night with a nightmare on my chest! and, after unheard-of miseries and tortures, found myself in the very depths of the earth, from which I was suddenly launched into planetary space, under the form of an eruptive rock!

Next day, the 23d June, Hans calmly awaited us outside the presbytery with his two companions loaded with provisions, tools, and instruments. Two iron-shod poles, two guns, and two large game bags, were reserved for my uncle and myself. Hans, who was a man who never forgot even the minutest precautions, had added to our baggage a large skin full of water, as an addition to our gourds. This assured us water for eight days.

It was nine o'clock in the morning when we were quite ready. The rector and his huge wife or servant, I never knew which, stood at the door to see us off. They appeared to be about to inflict on us the usual final kiss of the Icelanders. To our supreme astonishment their adieu took the shape of a formidable bill, in which they even counted the use of the pastoral house, really and truly the most abominable and dirty place I ever was in. The worthy couple cheated and robbed us like a Swiss innkeeper, and made us feel, by the sum we had to pay, the splendors of their hospitality. My uncle, however, paid without bargaining. A man who had made up his mind to undertake a voyage into the Interior of the Earth, is not the man to haggle over a few miserable rix-dollars.

This important matter settled, Hans gave the signal for departure, and some few moments later we had left Stapi.

CHAPTER XII
THE ASCENT OF MOUNT SNEFFELS

THE huge volcano which was the first stage of our daring experiment, is above five thousand feet high. Sneffels is the termination of a long range of volcanic mountains, of a different character to the system of the island itself. One of its peculiarities is its two huge pointed summits. From where we started it was impossible to make out the real outlines of the peak against the gray field of sky. All we could distinguish was a vast dome of white, which fell downwards from the head of the giant. The commencement of the great undertaking filled me with awe. Now that we had actually started, I began to believe in the reality of the undertaking!

Our party formed quite a procession. We walked in single file, preceded by Hans, the imperturbable eider-duck hunter. He calmly led us by narrow paths where two persons could by no possibility walk abreast. Conversation was wholly impossible. We had all the more opportunity to reflect, and to admire the awful grandeur of the scene around.

As we advanced, the road became every moment more difficult. The soil was broken and dangerous. The rocks broke and gave way under our feet, and we had to be scrupulously careful in order to avoid dangerous and constant falls. Hans advanced as calmly as if he had been walking over Salisbury Plain; sometimes he would disappear behind huge blocks of stone, and we momentarily lost sight of him. There was a little period of anxiety and then there was a shrill whistle, just to tell us where to look for him.

Occasionally he would take it into his head to stop to

pick up lumps of rock, and silently pile them up into small heaps, *in order that we might not lose our way on our return.* He had no idea of the journey we were about to undertake. At all events, the precaution was a good one; though how utterly useless and unnecessary—but I must not anticipate.

Three hours of terrible fatigue, walking incessantly, had only brought us to the foot of the great mountain. This will give some notion of what we had still to undergo.

Suddenly, however, Hans cried a halt—that is, he made signs to that effect—and a summary kind of breakfast was laid out on the lava before us. My uncle, who now was simply Professor Hardwigg, was so eager to advance, that he bolted his food like a greedy clown. This halt for refreshment was also a halt for repose. The Professor was therefore compelled to wait the good pleasure of his imperturbable guide, who did not give the signal for departure for a good hour. The three Icelanders, who were as taciturn as their comrade, did not say a word; but went on eating and drinking very quietly and soberly.

From this, our first real stage, we began to ascend the slopes of the Sneffels volcano. Its magnificent snowy night-cap, as we began to call it, by an optical delusion very common in mountains, appeared to me to be close at hand; and yet how many long weary hours must elapse before we reached its summit. What unheard-of fatigue must we endure!

The stones on the mountain side, held together by no cement of soil, bound together by no roots or creeping herbs, gave way continually under our feet, and went rushing below into the plains, like a series of small avalanches. In certain places the sides of this stupendous mountain were at an angle so steep that it was impossible to climb upwards, and we were compelled to get round these obstacles as best we might. Those who understand Alpine climbing will comprehend our difficutlies. Often we were obliged to help each other along by means of our climbing poles.

I must say this for my uncle, that he stuck as close to me as possible. He never lost sight of me, and on many occasions his arm supplied me with firm and solid support. He was strong, wiry, and apparently insensible to fatigue. Another great advantage with him was that he had the innate sentiment of equilibrium—for he never slipped or failed in his steps. The Icelanders, though heavily loaded, climbed with the agility of mountaineers.

Looking up, every now and then, at the height of the great volcano of Sneffels, it appeared to me wholly impossible to reach to the summit on that side; at all events, if the angle of inclination did not speedily change.

Fortunately, after an hour of unheard-of fatigues, and of gymnastic exercises that would have been trying to an acrobat, we came to a vast field of ice, which wholly surrounded the bottom of the cone of the volcano. The natives called it the table-cloth, probably from some such reason as the dwellers in the Cape of Good Hope call their mountain Table Mountain, and their roads Table Bay.

Here, to our mutual surprise, we found an actual flight of stone steps, which wonderfully assisted our ascent. This singular flight of stairs was, like everything else, volcanic. It had been formed by one of those torrents of stones cast up by the eruptions, and of which the Icelandic name is stinâ. If this singular torrent had not been checked in its descent by the peculiar shape of the flanks of the mountain, it would have swept into the sea, and would have formed new islands. Such as it was, it served us admirably. The abrupt character of the slopes momentarily increased, but these remarkable stone steps, a little less difficult than those of the Egyptian pyramids, were the one simple natural means by which we were enabled to proceed.

About seven in the evening of that day, after having clambered up two thousand of these rough steps, we found ourselves overlooking a kind of spur or projection of the mountain—a sort of buttress upon which the cone-like crater, properly so called, leaned for support.

The ocean lay beneath us at a depth of more than three thousand two hundred feet—a grand and mighty spectacle. We had reached the region of eternal snows. The cold was keen, searching and intense. The wind blew with extraordinary violence. I was utterly exhausted.

My worthy uncle, the Professor, saw clearly that my legs refused further service, and that, in fact, I was utterly exhausted. Despite his hot and feverish impatience, he decided, with a sigh, upon a halt. He called the eider-duck hunter to his side.   That worthy, however, shook his head.

"Ofvanfor," was his sole spoken reply.

"It appears," says my uncle with a woe-begone look, "that we must go higher."

He then turned to Hans, and asked him to give some reason for this decisive response.

"Mistour," replied the guide.

"*Ja mistour*—yes, the mistour," cried one of the Icelandic guides in a terrified tone.

It was the first time he had spoken.

"What does this mysterious word signify?" I anxiously inquired.

"Look," said my uncle.

I looked down upon the plain below, and I saw a vast, a prodigious volume of pulverized pumice-stone, of sand, of dust, rising to the heavens in the form of a mighty waterspout. It resembled the fearful phenomenon of a similar character known to the travelers in the desert of the great Sahara.

The wind was driving it directly towards that side of Sneffels on which we were perched. This opaque veil standing up between us and the sun projected a deep shadow on the flanks of the mountain. If this sand-spout broke over us, we must all be infallibly destroyed, crushed in its fearful embraces. This extraordinary phenomenon, very common when the wind shakes the glaciers, and sweeps over the arid plains, is in the Icelandic tongue called *mistour*.

"Hastigt, Hastigt!" cried our guide.

Now I certainly knew nothing of Danish, but I thoroughly understood that his gestures were meant to quicken us. The guide turned rapidly in a direction which would take us to the back of the crater, all the while ascending slightly. We followed rapidly, despite our excessive fatigue.

A quarter of an hour later Hans paused to enable us to look back. The mighty whirlwind of sand was spreading up the slope of the mountain to the very spot where we had proposed to halt. Huge stones were caught up, cast into the air, and thrown about as during an eruption. We were happily a little out of the direction of the wind, and therefore out of reach of danger. But for the precaution and knowledge of our guide, our dislocated bodies, our crushed and broken limbs, would have been cast to the wind, like dust from some unknown meteor.

Hans, however, did not think it prudent to pass the night on the bare side of the cone. We therefore continued our journey in a zigzag direction. The fifteen hundred feet which remained to be accomplished took us at least five hours. The turnings and windings, the no-thoroughfares, the marches and marches, turned that insignificant distance into at least three leagues. I never felt such misery, fatigue and exhaustion in my life. I was ready to faint from hunger and cold. The rarefied air at the same time painfully acted upon my lungs.

At last, when I thought myself at my last gasp, about eleven at night, it being in that region quite dark, we reached the summit of Mount Sneffels! it was in an awful mood of mind, that despite my fatigue, before I descended into the crater which was to shelter us for the night, I paused to behold the sun rise at midnight on the very day of its lowest declension, and enjoyed the spectacle of its ghastly pale rays cast upon the isle which lay sleeping at our feet!

I no longer wondered at people traveling all the way from England to Norway, to behold this magical and wondrous spectacle.

CHAPTER XIII
THE SHADOW OF SCARTARIS

OUR supper was eaten with ease and rapidity, after which everybody did the best he could for himself within the hollow of the crater. The bed was hard, the shelter unsatisfactory, the situation painful—lying in the open air, five thousand feet above the level of the sea! Nevertheless, it has seldom happened to me to sleep so well as I did on that particular night. I did not even dream. So much for the effects of what my uncle called "wholesome fatigue."

Next day, when we awoke under the rays of a bright and glorious sun, we were nearly frozen by the keen air. I left my granite couch and made one of the party to enjoy a view of the magnificent spectacle which developed itself, panorama-like, at our feet.

I stood upon the lofty summit of Mount Sneffels' southern peak. Thence I was able to obtain a view of the greater part of the island. The optical delusion, common to all lofty heights, raised the shores of the island, while the central portions appeared depressed. It was by no means too great a flight of fancy to believe that a giant picture was stretched out before me. I could see the deep valleys that crossed each other in every direction. I could see precipices looking like sides of wells, lakes that seemed to be changed into ponds, ponds that looked like puddles, and rivers that were transformed into petty brooks. To my right were glaciers upon glaciers, and multiplied peaks, topped with light clouds of smoke.

The undulation of these infinite numbers of mountains, whose snowy summits make them look as if covered by foam, recalled to my remembrance the surface of a storm-beaten ocean. If I looked towards the west, the ocean lay before me in all its majesty grandeur, a continuation as it were, of these fleecy hill-tops. Where the earth ended and the sea began it was impossible for the eye to distinguish.

I soon felt that strange and mysterious sensation which is awakened in the mind when looking down from lofty hill tops, and now I was able to do so without any feeling of nervousness, having fortunately hardened myself to that kind of sublime contemplation. I wholly forgot who I was, and where I was. I became intoxicated with a sense of lofty sublimity, without thought of the abysses into which my daring was soon about to plunge me. I was presently, however, brought back to the realities of life by the arrival of the Professor and Hans, who joined me upon the lofty summit of the peak.

My uncle, turning in a westerly direction, pointed out to me a light cloud of vapor, a kind of haze, with a faint outline of land rising out of the waters. " Greenland! " said he.

" Greenland? " cried I in reply.

" Yes," continued my uncle, who always when explaining anything spoke as if he were in a Professor's chair; " we are not more than thirty-five leagues distant from that wonderful land. When the great annual break up of the ice takes place, white bears come over to Iceland, carried by the floating masses of ice from the north. This, however, is a matter of little consequence. We are now on the summit of the great, the transcendent Sneffels, and here are its two peaks, north and south. Hans will tell you the name by which the people of Iceland call that on which we stand."

My uncle turned to the imperturbable guide, who nodded, and spoke as usual—one word. *"Scartaris."*

My uncle looked at me with a proud and triumphant glance. "A crater," he said, "you hear?"

I did hear, but I was totally unable to make reply.

The crater of Mount Sneffels represented an inverted cone, the gaping orifice apparently half a mile across; the depth indefinite feet. Conceive what this *hole* must have been like when full of flame and thunder and lightning. The bottom of the funnel-shaped hollow was about five hundred feet in circumference, by which it will be seen that the slope from the summit to the bottom was very gradual, and we were therefore clearly able to get there without much fatigue or difficulty. Involuntarily, I compared this crater to an enormous loaded cannon; and the comparison completely terrified me.

"To descend into the interior of a cannon," I thought to myself, "when perhaps it is loaded, and will go off at the least shock, is the act of a madman."

But there was no longer any opportunity for me to hesitate. Hans, with a perfectly calm and indifferent air, took his usual post at the head of the adventurous little band. I followed without uttering a syllable. I felt like the lamb led to the slaughter.

In order to render the descent less difficult, Hans took his way down the interior of the cone in rather a zigzag fashion, making, as the sailors say, long tacks to the eastward, followed by equally long ones to the west. It was necessary to walk through the midst of eruptive rocks, some of which, shaken in their balance, went rolling down with thundering clamor to the bottom of the abyss. These continual falls awoke echoes of singular power and effect.

Many portions of the cone consisted of inferior glaciers. Hans, whenever he met with one of these obstacles advanced with a great show of precaution, sounding the soil with his long iron pole in order to discover fissures and layers of deep soft snow. In many doubtful or dangerous places, it became necessary for us to be tied together by a long rope in order that should any one of us be unfortunate enough to slip, he would be supported by his companions. This connecting link was doubtless a prudent precaution, but not by any means unattended with danger.

Nevertheless, despite all the manifold difficulties of the descent, along slopes with which our guide was wholly unacquainted, we made considerable progress without accident. One of our great parcels of rope slipped from one of the Iceland porters, and rushed by a short cut to the bottom of the abyss.

By mid-day we were at the end of our journey. I looked upwards, and saw only the upper orifice of the cone, which served as a circular frame to a very small portion of the sky—a portion which seemed to me singularly beautiful. Should I ever again gaze on that lovely sunlit sky!

The only exception to this extraordinary landscape, was the Peak of Scartaris, which seemed lost in the great void of the heavens.

The bottom of the crater was composed of three separate shafts, through which, during periods of eruption, when Sneffels was in action, the great central furnace sent forth its burning lava and poisonous vapors. Each of these chimneys or shafts gaped open-mouthed in our path. I kept as far away from them as possible, not even venturing to take the faintest peep downwards.

As for the Professor, after a rapid examination of their disposition and characteristics, he became breathless and panting. He ran from one to the other like a delighted school-boy, gesticulating wildly, and uttering incomprehensible and disjointed phrases in all sorts of languages. Hans, the guide, and his humbler companions seated themselves on some piles of lava and looked silently on. They clearly took my uncle for a lunatic; and—waited the result.

Suddenly the Professor uttered a wild, unearthly cry. At first I imagined he had lost his footing, and was falling headlong into one of the yawning gulfs. Nothing of the kind. I saw him, his arms spread out to their widest extent, his legs stretched apart, standing upright before an enormous pedestal, high enough and black enough to bear a gigantic statue of Pluto. His attitude and mien were that of a man utterly stupefied. But his stupefaction was speedily changed to the wildest joy. "Harry! Harry! come here!" he cried; "make haste—wonderful—wonderful!"

Unable to understand what he meant, I turned to obey his commands. Neither Hans, nor the other Icelanders moved a step.

"Look!" said the Professor, in something of the manner of the French general, pointing out the pyramids to his army. And fully partaking his stupefaction, if not his joy, I read on the eastern side of the huge block of stone, the same characters, half eaten away by the corrosive action of time, the name, to me a thousand times accursed—

ᚾᛃᚾᛏ ᚼᛃᚱᛃᚾᚾᛃᛏᚷ

"Arne Saknussemm!" cried my uncle, "now, unbeliever, do you begin to have faith?"

It was totally impossible for me to answer a single word. I went back to my pile of lava, in a state of silent awe. The evidence was unanswerable, overwhelming!

In a few moments, however, my thoughts were far away, back in my German home, with Gretchen and the old cook. What would I have given for one of my cousin's smiles, for one of the ancient domestic's omelettes, and for my own feather bed! How long I remained in this state I know not. All I can say is, that when at last I raised my head from between my hands, there remained at the bottom of the crater only myself, my uncle and Hans. The Icelandic porters had been dismissed and were now descending the exterior slopes of Mount Sneffels, on their way to Stapi. How heartily did I wish myself with them!

Hans slept tranquilly at the foot of a rock in a kind of rill of lava, where he had made himself a rough and ready bed. My uncle was walking about the bottom of the crater like a wild beast in a cage. I had no desire, neither had I the strength, to move from my recumbent position. Taking example by the guide, I gave way to a kind of painful somnolency, during which I seemed both to hear and feel continual heavings and shudderings in the mountain. In this way we passed our first night in the interior of a crater.

Next morning, a gray, cloudy, heavy sky hung like a funeral-pall over the summit of the volcanic cone. I did not notice it so much from the obscurity that reigned around us, as from the rage with which my uncle was devoured.

I fully understood the reason, and again a glimpse of hope made my heart leap with joy. I will briefly explain the cause. Of the three openings which yawned beneath our steps, only one could have been followed by the adventurous Saknussemm. According to the words of the learned Icelander, it was only to be known by that one particular mentioned in the cryptograph, that the shadow of Scartaris fell upon it, just touching its mouth in the last days of the month of June. We were, in fact, to consider the pointed peak as the *stylus* of an immense sun-dial, the shadow of which pointed on one given day, like the inexorable finger of fate, to the yawning chasm which led into the interior of the earth.

Now, as often happens in these regions, should the sun fail to burst through the clouds, no shadow. Consequently, no chance of discovering the right aperture. We had already reached the 25th June. If the kindly heavens would only remain densely clouded for six more days, we should have to put off our voyage of discovery for another year, when certainly there would be one person fewer in the party. I already had sufficient of the mad and monstrous enterprise.

It would be utterly impossible to depict the impotent rage of Professor Hardwigg. The day passed away, and not the faintest outline of a shadow could be seen at the bottom of the crater. Hans the guide never moved from his place. He must have been curious to know what we were about, if indeed he could believe we were about anything. As for my uncle, he never addressed a word to me. He was nursing his wrath to keep it warm! His eyes fixed on the black and foggy atmosphere, his complexion hideous with suppressed passion. Never had his eyes appeared so fierce, his nose so aquiline, his mouth so hard and firm.

On the 26th no change for the better. A mixture of rain and snow fell during the whole day. Hans very quietly built himself a hut of lava into which he retired like Diogenes into his tub. I took a malicious delight in watching the thousand little cascades that flowed down the side of the cone, carrying with them at times a stream of stones into the " vasty deep " below.

My uncle was almost frantic: to be sure it was enough to make even a patient man angry. He had reached to a certain extent the goal of his desires, and yet he was likely to be wrecked in port.

But if the heavens and the elements are capable of causing us much pain and sorrow, there are two sides to a medal. And there was reserved for Professor Hardwigg a brilliant and sudden surprise which was to compensate him for all his sufferings. Next day the sky was still overcast, but on Sunday, the 26th, the last day but one of the month, with a sudden change of wind and a new moon there came a change of weather. The sun poured its beaming rays to the very bottom of the crater.

Each hillock, every rock, every stone, every asperity of the soil had its share of the luminous effulgence, and its shadow fell heavily on the soil. Among others, to his insane delight, the shadow of Scartaris was marked and clear, and moved slowly with the radiant star of day.

My uncle moved with it in a state of mental ecstasy. 'At twelve o'clock exactly, when the sun had attained its highest altitude for the day, the shadow fell upon the edge of the central pit!

" Here it is," gasped the Professor in an agony of joy, " here it is—we have found it. Forward, my friends, into the Interior of the Earth."

I looked curiously at Hans to see what reply he would make to this terrific announcement. " Forut," said the guide tranquilly.

" Forward it is," answered my uncle, who was now in the seventh heaven of delight.

When we were quite ready, our watches indicated thirteen minutes past one!

CHAPTER XIV
THE REAL JOURNEY COMMENCES

OUR real journey now commenced. Hitherto our courage and determination had overcome all difficulties. We were fatigued at times; and that was all. Now, unknown and fearful dangers were to be encountered.

I had not as yet ventured to take a glimpse down the horrible abyss into which in a few minutes more I was about to plunge. The fatal moment had, however, at last arrived. I had still the option of refusing or accepting a share in this foolish and audacious enterprise. But I was ashamed to show more fear than the eider-duck hunter. Hans seemed to accept the difficulties of the journey so tranquilly, with such calm indifference, with such perfect recklessness of all danger, that I actually blushed to appear less of a man than he! Had I been alone with my uncle, I should certaily have sat down and argued the point fully; but in the presence of the guide I held my tongue. I gave one moment to the thought of my charming cousin, and then I advanced to the mouth of the central shaft.

It measured about a hundred feet in diameter, which made about three hundred in circumference. I leaned over a rock which stood on its edge, and looked down. My hair stood on end, my teeth chattered, my limbs trembled, I seemed utterly to lose my center of gravity, while my head was in a sort of whirl, like that of a drunken man. There is nothing more powerful than this attraction towards an abyss. I was about to fall headlong into the gaping well, when I was drawn back by a firm and powerful hand. It was that of Hans. I had not taken lessons enough at the Frelser's-kirk of Copenhagen in the art of looking down from lofty eminences without blinking!

However, few as the minutes were during which I gazed down this tremendous and even wondrous shaft, I had a sufficient glimpse of it to give me some idea of its physical conformation. Its sides, which were almost as perpendicular as those of a well, presented numerous projections which doubtless would assist our descent.

It was a sort of wild and savage staircase, without bannister or fence. A rope fastened above, near the surface, would certainly support our weight and enable us to reach the bottom, but how, when we had arrived at its utmost depth, were we to loosen it above? This was, I thought, a question of some importance.

My uncle, however, was one of those men who are nearly always prepared with expedients. He hit upon a very simple method of obviating this difficulty. He unrolled a cord about as thick as my thumb, and at least four hundred feet in length. He allowed about half of it to go down the pit and catch in a hitch over a great block of lava which stood on the edge of the precipice. This done, he threw the second half after the first.

Each of us could now descend by catching the two cords in one hand. When about two hundred feet below, all the explorer had to do was to let go one end and pull away at the other, when the cord would come falling at his feet. In order to go down farther, all that was necessary was to continue the same operation. Going down thus appeared to me easy enough, it was the coming up again that now occupied my thoughts.

"Now," said my uncle, as soon as he had completed this important preparation, "let us see about the baggage. It must be divided into three separate parcels, and each of us must carry one on his back. I allude to the more important and fragile articles." My worthy and ingenious uncle did not appear to consider that we came under that denomination. "Hans," he continued, "you will take charge of the tools and some of the provisions; you, Harry, must take possession of another third of the provisions and of the arms. I will load myself with the rest of the eatables, and with the more delicate instruments."

"But," I exclaimed, "our clothes, this mass of cord and ladders—who will undertake to carry them down?"

"They will go down of themselves."

"And how so?" I asked.

"You shall see." My uncle was not fond of half measures, nor did he like anything in the way of hesitation. Giving his orders to Hans he had the whole of the non-fragile articles made up into one bundle; and the packet firmly and solidly fastened, was simply pitched over the edge of the gulf.

I heard the moaning of the suddenly displaced air, and the noise of falling stones. My uncle leaning over the abyss followed the descent of his luggage with a perfectly self-satisfied air, and did not rise until it had completely disappeared from sight. " Now then," he cried, " it is our turn."

I put it in good faith to any man of common sense—was it possible to hear this energetic cry without a shudder? The Professor fastened his case of instruments on his back. Hans took charge of the tools, I of the arms. The descent then commenced in the following order: Hans went first, my uncle followed, and I went last. Our progress was made in profound silence—a silence only troubled by the fall of pieces of rock, which breaking from the jagged sides, fell with a roar into the depths below.

I allowed myself to slide, so to speak, holding frantically on the double cord with one hand and with the other keeping myself off the rocks by the assistance of my iron-shod pole. One idea was all the time impressed upon my brain. I feared that the upper support would fail me. The cord appeared to me far too fragile to bear the weight of three such persons as we were, with our luggage. I made as little use of it as possible, trusting to my own agility and doing miracles in the way of feats of dexterity and strength upon the projecting shelves and spurs of lava which my feet seemed to clutch as strongly as my hands.

The guide went first as I have said, and when one of the slippery and frail supports broke from under his feet he had recourse to his usual monosyllabic way of speaking. " Gifakt——"

" Attention—look out," repeated my uncle.

In about half an hour we reached a kind of small terrace formed by a fragment of rock projecting some distance from the sides of the shaft. Hans now began to haul upon the cord on one side only, the other going as quietly upward as the other came down. It fell at last, bringing with it a shower of small stones, lava and dust, a disagreeable kind of rain or hail.

While we were seated on this extraordinary bench I ventured once more to look downwards. With a sigh I discovered that the bottom was still wholly invisible. Were we, then, going direct to the interior of the earth?

The performance with the cord recommenced, and a quarter of an hour later we had descended another two hundred feet.

I have very strong doubts if the most determined geologist would, during that descent have studied the nature of the different layers of earth around him.   I did not trouble my head much about the matter; whether we were among the combustible carbon, silurians, or primitive soil, I neither knew nor cared to know.

Not so the inveterate Professor.   He must have taken notes all the way down, for, at one of our halts, he began a brief lecture.   " The farther we advance," said he, " the greater is my confidence in the result.   The disposition of these volcana strata absolutely confirms the theories of Sir Humphrey Davy.   We are still within the region of the primordial soil, the soil in which took place the chemical operation of metals becoming inflamed by coming in contact with the air and water.   I at once regret the old and now for ever exploded theory of a central fire.   At all events, we shall soon know the truth."

Such was the conclusion to which he came.   I, however, was very far from being in humor to discuss the matter. I had something else to think of.   My silence was taken for consent; and still we continued to go down.

At the expiration of three hours, we were, to all appearance, as far off as ever from the bottom of the well.   When I looked upwards, however, I could see that the upper orifice was every minute decreasing in size.   The sides of the shaft were getting closer and closer together, we were approaching the regions of eternal night!

And still we continued to descend!   At length, I noticed that when pieces of stone were detached from the sides of this stupendous precipice, they were swallowed up with less noise than before.   The final sound was sooner heard.   We were approaching the bottom of the abyss!

As I had been very careful to keep account of all the changes of cord which took place, I was able to tell exactly what was the depth we had reached, as well as the time it had taken.   We had shifted the rope twenty-eight times, each operation taking a quarter of an hour, which in all made seven hours.   To this had to be added twenty-eight pauses; in all ten hours and a half.   We started at one, it was now, therefore, about eleven o'clock at night.

It does not require great knowledge of arithmetic to know that twenty-eight times two hundred feet makes five thousand six hundred feet in all (more than an English mile).

While I was making this mental calculation a voice broke the silence. It was the voice of Hans. " Halt ! " he cried.

I checked myself very suddenly, just at the moment when I was about to kick my uncle on the head.

" We have reached the end of our journey," said the worthy Professor in a satisfied tone.

" What, the interior of the earth ? " said I, slipping down to his side.

" No, you stupid fellow ! but we have reached the bottom of the well."

" And I suppose there is no farther progress to be made ? " I hopefully exclaimed.

" Oh, yes, I can dimly see a sort of tunnel, which turns off obliquely to the right. At all events, we must see about that to-morrow. Let us sup now, and seek slumber as best we may."

I thought it time, but made no observations on that point. I was fairly launched on a desperate course, and all I had to do was to go forward hopefully and trustingly.

It was not even now quite dark, the light filtering down in a most extraordinary manner. We opened the provision bag, ate a frugal supper, and each did his best to find a bed amid the pile of stones, dirt, and lava which had accumulated for ages at the bottom of the shaft. I happened to grope out the pile of ropes, ladders, and clothes which we had thrown down ; and upon them I stretched myself. After such a day's labor, my rough bed seemed as soft as down !

For a while I lay in a sort of pleasant trance. Presently, after lying quietly for some minutes, I opened my eyes and looked upwards. As I did so I made out a brilliant little dot, at the extremity of this long, gigantic telescope.

It was a star without scintillating rays. According to my calculation, it must be in the constellation of the Little Bear. After this little bit of astronomical recreation, I dropped into a sound sleep.

CHAPTER XV
WE CONTINUE OUR DESCENT

At eight o'clock the next morning, a faint kind of dawn awoke us. The thousand and one prisms of the lava collected the light as it passed and brought it to us like a shower of sparks. We were able with ease to see objects around us.

"Well, Harry, my boy," cried the delighted Professor, rubbing his hands together, "what say you now? Did you ever pass a more tranquil night in our house in the König Strasse? No deafening sounds of cart-wheels, no cries of hawkers, no bad language from boatmen or watermen!"

"Well, uncle, we are quiet at the bottom of this well—but to me there is something terrible in this calm."

"Why," said the Professor, hotly, "one would say you were already beginning to be afraid. How will you get on presently? Do you know, that as yet, we have not penetrated one inch into the bowels of the earth."

"What can you mean, sir?" was my bewildered and astonished reply.

"I mean to say that we have only just reached the soil of the island itself. This long vertical tube, which ends at the bottom of the crater of Sneffels, ceases here just about on a level with the sea."

"Are you sure, sir?"

"Quite sure. Consult the barometer."

It was quite true that the mercury, after rising gradually in the instrument, as long as our descent was taking place, had stopped precisely at twenty-nine degrees. "You perceive," said the Professor, "we have as yet only to endure the pressure of air. I am curious to replace the barometer by the manometer." The barometer, in fact, was about to become useless—as soon as the weight of the air was greater than what was calculated as above the level of the ocean.

"But," said I, "is it not very much to be feared that this ever-increasing pressure may not in the end turn out very painful and inconvenient?"

"No," said he. "We shall descend very slowly, and our lungs will be gradually accustomed to breathe compressed air. It is well known that aëronauts have gone so high as to be nearly without air at all—why, then, should we not accustom ourselves to breathe when we have, say, a little too much of it? For myself, I am certain I shall prefer it. Let us not lose a moment. Where is the packet which preceded us in our descent?"

I smilingly pointed it out to my uncle. Hans had not seen it, and believed it caught somewhere above us; "huppe" as he phrased it.

"Now," said my uncle, "let us breakfast, and breakfast like people who have a long day's work before them."

Biscuit and dried meat, washed down by some mouthfuls of water flavored with schiedam, was the material of our luxurious meal. As soon as it was finished, my uncle took from his pocket a note-book destined to be filled by memoranda of our travels. He had already placed his instruments in order, and this is what he wrote:—Monday, July 1st. Chronometer, 8h. 17m. morning. Barometer, 29 degrees. Thermometer, 43 degrees Fahr. Direction, E. S. E.

This last observation referred to the obscure gallery, and was indicated to us by the compass.

"Now, Harry," cried the Professor, in an enthusiastic tone of voice, "we are truly about to take our first step into the Interior of the Earth; never before visited by man since the first creation of the world. You may consider, therefore, that at this precise moment our travels really commence."

As my uncle made this remark, he took in one hand the Ruhmkorff coil apparatus, which hung round his neck, and with the other he put the electric current into communication with the worm of the lantern. And a bright light at once illumined that dark and gloomy tunnel! The effect was magical!

Hans, who carried the second apparatus, had it also put into operation. This ingenious application of electricity to practical purposes enabled us to move along by the light of an artificial day, amid even the flow of the most inflammable and combustible gases.

"Forward!" cried my uncle. Each took up his burden. Hans went first, my uncle followed, and I going third, we entered the somber gallery! Just as we were about to engulf ourselves in this dismal passage, I lifted up my head, and through the tubelike shaft I saw that Iceland sky I was never to see again! Was it the last I should ever see of any sky?

The stream of lava flowing from the bowels of the earth in 1229, had forced itself a passage through the tunnel. It lined the whole of the inside with its thick and brilliant coating. The electric light added very greatly to the brilliancy of the effect. The great difficulty of our journey now began. How were we to prevent ourselves from slipping down the steeply-inclined plane? Happily some cracks, abrasures of the soil, and other irregularities, served the place of steps; and we descended slowly; allowing our heavy luggage to slip on before, at the end of a long cord.

But that which served as steps under our feet, became in other places stalactites. The lava, very porous in certain places, took the form of little round blisters. Crystals of opaque quartz, adorned with limpid drops of natural glass suspended to the roof like lusters, seemed to take fire as we passed beneath them. One would have fancied that the genii of romance were illuminating their underground palaces to receive the sons of men.

" Magnificent, glorious!" I cried in a moment of involuntary enthusiasm, "what a spectacle, uncle! Do you not admire these variegated shades of lava, which run through a whole series of colors, from reddish brown to pale yellow —by the most insensible degrees? And these crystals, they appear like luminous globes."

" You are beginning to see the charms of travel, Master Harry," cried my uncle. "Wait a bit, until we advance farther. What we have as yet discovered is nothing—onwards, my boy, onwards!"

It would have been a far more correct and appropriate expression, had he said, "let us slide," for we were going down an inclined plane with perfect ease. The compass indicated that we were moving in a south-easterly direction. The flow of lava had never turned to the right or the left. It had the inflexibility of a straight line.

Nevertheless, to my surprise, we found no perceptible increase in heat. This proved the theories of Humphrey Davy to be founded on truth, and more than once I found myself examining the thermometer in silent astonishment. Two hours after my departure it only marked 54 degrees Fahrenheit. I had every reason to believe from this that our descent was far more horizontal than vertical. As for discovering the exact depth to which we had attained, nothing could be easier. The Professor, as he advanced measured the angles of deviation and inclination; but he kept the result of his observations to himself.

About eight o'clock in the evening, my uncle gave the signal for the night's rest. Hans seated himself on the ground. The lamps were hung to fissures in the lava rock. We were now in a large cavern where air was not wanting. On the contrary, it abounded. What could be the cause of this—to what atmospheric agitation could be ascribed this draught? But this was a question which I did not care to discuss just then. Fatigue and hunger made me incapable of reasoning. An almost unceasing march of twelve hours had not been kept up without great exhaustion. I was really and truly worn out; and delighted enough I was to hear the word Halt.

Hans laid out some provisions on a lump of lava, and we each supped with keen relish. One thing, however, caused us great uneasiness—our water reserve was already half exhausted. My uncle had full confidence in finding subterranean resources, but hitherto we had completely failed in so doing. I could not help calling my uncle's attention to the circumstance. "And you are surprised at this total absence of springs?" he said.

"Doubtless—I am very uneasy on the point. We have certainly not enough water to last us five days."

"Be quite easy on that matter," continued my uncle. "I answer for it we shall find plenty of water—in fact, far more than we shall want."

"But when?"

"When we once get through this crust of lava. How can you expect springs to force their way through these solid stone walls?"

"But what is there to prove that this concrete mass of lava does not extend to the center of the earth? I don't think we have as yet done much in a vertical way."

"What puts that into your head, my boy?" asked my uncle, mildly.

"Well, it appears to me that if we had descended very far below the level of the sea—we should find it rather hotter than we have."

"'According to your system," said my uncle; "but what does the thermometer say?"

"Scarcely 15 degrees by Reaumur, which is only an increase of 9 since our departure."

"Well, and what conclusion does that bring you to?" inquired the Professor.

"The deduction I draw from this is very simple. According to the most exact observations, the augmentation of the temperature of the interior of the earth is 1 degree for every hundred feet. But certain local causes may considerably modify this figure. The difference evidently depends on the conductibility of certain rocks. In the neighborhood of an extinct volcano, it has been remarked that the elevation of temperature was only 1 degree in every 125 feet. Let us, then, go upon this calculation—which is the most favorable—and calculate."

"Calculate away, my boy."

"Nothing easier," said I, pulling out my note-book and pencil. "Nine times one hundred and twenty-five feet, make a depth of eleven hundred and twenty-five feet."

"'Archimedes could not have spoken more geometrically."

"Well?"

"Well, according to my observations, we are at least ten thousand feet below the level of the sea."

"Can it be possible?"

"Either my calculation is correct, or there is no truth in figures."

The calculations of the Professor were perfectly correct. We were already six thousand feet deeper down in the bowels of the earth than anyone had ever been before. The lowest known depth to which man had hitherto penetrated was in the mines of Kitz-Bahl, on the Tyrol, and those of Württemburg in Bohemia.

The temperature, which should have been eighty-one, was in this place only fifteen. This was a matter for serious consideration.

CHAPTER XVI
THE EASTERN TUNNEL

THE next day was Tuesday, the 2d of July—and at six o'clock in the morning we resumed our journey. We still continued to follow the gallery of lava, a perfect natural pathway, as easy of descent as some of those inclined planes which, in very old German houses, serve the purpose of staircases. This went on until seventeen minutes past twelve, the precise instant at which we rejoined Hans, who having been somewhat in advance, had suddenly stopped.

" At last," cried my uncle, " we have reached the end of the shaft."

I looked wonderingly about me. We were in the center of four cross paths—somber and narrow tunnels. The question now arose as to which it was wise to take; and this of itself was no small difficulty. My uncle, who did not wish to appear to have any hesitation about the matter before myself or the guide, at once made up his mind. He pointed quietly to the eastern tunnel; and, without delay, we entered within its gloomy recesses.

Besides, had he entertained any feeling of hesitation it might have been prolonged indefinitely, for there was no indication by which to determine on a choice. It was absolutely necessary to trust to chance and good fortune!

The descent of this obscure and narrow gallery was very gradual and winding. Sometimes we gazed through a succession of arches, its course very like the aisles of a Gothic cathedral. The great artistic sculptors and builders of the middle ages might have here completed their studies with advantage. Many most beautiful and suggestive ideas of architectural beauty would have been discovered by them. After passing through this phase of the cavernous way, we suddenly came, about a mile farther on, upon a square system of arch, such as that adopted by the early Romans, projecting from the solid rock, and keeping up the weight of the roof. Suddenly we would come upon a series of low subterranean tunnels which looked like beaver holes, or the work of foxes. Through these narrow and winding ways we had literally to crawl!

The heat still remained at quite a supportable degree. With an involuntary shudder, I reflected on what the heat

must have been when the volcano of Sneffels was pouring
its smoke, flames, and streams of boiling lava—all of which
must have come up by the road we were now following.   I
could imagine the torrents of hot seething stone darting on,
bubbling up with accompaniments of smoke, steam, and
sulphurous stench!   "Only to think of the consequences,"
I mused, "if the old volcano were once more to set to
work."

I did not communicate these rather unpleasant reflections
to my uncle.   His only idea was to go ahead.   He walked,
he slid, he clambered over piles of fragments, he rolled down
heaps of broken lava, with an earnestness and conviction it
was impossible not to admire.

At six o'clock in the evening, after a very wearisome
journey, but one not so fatiguing as before, we had made
six miles towards the southward, but had not gone more
than a mile downwards.

My uncle, as usual, gave the signal to halt.   We ate our
meal in thoughtful silence, and then retired to sleep.   Our
arrangements for the night were very primitive and simple.
A traveling rug, in which each rolled himself, was all our
bedding.   We had no necessity to fear cold or any unpleasant visit.   Travelers who bury themselves in the wilds
and depths of the African desert, who seek profit and
pleasure in the forests of the New World, are compelled
to take it in turn to watch during the hours of sleep; but in
this region of the earth absolute solitude and complete se-
curity reigned supreme.

After a night's sweet repose, we awoke fresh and ready
for action.   There being nothing to detain us, we started
on our journey.   We continued to burrow through the lava
tunnel as before.   It was impossible to make out through
what soil we were making way.   The tunnel, moreover, instead of going down into the bowels of the earth, became
absolutely horizontal.   I even thought, after some examination, that we were actually tending upwards.   About ten
o'clock in the day this state of things became so clear, that
finding the change very fatiguing I was obliged to slacken
my pace and finally to come to a halt.   "Well," said the
Professor quickly, "what is the matter?"

"The fact is, I am dreadfully tired," was my earnest
reply.

" What," cried my uncle, " tired after a three hours' walk, and by so easy a road? "

" Easy enough, I dare say, but very fatiguing."

" But how can that be, when all we have to do is to go downwards."

" I beg your pardon, sir. For some time I have noticed that we are going upwards."

" Upwards," cried my uncle, shrugging his shoulders, " how can that be? "

" There can be no doubt about it. For the last half hour the slopes have been upward—and if we go on in this way much longer we shall find ourselves back in Iceland."

My uncle shook his head with the air of a man who does not want to be convinced. I tried to continue the conversation. He would not answer me, but once more gave the signal for departure. His silence I thought was only caused by concentrated ill-temper.

However this might be, I once more took up my load, and resolutely followed Hans, who was now in advance of my uncle. I did not like to be beaten or even distanced. The very idea of being left behind, lost in that terrible labyrinth, made me shiver as with the ague. Besides, if the ascending path was more arduous and painful to clamber, I had one source of secret consolation and delight. It was to all appearance taking us back to the surface of the earth. That of itself was hopeful. Every step I took confirmed me in my belief, and I began already to build castles in the air in relation to my marriage with my pretty little cousin.

About twelve o'clock there was a great and sudden change in the aspect of the rocky sides of the gallery. I first noticed it from the diminution of the rays of light which cast back the reflection of the lamp. From being coated with shining and resplendent lava, it became living rock. The sides were sloping walls, which sometimes became quite vertical. We were now in what the geological professors call a state of transition, in the period of Silurian stones. " I can see, clearly now," I cried; " the sediment from the waters which once covered the whole earth, formed during the second period of its existence, these schists and these calcareous rocks. We are turning our backs on the granite rocks."

I might just as well have kept my observations to myself. My geological enthusiasm got the better, however, of my cooler judgment, and Professor Hardwigg heard my observations. "What is the matter now?" he said, in a tone of great gravity.

"Well," cried I, "do you not see these different layers of calcareous rocks and the first indication of slate strata?"

"Well; what then?"

"We have arrived at that period of the world's existence when the first plants and the first animals made their appearance."

"You think so?"

"Yes, look; examine and judge for yourself."

I induced the Professor with some difficulty to cast the light of his lamp on the sides of the long winding gallery. I expected some exclamation to burst from his lips. I was very much mistaken. The worthy Professor never spoke a word.

It was impossible to say whether he understood me or not. Perhaps it was possible that in his pride—my uncle and a learned professor—he did not like to own that he was wrong in having chosen the eastern tunnel, or was he determined at any price to go to the end of it? It was quite evident we had left the region of lava, and that the road by which we were going could not take us back to the great crater of Mount Sneffels. "At all events, if I am right," I thought to myself, "I must certainly find some remains of primitive plants ,and it will be absolutely necessary to give way to such indubitable evidence. Let us have a good search."

I accordingly lost no opportunity of searching, and had not gone more than about a hundred yards, when the evidence I sought for cropped up in the most incontestable manner before my eyes. It was quite natural that I should expect to find these signs, for during the Silurian period the seas contained no fewer than fifteen hundred different animal and vegetable species. My feet so long accustomed to the hard and arid lava soil, suddenly found themselves treading on a kind of soft dust, the remains of plants and shells. Upon the walls themselves I could clearly make out the outline, as plain as a sun picture, of the fucus and the lycopodes. The worthy and excellent Professor Hardwigg could not of course make any mistake about the matter; but

I believe he deliberately closed his eyes, and continued on his way with a firm and unalterable step.

I began to think that he was carrying his obstinacy a great deal too far. I could no longer act with prudence or composure. I stooped on a sudden and picked up an almost perfect shell, which had undoubtedly belonged to some animal very much resembling some of the present day. Having secured the prize, I followed in the wake of my uncle. "Do you see this?" I said.

"Well," said the Professor, with the most imperturbable tranquillity, "it is the shell of a crustaceous animal of the extinct order of the trilobites; nothing more I assure you."

"But," cried I, much troubled at his coolness, "do you draw no conclusion from it?"

"Well, if I may ask, what conclusion do you draw from it yourself?"

"Well, I thought——"

"I know, my boy, what you would say, and you are right, perfectly and incontestably right. We have finally abandoned the crust of lava and the road by which the lava ascended. It is quite possible that I may have been mistaken, but I shall be unable to discover my error until I get to the end of this gallery."

"You are quite right as far as that is concerned," I replied, "and I should highly approve of your decision, if we had not to fear the greatest of all dangers."

"And what is that?"

"Want of water."

"Well, my dear Henry, it can't be helped. We must put ourselves on rations."

And on he went.

CHAPTER XVII
DEEPER AND DEEPER—THE COAL MINE

IN truth, we were compelled to put ourselves upon rations. Our supply would certainly last not more than three days. I found this out about supper time. The worst part of the matter was, that in what is called the transition rocks, it was hardly to be expected we should meet with water! I had read of the horrors of thirst, and

I knew that where we were, a brief trial of its sufferings would put an end to our adventures—and our lives! But it was utterly useless to discuss the matter with my uncle. He would have answered by some axiom from Plato.

During the whole of the next day we proceeded on our journey through this interminable gallery, arch after arch, tunnel after tunnel. We journeyed without exchanging a word. We had become as mute and reticent as Hans our guide. The road had no longer an upward tendency; at all events, if it had, it was not to be made out very clearly. Sometimes there could be no doubt that we were going downwards. But this inclination was scarcely to be distinguished, and was by no means reassuring to the Professor, because the character of the strata was in no wise modified, and the transition character of the rocks became more and more marked.

It was a glorious sight to see how the electric light brought out the sparkles in the walls of the calcareous rocks, and the old red sandstone. One might have fancied oneself in one of those deep cuttings in Devonshire, which have given their name to this kind of soil. Some magnificent specimens of marble projected from the sides of the gallery; some of an agate gray with white veins of variegated character, others of a yellow spotted color, with red veins; farther off might be seen samples of color in which cherry-tinted seams were to be found in all their brightest shades.

The greater number of these marbles were stamped with the marks of primitive animals. Since the previous evening, nature and creation had made considerable progress. Instead of the rudimentary trilobites, I perceived the remains of a more perfect order. Among others, the fish in which the eye of a geologist has been able to discover the first form of the reptile. It was quite evident to me that we were ascending the scale of animal life of which man forms the summit. My excellent uncle, the Professor, appeared not to take notice of these warnings. He was determined at any risk to proceed.

He must have been in expectation of one of two things; either that a vertical well was about to open under his feet, and thus allow him to continue his descent, or that some insurmountable obstacle would compel us to stop

and go back by the road we had so long traveled. But
evening came again, and, to my horror, neither hope was
doomed to be realized!

On Friday, after a night when I began to feel the gnaw-
ing agony of thirst, and when in consequence appetite de-
creased, our little band rose and once more followed the
turnings and windings, the ascents and descents, of this
interminable gallery. All were silent and gloomy. I could
see that even my uncle felt we had ventured too far.

After about ten hours of further progress,—a progress
dull and monotonous to the last degree—I remarked that
the reverberation, and reflection of our lamps upon the
sides of the tunnel had singularly diminished. The marble,
the schist, the calcareous rocks, the red sandstone, had disappeared, leaving in their places a dark and gloomy wall,
sombre and without brightness. When we reached a remarkably narrow part of the tunnel, I leaned my left hand
against the rock. When I took my hand away, and happened to glance at it, it was quite black. We had reached
the coal strata of the Central Earth. "A coal mine!" I
cried.

"A coal mine without miners," responded my uncle, a
little severely.

"How can we tell?"

"I can tell," replied my uncle, in a sharp and doctorial
tone. "I am perfectly certain that this gallery through
successive layers of coal, was not cut by the hand of man.
But whether it is the work of nature or not is of little
concern to us. The hour for our evening meal has come
—let us sup."

Hans, the guide, occupied himself in preparing food. I
had come to that point when I could no longer eat. All I
cared about were the few drops of water which fell to my
share. What I suffered it is useless to record. The
guide's gourd, not quite half full, was all that was left for
us three! Having finished their repast, my two companions laid themselves down upon their rugs, and found
in sleep a remedy for their fatigue and sufferings. As for
me, I could not sleep, I lay counting the hours until morning.

The next morning, Saturday, at six o'clock, we started
again. Twenty minutes later we suddenly came upon a
vast excavation. From its mighty extent I saw at once

that the hand of man could have had nothing to do with this coal mine; the vault above would have fallen in; as it was, it was only held together by some miracle of nature. This mighty natural cavern was about a hundred feet wide, by about a hundred and fifty high. The earth had evidently been cast apart by some violent subterranean commotion. The mass, giving way to some prodigious upheaving of nature, had split in two, leaving the vast gap into which we inhabitants of the earth had penetrated for the first time.

The whole singular history of the coal period was written on those dark and gloomy walls. A geologist would have been able easily to follow the different phases of its formation. The seams of coal were separated by strata of sandstone, a compact clay, which appeared to be crushed down by the weight from above.

While we still continued our journey, I forgot the length of the road, by giving myself up wholly to these geological considerations. The temperature continued to be very much the same as while we were traveling amid the lava and the schists. On the other hand my sense of smell was much affected by a very powerful odor. I immediately knew that the gallery was filled to overflowing with that dangerous gas the miners call fire-damp, the explosion of which has caused such fearful and terrible accidents, making a hundred widows, and hundreds of orphans in a single hour.

Happily, we were able to illume our progress by means of the Ruhmkorff apparatus. If we had been so rash and imprudent as to explore this gallery, torch in hand, a terrible explosion would have put an end to our travels, simply because no travelers would be left.

Our excursion through this wondrous coal mine in the very bowels of the earth lasted until evening. My uncle was scarcely able to conceal his impatience and dissatisfaction at the road continuing still to advance in a horizontal direction. The darkness, dense and opaque, a few yards in advance and in the rear, rendered it impossible to make out what was the length of the gallery. For myself, I began to believe that it was simply interminable, and would go on in the same manner for months.

Suddenly, however, at six o'clock, we stood in front of a

wall. To the right, to the left, above, below, nowhere was there any passage. We had reached a spot where the rocks said in unmistakable accents—No Thoroughfare. I stood stupefied. The guide simply folded his arms. My uncle was silent.

"Well, well, so much the better," cried my uncle, at last, "I now know what we are about. We are decidedly not upon the road followed by Saknussemm. All we have to do is to go back. Let us take one night's good rest, and before three days are over, I promise you we shall have regained the point where the galleries divided."

"Yes, we may, if our strength lasts as long," I cried, in a lamentable voice.

"And why not?"

"To-morrow, among us three, there will not be a drop of water. It is just gone."

"And your courage with it," said my uncle, speaking in a severe tone.

What could I say? I turned round on my side, and from sheer exhaustion fell into a heavy but troubled sleep. Dreams of water! And I awoke unrefreshed. I would have bartered a diamond mine for a glass of pure spring water!

CHAPTER XVIII
THE WRONG ROAD

NEXT day, our departure took place at a very early hour. There was no time for the least delay. According to my account, we had five days' hard work to get back to the place where the galleries divided.

I can never tell all the sufferings we endured upon our return. My uncle bore them like a man who has been in the wrong—that is, with concentrated and suppressed anger; Hans, with all the resignation of his pacific character; and I—I confess that I did nothing but complain, and despair. I had no heart for this bad fortune. But there was one consolation. Defeat at the outset would probably upset the whole journey!

As I had expected from the first, our supply of water gave completely out on our first day's march. Our provision of liquids was reduced to our supply of schiedam;

but this horrible—nay, I will say it—this infernal liquor burnt the throat, and I could not even bear the sight of it. I found the temperature to be stifling. I was paralyzed with fatigue. More than once I was about to fall insensible to the ground. The whole party then halted, and the worthy Icelander and my excellent uncle did their best to console and comfort me. I could, however, plainly see that my uncle was contending painfully against the extreme fatigues of our journey, and the awful torture generated by the absence of water. At length a time came when I ceased to recollect anything—when all was one awful, hideous, fantastic dream!

At last, on Tuesday, the eighth of the month of July, after crawling on our hands and knees for many hours, more dead than alive, we reached the point of junction between the galleries. I lay like a log, an inert mass of human flesh on the arid lava soil. It was then ten in the morning.

Hans and my uncle, leaning against the wall, tried to nibble away at some pieces of biscuit, while deep groans and sighs escaped from my scorched and swollen lips. Then I fell off into a kind of deep lethargy. Presently I felt my uncle approach, and lift me up tenderly in his arms. "Poor boy," I heard him say in a tone of deep commiseration.

I was profoundly touched by these words, being by no means accustomed to signs of womanly weakness in the Professor. I caught his trembling hands in mine and gave them a gentle pressure. He allowed me to do so without resistance, looking at me kindly all the time. His eyes were wet with tears. I then saw him take the gourd which he wore at his side. To my surprise, or rather to my stupefaction, he placed it to my lips. "Drink, my boy," he said.

Was it possible my ears had not deceived me? Was my uncle mad? I looked at him, with, I am sure, quite an idiotic expression. I would not understand him. I too much feared the counteraction of disappointment.

"Drink," he said again.

Had I hear aright? Before, however, I could ask myself the question a second time, a mouthful of water cooled my parched lips and throat—one mouthful, but I do believe it brought me back to life. I thanked my uncle by clasping my hands. My heart was too full to speak.

"Yes," said he, "one mouthful of water, the very last—do you hear, my boy—the very last! I have taken care of it at the bottom of my bottle as the apple of my eye. Twenty times, a hundred times, I have resisted the fearful desire to drink it. But—no—no, Harry, I saved it for you."

"My dear uncle," I exclaimed, and the big tears rolled down my hot and feverish cheeks.

"Yes, my poor boy, I knew that when you reached this place, this cross road in the earth, you would fall down half dead, and I saved my last drop of water in order to restore you."

"Thanks," I cried; "thanks from my heart."

As little as my thirst was really quenched, I had nevertheless partially recovered my strength. The contracted muscles of my throat relaxed—and the inflammation of my lips in some measure subsided. At all events, I was able to speak. "Well," I said, "there can be no doubt now as to what we have to do. Water has utterly failed us; our journey is therefore at an end. Let us return."

While I spoke thus, my uncle evidently avoided my face: he held down his head; his eyes were turned in every possible direction but the right one.

"Yes," I continued, getting excited by my own words, "we must go back to Sneffels. May heaven give us strength to enable us once more to revisit the light of day. Would that we now stood on the summit of the crater."

"Go back," said my uncle speaking to himself—"and must it be so?"

"Go back—yes, and without losing a single moment," I vehemently cried.

For some moments there was silence under that dark and gloomy vault. "So, my dear Harry," said the Professor in a very singular tone of voice, "those few drops of water have not sufficed to restore your energy and courage."

"Courage!" I cried.

"I see that you are quite as downcast as before—and still give way to discouragement and despair.

What, then, was the man made of, and what other pro-

jects were entering his fertile and audacious brain! "You
are not discouraged, sir?"

"What! give up just as we are on the verge of success,"
he cried, "never, never shall it be said that Professor Hardwigg retreated."

"Then we must make up our minds to perish," I cried
with a helpless sigh.

"No, Harry, my boy, certainly not. Go, leave me, I am
very far from desiring your death. Take Hans with you,
I will go on alone."

"You ask us to leave you?"

"Leave me, I say. I have undertaken this dangerous
and perilous adventure. I will carry it to the end—or I
will never return to the surface of Mother Earth. Go—
Harry—once more I say to you—go!"

My uncle as he spoke was terribly excited. His voice,
which before had been tender, almost womanly, became
harsh and menacing. He appeared to be struggling with
desperate energy against the impossible. I did not wish
to abandon him at the bottom of that abyss, while, on
the other hand, the instinct of preservation told me
to fly.

Meanwhile, our guide was looking on with profound
calmness and indifference. He appeared to be an unconcerned party, and yet he perfectly well knew what was going on between us. Our gestures sufficiently indicated the
different roads each wished to follow—and which each tried
to influence the other to undertake. But Hans appeared
not to take the slightest interest in what was really a question of life and death for us all, but waited quite ready to
obey the signal which should say go aloft, or to resume
his desperate journey into the interior of the earth.

How then I wished with all my heart and soul that I
could make him understand my words. My representations, my sighs and groans, the earnest accents in which I
should have spoken would have convinced that cold hard
nature. Those fearful dangers and perils of which the
stolid guide had no idea, I would have pointed them out to
him—I would have, as it were, made him see and feel.
Between us, we might have convinced the obstinate Professor. If the worst had come to the worst, we could have
compelled him to return to the summit of Sneffels. I ap-

proached Hans. I caught his hand in mine. He never moved a muscle. I indicated to him the road to the top of the crater. He remained motionless. My panting form, my haggard countenance, must have indicated the extent of my sufferings. The Icelander gently shook his head and pointed to my uncle. *"Master,"* he said.

" The master! " I cried, beside myself with fury—" madman! no—I tell you he is not the master of our lives; we must fly! we must drag him with us! do you hear me? Do you understand me, I say?"

I have already explained that I held Hans by the arm. I tried to make him rise from his seat. I struggled with him and tried to force him away. My uncle now interposed. " My good Henry, be calm," he said. " You will obtain nothing from my devoted follower; therefore, listen to what I have to say."

I folded my arms, as well as I could, and looked my uncle full in the face.

" This wretched want of water," he said, " is the sole obstacle to the success of my project. In the entire gallery, composed of lava, schist, and coal, it is true we found not one liquid molecule. It is quite possible that we may be more fortunate in the western tunnel."

My sole reply was to shake my head with an air of incredulity.

" Listen to me to the end," said the Professor in his well known lecturing voice. " While you lay yonder without life or motion, I undertook a reconnoitering journey into the conformation of this other gallery. I have discovered that it goes directly downwards into the bowels of the earth, and in a few hours will take us to the old granitic formation. In this we shall undoubtedly find innumerable springs. The nature of the rock makes this a mathematical certainty, and instinct agrees with logic to say that it is so. Now, this is the serious proposition which I have to make to you. When Christopher Columbus asked of his men three days to discover the land of promise, his men ill, terrified, and hopeless, yet gave him three days—and the New World was discovered. Now I, the Christopher Columbus of this subterranean region, only ask of you one more day. If, when that time is expired, I have not found the water of which we are in search, I swear to you, I will give up my mighty enterprise and return to the earth's surface."

Despite my irritation and despair, I knew how much it cost my uncle to make this proposition, and to hold such conciliatory language. Under the circumstances, what could I do, but yield?

"Well," I cried, "let it be as you wish, and may heaven reward your superhuman energy. But as, unless we discover water, our hours are numbered, let us lose no time, but go ahead."

CHAPTER XIX
THE WESTERN GALLERY—A NEW ROUTE

OUR descent was now resumed by means of the second gallery. Hans took up his post in front as usual. We had not gone more than a hundred yards when the Professor carefuly examined the walls. "This is the primitive formation—we are on the right road—onwards is our hope!"

When the whole earth got cool in the first hours of the world's morning, the diminution of the volume of the earth produced a state of dislocation in its upper crust, followed by ruptures, crevasses and fissures. The passage was a fissure of this kind, through which, ages ago, had flowed the eruptive granite. The thousand windings and turnings formed an inextricable labyrinth through the ancient soil. As we descended, successions of layers composing the primitive soil appeared with the utmost fidelity of detail.

No mineralogists had ever found themselves placed in such a marvelous position to study nature in all her real and naked beauty. The sounding rod, a mere machine, could not bring to the surface of the earth the objects of value for the study of its internal structure, which we were about to see with our own eyes, to touch with our own hands. Remember that I am writing this *after* the journey.

Across the streak of the rocks, colored by beautiful green tints, wound metallic threads of copper, of manganese, with traces of platinum and gold. I could not help gazing at these riches buried in the entrails of mother earth, and of which no man would have the enjoyment to the end of time! These treasures—mighty and inexhaustible, were buried in the morning of the earth's history, at such awful depths, that no crowbar or pickax will ever drag them from their tomb! The light of our Ruhmkorf's coil, increased tenfold by the myriad of prismatic masses of rock, sent their jets of fire in every direction, and I could fancy myself traveling through a huge hollow diamond, the rays of which produced myriads of extraordinary effects. Towards six o'clock, this festival of light began sensibly and visibly to decrease, and soon almost ceased. The sides of the gallery assumed a crystallized tint, with a somber hue; white mica began to commingle more freely with feldspar and quartz, to form what may be called the true rock—the stone which is hard above all, that supports, without being crushed, the four stories of the earth's soil. We were walled by an immense prison of granite!

It was now eight o'clock, and still there was no sign of water. The sufferings I endured were horrible. My uncle now kept at the head of our little column. Nothing could induce him to stop. I, meanwhile, had but one real thought. My ear was keenly on the watch to catch the sound of a spring. But no pleasant sound of falling water fell upon my listening ear.

At last the time came when my limbs refused to longer carry me. I contended heroically against the terrible tortures I endured, because I did not wish to compel my uncle to halt. To him I knew this would be the last fatal stroke. Suddenly I felt a deadly faintness come over me. My eyes could no longer see; my knees shook. I gave one despairing cry—and fell!

"Help, help, I am dying!"

My uncle turned and slowly retraced his steps. He looked at me with folded arms, and then allowed one sentence to escape, in hollow accents, from his lips—"All is over."

The last thing I saw was a face fearfully distorted with pain and sorrow; and then my eyes closed.

When I again opened them, I saw my companions lying near me, motionless, wrapped in their huge traveling rugs. Were they asleep or dead? For myself, sleep was wholly out of the question. My fainting fit over, I was wakeful as the lark. I suffered too much for sleep to visit my eyelids—the more, that I thought myself sick unto death—dying. The last words spoken by my uncle seemed to be buzzing in my ears—*all is over!* It was probable that he was right. In the state of prostration to which I was reduced, it was madness to think of ever again seeing the light of day. Above were miles upon miles of the earth's crust. As I thought of it, I could fancy the whole weight resting on my shoulders. I was crushed, annihilated! and exhausted myself in vain attempts to turn in my granite bed.

Hours upon hours passed away. A profound and terrible silence reigned around us—a silence of the tomb. Nothing could make itself heard through these gigantic walls of granite. The very thought was stupendous.

Presently, despite my apathy, despite the kind of deadly calm into which I was cast, something aroused me. It was a slight but peculiar noise. While I was watching intently, I observed that the tunnel was becoming dark. Then gazing through the dim light that remained, I thought I saw the Icelander taking his departure, lamp in hand.

Why had he acted thus? Did Hans the guide mean to abandon us? My uncle lay fast asleep—or dead. I tried to cry out, and arouse him. My voice, feebly issuing from my parched and fevered lips, found no echo in that fearful place. My throat was dry, my tongue stuck to the roof of my mouth. The obscurity had by this time become intense, and at last even the faint sound of the guide's footsteps was lost in the blank distance. My soul seemed filled with anguish, and death appeared welcome, only let it come quickly.

"Hans is leaving us," I cried. "Hans—Hans, if you are a man, come back."

These words were spoken to myself. They could not be heard aloud. Moreover, a moment's reflection re-assured me. Hans's departure could not be a flight. Instead of ascending the gallery, he was going deeper down into the gulf. Had he had any bad design, his way would have been upwards.

This reasoning calmed me a little and I began to hope! The good, and peaceful, and imperturbable Hans would certainly not have arisen from his sleep without some serious and grave motive. Was he bent on a voyage of discovery? During the deep, still silence of the night had he at last heard that sweet murmur about which we were all so anxious?

CHAPTER XX
WATER, WHERE IS IT? A BITTER DISAPPOINTMENT

DURING a long, long, weary hour, there crossed my wildly delirious brain all sorts of reasons as to what could have aroused our quiet and faithful guide. The most absurd and ridiculous ideas passed through my head, each more impossible than the other. I believe I was either half or wholly mad. Suddenly, however, there arose, as it were from the depths of the earth, a voice of comfort. It was the sound of footsteps! Hans was returning. Presently the uncertain light began to shine upon the walls of the passage, and then it came in view far down the sloping tunnel. At length Hans himself appeared.

He approached my uncle, placed his hand upon his shoulder, and gently awakened him. My uncle, as soon as he saw who it was, instantly rose. " Well!" exclaimed the Professor.

" *Vatten,*" said the hunter.

I did not know a single word of the Danish language, and yet by a sort of mysterious instinct I understood what the guide had said.

" Water, water!" I cried, in a wild and frantic tone, clapping my hands, and gesticulating like a madman.

" Water!" murmured my uncle, in a voice of deep emotion and gratitude. " *Hvar?* "

" *Nedat.*"

" Where? below!" I understood every word. I had caught the hunter by the hands, and I shook them heartily, while he looked on with perfect calmness.

The preparations for our departure did not take long, and we were soon making a rapid descent into the tunnel. An hour later we had advanced a thousand yards, and descended two thousand feet. At this moment I heard an accustomed and well-known sound running along the floors of the granite rock—a kind of dull and sullen roar, like that of a distant waterfall.

During the first half-hour of our advance, not finding the discovered spring, my feelings of intense suffering returned. Once more I began to lose all hope. My uncle, however, observing how down-hearted I was again becoming, took up the conversation. "Hans was right," he exclaimed, enthusiastically; "that is the dull roaring of a torrent."

"A torrent," I cried, delighted at even hearing the welcome words.

"There's not the slightest doubt about it," he replied, "a subterranean river is flowing beside us."

I made no reply, but hastened on, once more animated by hope. I did not even feel the deep fatigue which hitherto had overpowered me. The very sound of this glorious murmuring water already refreshed me. We could hear it increasing in volume every moment. The torrent, which for a long time could be heard flowing over our heads, now ran distinctly along the left wall, roaring, rushing, spluttering, and still falling.

Several times I passed my hand across the rock hoping to find some trace of humidity—of the slightest percolation. Alas! in vain. Again a half hour passed in the same weary toil. Again we advanced.

It now became evident that the hunter, during his absence, had not been able to carry his researches any farther. Guided by an instinct peculiar to the dwellers in mountain regions and water finders, he "smelt" the living spring through the rock. Still he had not seen the precious liquid. He had neither quenched his own thirst nor brought us one drop in his gourd.

Moreover, we soon made the disastrous discovery, that if our progress continued, we should soon be moving away from the torrent, the sound of which gradually diminished. We turned back. Hans halted at the precise spot where the sound of the torrent appeared nearest.

I could bear the suspense and suffering no longer, and seated myself against the wall, behind which I could hear the water seething and effervescing not two feet away. But a solid wall of granite still separated us from it!

Hans looked keenly at me, and, strange enough, for once I thought I saw a smile on his imperturbable face. He rose from a stone on which he had been seated, and took up the lamp. I could not help rising and following. He moved slowly along the firm and solid granite wall. I watched him with mingled curiosity and eagerness. Presently he halted and placed his ear against the dry stone, moving slowly along and listening with the most extreme care and attention. I understood at once that he was searching for the exact spot where the torrent's roar was most plainly heard. This point he soon found in the lateral wall on the left side, about three feet above the level of the tunnel floor.

I was in a state of intense excitement. I scarcely dared believe what the eider-duck hunter was about to do. It was, however, impossible in a moment more not to both understand and applaud, and even to smother him in my embraces, when I saw him raise the heavy crowbar and commence an attack upon the rock itself.

" Saved," I cried.

" Yes," cried my uncle, even more excited and delighted than myself; " Hans is quite right. Oh, the worthy, excellent man! We should never have thought of such an idea."

And nobody else, I think, would have done so. Such a process, simple as it seemed, would most certainly not have entered our heads. Nothing could be more dangerous than to begin to work with pickaxes in that particular part of the globe. Supposing while he was at work a break-up were to take place, and supposing the torrent once having gained an inch were to take an ell, and come pouring bodily through the broken rock!

Not one of these dangers was chimerical. They were only too real. But at that moment no fear of falling in of roof, or even of inundation was capable of stopping us. Our thirst was so intense, that to quench it we would have dug below the bed of old Ocean itself.

Hans went quietly to work—a work which neither my uncle nor I could have undertaken. Our impatience was so great, that if we had once begun with pickax and crowbar, the rock would soon have split into a hundred fragments. The guide, on the contrary, calm, ready, moderate, wore away the hard rock by little steady blows of his instrument, making no attempt at a larger hole than about six inches. As I stood, I heard, or I thought I heard, the roar of the torrent momentarily increasing in loudness, and at times

I almost felt the pleasant sensation of water upon my parched lips.

At the end of what appeared an age, Hans had made a hole, which enabled his crowbar to enter two feet into the solid rock. He had been at work exactly an hour. It appeared a dozen. I was getting wild with impatience. My uncle began to think of using more violent measures. I had the greatest difficulty in checking him. He had indeed just got hold of his crowbar when a loud and welcome hiss was heard. Then a stream, or rather a jet of water burst through the wall and came out with such force as to hit the opposite side!

Hans, the guide, who was half upset by the shock, was scarcely able to keep down a cry of pain and grief. I understood his meaning when plunging my hands into the sparkling jet I myself gave a wild and frantic cry. The water was scalding hot! "Boiling," I cried, in bitter disappointment.

"Well, never mind," said my uncle, "it will soon get cool."

The tunnel began to be filled by clouds of vapor, while a small stream ran away into the interior of the earth. In a short time we had some sufficiently cool to drink. We swallowed it in huge mouthfuls.

Oh what exalted delight—what rich and incomparable luxury! What was this water, whence did it come? To us what was that? The simple fact was—it was water; and, though still with a tinge of warmth about it, it brought back to the heart, that life which, but for it, must surely have faded away. I drank greedily, almost without tasting it.

When, however, I had almost quenched my ravenous thirst, I made a discovery. "Why, it is ferruginous water."

"Most excellent stomachic," replied my uncle, "and highly mineralized. Here is a journey worth twenty to Spa."

"It's very good," I replied.

"I should think so. Water found six miles under ground. There is a peculiarly inky flavor about it, which is by no means disagreeable. Hans may congratulate himself on having made a rare discovery. What do you say, nephew, according to the usual custom of travelers, to name the stream after him?"

"Good," said I. And the name of "Hans-bach" was at once agreed upon.

Hans was not a bit more proud after hearing our determination than he was before. After having taken a very small modicum of the welcome refreshment, he had seated himself in a corner with his usual imperturbable gravity.

"Now," said I, "it is not worth while letting this water run to waste."

"What is the use," replied my uncle, "the source from which this river rises is inexhaustible."

"Never mind," I continued, "let us fill our goat skin and gourds, and then try to stop the opening up."

My plan, after some hesitation, was followed or attempted. Hans picked up all the broken pieces of granite he had knocked out, and using some tow he happened to have about him, tried to shut up the fissure he had made in the wall. All he did was to scald his hands. The pressure was too great, and all our attempts were utter failures.

"It is evident," I remarked, "that the upper surface of these springs is situated at a very great height above—as we may fairly infer from the great pressure of the jet."

"That is by no means doubtful," replied my uncle, "if this column of water is about thirty-two thousand feet high, the atmospheric pressure must be something enormous. But a new idea has just struck me."

"And what is that?"

"Why be at so much trouble to close this aperture?"

"Because——" I hesitated and stammered, having no real reason.

"When our water bottles are empty, we are not at all sure that we shall be able to fill them," observed my uncle.

"I think that is very probable."

"Well, then, let this water run. It will, of course, naturally follow in our track, and will serve to guide and refresh us."

"I think the idea a good one," I cried, in reply, "and with this rivulet as a companion, there is no further reason why we should not succeed in our marvellous project."

"Ah, my boy," said the professor, laughing, "after all, you are coming round."

"More than that, I am now confident of ultimate success. Forward."

"One moment, nephew mine. Let us begin by taking some hours of repose."

I had utterly forgotten that it was night. The chronometer, however, informed me of the fact. Soon we were sufficiently restored and refreshed, and had all fallen into a profound sleep.

CHAPTER XXI
UNDER THE OCEAN

By the next day we had nearly forgotten our past sufferings. The first sensation I experienced was surprise at not being thirsty, and I actually asked myself the reason. The running stream, which flowed in rippling wavelets at my feet, was the satisfactory reply.

We breakfasted with a good appetite, and then drank our fill of the excellent water. I felt myself quite a new man, ready to go anywhere my uncle chose to lead. I began to think. Why should not a man as seriously convinced as my uncle, succeed, with so excellent a guide as worthy Hans, and so devoted a nephew as myself? These were the brilliant ideas which now invaded my brain. Had the proposition now been made to go back to the summit of Mount Sneffels, I should have declined the offer in a most indignant manner. But fortunately there was no question of going up. We were about to descend farther into the interior of the earth. "Let us be moving," I cried, awakening the echoes of the old world.

We resumed our march on Thursday at eight o'clock in the morning. The great granite tunnel went round by sinuous and winding ways, presenting every now and then sharp turns, and in fact had all the appearance of a labyrinth. Its direction, however, was in general towards the southwest. My uncle made several pauses in order to consult his compass. The gallery now began to trend downwards in a horizontal direction, with about two inches of fall in every furlong. The murmuring stream flowed quietly at our feet. I could not but compare it to some familiar spirit, guiding us through the earth, and I dabbled my fingers in its tepid water, which sang like a naiad as we progressed. My good humor began to assume a mythological character.

As for my uncle he began to complain of the horizontal character of the road. His route he found began to be indefinitely prolonged, instead of "sliding down the celestial ray," according to his expression.

But we had no choice; and as long as our road led towards the center—however little progress we made, there was no reason to complain. Moreover, from time to time the slopes were much greater; the naiad sang more loudly, and we began to dip downwards in earnest. I felt, however, no further painful sensation. I had not got over the excitement of the discovery of water.

That day and the next we did a considerable amount of horizontal, and relatively very little vertical, traveling. On Friday evening, the tenth of July, according to our estimation, we ought to have been thirty leagues to the southeast of Reykjawik, and about two leagues and a half deep. We now received a rather startling surprise.

Under our feet there opened a horrible well. My uncle was so delighted that he actually clapped his hands—as he saw how steep and sharp was the descent. "Ah, ah!" he cried, in rapturous delight; "this will take us a long way. Look at the projections of the rock. Hah!" he exclaimed, "it's a fearful staircase!"

Hans, however, who in all our troubles had never given up the ropes, took care so to dispose of them as to prevent any accidents. Our descent then began. I dare not call it a perilous descent, for I was already too familiar with that sort of work to look upon it as anything but a very ordinary affair. This well was a kind of narrow opening in the massive granite of the kind known as a fissure. The contraction of the terrestrial scaffolding, when it suddenly cooled, had been evidently the cause. If it had ever served in former times as a kind of funnel through which passed the eruptive masses vomited by Sneffels, I was at a loss to explain how it had left no mark. We were, in fact, descending a spiral, something like those winding staircases in use in modern houses.

We were compelled every quarter of an hour or thereabouts to sit down in order to rest our legs. Our calves ached. We then seated ourselves on some projecting rock with our legs hanging over, and gossiped while we ate a mouthful—drinking still from the pleasantly warm running stream which had not deserted us.

It is scarcely necessary to say, that in this curiously shaped fissure the Hansbach had become a cascade to the detriment of its size. It was still, however, sufficient, and more, for our wants. Besides we knew that, as soon as the declivity ceased to be so abrupt, the stream must resume its peaceful course. At this moment it reminded me of my uncle, his impatience and rage, while when it flowed more peacefully, I pictured to myself the placidity of the Icelandic guide.

During the whole of two days, the sixth and seventh of July, we followed the extraordinary spiral staircase of the fissure, penetrating two leagues farther into the crust of the earth, which placed us five leagues below the level of the sea. On the eighth, however, at twelve o'clock in the day, the fissure suddenly assumed a much more gentle slope still trending in a southeast direction. The road now became comparatively easy, and at the same time dreadfully monotonous. It would have been difficult for matters to have turned out otherwise. Our peculiar journey had no chance of being diversified by landscape and scenery. At all events, such was then my idea.

At length, on Wednesday the fifteenth, we were actually seven leagues (twenty-one miles) below the surface of the earth, and fifty leagues distant from the mountain of Sneffels. Though, if the truth be told, we were very tired, our health had resisted all suffering, and was in a most satisfactory state. Our traveler's box of medicaments had not even been opened. My uncle was careful to note every hour the indications of the compass, of the manometer, and of the thermometer, all which he afterwards published in his elaborate philosophical and scientific account of our remarkable voyage. He was therefore able to give an exact relation of the situation. When, therefore, he informed me that we were fifty leagues in a horizontal direction distant from our starting-point, I could not suppress a loud exclamation.

"What is the matter now?" cried my uncle.

" Nothing very important, only an idea has entered my head," was my reply.

" Well, out with it, my boy."

" It is my opinion that if your calculations are correct we are no longer under Iceland."

" Do you think so? "

" We can very easily find out," I replied, pulling out the map and compasses.

" You see," I said, after careful measurement, " that I am not mistaken. We are far beyond Cape Portland; and those fifty leagues to the southeast will take us into the open sea."

" Under the open sea," cried my uncle, rubbing his hands with a delighted air.

" Yes," I cried, " no doubt old ocean flows over our heads."

" Well, my dear boy, what can be more natural. Do you not know that in the neighborhood of Newcastle there are coal mines which have been worked far out under the sea? "

Now my worthy uncle, the Professor, no doubt regarded this discovery as a very simple fact, but to me the idea was by no means a pleasant one. And yet when one came to think the matter over seriously, what mattered it whether the plains and mountains of Iceland were suspended over our devoted heads, or the mighty billows of the Atlantic Ocean? The whole question rested on the solidity of the granite roof above us. However, I soon got used to the idea, for the passage now level, now running down, and still always to the southeast, kept going deeper and deeper into the profound abysses of Mother Earth.

Three days later, on the eighteenth day of July, on a Saturday, we reached a kind of vast grotto. My uncle here paid Hans his usual rix-dollars, and it was decided that the next day should be a day of rest.

I AWOKE on Sunday morning without any sense of hurry and bustle attendant on an immediate departure. Though the day to be devoted to repose and reflection was spent under such strange circumstances, and in so wonderful a place, the idea was a pleasant one. Besides, we all began to get used to this kind of existence. I had almost ceased to think of the sun, of the moon, of the stars, of the trees, houses, and towns; in fact, about any terrestrial necessities. In our peculiar position we were far above such reflections.

The grotto was a vast and magnificent hall. Along its granitic soil the stream flowed placidly and pleasantly. So great a distance was it now from its fiery source, that its water was scarcely lukewarm, and could be drank without delay or difficulty.

After a frugal breakfast, the Professor made up his mind to devote some hours to putting his notes and calculations in order. "In the first place," he said, "I have a good many to verify and prove, in order that we may know our exact position. I wish to be able on our return to the upper regions, to make a map of our journey, a kind of vertical section of the globe, which will be as it were the profile of the expedition."

"That would indeed be a curious work, uncle; but can you make your observations with anything like certainty and precision?"

"I can. I have never on one occasion failed to note with great care the angles and slopes. I am certain as to having made no mistake. Take the compass and examine how she points."

I looked at the instrument with care. "East one-quarter southeast."

"Very good," resumed the Professor, noting the observation, and going through some rapid calculations. "I make out that we have journeyed two hundred and fifty miles from the point of our departure."

"Then the mighty waves of the Atlantic are rolling over our heads?"

"Certainly."

"And at this very moment it is possible that fierce

tempests are raging above, and that men and ships are battling against the angry blasts just over our heads?"

"It is quite within the range of possibility," rejoined my uncle, smiling.

"And that whales are playing in shoals, thrashing the bottom of the sea, the roof of our adamantine prison?"

"Be quite at rest on that point; there is no danger of their breaking through. But to return to our calculations. We are to the southeast, two hundred and fifty miles from the base of Sneffels, and, according to my preceding notes, I think we have gone sixteen leagues in a downward direction."

"Sixteen leagues—fifty miles!" I cried.

"I am sure of it."

"But that is the extreme limit allowed by science for the thickness of the earth's crust," I replied, referring to my geological studies.

"I do not contravene that assertion," was his quiet answer.

"And at this stage of our journey, according to all known laws on the increase of heat, there should be here a temperature of *fifteen hundred* degrees of Reaumur."

"There should be—you say, my boy."

"In which case this granite would not exist, but be in a state of fusion."

"But you perceive, my boy, that it is not so, and that facts, as usual, are very stubborn things, overruling all theories."

"I am forced to yield to the evidence of my senses, but I am nevertheless very much surprised."

"What heat does the thermometer really indicate?" continued the philosopher.

"Twenty-seven six-tenths."

"So that science is wrong by fourteen hundred and seventy-four degrees and four-tenths. According to which, it is demonstrated that the proportional increase in temperature is an exploded error. Humphrey Davy here shines forth in all his glory. He is right, and I have acted wisely to believe him. Have you any answer to make to this statement?"

Had I chosen to have spoken, I might have said a great deal. I in no way admitted the theory of Humphrey

Davy—I still held out for the theory of proportional increase of heat, though I did not feel it.   I was far more
willing to allow that this chimney of an extinct volcano
was covered by lava of a kind refractory to heat—in
fact a bad conductor—which did not allow the great increase of temperature to percolate through its sides.   The
hot water jet supported my view of the matter.

But without entering on a long and useless discussion,
or seeking for new arguments to controvert my uncle, I
contented myself with taking up facts as they were.
" Well, sir, I take for granted that all your calculations are
correct, but allow me to draw from them a rigorous and
definite conclusion."

" Go on, my boy—have your say," cried my uncle, good-
humoredly.

" At the place where we now are, under the latitude of
Iceland, the terrestrial depth is about fifteen hundred and
eighty-three leagues."

" Fifteen hundred, eighty-three and a quarter."

" Well, suppose we say sixteen hundred in round numbers.   Now, out of a voyage of sixteen hundred leagues
we have completed sixteen."

" As you say, what then ? "

" At the expense of a diagonal journey of no less than
eighty-five leagues."

" Exactly."

" We have been twenty days about it."

" Exactly twenty days."

" Now sixteen is the hundredth part of our contemplated
expedition.   If we go on in this way we shall be two thousand days, that is about five years and a half, going down."

The Professor folded his arms, listened, but did not
speak.

" Without counting that if a vertical descent of sixteen
leagues costs us a horizontal of eighty-five, we shall have
to go about eight thousand leagues to the southeast, and
we must therefore come out somewhere in the circumference long before we can hope to reach the center."

" Bother your calculations," cried my uncle in one of his
old rages.   " On what basis do they rest?   How do you
know that this passage does not take us direct to the end
we require?   Moreover, I have in my favor, fortunately,

a precedent. What I have undertaken to do, another has done, and he having succeeded, why should I not be equally successful? "

" I hope, indeed, you will, but still, I suppose I may be allowed to——"

" You are allowed to hold your tongue," cried Professor Hardwigg, " when you talk so unreasonably as this."

I saw at once that the old doctorial Professor was still alive in my uncle—and fearful to rouse his angry passions, I dropped the unpleasant subject.

" Now, then," he explained, " consult the manometer. What does that indicate? "

" A considerable amount of pressure."

" Very good. You see, then, that by descending slowly, and by gradually accustoming ourselves to the density of this lower atmosphere, we shall not suffer.

" Well, I suppose not, except it may be a certain amount of pain in the ears," was my rather grim reply.

" That, my dear boy, is nothing, and you will easily get rid of that source of discomfort by bringing the exterior air in communication with the air contained in your lungs."

" Perfectly," said I, for I had quite made up my mind in no wise to contradict my uncle. " I should fancy almost that I should experience a certain amount of satisfaction in making a plunge into this dense atmosphere. Have you taken note of how wonderfully sound is propagated? "

" Of course I have. There can be no doubt that a journey into the interior of the earth would be an excellent cure for deafness."

" But then, uncle," I ventured mildly to observe, " this density will continue to increase."

" Yes—according to a law which, however, is scarcely defined. It is true that the intensity of weight will diminish just in proportion to the depth to which we go. You know very well that it is on the surface of the earth that its action is most powerfully felt, while on the contrary, in the very center of the earth bodies cease to have any weight at all."

" I know that is the case, but as we progress will not the atmosphere finally assume the density of water? "

"I know it; when placed under the pressure of seven hundred and ten atmospheres," cried my uncle with imperturbable gravity."

"And when we are still lower down?" I asked with natural anxiety."

"Well, lower down, the density will become even greater still."

"Then how shall we be able to make our way through this atmospheric fog?"

"Well, my worthy nephew, we must ballast ourselves by filling our pockets with stones," said Professor Hardwigg.

"Faith, uncle, you have an answer for everything," was my only reply. I began to feel that it was unwise in me to go any farther into the wide field of hypotheses, for I should certainly have revived some difficulty, or rather impossibility that would have enraged the Professor.

It was evident, nevertheless, that the air under a pressure which might be multiplied by thousands of atmospheres, would end by becoming perfectly solid, and that then admitting our bodies resisted the pressure, we should have to stop, in spite of all the reasonings in the world. Facts overcome all arguments.

But I thought it best not to urge this argument. My uncle would simply have quoted the example of Saknussemm. Supposing the learned Icelander's journey ever really to have taken place—there was one simple answer to be made:—In the sixteenth century neither the barometer nor the manometer had been invented—how, then, could Saknussemm have been able to discover when he did reach the center of the earth? This unanswerable and learned objection I, however, kept to myself, and bracing up my courage awaited the course of events—little aware of how adventurous yet were to be the incidents of our remarkable journey.

The rest of this day of leisure and repose was spent in calculation and conversation. I made it a point to agree with the Professor in everything; but I envied the perfect indifference of Hans, who without taking any such trouble about the cause and effect, went blindly onwards wherever destiny chose to lead.

CHAPTER XXIII
ALONE

It must in all truth be confessed, things as yet had gone on well, and I should have acted in bad taste to have complained. If our difficulties did not increase, it was within the range of possibility that we might ultimately reach the end of our journey. Then what glory would be ours! I began in the newly aroused ardor of my soul to speak enthusiastically to the Professor. Was I serious? The whole state in which we existed was a mystery—and it was impossible to know whether or not I was in earnest.

For several days after our memorable halt, the slopes became more rapid—some were even of a most frightful character—almost vertical, so that we were for ever going down into the solid interior mass. During some days, we actually descended a league and a half, even two leagues towards the center of the earth. The descents were sufficiently perilous, and while we were engaged in them we learned fully to appreciate the marvelous coolness of our guide, Hans. Without him we should have been wholly lost. The grave and impassible Icelander devoted himself to us with the most incomprehensible *sang froid* and ease; and, thanks to him, many a dangerous pass was got over, where, but for him, we should inevitably have stuck fast.

His silence increased every day. I think that we began to be influenced by this peculiar trait in his character. It is certain that the inanimate objects by which you are surrounded have a direct action on the brain. It must be that a man who shuts himself up between four walls must lose the faculty of associating ideas and words. How many persons condemned to the horrors of solitary confinement have gone mad—simply because the thinking faculties have lain dormant!

During the two weeks that followed our last interesting conversation, there occurred nothing worthy of being especially recorded. I have, while writing these memoirs, taxed my memory in vain for one incident of travel during this particular period.

But the next event to be related is terrible indeed. Its very memory, even now, makes my soul shudder, and my blood run cold. It was on the seventh of August. Our constant and successive descents had taken us quite thirty leagues into the interior of the earth, that is to say that there were above us thirty leagues, nearly a hundred miles, of rocks, and oceans, and continents, and towns, to say nothing of living inhabitants. We were in a southeasterly direction, about two hundred leagues from Iceland.

On that memorable day the tunnel had begun to assume an almost horizontal course. I was on this occasion walking on in front. My uncle had charge of one of the Ruhmkorf coils, I had possession of the other. By means of its light I was busy examining the different layers of granite. I was completely absorbed in my work. Suddenly halting and turning round, I found that I was alone!

"Well," thought I to myself, "I have certainly been walking too fast—or else Hans and my uncle have stopped to rest. The best thing I can do is to go back and find them. Luckily, there is very little ascent to tire me."

I accordingly retraced my steps, and while doing so, walked for at least a quarter of an hour. Rather uneasy, I paused and looked eagerly around. Not a living soul. I called aloud. No reply. My voice was lost amid the myriad cavernous echoes it aroused!

I began for the first time to feel seriously uneasy. A cold shiver shook my whole body, and perspiration, chill and terrible, burst upon my skin.

"I must be calm," I said, speaking aloud, as boys whistle to drive away fear. "There can be no doubt that I shall find my companions. There cannot be two roads. It is certain that I was considerably ahead; all I have to do is to go back."

Having come to this determination I ascended the tunnel for at least half an hour, unable to decide if I had ever seen certain landmarks before. Every now and then I paused to discover if any loud appeal was made to me, well knowing that in that dense and intensified atmosphere I should hear it a long way off. But no. The most extraordinary silence reigned in this immense gallery. Only the echoes of my own footsteps could be heard.

At last I stopped. I could scarcely realize the fact of my isolation. I was quite willing to think that I had made a mistake, but not that I was lost. If I had made a mistake, I might find my way: if lost—I shuddered to think of it.

"Come, come," said I to myself, "since there is only one road, and they must come by it, we shall at last meet. All I have to do is still to go upwards.   Perhaps, however, not seeing me, and forgetting I was ahead, they may have gone back in search of me.   Still even in this case, if I make haste, I shall get up to them.   There can be no doubt about the matter."

But as I spoke these last words aloud, it would have been quite clear to any listener—had there been one—that I was by no means convinced of the fact.   Moreover, in order to associate together these simple ideas and to reunite them under the form of reasoning, required some time.   I could not all at once bring my brain to think.

Then another dread doubt fell upon my soul.   After all, was I ahead.   Of course I was.   Hans was no doubt following behind, preceded by my uncle.   I perfectly recollected his having stopped for a moment to strap his baggage on his shoulder.   I now remembered this trifling detail.   It was, I believed, just at that very moment that I had determined to continue my route.

"Again," thought I, reasoning as calmly as was possible, "there is another sure means of not losing my way, a thread to guide me through the labyrinthine subterraneous retreat—one which I had forgotten—my faithful river."

This course of reasoning roused my drooping spirits, and I resolved to resume my journey without further delay.   No time was to be lost.   It was at this moment that I had reason to bless the thoughtfulness of my uncle, when he refused to allow the eider hunter to close the orifices of the hot spring—that small fissure in the great mass of granite.   This beneficent spring after having saved us from thirst during so many days would now enable me to regain the right road.   Having come to this mental decision, I made up my mind, before I started upwards, that ablution would certainly do me a great deal of good.

I stopped to plunge my hands and forehead in the pleasant water of the Hansbach stream, blessing its presence as a certain consolation.

Conceive my horror and stupefaction!—I was treading a hard, dusty, shingly road of granite. The stream on which I reckoned had wholly disappeared!

CHAPTER XXIV
LOST!

No words in any human language can depict my utter despair. I was literally buried alive; with no other expectation before me but to die in all the slow horrible torture of hunger and thirst. Mechanically I crawled about, feeling the dry and arid rock. Never to my fancy had I ever felt anything so dry.

But, I frantically asked myself, how had I lost the course of the flowing stream? There could be no doubt it had ceased to flow in the gallery in which I now was. Now I began to understand the cause of the strange silence which prevailed when last I tried if any appeal from my companions might perchance reach my ear.

It so happened that when I first took an imprudent step in the wrong direction, I did not perceive the absence of the all-important stream. It was now quite evident that when we halted, another tunnel must have received the waters of the little torrent, and that I had unconsciously entered a different gallery. To what unknown depths had my companions gone? Where was I?

How to get back! Clue or landmark there was absolutely none! My feet left no signs on the granite and shingle. My brain throbbed with agony as I tried to discover the solution of this terrible problem. My situation, after all sophistry and reflection, had finally to be summed up in three awful words—*Lost!* LOST!! LOST!!!

Lost at a depth which, to my infinite understanding, appeared to be immeasurable. These thirty leagues of the crust of the earth weighed upon my shoulders like the globe on the shoulders of Atlas. I felt myself crushed by the awful weight. It was indeed a position to drive the sanest man to madness.

I tried to bring my thoughts back to the things of the world so long forgotten. It was with the greatest difficulty that I succeeded in doing so. Hamburg, the house on the Königstrasse, my dear cousin Gretchen—all that world which had before vanished like a shadow floated before my now vivid imagination. There they were before me, but how unreal. Under the influence of a terrible hallucination I saw the whole incidents of our journey pass before me like the scenes of a panorama. The ship and its inmates, Iceland, M. Fridriksson, and the great summit of Mount Sneffels! I said to myself that if in my position, I retained the most faint and shadowy outline of a hope it would be a sure sign of approaching delirium. It were better to give way wholly to despair!

In fact, if I reasoned with calmness and philosophy, what human power was there in existence able to take me back to the surface of the earth, and ready too, to split asunder those huge and mighty vaults which stood above my head? Who could enable me to find my road—and regain my companions? Insensate folly and madness to entertain even a shadow of hope!

"Oh, uncle!" was my despairing cry. This was the only word of reproach which came to my lips; for I thoroughly understood how deeply and sorrowfully the worthy Professor would regret my loss, and how in his turn he would patiently seek for me.

When I at last began to resign myself to the fact that no further aid was to be expected from man, and knowing that I was utterly powerless to do anything for my own salvation, I kneeled with earnest fervor and asked assistance from Heaven. The remembrance of my innocent childhood, the memory of my mother, known only in my infancy, came welling forth from my heart. I had recourse to prayer. And little as I had right to be remembered by Him whom I had forgotten in the hour of prosperity, and whom I so tardily invoked, I prayed earnestly and sincerely.

This renewal of my youthful faith brought about a much greater amount of calm, and I was enabled to concentrate all my strength and intelligence on the terrible realities of my unprecedented situation. I had about me that which I had at first wholly forgotten—three days' provisions. Moreover, my water bottle was quite full. Nevertheless, the one thing which it was impossible to do was to remain alone. Try to find my companions I must, at any price. But which course should I take? Should I go upwards, or again descend? Doubtless it was right to retrace my steps in an upward direction.

By doing this with care and coolness, I must reach the point where I had turned away from the rippling stream. I must find the fatal bifurcation or fork. Once at this spot, once the river at my feet, I could, at all events, regain the awful crater of Mount Sneffels. Why had I not thought of this before? This, at last, was a reasonable hope of safety. The most important thing, then, to be done was to discover the bed of the Hansbach.

After a slight meal and a draught of water, I rose like a giant refreshed. Leaning heavily on my pole, I began the ascent of the gallery. The slope was very rapid and rather difficult. But I advanced hopefully and carefully, like a man who at last is making his way out of a forest, and knows there is only one road to follow.

During one whole hour nothing happened to check my progress. As I advanced I tried to recollect the shape of the tunnel—to recall to my memory certain projections of rocks—to persuade myself that I had followed certain winding routes before. But no one particular sign could I bring to mind, and I was soon forced to allow that this gallery would never take me back to the point at which I had separated myself from my companions. It was absolutely without issue—a mere blind alley in the earth.

The moment at length came when, facing the solid rock, I knew my fate, and fell inanimate on the arid floor!

To describe the horrible state of despair and fear into which I then fell would now be vain and impossible. My last hope, the courage which had sustained me, drooped before the sight of this pitiless granite rock! Lost in a vast labyrinth, the sinuosities of which spread in every direction, without guide, clue or compass, it was a vain and useless task to attempt flight. All that remained to me was to lie down and die. To lie down and die the most cruel and horrible of deaths!

In my state of mind, the idea came into my head that one day perhaps, when my fossil bones were found, their discovery so far below the level of the earth might give rise to solemn and interesting scientific discussions. I tried to cry aloud, but hoarse, hollow and inarticulate sounds alone could make themselves heard through my parched lips. I literally panted for breath.

In the midst of all these horrible sources of anguish and despair, a new horror took possession of my soul. My lamp, by falling down, had got out of order. I had no means of repairing it. Its light was already becoming paler and paler, and soon would expire. With a strange sense of resignation and despair, I watched the luminous current in the coil getting less and less. A procession of shadows moved flashing along the granite wall. I scarcely dared to lower my eyelids, fearing to lose the last spark of this fugitive light. Every instant it seemed to me that it was about to vanish and to leave me forever—in utter darkness!

At last, one final trembling flame remained in the lamp; I followed it with all my power of vision; I gasped for breath; I concentrated upon it all the power of my soul, as upon the last scintillation of light I was ever destined to see; and then I was to be lost forever in Cimmerian and tenebrous shades.

A wild and plaintive cry escaped my lips. On earth during the most profound and comparatively complete darkness, light never allows a complete destruction and extinction of its power. Light is so diffuse, so subtle, that it permeates everywhere, and whatever little may remain, the retina of the eye will succeed in finding it. In this place nothing—not the faintest ray of light. It mazed me!

My head was now wholly lost. I raised my arms, trying the effects of the feeling in getting against the cold stone wall. It was painful in the extreme. Madness must have taken possession of me. I knew not what I did. I began to run, to fly, rushing at haphazard in this inextricable labyrinth, always going downwards, running wildly underneath the terrestrial crust, like an inhabitant of the subterranean furnaces, screaming, roaring, howling, until bruised by the pointed rocks, falling and picking myself up all covered with blood, seeking madly to drink the blood which dripped from my torn features, mad because this blood trickled over my face, and watching always for this horrid wall which ever presented to me the fearful obstacle against which I could not dash my head.

Where was I going? It was impossible to say. Several hours passed in this way. After a long time, having utterly exhausted my strength, I fell a heavy inert mass along the side of the tunnel, and lost all consciousness of existence!

CHAPTER XXV
THE WHISPERING GALLERY

WHEN at last I came back to a sense of life and being, my face was wet; but wet as I soon knew with tears. How long this state of insensibility lasted, it is quite impossible for me now to say. I had no means left to me of taking any account of time. Never since the creation of the world, had such a solitude as mine existed. I was completely abandoned.

After my fall I had lost much blood. I had felt myself flooded with the life-giving liquid. My first sensation was perhaps a natural one. Why was I not dead? Because I was alive, there was something left to do. I tried to make up my mind to think no longer. As far as I was able, I drove away all ideas, and utterly overcome by pain and grief, crouched against the granite wall.

I commenced to feel the fainting coming on again, with the sensation that this was the last struggle before complete annihilation,—when, on a sudden, a violent uproar reached my ears. It had some resemblance to the prolonged rumbling voice of thunder, and I clearly distinguished sonorous voices, lost one after the other, in the distant depths of the gulf.

Whence came this noise? Again I listened with deep attention. I was extremely anxious to hear if the strange and inexplicable sound was likely to be renewed! A whole quarter of an hour elapsed in painful expectation. Deep and solemn silence reigned in the tunnel. So still that I could hear the beatings of my own heart! I waited, waited, waited with a strange kind of hopefulness.

Suddenly my ear, which leant accidentally against the wall, appeared to catch as it were the faintest echo of a sound. I thought that I heard vague, incoherent and distant voices. I quivered all over with excitement and hope!

"It must be hallucination," I cried. "It cannot be! it is not true!"

But no! By listening more attentively, I really did convince myself that what I heard was truly the sound of human voices. To make any meaning out of the sound, however, was beyond my power. I was too weak even to hear distinctly. Still it was a positive fact that some one was speaking. Of that I was quite certain.

There was a moment of fear. A dread fell upon my soul that it might be my own words brought back to me by a distant echo. Perhaps without knowing it, I might have been crying aloud. I resolutely closed my lips, and once more placed my ear to the huge granite wall. Yes, for certain. It was in truth the sound of human voices.

I now by the exercise of great determination dragged myself along the sides of the cavern, until I reached a point where I could hear more distinctly. But though I could detect the sound, I could only make out uncertain, strange, and incomprehensible words. They reached my ear as if they had been spoken in a low tone—murmured, as it were, afar off. At last, I made out the word *förlorad* repeated several times in a tone betokening great mental anguish and sorrow.

What could this word mean, and who was speaking it? It must be either my uncle or the guide Hans! If, therefore, I could hear them, they must surely be able to hear me. "Help," I cried at the top of my voice; "help, I am dying!"

I then listened with scarcely a breath; I panted for the slightest sound in the darkness—a cry, a sigh, a question! But silence reigned supreme. No answer came! In this way some minutes passed. A whole flood of ideas flashed through my mind. I began to fear that my voice weakened by sickness and suffering could not reach my companions who were in search of me.

"It must be them," I cried; "what other men can by possibility be buried a hundred miles below the level of the earth?" The mere supposition was preposterous. I began, therefore, to listen again with the most breathless attention. As I moved my ears along the side of the place I was in, I found a mathematical point as it were, where the voices appeared to attain their maximum of intensity. The word *förlorad* again distinctly reached my ear. Then came again that rolling noise like thunder which had awakened me out of torpor.

"I begin to understand," I said to myself, after some little time devoted to reflection; "it is not through the solid mass that the sound reaches my ears. The walls of my cavernous retreat are of solid granite, and the most fearful explosion would not make uproar enough to penetrate them. The sound must come along the gallery itself. The place I was in must possess some peculiar acoustic properties of its own."

Again I listened; and this time—yes, this time—I heard my name distinctly pronounced: cast as it were into space. It was my uncle the Professor who was speaking. He was in conversation with the guide, and the word which had so often reached my ears, *förlorad,* was a Danish expression.

Then I understood it all. In order to make myself heard, I too must speak as it were along the side of the gallery, which would carry the sound of my voice just as the wire carries the electric fluid from point to point. But there was no time to lose. If my companions were only to remove a few feet from where they stood, the acoustic effect would be over, my Whispering Gallery would be destroyed. I again therefore crawled towards the wall, and said as clearly and distinctly as I could—"Uncle Hardwigg."

I then awaited a reply.

Sound does not possess the property of traveling with such extreme rapidity. Besides the density of the air at that depth from light and motion, was very far from adding to the rapidity of circulation. Several seconds elapsed, which, to my excited imagination, appeared ages; and these words reached my eager ears, and moved my wildly beating heart—"Harry, my boy, is that you?"

A short delay between question and answer.

"Yes—yes."

"Where are you?"

"Lost!"

"And your lamp?"

"Out."

"But the guiding stream?"

" Is lost ! "

" Keep your courage, Harry. We will do our best."

" One moment, my uncle," I cried; " I have no longer
strength to answer your questions. But—for heaven's
sake—do you—continue—to speak—to me ! "

Absolute silence, I felt, would be annihilation.

" Keep up your courage," said my uncle. " As you are
so weak do not speak. We have been searching for you
in all directions, both by going upwards and downwards
in the gallery. My dear boy, I had begun to give over all
hope—and you can never know what bitter tears of sorrow
and regret I have shed. At last, supposing you to be still
on the road beside the Hansbach we again descended,
firing off guns as signals. Now, however, that we have
found you, and that our voices reach each other, it may
be a long time before we actually meet. We are convers-
ing by means of some extraordinary acoustic arrangement
of the labyrinth. But do not despair, my dear boy. It
is something gained even to hear each other."

While he was speaking my brain was at work reflecting.
A certain undefined hope, vague and shapeless as yet,
made my heart beat wildly. In the first place, it was absolutely necessary for me to know one thing. I once more
therefore leaned my head against the wall, which I almost
touched with my lips, and again spoke.

" Uncle."

" My boy," was his ready answer.

" It is of the utmost consequence that we should know
how far we are asunder."

" That is not difficult."

" You have your chronometer at hand ? " I asked.

" Certainly."

" Well, take it into your hand. Pronounce my name,
noting exactly the second at which you speak. I will
reply as soon as I hear your words—and you will then
note exactly the moment at which my reply reaches you."

" Very good; and the time between my question and your
answer will be the time occupied by my voice in reaching
you."

" That is exactly what I mean, uncle," was my eager
reply.

" Are you ready ? "

"Yes."

"Well, make ready, I am about to pronounce your name," said the Professor.

I applied my ear close to the sides of the cavernous gallery, and as soon as the word Harry reached my ear, I turned round, and placing my lips to the wall, repeated the sound.

"Forty seconds," said my uncle. "There has elapsed forty seconds between the two words. The sound, therefore, takes twenty seconds to ascend. Now, allowing a thousand and twenty feet for every second—we have twenty thousand four hundred feet—a league and a half and one-eighth."

These words fell on my soul like a kind of death-knell. "A league and a-half," I muttered in a low and despairing voice.

"It shall be got over, my boy," cried my uncle in a cheery tone; "depend on us."

"But do you know whether to ascend or descend?" I asked faintly enough.

"You have to descend, and I will tell you why. We have reached a vast open space, a kind of bare cross road, from which galleries diverge in every direction. That in which you are now lying, must necessarily bring you to this point, for it appears that all these mighty fissures, these fractures of the globe's interior radiate from the vast cavern which we at this moment occupy. Rouse yourself, then, have courage and continue your route. Walk if you can, if not drag yourself along—slide, if nothing else is possible. The slope must be rather rapid—and you will find strong arms to receive you at the end of your journey. Make a start, like a good fellow."

These words served to rouse some kind of courage in my sinking frame. "Farewell for the present, good uncle, I am about to take my departure. As soon as I start, our voices will cease to commingle. Farewell, then, until we meet again."

"Adieu, Harry—until we say Welcome." Such were the last words which reached my anxious ears, before I commenced my weary and almost hopeless journey.

This wonderful and surprising conversation which took place through the vast mass of the earth's labyrinth, these

words exchanged, the speakers being about five miles apart
—ended with hopeful and pleasant expressions. I breathed
one more prayer to Heaven, I sent up words of thanks-
giving—believing in my inmost heart that He had led me
to the only place where the voices of my friends could
reach my ears.

I accordingly rose to my feet. I soon found, however,
that I could not walk; that I must drag myself along.
The slope, as I expected, was very rapid; but I allowed
myself to slip down.

Soon the rapidity of the descent began to assume frightful proportions; and menaced a fearful fall. I clutched
at the sides; I grasped at projections of rocks; I threw
myself backwards. All in vain. My weakness was so
great I could do nothing to save myself.

Suddenly earth failed me. I was first launched into a
dark, and gloomy void. I then struck against the projecting asperities of a vertical gallery, a perfect well. My
head bounded against a pointed rock, and I lost all knowledge of existence. As far as I was concerned, death had
claimed me for his own.

CHAPTER XXVI
A RAPID RECOVERY

WHEN I returned to the consciousness of existence, I
found myself surrounded by a kind of semi-obscurity,
lying on some thick and soft coverlids. My uncle was
watching—his eyes fixed intently on my countenance, a
grave expression on his face; a tear in his eye. At the
first sigh which struggled from my bosom he took hold of
my hand. When he saw my eyes open and fix themselves
upon his, he uttered a loud cry of joy. " He lives! he
lives! "

" Yes, my good uncle," I whispered.

" My dear boy," continued the grim Professor, clasping
me to his heart, " you are saved! "

I was deeply and unaffectedly touched by the tone in
which these words were uttered, and even more by the
kindly care which accompanied them. The Professor was
one of those men who must be severely tried in order to

induce any display of affection or gentle emotion. At this moment our friend Hans, the guide, joined us. He saw my hand in that of my uncle, and I venture to say, that, taciturn as he was, his eyes beamed with lively satisfaction. "*God dag,*" he said.

"Good day, Hans, good day," I replied, in as hearty a tone as I could assume, "and now, uncle, that we are together, tell me where we are. I have lost all idea of our position, as of everything else."

"To-morrow, Harry, to-morrow," he replied. "To-day you are far too weak. Your head is surrounded with bandages and poultices that must not be touched. Sleep, my boy, sleep, and to-morrow you will know all that you require."

"But" I cried, "let me know what o'clock it is—what day it is?"

"It is now eleven o'clock at night, and this is once more Sunday. It is now the ninth of the month of August. And I distinctly prohibit you from asking any more questions until the tenth of the same."

I was, if the truth were told, very weak indeed, and my eyes soon closed involuntarily. I did require a good night's rest, and I went off reflecting at the last moment that my perilous adventure in the interior of the earth, in total darkness, had lasted four days!

On the morning of the next day, at my awakening, I began to look around me. My sleeping-place, made of all our traveling bedding, was in a charming grotto, adorned with magnificent stalagmites, glittering in all the colors of the rainbow, the floor of soft and silvery sand. A dim obscurity prevailed. No torch, no lamp was lighted, and yet certain unexplained beams of light penetrated from without, and made their way through the opening of the beautiful grotto.

I, moreover, heard a vague and indefinite murmur, like the ebb and flow of waves upon a strand, and sometimes I verily believed I could hear the sighing of the wind. I began to believe that, instead of being awake, I must be dreaming. Surely my brain had not been affected by my fall, and all that occurred during the last twenty-four hours was not the frenzied visions of madness? And yet after some reflection, a trial of my faculties, I came to the conclusion that I could not be mistaken. Eyes and ears could not surely both deceive me.

"It is a ray of the blessed daylight," I said to myself, "which has penetrated through some mighty fissure in the rocks. But what is the meaning of this murmur of waves, this unmistakable moaning of the salt sea billows? I can hear, too, plainly enough, the whistling of the wind. But can I be altogether mistaken? If my uncle, during my illness, has but carried me back to the surface of the earth! Has he, on my account, given up his wondrous expedition, or in some strange manner has it come to an end?"

I was puzzling my brain over these and other questions, when the Professor joined me. "Good-day, Harry," he cried in a joyous tone. "I fancy you are quite well."

"I am very much better," I replied, actually sitting up in my bed.

"I knew that would be the end of it, as you slept both soundly and tranquilly. Hans and I have each taken turn to watch, and every hour we have seen visible signs of amelioration."

"You must be right, uncle," was my reply, "for I feel as if I could do justice to any meal you could put before me. I am really hungry."

"You shall eat, my boy, you shall eat. The fever has left you. Our excellent friend Hans has rubbed your wounds and bruises, with I know not what ointment, of which the Icelanders alone possess the secret. And they have healed your bruises in the most marvelous manner. Ah, he's a wise fellow, is Master Hans."

While he was speaking, my uncle was placing before me several articles of food, which despite his earnest injunctions, I readily devoured. As soon as the first rage of hunger was appeased, I overwhelmed him with questions, to which he now no longer hesitated to give answers. I then learned, for the first time, that my providential fall had brought me to the bottom of an almost perpendicular gallery. As I came down, amidst a perfect shower of stones, the least of which falling on me would have crushed me to death, they came to the conclusion that I had carried with me an entire dislocated rock. Riding as it were on this terrible chariot, I was cast headlong into my uncle's arms. And into them I fell, insensible and covered with blood. " It is indeed a miracle," was the Professor's final remark, " that you were not killed a thousand times over. But let us take care never to separate; for surely we should risk never meeting again."

" Let us take care never again to separate." These words fell with a sort of chill upon my heart. The journey, then, was not over. I looked at my uncle with surprise and astonishment.

My uncle, after an instant's examination of my countenance, said—" What is the matter, Harry? "

" I want to ask you a very serious question. You say that I am all right in health? "

" Certainly you are."

" And all my limbs are sound and capable of new exertion? " I asked.

" Most undoubtedly."

" But what about my head? " was my next anxious question.

" Well, your head, except that you have one or two contusions, is exactly where it ought to be—on your shoulder," said my uncle, laughing.

" Well, my own opinion is that my head is not exactly right. In fact, I believe myself slightly delirious."

" What makes you think so? "

" I will explain why I fancy I have lost my senses," I cried, " have we not returned to the surface of mother earth? "

" Certainly not."

" Then truly I must be mad, for do I not see the light of day? do I not hear the whistling of the wind? and can I not distinguish the wash of a great sea? "

" And that is all that makes you uneasy? " said my uncle, with a smile.

" Can you explain? "

" I will not make any attempt to explain; for the whole matter is utterly inexplicable. But you shall see and judge for yourself. You will then find that geological science is as yet in its infancy—and that we are doomed to enlighten the world."

" Let us advance, then," I cried eagerly, no longer able to restrain my curiosity.

" Wait a moment, my dear Harry," he responded; " you

must take precautions after your illness before going into the open air."

" The open air? "

" Yes, my boy. I have to warn you that the wind is rather violent—and I have no wish for you to expose yourself without necessary precautions."

" But I beg to assure you that I am perfectly recovered from my illness."

" Have just a little patience, my boy. 'A' relapse would be inconvenient to all parties. We have no time to lose—as our approaching sea voyage may be of long duration."

" Sea voyage? " I cried, more bewildered than ever.

" Yes. You must take another day's rest, and we shall be ready to go on board by to-morrow," replied my uncle, with a peculiar smile.

Go on board! The words utterly astonished me. Go on board—what? and how? Had we come upon a river, a lake, had we discovered some inland sea? Was a vessel lying at anchor in some part of the interior of the earth?

My curiosity was worked up to the very highest pitch. My uncle made vain attempts to restrain me. When at last, however, he discovered that my feverish impatience would do more harm than good—and that the satisfaction of my wishes could alone restore me to a calm state of mind, he gave way.

I dressed myself rapidly—and then taking the precaution, to please my uncle, of wrapping myself in one of the coverlets, I rushed out of the grotto.

CHAPTER XXVII
THE CENTRAL SEA

AT first I saw absolutely nothing. My eyes, wholly unused to the effulgence of light, could not bear the sudden brightness; and I was compelled to close them. When I was able to re-open them, I stood still, far more stupefied than astonished. Not all the wildest effects of imagination could have conjured up such a scene! " The sea—the sea," I cried.

" Yes," replied my uncle, in a tone of pardonable pride; " The Central Sea. No future navigator will deny the fact of my having discovered it; and hence of acquiring a right of giving it a name."

It was quite true. A vast, limitless expanse of water, the end of a lake if not of an ocean, spread before us, until it was lost in the distance. The shore, which was very much indented, consisted of a beautiful soft golden sand, mixed with small shells, the long deserted homes of some of the creatures of a past age. The waves broke incessantly, and with a peculiarly sonorous murmur—to be found in underground localities. A slight frothy flake arose as the wind blew along the pellucid waters; and many a dash of spray was blown into my face. The mighty superstructure of rock which rose above to an inconceivable height, left only a narrow margin—but where we stood, there was a long beach of strand. On all sides were capes and promontories and enormous cliffs, partially worn by the eternal breaking of the waves, through countless ages! And as I gazed from side to side, the mighty rocks faded in the distance like a fleecy film of cloud.

It was in reality an ocean, with all the usual characteristics of an inland sea, only horribly wild—so rigid, cold and savage.

One thing startled and puzzled me greatly. How was it that I was able to look upon that vast sheet of water instead of being plunged in utter darkness? The vast landscape before me was lit up like day. But there was wanting the dazzling brilliancy, the splendid irradiation of the sun; the pale cold illumination of the moon; the brightness of the stars. The illuminating power in this subterraneous region, from its trembling and flickering character, its clear dry whiteness, the very slight elevation of its temperature, its great superiority to that of the moon, was evidently electric; something in the nature of the aurora borealis, only that its phenomena were constant, and able to light up the whole of the ocean cavern.

The tremendous vault above our heads, the sky, so to speak, appeared to be composed of a conglomeration of nebulous vapors, in constant motion. I should originally have supposed, that under such an atmospheric pressure as must exist in that place, the evaporation of water could not really take place; yet there were heavy and dense clouds rolling along that mighty vault, partially concealing the roof. Electric currents produced astonishing play of light and shade in the distance, especially around the heavier clouds. Deep shadows were cast beneath, and then suddenly, between two clouds, there would come a ray of unusual beauty, and remarkable intensity. Yet it was not like the sun, for it gave no heat.

The effect was sad and excruciatingly melancholy. Instead of a noble firmament of blue, studded with stars, there was above me a heavy roof of granite, which seemed to crush me. Gazing around, I began to think of the theory of the English captain, who compared the earth to a vast hollow sphere in the interior of which the air is retained in a luminous state by means of atmospheric pressure, while two stars, Pluto and Proserpine, circled there in their mysterious orbits. After all, suppose the old fellow was right!

In truth, we were imprisoned—bound as it were, in a vast excavation. Its width it was impossible to make out; the shore, on either hand, widening rapidly until lost to sight; while its length was equally uncertain. A haze on the distant horizon bounded our view. As to its height we could see that it must be many miles to the roof. Looking upward, it was impossible to discover where the stupendous roof began. The lowest of the clouds must have been floating at an elevation of two thousand yards, a height greater than that of terrestrial vapors, which circumstance was doubtless owing to the extreme density of the air.

I use the word cavern in order to give an idea of the place. I cannot describe its awful grandeur; human language fails to convey an idea of its savage sublimity. Whether this singular vacuum had or had not been caused by the sudden cooling of the earth when in a state of fusion, I could not say. I had read of most wonderful and gigantic caverns—but none in any way like this.

The great grotto of Guachara, in Colombia, visited by the learned Humboldt; the vast and partially explored Mammoth Cave in Kentucky; what were these holes in the earth to that in which I stood in speechless admiration! with its vapory clouds, its electric light, and the mighty ocean slumbering in its bosom! Imagination, not description, can alone give an idea of the splendor and vastness of the cave.

I gazed at these marvels in profound silence. Words were utterly wanting to indicate the sensations of wonder I experienced. I seemed, as I stood upon that mysterious shore, as if I were some wandering inhabitant of a distant planet, present for the first time at the spectacle of some terrestrial phenomena belonging to another existence. To give body and existence to such new sensations, would have required the coinage of new words—and here my feeble brain found itself wholly at fault. I looked on, I thought, I reflected, I admired, in a state of stupefaction not altogether unmingled with fear!

The unexpected spectacle restored some color to my pallid cheeks. I seemed to be actually getting better under the influence of this novelty. Moreover, the vivacity of the dense atmosphere reanimated my body, by inflating my lungs with unaccustomed oxygen.

It will be readily conceived that after an imprisonment of forty-seven days, in a dark and miserable tunnel, it was with infinite delight that I breathed this saline air. It was like the genial, reviving influence of the salt sea waves. My uncle had already got over the first surprise. With the Latin poet Horace his idea was that—

> " Not to admire, is all the art I know
> To make man happy and to keep him so."

" Well," he said, after giving me time thoroughly to appreciate the marvels of this underground sea, " do you feel strong enough to walk up and down? "

" Certainly," was my ready answer, " nothing would give me greater pleasure."

" Well, then, my boy," he said, " lean on my arm, and we will stroll along the beach."

I accepted his offer eagerly, and we began to walk along the shores of this extraordinary lake. To our left were abrupt rocks, piled one upon the other,—a stupendous titanic pile; down their sides leapt innumerable cascades, which at last, becoming limpid and murmuring streams, were lost in the waters of the lake. Light vapors, which rose here and there, and floated in fleecy clouds from rock to rock, indicated hot springs, which also poured their superfluity into the vast reservoir at our feet.

Among them I recognized our old and faithful stream,

the Hansbach, which, lost in that wild basin, seemed as if it had been flowing since the creation of the world.

"We shall miss our excellent friend," I remarked, with a deep sigh.

"Bah!" said my uncle, testily, "what matters it. That or another, it is all the same."

I thought the remark ungrateful, and felt almost inclined to say so; but I forbore. At this moment my attention was attracted by an unexpected spectacle. After we had gone about five hundred yards, we suddenly turned a steep promontory, and found ourselves close to a lofty forest! It consisted of straight trunks with tufted tops, in shape like parasols. The air seemed to have no effect upon these trees—which in spite of a tolerable breeze remained as still and motionless as if they had been petrified.

I hastened forward. I could find no name for these singular formations. Did they belong to the two thousand and more known trees—or were we to make the discovery of a new growth? When we at last reached the forest, and stood beneath the trees, my surprise gave way to admiration. In truth, I was simply in the presence of a very ordinary product of the earth, of singular and gigantic proportions. My uncle unhesitatingly called them by their real names. "It is only," he said, in his coolest manner, "a forest of mushrooms."

On close examination I found that he was not mistaken. Judge of the development attained by this product of damp hot soils. I had heard that the *lycoperdon giganteum* reaches nine feet in circumference, but here were white mushrooms, nearly forty feet high, and with tops of equal dimensions. They grew in countless thousands— the light could not make its way through their massive substance, and beneath them reigned a gloomy and mystic darkness.

Still I wished to go forward. The cold in the shades of this singular forest was intense. For nearly an hour we wandered about in this darkness visible. At length I left the spot, and once more returned to the shores of the lake, to light and comparative warmth.

The amazing vegetation of this subterraneous land was not confined to gigantic mushrooms. New wonders awaited us at every step. We had not gone many hundred yards, when we came upon a mighty group of other trees with discolored leaves—the common humble trees of mother earth, of an exorbitant and phenomenal size; mosses a hundred feet high; flowering ferns as tall as pines; gigantic grasses!

"Astonishing, magnificent, splendid!" cried my uncle; "here we have before us the whole Flora of the second period of the world, that of transition. Behold the humble plants of our gardens, which in the first ages of the world were mighty trees. Look around you, my dear Harry. No botanist ever before gazed on such a sight!"

My uncle's enthusiasm, usually a little more than was required, was now excusable. "You are right, uncle," I remarked. "Providence appears to have designed the preservation in this vast and mysterious hot-house of antediluvian plants, to prove the sagacity of learned men in figuring them so marvelously on paper."

"Well said, my boy—very well said; it is indeed a mighty hot-house;—but you would also be within the bounds of reason and common sense, if you also added—a vast menagerie."

I looked rather anxiously around. If the animals were as exaggerated as the plants, the matter would certainly be serious. "A menagerie?"

"Doubtless. Look at the dust we are treading under foot—behold the bones with which the whole soil of the seashore is covered——"

"Bones," I replied, "yes, certainly, the bones of antediluvian animals." I stooped down as I spoke, and picked up one or two singular remains, relics of a by-gone age. It was easy to give a name to these gigantic bones, in some instances as big as trunks of trees.

"Here is, clearly, the lower jaw-bone of a mastodon," I cried, almost as warmly and enthusiastically as my uncle, "here are the molars of the dinotherium; here is a leg-bone which belonged to the megatherium. You are right, uncle, it is indeed a menagerie; for the mighty animals to which these bones once belonged, have lived and died on the shores of this subterranean sea, under the shadow of these plants. Look, yonder are whole skeletons—and yet——"

"And yet, nephew?" said my uncle, noticing that I suddenly came to a full stop.

"I do not understand the presence of such beasts in granite caverns, however vast and prodigious," was my reply.

"Why not?" said my uncle, with very much of his old professional impatience.

"Because it is well known that animal life only existed on earth during the secondary period, when the sedimentary soil was formed by the alluviums, and thus replaced the hot and burning rocks of the primitive age."

"I have listened to you earnestly and with patience, Harry, and I have a simple and clear answer to your objections: and that is, that this itself is a sedimentary soil."

"How can that be at such enormous depth from the surface of the earth?"

"The fact can be explained both simply and geologically. At a certain period, the earth consisted only of an elastic crust, liable to alternative upward and downward movements in virtue of the law of attraction. It is very probable that many a landslip took place in those days, and that large portions of sedimentary soil were cast into huge and mighty chasms."

"Quite possible," I dryly remarked. "But, uncle, if these antediluvian animals formerly lived in these subterranean regions, what more likely than that one of these huge monsters may at this moment be concealed behind one of yonder mighty rocks."

As I spoke, I looked keenly around, examining with care every point of the horizon; but nothing alive appeared to exist on these deserted shores.

I now felt rather fatigued, and told my uncle so. The walk and excitement were too much for me in my weak state. I therefore seated myself at the end of a promontory, at the foot of which the waves broke in incessant rolls. I looked round a bay formed by projections of vast granitic rocks. At the extreme end was a little port protected by huge pyramids of stones. A brig and three or four schooners might have lain there with perfect ease. So natural did it seem, that every minute my imagination induced me to expect a vessel coming out under all sail and making for the open sea under the influence of a warm southerly breeze.

But the fantastic illusion never lasted more than a minute. We were the only living creatures in this subterranean world!

During certain periods there was an utter cessation of wind, when a silence deeper, more terrible than the silence of the desert fell upon these solitary and arid rocks—and seemed to hang like a leaden weight upon the waters of this singular ocean. I sought, amid the awful stillness, to penetrate through the distant fog, to tear down the veil which concealed the mysterious distance. What unspoken words were murmured by my trembling lips—what questions did I wish to ask and did not! Where did this sea end—to what did it lead? Should we ever be able to examine its distant shores?

But my uncle had no doubts about the matter. He was convinced that our enterprise would in the end be successful. For my part, I was in a state of painful indecision—I desired to embark on the journey and to succeed, and still I feared the result.

After we had passed an hour or more in silent contemplation of the wondrous spectacle, we rose and went down towards the bank on our way to the grotto, which I was not sorry to gain. After a slight repast, I sought refuge in slumber, and at length, after many and tedious struggles, sleep came over my weary eyes.

CHAPTER XXVIII
LAUNCHING THE RAFT

On the morning of the next day, to my great surprise, I awoke completely restored. I thought a bath would be delightful after my long illness and sufferings. So, soon after rising, I went and plunged into the waters of this new Mediterranean. The bath was cool, fresh and invigorating.

I came back to breakfast with an excellent appetite. Hans, our worthy guide, thoroughly understood how to cook such eatables as we were able to provide; he had both fire and water at discretion, so that he was enabled slightly to vary the weary monotony of our ordinary repast. Our morning meal was like a capital English breakfast, with coffee by way of a wind-up. And never had this delicious beverage been so welcome and refreshing.

My uncle had sufficient regard for my state of health not to interrupt me in the enjoyment of the meal, but he was evidently delighted when I had finished. "Now then," said he, "come with me. It is the height of the tide, and I am anxious to study its curious phenomena."

"What," I cried, rising in astonishment, "did you say the tide, uncle?"

"Certainly I did."

"You do not mean to say," I replied, in a tone of respectful doubt, "that the influence of the sun and moon is felt here below."

"And pray why not? Are not all bodies influenced by the law of universal attraction? Why should this vast underground sea be exempt from the general law, the rule of the universe? Besides, there is nothing like that which is proved and demonstrated. Despite the great atmospheric pressure down here, you will notice that this inland sea rises and falls with as much regularity as the Atlantic itself."

As my uncle spoke, we reached the sandy shore, and saw and heard the waves breaking monotonously on the beach. They were evidently rising.

"This is truly the flood," I cried, looking at the water at my feet.

"Yes, my excellent nephew," replied my uncle, rubbing his hands with the gusto of a philosopher, "and you see by these several streaks of foam, that the tide rises at least ten or twelve feet."

"It is indeed marvelous."

"By no means," he responded; "on the contrary, it is quite natural."

"It may appear so in your eyes, my dear uncle," was my reply, "but the whole phenomena of the place appear to me to partake of the marvelous. It is almost impossible to believe that which I see. Who in his wildest dreams could have imagined that, beneath the crust of our earth, there could exist a real ocean, with ebbing and flowing tides, with its changes of winds, and even its storms. I for one should have laughed the suggestion to scorn."

"But, Harry, my boy, why not?" inquired my uncle, with a pitying smile, "is there any physical reason in opposition to it?"

"Not if we give up the great theory of the central heat of the earth. That point once granted, I certainly can see no reason for doubting the existence of seas and other wonders, even countries, in the interior of the globe."

"That is so—but of course these varied countries are uninhabited?"

"Well, I grant that it is more likely than not: still, I do not see why this sea should not have given shelter to some species of unknown fish."

"Hitherto we have not discovered any, and the probabilities are rather against our ever doing so," observed the Professor.

I was losing my skepticism in the presence of these wonders. "Well, I am determined to solve the question. It is my intention to try my luck with my fishing line and hook."

"Certainly; make the experiment," said my uncle, pleased with my enthusiasm. "While we are about it, it will certainly be only proper to discover all the secrets of this extraordinary region."

"But, after all, where are we now?" I asked; "all this time I have quite forgotten to ask you a question, which, doubtless, your philosophical instruments have long since answered."

"Well," replied the Professor, "examining the situation from only one point of view, we are now distant three hundred and fifty leagues from Iceland."

"So much?" was my exclamation.

"I have gone over the matter several times, and am sure not to have made a mistake of five hundred yards," replied my uncle positively.

"And as to the direction—are we still going to the southeast?"

"Yes, with a western declination of nineteen degrees, forty-two minutes, just as it is above. As for the inclination I have discovered a very curious fact."

"What may that be, uncle? Your information interests me."

"Why that the needle, instead of dipping towards the

pole as it does on earth, in the northern hemisphere, has an upward tendency."

"This proves," I cried, "that the great point of magnetic attraction lies somewhere between the surface of the earth and the spot we have succeeded in reaching."

"Exactly, my observant nephew," exclaimed my uncle, elated and delighted, "and it is quite probable that if we succeed in getting toward the polar regions—somewhere near the seventy-third degree of latitude, where Sir James Ross discovered the magnetic pole, we shall behold the needle point directly upward. We have therefore discovered that this great center of attraction is not situated at a very great depth."

"Well," said I, rather surprised, "this discovery will astonish experimental philosophers. It was never suspected."

"Science, great, mighty and in the end unerring," replied my uncle dogmatically, "science has fallen into many errors—errors which have been fortunate and useful rather than otherwise, for they have been the stepping-stones to truth."

After some further discussion, I turned to another matter. "Have you any idea of the depth we have reached?"

"We are now," continued the Professor, "exactly thirty-five leagues—above a hundred miles—down into the interior of the earth."

"So," said I, after measuring the distance on the map, "we are now beneath the Scottish Highlands, and have over our heads the lofty Grampian hills."

"You are quite right," said the Professor, laughing, "it sounds very alarming, the weight being heavy—but the vault which supports this vast mass of earth and rock is solid and safe—the mighty Architect of the Universe has constructed it of solid materials. Man, even in his highest flights of vivid and poetic imagination, never thought of such things! What are the finest arches of our bridges, what the vaulted roofs of our cathedrals, to that mighty dome above us, and beneath which floats an ocean with its storms and calms and tides!"

"I admire it all as much as you can, uncle, and have no fear that our granite sky will fall upon our heads. But now that we have discussed matters of science and dis-

covery, what are your future intentions? Are you not
thinking of getting back to the surface of our beautiful
earth?" This was said more as a feeler than with any
hope of success.

"Go back, nephew," cried my uncle in a tone of alarm,
"you are not surely thinking of anything so absurd or
cowardly. No, my intention is to advance and continue
our journey. We have as yet been singularly fortunate,
and henceforth I hope we shall be more so."

"But," said I, "how are we to cross yonder liquid
plain?"

"It is not my intention to leap into it head foremost, or
even to swim across it, like Leander over the Hellespont.
But as oceans are, after all, only great lakes, inasmuch as
they are surrounded by land, so does it stand to reason, that
this central sea is circumscribed by granite surroundings."

"Doubtless," was my natural reply.

"Well, then, do you not think that when once we reach
the other end, we shall find some means of continuing our
journey?"

"Probably, but what extent do you allow to this internal
ocean?"

"I should fancy it to extend about forty or fifty leagues
—more or less."

"But even supposing this approximation to be a correct
one—what then?" I asked.

"My dear boy, we have no time for further discussion.
We shall embark to-morrow."

I looked around with surprise and incredulity. I could
see nothing in the shape of boat or vessel. "What!" I
cried, "we are about to launch out upon an unknown sea;
and where, if I may ask, is the vessel to carry us?"

"Well, my dear boy, it will not be exactly what you
would call a vessel. For the present we must be content
with a good and solid raft."

"A raft," I cried, incredulously, "but down here a raft
is as impossible of construction as a vessel—and I am at a
loss to imagine——"

"My good Harry—if you were to listen instead of talking so much, you would hear," said my uncle, waxing a little impatient.

"I should hear?"

"Yes—certain knocks with the hammer, which Hans is now employing to make the raft. He has been at work for many hours."

"But where has he found trees suitable for such a construction?"

"He found the trees all ready to his hand. Come, and you shall see our excellent guide at work."

More and more amazed at what I heard and saw, I followed my uncle like one in a dream. After a walk of about a quarter of an hour, I saw Hans at work on the other side of the promonotory which formed our natural port. A few minutes more and I was beside him. To my great surprise, on the sandy shore lay a half-finished raft. It was made from beams of a very peculiar wood, and a great number of limbs, joints, boughs, and pieces lay about, sufficient to have constructed a fleet of ships and boats.

I turned to my uncle, silent with astonishment and awe. "Where did all this wood come from?" I cried; "what wood is it?"

"Well, there is pine-wood, fir, and the palms of the northern regions, mineralized by the action of the sea," he replied, sententiously.

"Can it be possible?"

"Yes," said the learned Professor, "what you see is called fossil wood."

"But then," cried I, after reflecting for a moment, "like the lignites, it must be as hard and as heavy as iron, and therefore will certainly not float."

"Sometimes that is the case. Many of these woods have become true anthracites, but others again, like those you see before you, have only undergone one phase of fossil transformation. But there is no proof like demonstration," added my uncle, picking one or two of these precious waifs and casting them into the sea.

The piece of wood, after having disappeared for a moment, came to the surface, and floated about with the oscillation produced by wind and tide. "Are you convinced?" said my uncle, with a self-satisfied smile.

"I am convinced," I cried, "that what I see is incredible."

The fact was that my journey into the interior of the earth was rapidly changing all preconceived notions, and day by day preparing me for the marvelous. I should not have been surprised to have seen a fleet of native canoes afloat upon that silent sea.

The very next evening, thanks to the industry and ability of Hans, the raft was finished. It was about ten feet long and five feet wide. The beams bound together with stout ropes, were solid and firm, and once launched by our united efforts, the improvised vessel floated tranquilly upon the waters of what the Professor had well named the Central Sea.

CHAPTER XXIX
ON THE WATERS.—A RAFT VOYAGE

On the 13th of August we were up betimes. There was no time to be lost. We now had to inaugurate a new kind of locomotion, which would have the advantage of being rapid and not fatiguing. A mast, made of two pieces of wood fastened together, to give additional strength, a yard made from another one, the sail a linen sheet from our bed. We were fortunately in no want of cordage, and the whole on trial appeared solid and seaworthy.

At six o'clock in the morning, when the eager and enthusiastic Professor gave the signal to embark, the victuals, the luggage, all our instruments, our weapons, and a goodly supply of sweet water, which we had collected from springs in the rocks, were placed on the raft. Hans had, with considerable ingenuity, contrived a rudder, which enabled him to guide the floating apparatus with ease. He took the tiller, as a matter of course. The worthy man was as good a sailor as he was a guide and duck-hunter. I then let go the painter which held us to the shore, the sail was brought to the wind, and we made a rapid offing. Our sea voyage had at length commenced; and once more we were making for distant and unknown regions.

Just as we were about to leave the little port where the raft had been constructed, my uncle, who was very strong as to geographic nomenclature, wanted to give it a name, and among others, suggested mine.

" Well," said I, " before you decide I have another to propose."

" Well; out with it."

" I should like to call it Gretchen. Port Gretchen will sound very well on our future map."

" Well, then, Port Gretchen let it be," said the Professor. And thus it was that the memory of my dear girl was attached to our adventurous and memorable expedition.

When we left the shore the wind was blowing from the northward and eastward. We went directly before the wind at a much greater speed than might have been expected from a raft. The dense layers of atmosphere at that depth had great propelling power and acted upon the sail with considerable force. At the end of an hour, my uncle, who had been taking careful observations, was enabled to judge of the rapidity with which we moved. It was far beyond anything seen in the upper world.

" If," he said, " we continue to advance at our present rate, we shall have traveled at least thirty leagues in twenty-four hours. With a mere raft this is an almost incredible velocity."

I certainly was surprised, and without making any reply went forward upon the raft. Already the northern shore was fading away on the edge of the horizon. The two shores appeared to separate more and more, leaving a wide and open space for our departure. Before me I could see nothing but the vast and apparently limitless sea—upon which we floated—the only living objects in sight.

Huge and dark clouds cast their gray shadows below—shadows which seemed to crush that colorless and sullen water by their weight. Anything more suggestive of gloom and of regions of nether darkness I never beheld. Silvery rays of electric light, reflected here and there upon some small spots of water, brought up luminous sparkles in the long wake of our cumbrous bark. Presently we were wholly out of sight of land, not a vestige could be seen, nor any indication of where we were going. So still and motionless did we seem without any distant point to fix our eyes on, that but for the phosphoric light at the wake of the raft I should have fancied that we were still and motionless.

But I knew that we were advancing at a very rapid rate. About twelve o'clock in the day, vast collections of seaweed were discovered surrounding us on all sides. I was aware of the extraordinary vegetative power of these plants, which have been known to creep along the bottom of the great ocean, and stop the advance of large ships. But never were seaweeds ever seen, so gigantic and wonderful as those of the Central Sea. I could well imagine how, seen at a distance, tossing and heaving on the summit of the billows, the long lines of Algæ have been taken for living things, and thus have been the fertile sources of the belief in sea serpents.

Our raft swept past great specimens of fucæ or seawrack, from three to four thousand feet in length, immense, incredibly long, looking like snakes that stretched out far beyond our horizon. It afforded me great amusement to gaze on their variegated ribbon-like endless lengths. Hour after hour passed without our coming to the termination of these floating weeds. If my astonishment increased, my patience was well-nigh exhausted.

What natural force could possibly have produced such abnormal and extraordinary plants? What must have been the aspect of the globe, during the first centuries of its formation, when under the combined action of heat and humidity, the vegetable kingdom occupied its vast surface to the exclusion of everything else? These were considerations of never-ending interest for the geologist and the philosopher.

All this while we were advancing on our journey; and at length night came; but as I had remarked the evening before, the luminous state of the atmosphere was in nothing diminished. Whatever was the cause, it was a phenomenon upon the duration of which we could calculate with certainty.

As soon as our supper had been disposed of, and some little speculative conversation indulged in, I stretched myself at the foot of the mast and presently went to sleep. Hans remained motionless at the tiller, allowing the raft to rise and fall on the waves. The wind being aft, and the sail square, all he had to do was to keep his oar in the center.

Ever since we had taken our departure from the newly named Port Gretchen, my worthy uncle had directed me to keep a regular log of our day's navigation, with instructions to put down even the most minute particulars, every interesting and curious phenomenon, the direction of the wind, our rate of sailing, the distance we went; in a word, every incident of our extraordinary voyage. From our log, therefore, I tell the story of our voyage on the Central Sea.

Friday, August 14th. A steady breeze from the northwest. Raft progressing with extreme rapidity, and going perfectly straight. Coast still dimly visible about thirty miles to leeward. Nothing to be seen beyond the horizon in front. The extraordinary intensity of the light neither increases nor diminishes. It is singularly stationary. The weather remarkably fine; that is to say, the clouds have ascended very high, and are light and fleecy, and surrounded by an atmosphere resembling silver in fusion. Thermometer + 32 degrees centigrade.

About twelve o'clock in the day our guide, Hans, having prepared and baited a hook, cast his line into the subterranean waters. The bait he used was a small piece of meat, by means of which he concealed his hook. Anxious as I was, I was for a long time doomed to disappointment. Were these waters supplied with fish or not? That was the important question. No—was my decided answer. Then there came a sudden and rather hard tug. Hans coolly drew it in, and with it a fish, which struggled violently to escape.

"A fish," cried my uncle, putting on his spectacles to examine it.

"It is a sturgeon!" I cried, "certainly a small sturgeon."

The Professor examined the fish carefully, noting every characteristic; and he did not coincide in my opinion. The fish had a flat head, round body, and the lower extremities covered with bony scales; its mouth was wholly without teeth, the pectoral fins, which were highly developed, sprouted direct from the body, which properly speaking had no tail. The animal certainly belonged to the order in which naturalists class the sturgeon, but it differed from that fish in many essential particulars. My uncle, after all, was not mistaken. After a long and patient examination, he said: "This fish, my dear boy, belongs to a family which has been extinct for ages, and of which no trace has ever been found on earth, except fossil remains in the Devonian strata."

"You do not mean to say," I cried, "that we have captured a live specimen of a fish belonging to the primitive stock that existed before the deluge?"

"We have," said the Professor, who all this time was continuing his observations, "and you may see by careful examination that these fossil fish have no identity with existing species. To hold in one's hand, therefore, a living specimen of the order, is enough to make a naturalist happy for life. Moreover this fish offers to our notice a remarkable peculiarity, never known to exist in any other fish but those which are the natives of subterranean waters, wells, lakes, in caverns, and such like hidden pools."

"And what may that be?"

"It is blind."

"Blind!" I cried, much surprised.

"Not only blind," continued the Professor, "but absolutely without organs of sight."

I now examined our discovery for myself. It was singular, to be sure, but it was really a fact. This, however, might be a solitary instance, I suggested. The hook was baited again and once more thrown into the water. This subterranean ocean must have been tolerably well supplied with fish, for in two hours we took a large number of similar fish. All, without exception, however, were blind. This unexpected capture enabled us to renew our stock of provisions in a very satisfactory way.

We were now convinced that this Subterranean Sea contained only fish known to us as fossil specimens—and fish and reptiles alike, were all the more perfect the farther back they dated their origin. We began to hope that we should find some of those Saurians which science has succeeded in reconstructing from bits of bone or cartilage. I took up the telescope and carefully examined the horizon —looked over the whole sea; it was utterly and entirely deserted. Doubtless we were still too near the coast.

After an examination of the ocean, I looked upward, towards the strange and mysterious sky. Why should not one of the birds, reconstructed by the immortal Cuvier, flap his stupendous wings aloft in the dull strata of subterranean air? It would, of course, find quite sufficient food

from the fish in the sea. I gazed for some time upon the
void above. It was as silent and as deserted as the shores
we had but lately left.

Nevertheless, though I could neither see nor discover
anything, my imagination carried me away into wild
hypotheses. I was in a kind of waking dream. I thought
I saw on the surface of the water those enormous antediluvian turtles as big as floating islands. Upon those dull
and somber shores passed a spectral row of the mammifers
of early days, the great Leptotherium found in the cavernous hollow of the Brazilian hills, the Mesicotherium, a
native of the glacial regions of Siberia. Farther on, the
pachydermatous Lophrodon, that gigantic tapir, which
concealed itself behind rocks, ready to do battle for its
prey with the Anoplotherium, a singular animal partaking
of the nature of the rhinoceros, the horse, the hippopot-
amus and the camel.

I thought, such was the effect of my imagination, that I
saw this whole tribe of antediluvian creatures. I carried
myself back to far ages, long before man existed—when,
in fact, the earth was in too imperfect a state for him to
live upon it. The whole panorama of the world's life
before the historic period, seemed to be born over again,
and mine was the only human heart that beat in this un-
peopled world! There were no more seasons; there were
no more climates; the natural heat of the world increased
unceasingly, and neutralized that of the great radiant Sun.

Next, unrolled before me like a panorama, came the
great and wondrous series of terrestrial transformations.
Plants disappeared; the granitic rocks lost all trace of
solidity; the liquid state was suddenly substituted for that
which had before existed. This was caused by intense
heat acting on the organic matter of the earth. The
waters flowed over the whole surface of the globe; they
boiled; they were volatilized, or turned into vapor; a kind
of steam-cloud wrapped the whole earth, the globe itself
becoming at last nothing but one huge sphere of gas,
indescribable in color, between white heat and red, as big
and as brilliant as the sun.

What an extraordinary dream! Where would it finally
take me? My feverish hand began to write down the marvelous details—details more like the imaginings of a luna-

tic than anything sober and real. I had during this period of hallucination forgotten everything—the Professor, the guide, and the raft on which we were floating. My mind was in a state of semi-oblivion.

"What is the matter, Harry?" said my uncle, suddenly.

My eyes, which were wide opened like those of a somnambulist, were fixed upon him, but I did not see him, nor could I clearly make out anything around me.

"Take care, my boy," again cried my uncle, "you will fall into the sea."

As he uttered these words, I felt myself seized on the other side by the firm hand of our devoted guide. Had it not been for the presence of mind of Hans, I must infallibly have fallen into the waves and been drowned.

"Have you gone mad?" cried my uncle, shaking me on the other side.

"What—what is the matter?" I said at last, coming to myself.

"Are you ill, Henry?" continued the Professor in an anxious tone.

"No—no; but I have had an extraordinary dream. It, however, has passed away. All now seems well," I added, looking around me with strangely puzzled eyes.

"All right," said my uncle; "a beautiful breeze, a splendid sea. We are going along at a rapid rate, and if I am not out in my calculations we shall soon see land. I shall not be sorry to exchange the narrow limits of our raft for the mysterious strand of the Subterranean Ocean."

As my uncle uttered these words, I rose and carefully scanned the horizon. But the line of water was still confounded with the lowering clouds that hung aloft, and in the distance appeared to touch the edge of the water.

CHAPTER XXX
TERRIFIC SAURIAN COMBAT

SATURDAY, August 15. The sea still retains its uniform monotony. The same leaden hue, the same eternal glare from above. No indication of land being in sight. The horizon appears to retreat before us, more and more as we advance.

My head is still dull and heavy from the effects of my extraordinary dream, which I cannot as yet banish from my mind. The Professor, who has not dreamed, is, however, in one of his morose and unaccountable humors. Spends his time in scanning the horizon, at every point of the compass. His telescope is raised every moment to his eyes, and when he finds nothing to give any clew to our whereabouts, he assumes a Napoleonic attitude and walks anxiously.

I remarked that my uncle, the Professor, had a strong tendency to resume his old impatient character, and I could not but make a note of this disagreeable circumstance. I saw clearly that it had required all the influence of my danger and suffering, to extract from him one scintillation of humane feeling. Now that I was quite recovered, his original nature had conquered and obtained the upper hand.

"You seem uneasy, uncle," said I, when for about the hundredth time he put down his telescope and walked up and down, muttering to himself.

"No, I am not uneasy," he replied in a dry harsh tone, "by no means."

"Perhaps I should have said impatient," I replied, softening the force of my remark.

"Enough to make me so, I think."

"And yet we are advancing at a rate seldom attained by a raft," I remarked.

"What matters that?" cried my uncle. "I am not vexed at the rate we go at, but I am annoyed to find the sea so much vaster than I expected."

I then recollected that the Professor, before our departure, had estimated the length of this Subterranean Ocean, as at most about fifty leagues. Now we had traveled at least over thrice that distance without discovering any trace of the distant shore. I began to understand my uncle's anger.

"We are not going down," suddenly exclaimed the Professor. "We are not progressing with our great discoveries. All this is utter loss of time. After all, I did not come from home to undertake a party of pleasure. This voyage on a raft over a pond annoys and wearies me."

He called this adventurous journey a party of pleasure, and this great Inland Sea a pond! "But," argued I, "if we have followed the route indicated by the great Saknussemm, we cannot be going far wrong."

"'That is the question,' as the great, the immortal Shakespeare, has it. Are we following the route indicated by that wondrous sage? Did Saknussemm ever fall in with this great sheet of water? If he did, did he cross it? I begin to fear that the rivulet we adopted for a guide has led us wrong."

"In any case, we can never regret having come thus far. It is worth the whole journey to have enjoyed this magnificent spectacle—it is something to have seen."

"I care nothing about seeing, nor about magnificent spectacles. I came down into the interior of the earth with an object, and that object I mean to attain. Don't talk to me about admiring scenery, or any other sentimental trash."

After this I thought it well to hold my tongue, and allow the Professor to bite his lips until the blood came, without further remark.

At six o'clock in the evening, our matter-of-fact guide, Hans, asked for his week's salary, and receiving his three rix-dollars, put them carefully in his pocket. He was perfectly contented and satisfied.

Sunday, 16th August. Nothing new to record. The same weather as before. The wind has a slight tendency to freshen up, with signs of an approaching gale. When I awoke, my first observation was in regard to the intensity of the light. I keep on fearing, day after day, that the extraordinary electric phenomenon should become first obscured, and then go wholly out, leaving us in total darkness. Nothing, however, of the kind occurs. The shadow of the raft, its mast and sails, is clearly distinguished on the surface of the water.

This wondrous sea is, after all, infinite in its extent. It must be quite as wide as the Mediterranean—or perhaps even as the great Atlantic Ocean. Why, after all, should it not be so? My uncle has on more than one occasion, tried deep sea soundings. He tied the cross of one of our heaviest crowbars to the extremity of a cord, which he allowed to run out to the extent of two hundred fathoms.

We had the greatest difficulty in hoisting in our novel kind of lead.

When the crowbar was finally dragged on board, Hans called my attention to some singular marks upon its surface. The piece of iron looked as if it had been crushed between two very hard substances. I looked at our worthy guide with an inquiring glance. "Tander," said he.

Of course I was at a loss to understand. I turned round towards my uncle, absorbed in gloomy reflections. I had little wish to disturb him from his reverie. I accordingly turned once more toward our worthy Icelander. Hans very quietly and significantly opened his mouth once or twice, as if in the act of biting, and in this way made me understand his meaning.

"Teeth!" cried I, with stupefaction, as I examined the bar of iron with more attention.

Yes. There can be no doubt about the matter. The indentations on the bar of iron are the marks of teeth! What jaws must the owner of such molars be possessed of! Have we, then, come upon a monster of unknown species, which still exists within the vast waste of waters —a monster more voracious than a shark, more terrible and bulky than the whale. I am unable to withdraw my eyes from the bar of iron, actually half-crushed!

Is, then, my dream about to come true—a dread and terrible reality? All day my thoughts were bent upon these speculations, and my imagination scarcely regained a degree of calmness and power of reflection until after a sleep of many hours. This day, as on other Sundays, we observed as a day of rest and pious meditation.

Monday, August 17th. I have been trying to realize from memory the particular instincts of those antediluvian animals of the secondary period, which succeeding to the mollusca, to the crustacea, and to the fish, preceded the appearance of the race of mammifers. The generation of reptiles then reigned supreme upon the earth. These hideous monsters ruled everything in the seas of the secondary period, which formed the strata of which the Jura mountains are composed. What a gigantic structure was theirs; what vast and prodigious strength they possessed! The existing Saurians, which include all such reptiles as lizards, crocodiles, and alligators, even the largest and most formidable of their class, are but feeble imitations of their mighty sires, the animals of ages long ago. If there were giants in the days of old, there were also gigantic animals.

I shuddered as I evolved from my mind the idea and recollection of these awful monsters. No eye of man had seen them in the flesh. They took their walks abroad upon the face of the earth thousands of ages before man came into existence, and their fossil bones, discovered in the limestone, have allowed us to reconstruct them anatomically, and thus to get some faint idea of their colossal formation.

I recollect once seeing in the great Museum of Hamburg the skeleton of one of these wonderful Saurians. It measured no less than thirty feet from the nose to the tail. Am I, then, an inhabitant of the earth of the present day, destined to find myself face to face with a representative of this antediluvian family? I can scarcely believe it possible; can hardly believe it true. And yet these marks of powerful teeth upon the bar of iron! can there be a doubt from their shape that the bite is the bite of a crocodile?

My eyes stare wildly and with terror upon the subterranean sea. Every moment I expect one of these monsters to rise from its vast cavernous depths. I fancy that the worthy Professor in some measure shares my notions, if not my fears, for, after an attentive examination of the crowbar, he cast his eyes rapidly over the mighty and mysterious ocean.

"What could possess him to leave the land," I thought, "as if the depth of this water was of any importance to us. No doubt he has disturbed some terrible monster in his watery home, and perhaps we may pay dearly for our temerity." Anxious to be prepared for the worst, I examined our weapons, and saw that they were in a fit state for use. My uncle looked on at me and nodded his head approvingly. He, too, had noticed what we had to fear.

Already the uplifting of the waters on the surface indicates that something is in motion below. The danger approaches. It comes nearer and nearer. It behooves us to be on the watch.

Tuesday, August 18. Evening came at last, the hour, when the desire for sleep caused our eyelids to be heavy. Night there is not, properly speaking, in this place, any more than there is in summer in the arctic regions. Hans, however, is immovable at the rudder. When he snatches a moment of rest I really cannot say. I took advantage of his vigilance to take some little repose.

Two hours after, I was awakened from a heavy sleep by an awful shock. The raft appeared to have struck upon a sunken rock. It was lifted right out of the water by some wondrous and mysterious power, and then started off twenty fathoms distant.

"Eh, what is it?" cried my uncle, starting up, "are we shipwrecked, or what?"

Hans raised his hand and pointed to where, about two hundred yards off, a huge black mass was moving up and down. I looked with awe. My worst fears were realized.

"It is a colossal monster!" I cried, clasping my hands.

"Yes," cried the agitated Professor, "there yonder is a huge sea lizard of terrible size and shape."

"And farther on behold a prodigious crocodile. Look at his hideous jaws, and that row of monstrous teeth. Ha! he has gone."

"A whale! a whale!" shouted the Professor, "I can see her enormous fins. See, see, how she blows air and water!"

Two liquid columns rose to a vast height above the level of the sea, into which they fell with a terrific crash, waking up the echoes of that awful place. We stood still —surprised, stupefied, terror-stricken at the sight of what seemed a group of fearful marine monsters, more hideous in the reality than in my dream. They were of supernatural dimensions; the very smallest of the whole party could with ease have crushed our raft and ourselves with a single bite.

Hans, seizing the rudder which had flown out of his hand, puts it hard a-weather in order to escape from such dangerous vicinity; but no sooner does he do so, than he finds he is flying from Scylla to Charybdis. To leeward is a turtle about forty feet wide, and a serpent quite as long, with an enormous and hideous head peering from out the waters. Look which way we will, it is impossible for us to fly. The fearful reptiles advanced upon us; they turned and twisted about the raft with awful rapidity. They formed around our devoted vessel a series of concentric circles. I took up my rifle in desperation. But what effect can a rifle-ball produce upon the armor scales with which the bodies of these horrid monsters are covered?

We remain still and dumb from utter horror. They advance upon us, nearer and nearer. Our fate appears certain, fearful and terrible. On one side the mighty crocodile, on the other the great sea serpent. The rest of the fearful crowd of marine prodigies have plunged beneath the briny waves and disappeared!

I was about at all risks to fire, and try the effect of a shot. Hans, the guide, however, interfered by a sign to check me. The two hideous and ravenous monsters passed within fifty fathoms of the raft, and then made a rush at one another—their fury and rage preventing them from seeing us.

The combat commenced. We distinctly made out every action of the two hideous monsters. To my excited imagination the other animals appeared about to take part in the fierce and deadly struggle—the monster, the whale, the lizard, and the turtle. I distinctly saw them every moment. I pointed them out to the Icelander. But he only shook his head. " Tva," he said.

" What—two only does he say. Surely he is mistaken," I cried, in a tone of wonder.

" He is quite right," replied my uncle coolly and philosophically, examining the terrible duel with his telescope and speaking as if he were in a lecture room.

" How can that be? "

" Yes, it is so. The first of these hideous monsters has the snout of a porpoise, the head of a lizard, the teeth of a crocodile; and it is this that has deceived us. It is the most fearful of all antediluvian reptiles, the world-renowned Ichthyosaurus or Great Fish Lizard."

" And the other? "

" The other is a monstrous serpent, concealed under the hard vaulted shell of the turtle, the terrible enemy of its fearful rival, the Plesiosaurus, or Sea Crocodile."

Hans was quite right. The two monsters only, disturbed the surface of the sea! At last have mortal eyes gazed upon two reptiles of the great primitive ocean! I saw the flaming red eyes of the Ichthyosaurus, each as big, or bigger than a man's head. Nature in its infinite wisdom had gifted this wondrous marine animal with an optical apparatus of extreme power, capable of resisting the pressure of the heavy layers of water which rolled over him in the depth of the ocean where he usually fed. It has by some authors truly been called the whale of the Saurian race, for it is as big and quick in its motions as our king of the seas. This one measured not less than a hundred feet in length, and I could form some idea of his girth, when I saw him lift his prodigious tail out of the waters. His jaw is of awful size and strength, and according to the best-informed naturalists, it does not contain less than a hundred and eighty-two teeth.

The other was the mighty Plesiosaurus, a serpent with a cylindrical trunk, with a shorty stumpy tail, with fins like a bank of oars in a Roman galley. Its whole body was covered by a carapace or shell; and its neck, as flexible as that of a swan, rose more than thirty feet above the waves, a tower of animated flesh!

These animals attacked one another with inconceivable fury. Such a combat was never seen before by mortal eyes, and to us who did see it, it appeared more like the phantasmagoric creation of a dream than anything else. They raised mountains of water, which dashed in spray over the raft, already tossed to and fro by the waves. Twenty times we seemed on the point of being upset and hurled headlong into the waves. Hideous hisses appeared to shake the gloomy granite roof of that mighty cavern—hisses which carried terror to our hearts. The awful combatants held each other in a tight embrace. I could not make out one from the other. Still the combat could not last for ever; and woe unto us, whichsoever became the victor.

One hour, two hours, three hours passed away, without any decisive result. The struggle continued with the same deadly tenacity, but without apparent result. The deadly opponents now approached, now drew away from the raft. Once or twice we fancied they were about to leave us altogether, but instead of that, they came nearer and nearer. We crouched on the raft ready to fire at them at a moment's notice, poor as the prospect of hurting or terrifying them was. Still we were determined not to perish without a struggle.

Suddenly the Ichthyosaurus and the Plesiosaurus disappeared beneath the waves, leaving behind them a maelstrom in the midst of the sea. We were very nearly drawn down by the indraught of the water!

Several minutes elapsed before anything was again seen. Was this wonderful combat to end in the depths of the ocean? Was the last act of this terrible drama to take place without spectators? It was impossible for us to say.

Suddenly, at no great distance from us, an enormous mass rose out of the waters—the head of the great Plesiosaurus. The terrible monster was wounded unto death. I could see nothing of his enormous body. All that could be distinguished was his serpent-like neck, which he twisted and curled in all the agonies of death. Now he struck the waters with it as if it had been a gigantic whip, and then again wriggled like a worm cut in two. The water was spurted up to a great distance in all directions. A great portion of it swept over our raft and nearly blinded us. But soon the end of the beast approached nearer and nearer; his movements slackened visibly; his contortions almost ceased; and at last the body of the mighty snake lay an inert, dead mass on the surface of the now calm and placid waters.

As for the Ichthyosaurus, has he gone down to his mighty cavern under the sea to rest, or will he reappear to destroy us? This question remained unanswered. And we had breathing time.

CHAPTER XXXI
THE SEA MONSTER

WEDNESDAY, August 19. Fortunately the wind, which at the present blows with great violence, allowed us to escape from the scene of the unparalleled and extraordinary struggle. Hans with his usual imperturbable calm remained at the helm. My uncle, who for a short time had been withdrawn from his absorbing reverie by the novel incidents of this sea-fight, fell back again apparently into a brown study. All this time, however, his eyes were fixed impatiently on the wide-spread ocean.

Our voyage now became monotonous and uniform. Dull

as it has become, I have no desire to have it broken by any repetition of the perils and adventures of yesterday.

Thursday, August 20. The wind is now N. N. E., and blows very irregularly. It has changed to fitful gusts. The temperature is exceedingly high. We are now progressing at the average rate of about ten miles and a half per hour. About twelve o'clock a distant sound as of thunder fell upon our ears. I make a note of the fact without even venturing a suggestion as to its cause. It was one continuous roar as of a sea falling over mighty rocks.

"Far off in the distance," said the Professor dogmatically, "there is some rock or some island against which the sea, lashed to fury by the wind, is breaking violently."

Hans, without saying a word, clambered to the top of the mast, but could make out nothing. The ocean was level in every direction as far as the eye could reach.

Three hours passed away without any sign to indicate what might be before us. The sound began to assume that of a mighty cataract. I expressed my opinion on this point strongly to my uncle. He merely shook his head. Are we advancing towards some mighty waterfall which shall cast us into the abyss? Probably this mode of descending into the abyss may be agreeable to the Professor, because it would be something like the vertical descent he is so eager to make. I entertain a very different view. Whatever be the truth, it is certain that not many leagues distant there must be some very extraordinary phenomenon, for as we advance the roar becomes something mighty and stupendous. Is it in the water, or in the air?

I cast hasty glances aloft at the suspended vapors, and I seek to penetrate their mighty depths. But the vault above is tranquil. The clouds, which are now elevated to the very summit, appear utterly still and motionless, and completely lost in the irradiation of electric light. It is necessary, therefore, to seek for the cause of this phenomenon elsewhere.

I examine the horizon, now perfectly calm, pure and free from all haze. Its aspect still remains unchanged. But if this awful noise proceeds from a cataract—if, so to speak in plain English, this vast interior ocean is precipitated into a lower basin—if these tremendous roars are produced by the noise of falling waters, the current would increase in activity, and its increasing swiftness would give me some idea of the extent of the peril with which we are menaced. I consult the current. It simply does not exist: there is no such thing. An empty bottle cast into the water lies to leeward without motion.

About four o'clock Hans rises, clambers up the mast and reaches the truck itself. From this elevated position his looks are cast around. They take in a vast circumference of the ocean. At last, his eyes remain fixed. His face expresses no astonishment, but his eyes slightly dilate.
" He has seen something at last," cried my uncle.

" I think so," I replied.

Hans came down, stood beside us and pointed with his right hand to the south. " *Der nere*," he said.

" There," replied my uncle. And seizing his telescope he looked at it with great attention for about a minute, which to me appeared an age. I knew not what to think or expect.

" Yes, yes," he cried in a tone of considerable surprise, " there it is."

" What ? " I asked.

" A tremendous spurt of water rising out of the waves."

" Some other marine monster," I cried, already alarmed.

" Perhaps."

" Then let us steer more to the westward, for we know what we have to expect from antediluvian animals," was my eager reply.

" Go ahead," said my uncle.

I turned towards Hans. Hans was at the tiller steering with his usual imperturbable calm. Nevertheless, if from the distance which separated us from this creature, a distance which must be estimated at not less than a dozen leagues, and this spurting of water proceeded from the pranks of some antediluvian animal, his dimensions must be something preternatural. To fly is, therefore, the course to be suggested by ordinary prudence. But we have not come into that part of the world to be prudent. Such is my uncle's determination.

We, accordingly, continued to advance. The nearer we come, the loftier is the spouting water. What monster can fill himself with such huge volumes of water, and then unceasingly spout them out in such lofty jets?

At eight o'clock in the evening, reckoning as above

ground, where there is day and night, we are not more than two leagues from the mighty beast. Its long, black, enormous, mountainous body, lies on the top of the water like an island. But then sailors have been said to have gone ashore on sleeping whales, mistaking them for land. Is it illusion, or is it fear? Its length cannot be less than a thousand fathoms. What, then, is this cetaceous monster of which no Cuvier ever thought? It is quite motionless and presents the appearance of sleep. The sea seems unable to lift him upwards; it is rather the waves which break on his huge and gigantic frame. The water-spout, rising to a height of five hundred feet, breaks in spray with a dull, sullen roar. We advance, like senseless lunatics, towards this mighty mass.

I honestly confess that I was abjectly afraid. I declared that I would go no farther. I threatened in my terror to cut the sheet of the sail. I attacked the Professor with considerable acrimony, calling him foolhardy, mad, I know not what. He made no answer. Suddenly the imperturbable Hans once more pointed his finger to the menacing object. *"Holme!"*

" An island! " cried my uncle.

" An island? " I replied, shrugging my shoulders at this poor attempt at deception.

" Of course it is," cried my uncle, bursting into a loud and joyous laugh.

" But the water spout? "

" Geyser," said Hans.

" Yes, of course—a geyser," replied my uncle, still laughing, " a geyser like those common in Iceland. Jets like this are the great wonders of the country."

At first I would not allow that I had been so grossly deceived. What could be more ridiculous than to have taken an island for a marine monster? But kick as one may, one must yield to evidence, and I was finally convinced of my error. It was nothing, after all, but a natural phenomenon.

As we approached nearer and nearer, the dimensions of the liquid sheaf of waters became truly grand and stupendous. The island had, at a distance, presented the appearance of an enormous whale, whose head rose high above the waters. The geyser, a word which signifies fury, rose majestically from its summit. Dull detonations are heard every now and then, and the enormous jet, taken as it were with sudden fury, shakes its plume of vapor, and bounds into the first layer of the clouds. It is alone. Neither spurts of vapor nor hot springs surround it, and the whole volcanic power of that region is concentrated in one sublime column. The rays of electric light mix with this dazzling sheaf, every drop as it falls assuming the prismatic colors of the rainbow.

"Let us go on shore," said the Professor, after some minutes of silence. It was necessary, however, to take great precaution, in order to avoid the weight of falling waters, which would cause the raft to founder in an instant. Hans, however, steered admirably, and brought us to the other extremity of the island.

I was the first to leap on the rock. My uncle followed, while the eider-duck hunter remained still, like a man above any childish sources of astonishment. We were now walking on granite mixed with silicious sandstone; the soil shivered under our feet like the sides of boilers in which over-heated steam is forcibly confined. It was burning. We soon came in sight of the little central basin from which rose the geyser. I plunged a thermometer into the water which ran bubbling from the center, and it marked a heat of a hundred and sixty-three degrees! This water, therefore, came from some place where the heat was intense. This was singularly in contradiction with the theories of Professor Hardwigg. I could not help telling him my opinion on the subject.

"Well," said he sharply, "and what does this prove against my doctrine?"

"Nothing," replied I dryly, seeing that I was running my head against a foregone conclusion. I am compelled to confess that until now we have been most remarkably fortunate, and that this voyage is being accomplished in most favorable conditions of temperature; but it appears evident, in fact, certain, that we shall sooner or later arrive at one of those regions, where the central heat will reach its utmost limits, and will go far beyond all the possible gradations of thermometers. Visions of the Hades of the ancients, believed to be in the center of the earth, floated through my imagination.

We shall, however, see what we shall see. That is the Professor's favorite phrase now. Having christened the volcanic island by the name of his nephew, the leader of the expedition turned away and gave the signal for embarkation. We went carefully round the projecting, and rather dangerous, rocks of the southern side. Hans had taken advantage of this brief halt to repair the raft. Not before it was required.

Before we took our final departure from the island, however, I made some observations to calculate the distance we had gone over, and I put them down in my Journal. Since we left Port Gretchen, we had traveled two hundred and seventy leagues—more than eight hundred miles—on this great inland sea; we were, therefore, six hundred and twenty leagues from Iceland, and exactly under England.

CHAPTER XXXII
THE BATTLE OF THE ELEMENTS

FRIDAY, August 21st. This morning the magnificent geyser had wholly disappeared. The wind had freshened up, and we were fast leaving the neighborhood of Henry's Island. Even the roaring sound of the mighty column was lost to the ear.

The weather, if, under the circumstances, we may use such an expression, is about to change very suddenly. The atmosphere is being gradually loaded with vapors, which carry with them the electricity formed by the constant evaporation of the saline waters; the clouds are slowly but sensibly falling towards the sea, and are assuming a dark olive texture; the electric rays can scarcely pierce through the opaque curtain which has fallen like a drop-scene before this wondrous theater, on the stage of which another and terrible drama is soon to be enacted. This time it is no fight of animals; it is the fearful battle of the elements.

In the distance, the clouds have assumed the appearance of enormous balls of cotton, or rather pods, piled one above the other in picturesque confusion. By degrees, they appear to swell out, break, and gain in number what they lose in grandeur; their heaviness is so great that they are unable to lift themselves from the horizon; but under the influence of the upper currents of air, they are gradually broken up, become much darker, and then present the appearance of one single layer of a formidable character; now and then a lighter cloud, still lit up from above, rebounds upon this gray carpet, and is lost in the opaque mass.

There can be no doubt that the entire atmosphere is saturated with electric fluid; I am myself wholly impregnated; my hairs literally stand on end as if under the influence of a galvanic battery.   If one of my companions ventured to touch me, I think he would receive rather a violent and unpleasant shock.

About ten o'clock in the morning, the symptoms of the storm became more thorough and decisive; the wind appeared to soften down as if to take breath for a renewed attack; the vast funereal pall above us looked like a huge bag—like the cave of Æolus, in which the storm was collecting its forces for the attack.   I tried all I could not to believe in the menacing signs of the sky, and yet I could not avoid saying, as it were involuntarily—"I believe we are going to have bad weather."

The Professor made me no answer.   He was in a horrible, in a detestable humor—to see the ocean stretching interminably before his eyes.   On hearing my words he simply shrugged his shoulders.

"We shall have a tremendous storm," I said again, pointing to the horizon.   "These clouds are falling lower and lower upon the sea, as if to crush it."

'A' great silence prevailed.   The wind wholly ceased. Nature assumed a dead calm, and ceased to breathe.   Upon the mast, where I noticed a sort of slight *ignis fatuus*, the sail hung in loose heavy folds.   The raft lay motionless in the midst of a dark heavy sea—without undulation, without motion.   It was as still as glass.   "Let us lower the sail," I said, "it is only an act of common prudence."

"No—no," cried my uncle, in an exasperated tone, "a hundred times, no.   Let the wind strike us and do its worst, let the storm sweep us away where it will—only let me see the glimmer of some coast—of some rocky cliffs, even if they dash our raft into a thousand pieces.   No! keep up the sail—no matter what happens."

These words were scarcely uttered, when the southern

horizon underwent a sudden and violent change.   The long accumulated vapors were resolved into water, and the air required to fill up the void produced became a wild and raging tempest.   It came from the most distant corners of the mighty cavern.   It raged from every point of the compass.   It roared; it yelled; it shrieked with glee as of demons let loose.   The darkness increased and became indeed darkness visible.

The raft rose and fell with the storm, and bounded over the waves.   My uncle was cast headlong upon the deck. I with great difficulty dragged myself towards him.   He was holding on with might and main to the end of a cable, and appeared to gaze with pleasure and delight at the spectacle of the unchained elements.

Hans never moved a muscle.   His long hair driven hither and thither by the tempest and scattered wildly over his motionless face, gave him a most extraordinary appearance—for every single hair was illuminated by little sparkling sprigs.   His countenance presented the extraordinary appearance of an antediluvian man, a true contemporary of the megatherium.

Still the mast holds good against the storm.   The sail spreads out and fills like a soap bubble about to burst.   The raft rushes on at a pace impossible to estimate.

"The sail, the sail!" I cried, making a trumpet of my hands, and then endeavoring to lower it.

"Let it alone!" said my uncle, more exasperated than ever.

"*Nej,*" said Hans, gently shaking his head.

The rain formed a roaring cataract before this horizon of which we were in search, and to which we were rushing like madmen.   But before this wilderness of waters reached us, the mighty veil of cloud was torn in twain; the sea began to foam wildly.   To the fearful claps of thunder were added dazzling flashes of lightning, such as I had never seen.   The flashes crossed one another, hurled from every side; while the thunder came pealing like an echo.

The mass of vapor becomes incandescent; the hail-stones which strike the metal of our boots and our weapons, are actually luminous; the waves as they rise appear to be fire-eating monsters, beneath which seethes an intense fire, their crests surmounted by combs of flame. My eyes are dazzled, blinded by the intensity of light, my ears are deafened by the awful roar of the elements. I am compelled to hold on to the mast, which bends like a reed beneath the violence of the storm, to which none ever before seen by mariners bore any resemblance.

.   .   .   .

Here my traveling notes become very incomplete, loose and vague. I have only been able to make out one or two fugitive observations, dotted down in a mere mechanical way. But even their brevity, even their obscurity, show the emotions which overcame me.

.   .   .   .

Sunday, August 23d. Where have we got to? In what region are we wandering? We are still carried forward with inconceivable rapidity. The night has been fearful, something not to be described. The storm shows no signs of cessation. We exist in the midst of an uproar which has no name. The detonations as of artillery are incessant. Our ears literally bleed. We are unable to exchange a word, or hear each other speak. The lightning never ceases to flash for a single instant. I can see the zigzags after a rapid dart, strike the arched roof of this mightiest of mighty vaults. If it were to give way and fall upon us! Other lightnings plunge their forked streaks in every direction, and take the form of globes of fire, which explode like bomb-shells over a beleaguered city. The general crash and roar do not apparently increase; it has already gone far beyond what human ear can appreciate. If all the powder-magazines in the world were to explode together, it would be impossible for us to hear worse noise.

There is a constant emission of light from the storm-clouds; the electric matter is incessantly released; innumerable columns of water rush up like waterspouts, and fall back upon the surface of the ocean in foam. Whither are we going? My uncle still lies at full length upon the raft, without speaking—without taking any note of time.

Monday, August 24. This terrible storm will never end. Why should not this state of the atmosphere, so dense and murky, once modified, again remain definitive?

We are utterly broken and harassed by fatigue. Hans remains just as usual. The raft runs to the south-east invariably. We have now already run two hundred leagues from the newly-discovered island.

About twelve o'clock the storm becomes worse than ever. We are obliged to fasten every bit of cargo tightly on the deck of the raft, or everything would be swept away. We tie ourselves to the mast, each man lashing the other. The waves drive over us, so that several times we are actually under water.

We had been under the painful necessity of abstaining from speech for three days and three nights. We opened our mouths, we moved our lips, but no sound came. Even when we placed our mouths to each other's ears it was the same. The wind carried the voice away. My uncle once contrived to get his head close to mine after several almost vain endeavors. He appeared to my nearly exhausted senses to articulate some word. I had a notion, more from intuition than anything else, that he said to me, " we are lost."

I took out my note book, from which under the most desperate circumstances I never parted, and wrote a few words as legibly as I could—" Take in sail." With a deep sigh he nodded his head and acquiesced.

His head had scarcely time to fall back in the position from which he had momentarily raised it, than a disc or ball of fire appeared on the very edge of the raft—our devoted, our doomed craft. The mast and sail were carried away bodily, and I saw them swept away to a prodigious height like a kite.

We were frozen, actually shivered with terror. The ball of fire, half white, half azure-colored, about the size of a ten-inch bomb-shell, moved along, turning with prodigious rapidity to leeward of the storm. It ran about here, there and everywhere, it clambered up one of the bulwarks of the raft, it leaped upon the sack of provisions, and then finally descended lightly, fell like a foot ball and landed on our powder barrel.

Horrible situation. An explosion of course seemed now inevitable. The dazzling disc moved to one side, it approached Hans, who looked at it with singular fixity; then it approached my uncle, who cast himself on his knees to avoid it; it came towards me, as I stood pale and shuddering in the dazzling light and heat; it pirouetted round my feet, which I endeavored to withdraw. An odor of nitrous gas filled the whole air; it penetrated to the throat, to the lungs. I felt ready to choke.

Why is it that I cannot withdraw my feet? Are they riveted to the flooring of the raft? No. The fall of the electric globe has turned all the iron on board into loadstones—the instruments, the tools, the arms are clanging together with awful and horrible noise; the nails of my heavy boots adhere closely to the plate of iron incrustated in the wood. I cannot withdraw my foot.

At last, by a violent and almost superhuman effort, I tear it away just as the ball which is still executing its gyratory motions is about to run round it and drag me with it—if——

O what intense stupendous light! The globe of fire bursts—we are enveloped in cascades of living fire, which flood the space around with luminous matter.

Then all went out and darkness once more fell upon the deep! I had just time to see my uncle once more cast apparently senseless on the flooring of the raft, Hans at the helm, " spitting fire " under the influence of the electricity which seemed to have gone through him.

Tuesday, August 25. I have just come out of a long fainting fit. The awful and hideous storm still continues; the lightning has increased in vividness, and pours out its fiery wrath like a brood of serpents let loose in the atmosphere.

Are we still upon the sea? Yes, and being carried along with incredible velocity. We have passed under England, under the Channel, under France, probably under the whole extent of Europe.

.   .   .   .   .

Another awful clamor in the distance. This time it is certain that the sea is breaking upon the rocks at no great distance. Then——

CHAPTER XXXIII
OUR ROUTE REVERSED

HERE ends what I call My Journal of our voyage on board the raft, which Journal was happily saved from the wreck. I proceed with my narrative as I did before I commenced my daily notes.

What happened when the terrible shock took place, when the raft was cast upon the rocky shore, it would be impossible for me now to say. I felt myself precipitated violently into the boiling waves, and if I escaped from a certain and cruel death, it was wholly owing to the determination of the faithful Hans, who clutching me by the arm, saved me from the yawning abyss.

The courageous Icelander then carried me in his powerful arms, far out of the reach of the waves, and laid me down upon a burning expanse of sand, where I found myself some time afterwards in the company of my uncle the Professor. Then Hans quietly returned towards the fatal rocks, against which the furious waves were beating, in order to save any stray waifs from the wreck. This man was always practical and thoughtful.

I could not utter a word; I was quite overcome with emotion; my whole body was broken and bruised with fatigue; it took hours before I was anything like myself. Meanwhile, there fell a fearful deluge of rain, drenching us to the skin. Its very violence, however, proclaimed the approaching end of the storm. Some overhanging rocks afforded us a slight protection from the torrents.

Under this shelter, Hans prepared some food, which, however, I was unable to touch; and, exhausted by the three weary days and nights of watching, we fell into a deep and painful sleep. My dreams were fearful, but at last exhausted nature asserted her supremacy, and I slumbered.

Next day when I awoke the change was magical. The weather was magnificent. Air and sea, as if by mutual consent, had regained their serenity. Every trace of the storm, even the faintest, had disappeared. I was saluted on my awakening by the first joyous tones I had heard from the Professor for many a day. His gayety, indeed, was something terrible. "Well, my lad," he cried, rubbing his hands together, "have you slept soundly?"

Might it not have been supposed that we were in the old house on the Königstrasse; that I had just come down quietly to my breakfast, and that my marriage with Gretchen was to take place that very day? My uncle's coolness was exasperating.

Alas, considering how the tempest had driven us in an easterly direction, we had passed under the whole of Germany, under the city of Hamburg where I had been so happy, under the very street which contained all I loved and cared for in the world. It was a positive fact that I was only separated from her by a distance of forty leagues. But these forty leagues were of hard impenetrable granite! All these dreary and miserable reflections passed through my mind, before I attempted to answer my uncle's question.

"Why, what is the matter?" he cried, "cannot you say whether you have slept well or not?"

"I have slept very well," was my reply, "but every bone in my body aches. I suppose that will lead to nothing."

"Nothing at all, my boy. It is only the result of the fatigue of the last few days—that is all."

"You appear—if I may be allowed to say so—to be very jolly this morning," I said.

"Delighted, my dear boy, delighted. Was never happier in my life. We have at last reached the wished-for port."

"The end of our expedition?" cried I, in a tone of considerable surprise.

"No; but to the confines of that sea which I began to fear would never end, but go round the whole world. We will now tranquilly resume our journey by land, and once again endeavor to dive into the center of the Earth."

"My dear uncle," I began, in a hesitating kind of way, "allow me to ask you one question?"

"Certainly, Harry; a dozen if you think proper."

"One will suffice. How about getting back?" I asked.

"How about getting back? What a question to ask. We have not as yet reached the end of our journey."

"I know that. All I want to know is, how you propose we shall manage the return voyage?"

"In the most simple manner in the world," said the imperturbable Professor. "Once we reach the exact center of this sphere, either we shall find a new road by which to ascend to the surface, or we shall simply turn round and go back by the way we came. I have every reason to believe that while we are traveling forward, it will not close behind us."

" Then one of the first matters to see to will be to repair the raft," was my rather melancholy response.

" Of course. We must attend to that above all things," continued the Professor.

" Then comes the all-important question of provisions," I urged. " Have we anything like enough left to enable us to accomplish such great, such amazing, designs as you contemplate carrying out? "

" I have seen into the matter, and my answer is in the affirmative. Hans is a very clever fellow, and has saved the greater part of the cargo. But the best way to satisfy your scruples, is to come and judge for yourself." Saying which, he led the way out of the kind of open grotto in which we had taken shelter. I had almost begun to hope that which I should rather have feared, the impossibility of such a shipwreck leaving even the slightest signs of what it had carried as freight.

As soon as I reached the shores of this inland sea, I found Hans standing gravely in the midst of a large number of things laid out in complete order. My uncle wrung his hands with deep and silent gratitude. His heart was too full for speech. This man, whose superhuman devotion to his employers, I never saw surpassed, nor even equaled, had been hard at work all the time we slept, and at the risk of his life had succeeded in saving the most precious articles of our cargo.

Of course, under the circumstances, we necessarily experienced several severe losses. Our weapons had wholly vanished. But experience had taught us to do without them. The provision of powder had, however, remained intact, after having narrowly escaped blowing us all to atoms in the storm.

" Well," said the Professor, who was now ready to make the best of everything, " as we have no guns, all we have to do is to give up all idea of hunting."

" Yes, my dear sir, we can do without them, but what about all our instruments? "

" Here is the manometer, the most useful of all, which

I gladly accept in lieu of the rest. With it alone I can calculate the depth as we proceed; by its means alone I shall be able to decide when we have reached the center of the earth. Ha, ha! but for this little instrument we might make a mistake, and run the risk of coming out at the antipodes!" All this was said amid bursts of unnatural laughter.

"But the compass," I cried, "without that what can we do?"

"Here it is safe and sound!" he cried, with real joy, "ah, ah, and here we have the chronometer and the thermometers. Hans the hunter is indeed an invaluable man!"

It was impossible to deny this fact. As far as the nautical and other instruments were concerned, nothing was wanting. Then on further examination, I found ladders, cords, pickaxes, crowbars, and shovels, all scattered about on the shore. "But what are we to do for food?" I asked.

"Let us see to the commissariat department," replied my uncle gravely. The boxes which contained our supply of food for the voyage were placed in a row along the strand, and proved in a capital state of preservation; the sea had in every case respected their contents. Taking into consideration, biscuits, salt meat, schiedam and dried fish, we could still calculate on having about four months' supply, if used with prudence and caution.

"Four months," cried the sanguine Professor, in high glee, "then we shall have plenty of time both to go and to come, and with what remains I undertake to give a grand dinner to my colleagues of the Johanneum."

I sighed. I should by this time have used myself to the temperament of my uncle, and yet this man astonished me more and more every day. He was the greatest human enigma I ever had known.

"Now," said he, "before we do anything else we must lay in a stock of fresh water. The rain has fallen in abundance, and filled the hollows of the granite. There is a rich supply of water, and we have no fear of suffering from thirst, which in our circumstances is of the last importance. As for the raft, I shall recommend Hans to repair it to the best of his abilities; though I have every reason to believe we shall not require it again."

"How is that?" I cried, more amazed than ever at my uncle's style of reasoning.

"I have an idea, my dear boy; it is none other than this simple fact: we shall not come out by the same opening as that by which we entered."

I began to look at my uncle with vague suspicion. An idea had more than once taken possession of me; and this was, that he was going mad. Little did I think how true and prophetic his words were doomed to be.

"And now," he said, "having seen to all these matters of detail, to breakfast." I followed him to a sort of projecting cape, after he had given his last instructions to our guide. In this original position, with dried meat, biscuit, and a delicious cup of tea, we made a satisfactory meal— I may say one of the most welcome and pleasant I ever remember. Exhaustion, the keen atmosphere, the state of calm after so much agitation, all contributed to give me an excellent appetite. Indeed, it contributed very much to producing a pleasant and cheerful state of mind.

While breakfast was in hand, and between the sips of warm tea, I asked my uncle if he had any idea of how we now stood in relation to the world above. "For my part," I added, "I think it will be rather difficult to determine."

"Well, if we were compelled to fix the exact spot," said my uncle, "it might be difficult, since during the three days of that awful tempest I could keep no account either of the quickness of our pace, or of the direction in which the raft was going. Still, we will endeavor to approximate to the truth. We shall not, I believe, be so very far out."

"Well, if I recollect rightly," I replied, "out last observation was made at the Geyser island."

"Harry's Island, my boy! Harry's Island. Do not decline the honor of having named it; given your name to an island discovered by us, the first human beings who trod it since the creation of the world!"

"Let it be so, then. At Harry's Island we had already gone over two hundred and seventy leagues of sea, and we were, I believe, about six hundred leagues, more or less, from Iceland."

"Good. I am glad to see that you remember so well. Let us start from that point, and let us count four days of storm, during which our rate of traveling must have been very great. I should say that our velocity must have been about eighty leagues to the twenty-four hours."

I agreed that I thought this a fair calculation. There were then three hundred leagues to be added to the grand total.

"Yes, and the Central Sea must extend at least six hundred leagues from side to side. Do you know, my boy, Harry, that we have discovered an inland lake larger than the Mediterranean?"

"Certainly, and we only know of its extent in one way. It may be hundreds of miles in length."

"Very likely."

"Then," said I, after calculating for some minutes, "if your previsions are right, we are at this moment exactly under the Mediterranean itself."

"Do you think so?"

"Yes, I am almost certain of it. Are we not nine hundred leagues distant from Reykjawik?"

"That is perfectly true, and a famous bit of road we have traveled, my boy. But why we should be under the Mediterranean more than under Turkey or the Atlantic Ocean can only be known when we are sure of not having deviated from our course; and of this we know nothing."

"I do not think we were driven very far from our course: the wind appears to me to have been always about the same. My opinion is that this shore must be situated to the southeast of Port Gretchen."

"Good—I hope so. It will, however, be easy to decide the matter by taking the bearings from our departure by means of the compass. Come along, and we will consult that invaluable invention." The Professor now walked eagerly in the direction of the rock where the indefatigable Hans had placed the instruments in safety. My uncle was gay and light-hearted; he rubbed his hands, and assumed all sorts of attitudes. He was to all appearance once more a young man. Since I had known him never had he been so amiable and pleasant. I followed him, rather curious to know whether I had made any mistake in my estimation of our position. As soon as we had reached the rock, my uncle took the compass, placed it horizontally before him and looked keenly at the needle. As he had at first shaken it to give it vivacity, it oscillated considerably, and then slowly assumed its right position under the influence of the magnetic power.

The Professor bent his eyes curiously over the wondrous instrument. A violent start immediately showed the extent of his emotion. He closed his eyes, rubbed them, and took another and a keener survey. Then he turned slowly round to me, stupefaction depicted on his countenance.

" What is the matter? " said I, beginning to be alarmed.

He could not speak. He was too overwhelmed for words. He simply pointed to the instrument. I examined it eagerly according to his mute directions, and a loud cry of surprise escaped my lips. The needle of the compass pointed due north, in the direction we expected was the south! It pointed to the shore instead of to the high seas.

I shook the compass; I examined it with a curious and anxious eye. It was in a state of perfection. No blemish in any way explained the phenomenon. Whatever position we forced the needle into, it returned invariably to the same unexpected point.

It was useless attempting to conceal from ourselves the fatal truth. There could be no doubt, unwelcome as was the fact, that during the tempest, there had been a sudden slant of wind, of which we had been unable to take any account, and thus the raft had carried us back to the shores we had left, apparently for ever, so many days before!

CHAPTER XXXIV
A VOYAGE OF DISCOVERY

IT would be altogether impossible for me to give any idea of the utter astonishment which overcame the Professor on making this extraordinary discovery. Amazement, incredulity, and rage were blended in such a way as to alarm me. During the whole course of my life I had never seen a man at first so chapfallen; and then so furiously indignant.

The terrible fatigues of our sea voyage, the fearful dangers we had passed through, had all, all, gone for nothing. We had to begin them all over again. Instead of progressing, as we fondly expected, during a voyage of so many

days, we had retreated. Every hour of our expedition on
the raft had been so much lost time!

Presently, however, the indomitable energy of my uncle
overcame every other consideration. " So," he said, between his set teeth, " fatality will play me these terrible
tricks. The elements themselves conspire to overwhelm me
with mortification. Air, fire, and water combine their
united efforts to oppose my passage. Well, they shall see
what the earnest will of a determined man can do. I will
not yield, I will not retreat even one inch; and we shall
see who shall triumph in this great contest—man or nature."

Standing upright on a rock, irritated and menacing, Professor Hardwigg, like the ferocious Ajax, seemed to defy
the fates. I, however, took upon myself to interfere, and
to impose some sort of check upon such insensate enthusiasm.

" Listen to me, uncle," I said, in a firm but temperate
tone of voice, " there must be some limit to ambition here
below. It is utterly useless to struggle against the impossible. Pray listen to reason. We are utterly unprepared
for a sea voyage; it is simple madness to think of per-
forming a second journey of five hundred leagues upon a
wretched pile of beams, with a counterpane for a sail, a
paltry stick for a mast, and a tempest to contend with. As
we are totally incapable of steering our frail craft, we shall
become the mere plaything of the storm, and it is acting the
part of madmen if we, a second time, run any risk upon
this dangerous and treacherous Central Sea."

These are only a few of the reasons and arguments I put
together—reasons and arguments which to me appeared
unanswerable. I was allowed to go on without interrup-
tion for about ten minutes. The explanation to this I soon
discovered. The Professor was not even listening, and did
not hear a word of all my eloquence.

" To the raft!" he cried, in a hoarse voice, when I paused
for a reply.

Such was the result of my strenuous effort to resist his
iron will. I tried again; I begged and implored him; I
got into a passion; but I had to deal with a will more determined than my own. I seemed to feel like the waves
which fought and battled against the huge mass of granite

at our feet, which had smiled grimly for so many ages at their puny efforts.

Hans, meanwhile, without taking part in our discussion, had been repairing the raft. One would have supposed that he instinctively guessed at the further projects of my uncle. By means of some fragments of cordage, he had again made the raft sea-worthy. While I had been speaking he had hoisted a new mast and sail, the latter already fluttering and waving in the breeze.

The worthy Professor spoke a few words to our imperturbable guide, who immediately began to put our baggage on board, and to prepare for our departure. The atmosphere was now tolerably clear and pure, and the north-east wind blew steadily and serenely. It appeared likely to last for some time.

What, then, could I do? Could I undertake to resist the iron will of two men? It was simply impossible; if even I could have hoped for the support of Hans. This, however, was out of the question. It appeared to me that the Icelander had set aside all personal will and identity. He was a picture of abnegation. I could hope for nothing from one so infatuated with and devoted to his master. All I could do, therefore, was to swim with the stream. In a mood of stolid and sullen resignation, I was about to take my accustomed place on the raft, when my uncle placed his hand upon my shoulder. "There is no hurry, my boy," he said, "we shall not start until to-morrow."

I looked the picture of resignation to the dire will of fate. "Under the circumstances," he said, "I ought to neglect no precautions. As fate has cast me upon these shores, I shall not leave without having completely examined them."

In order to understand this remark, I must explain that though we had been driven back to the northern shore, we had landed at a very different spot from that which had been our starting point. Port Gretchen must, we calculated, be very much to the westward. Nothing, therefore, was more natural and reasonable than that we should reconnoiter this new shore upon which we had so unexpectedly landed. "Let us go on a journey of discovery," I cried.

And leaving Hans to his important operation, we started on our expedition. As we trudged along, our feet crushed

.innumerable shells of every shape and size—once the dwelling place of animals of every period of creation. I particularly noticed some enormous shells—carapaces (turtle and tortoise species) the diameter of which exceeded fifteen feet.

They had in past ages belonged to those gigantic glyptodons of the pliocene period, of which the modern turtle is but a minute specimen. In addition, the whole soil was covered by a vast quantity of stony relics, having the appearance of flints worn by the action of the waves, and lying in successive layers one above the other. It appeared clear that we were walking upon a kind of sediment, formed like all the soils of that period, so frequent on the surface of the globe, by the subsidence of the waters. The Professor, who was now in his element, carefully examined every rocky fissure. Let him only find an opening and it directly became important to him to examine its depth.

For a whole mile we followed the windings of the Central Sea, when suddenly an important change took place in the aspect of the soil. It seemed to have been rudely cast up, convulsionized, as it were, by a violent upheaving of the lower strata. In many places, hollows here, and hillocks there, attested great dislocations at some other period of the terrestrial mass. We advanced with great difficulty over the broken masses of granite mixed with flint, quartz and alluvial deposits, when a large field, more even than a field, a plain of bones, appeared suddenly before our eyes! It looked like an immense cemetery, where generation after generation had mingled their mortal dust.

Lofty barrows of early remains rose at intervals. They undulated away to the limits of the distant horizon and were lost in a thick and brown fog. On that spot, some three square miles in extent, was accumulated the whole history of animal life—scarcely one creature still a habitant of the comparatively modern soil of the upper and inhabited world, had there existed.

We were drawn forward by an all-absorbing and impatient curiosity. Our feet crushed with a dry and crackling sound the remains of those prehistoric fossils, for which the museums of great cities quarrel, even when they obtain only rare and curious morsels. I was utterly confounded. My uncle stood for some minutes with his arms raised on high towards the thick granite vault which served us for a sky. His mouth was wide open; his eyes sparkled wildly behind his spectacles (which he had fortunately saved), his head bobbed up and down and from side to side, while his whole attitude and mien expressed unbounded astonishment.

He stood in the presence of an endless, wondrous and inexhaustibly rich collection of antediluvian monsters, piled up for his own private and peculiar satisfaction. Fancy an enthusiastic lover of books carried suddenly into the very midst of the famous library of Alexandria burned by the sacrilegious Omar, and which some miracle had restored to its pristine splendor! Such was something of the state of mind in which uncle Hardwigg was now placed.

For some time he stood thus, literally aghast at the magnitude of his discovery.

But it was even a greater excitement when, darting wildly over this mass of organic dust, he caught up a naked skull and addressed me in a quivering voice—" Harry, my boy—Harry—this is a human head!"

CHAPTER XXXV
DISCOVERY UPON DISCOVERY

It will be easy to understand the Professor's mingled astonishment and joy when, on advancing about twenty yards further, he found himself in the presence of, I may say face to face with an entire fossil of the human race, actually belonging to the quarternary period!

The human skull was perfectly recognizable. Had a soil of very peculiar nature, like that of the cemetery of St. Michel at Bordeaux, preserved it during countless ages? This was the question I asked myself, but which I was wholly unable to answer. This head with stretched and parchmenty skin, with the teeth whole, the hair abundant, was before our eyes as in life!

I stood mute, almost paralyzed with wonder and awe before this dread apparition of another age. My uncle, who on almost every occasion was a great talker, remained for a time completely dumbfounded. He was too full of emotion for speech to be possible. After a while, however, we raised up the body to which the skull belonged. We stood it on end.   It seemed, to our excited imaginations, to look at us with its terrible hollow eyes.

After some minutes of silence, the man was vanquished by the Professor.   Human instincts succumbed to scientific pride and exultation.   Professor Hardwigg, carried away by his enthusiasm, forgot all the circumstances of our journey, the extraordinary position in which we were placed, the immense cavern which stretched far away over our heads.   There can be no doubt that he thought himself at the institution addressing his attentive pupils, for he put on his most doctorial style, waved his hand, and began——

"Gentlemen, I have the honor on this auspicious occasion to present to you a man of the quartenary period of our globe.   Many learned men have denied his very existence, while other able persons, perhaps of even higher authority, have affirmed their belief in the reality of his life.   If the St. Thomases of palæontology were present, they would reverentially touch him with their fingers and believe in his existence, thus acknowledging their obstinate heresy.   I know that science should be careful in relation to all discoveries of this nature.   I am not without having heard of the many Barnums and other quacks who have made a trade of such like pretended discoveries.   I have, of course, heard of the discovery of the knee-bones of Ajax, of the pretended finding of the body of Orestes by the Spartiates, and of the body of Asterius, ten spans long, fifteen feet—of which we read in Pausanias.

"I have read everything in relation to the skeleton of Trapani, discovered in the fourteenth century, and which many persons chose to regard as that of Polyphemus, and the history of the giant dug up during the sixteenth century in the environs of Palmyra.   You are as well aware as I am, gentlemen, of the existence of the celebrated analysis made near Lucerne, in 1577, of the great bones which the celebrated Doctor Felix Plater declared belonged to a giant about nineteen feet high.   I have devoured all the treatises of Cassanion, and all those memoirs, pamphlets, speeches, and replies, published in reference to the skeleton of Teutobochus, king of the Cimbri, the invader of Gaul, dug out of a gravel pit in Dauphiny, in 1613.   In the eighteenth century I should have denied, with Peter Cam-

pet, the existence of the preadamites of Scheuchzer.   I
have had in my hands the writing called Gigans——"

Here my uncle was afflicted by the natural infirmity
which prevented him from pronouncing difficult words in
public.   It was not exactly stuttering, but a strange sort
of constitutional hesitation.   "The writing named Gigans——" he repeated.

He, however, could get no further.   "*Giganteo*——"

Impossible!   The unfortunate word would not come out.
There would have been great laughter at the Institution,
had the mistake happened there.   "Gigantosteology!" at
last exclaimed Professor Hardwigg, between two savage
growls.

"Yes, gentlemen, I am well acquainted with all these
matters, and know, also, that Cuvier and Blumenbach fully
recognized in these bones, the undeniable remains of mam-
moths of the quaternary period.   But after what we now
see, to allow a doubt is to insult scientific inquiry.   There is
the body; you can see it; you can touch it.   It is not a skeleton, it is a complete and uninjured body, preserved with an
anthropological object."   I did not attempt to controvert
this singular and astounding assertion.

"If I could but wash this corpse in a solution of sul-
phuric acid," continued my uncle, "I would undertake to
remove all the earthy particles, and these resplendent shells,
which are incrusted all over this body.   But I am without
this precious dissolving medium.   Nevertheless, such as
it is, this body will tell its own history."

Here the Professor held up the fossil body, and exhibited
it with rare dexterity.   No professional showman could
have shown more activity.

"As on examination you will see," my uncle continued,
"it is only about six feet in length, which is a long way
from the pretended giants of early days.   As to the particular race to which it belonged, it is incontestably Cau-
casian.   It is of the white race, that is, of our own.   The
skull of this fossil being is a perfect ovoid without any remarkable or prominent development of the cheek bones,
and without any projection of the jaw.   But I will advance still farther on the road of inquiry and deduction,
and I dare venture to say that this human sample or specimen belongs to the Japhetic family, which spread over the

world from India to the uttermost limits of western
Europe. There is no occasion, gentlemen, to smile at my
remarks."

Of course nobody smiled. But the excellent Professor
was so accustomed to beaming countenances at his lectures,
that he believed he saw all his audience laughing during
the delivery of his learned dissertation.

"Yes," he continued, with renewed animation, "this is a
fossil man, a contemporary of the mastodons, with the bones
of which this whole amphitheater is covered. But if I am
called on to explain how he came to this place, how these
various strata by which he is covered have fallen into this
vast cavity, I can undertake to give you no explanation.
But there is the man, surrounded by the works of his hands,
his hatchets, and his carved flints, which belong to the stone
period; and the only rational supposition is, that, like myself, he visited the center of the earth as a traveling tourist,
a pioneer of science. At all events, there can be no doubt
of his great age, and of his being one of the oldest race of
human beings."

The Professor with these words ceased his oration, and I
burst forth into loud and "unanimous" applause. Besides, after all, my uncle was right. Much more learned
men than his nephew would have found it rather hard to
refute his facts and arguments.

Another circumstance soon presented itself. This fos-
silized body was not the only one in this vast plain of bones
—the cemetery of an extinct world. Other bodies were
found, as we trod the dusty plain, and my uncle was able
to choose the most marvelous of these specimens in order
to convince the most incredulous.

In truth, it was a surprising spectacle, the successive remains of generations and generations of men and animals
confounded together in one vast cemetery. But a great
question now presented itself to our notice, and one we
were actually afraid to contemplate in all its bearings. Had
these once animated beings been buried so far beneath the
soil by some tremendous convulsion of nature, after they
had been earth to earth and ashes to ashes, or had they
lived here below, in this subterranean world, under this
factitious sky, born, married, and given in marriage, and
dying at last, just like ordinary inhabitants of the earth?

Up to the present moment, marine monsters, fish, and such like animals, had alone been seen alive! The question which rendered us rather uneasy, was a pertinent one. Were any of these men of the abyss wandering about the deserted shores of this wondrous sea of the center of the earth? This was a question which rendered me very uneasy and uncomfortable. How, should they really be in existence, would they receive us men from above?

CHAPTER XXXVI

WHAT IS IT?

FOR a long and weary hour we tramped over this great bed of bones. We advanced regardless of everything, drawn on by ardent curiosity. What other marvels did this great cavern contain—what other wondrous treasures for the scientific man? My eyes were quite prepared for any number of surprises, my imagination lived in expectation of something new and wonderful.

The borders of the great Central Ocean had for some time disappeared behind the hills that were scattered over the ground occupied by the plane of bones. The imprudent and enthusiastic Professor, who did not care whether he lost himself or not, hurried me forward. We advanced silently, bathed in waves of electric fluid. The light illumined equally the sides of every hill and rock. The appearance presented was that of a tropical country at mid-day in summer—in the midst of the equatorial regions and under the vertical rays of the sun. The rocks, the distant mountains, some confused masses of far-off forests, assumed a weird and mysterious aspect under this equal distribution of the luminous fluid! We resembled, to a certain extent, the mysterious personage in one of Hoffmann's fantastic tales—the man who lost his shadow.

After we had walked about a mile farther, we came to the edge of a vast forest, not, however, one of the vast mushroom forests we had discovered near Port Gretchen. It was the glorious and wild vegetation of the tertiary period, in all its superb magnificence. Huge palms, of a species now unknown, superb palmacites—a genus of fossil palms from the coal formation—pines, yews, cypress, and conifers or cone-bearing trees, the whole bound together by an inextricable and complicated mass of creeping plants. A beautiful carpet of mosses and ferns grew beneath the trees. Pleasant brooks murmured beneath umbrageous boughs, little worthy of this name, for no shade did they give. Upon their borders grew small tree-like shrubs, such as are seen in the hot countries on our own inhabited globe.

The one thing wanted to these plants, these shrubs, these trees—was color! Forever deprived of the vivifying warmth of the sun, they were vapid and colorless. All shade was lost in one uniform tint, of a brown and faded character. The leaves were wholly devoid of green, and the flowers, so numerous during the tertiary period which gave them birth, were without color and without perfume, something like paper discolored by long exposure to the atmosphere.

My uncle ventured beneath the gigantic groves. I followed him, though not without a certain amount of apprehension. Since nature had shown herself capable of producing such stupendous vegetable productions, why might we not meet with animals as large, and therefore dangerous.

Suddenly I stopped short and restrained my uncle. The extreme diffuseness of the light enabled me to see the smallest objects in the distant copse. I thought I saw—no, I really did see with my own eyes,—immense, gigantic animals moving about under the mighty trees. Yes, they were truly gigantic animals, a whole herd of mastodons, not fossils, but living.

Yes, I could see these enormous elephants, whose trunks were tearing down large boughs, and working in and out the trees like a legion of serpents. I could hear the sounds of the mighty tusks uprooting huge trees! The boughs crackled, and the whole masses of leaves and green branches went down the capacious throats of these terrible monsters!

That wondrous dream, when I saw the ante-historical times revivified, when the tertiary and quaternary periods passed before me, was now realized! And there we were alone, far down in the bowels of the earth, at the mercy of its ferocious inhabitants!

My uncle paused, full of wonder and astonishment. "Come," he said at last, when his first surprise was over, "come along, my boy, and let us see them nearer."

"No," replied I, restraining his efforts to drag me forward, "we are wholly without arms. What should we do in the midst of that flock of gigantic quadrupeds? Come away, uncle, I implore you. No human creature can with impunity brave the ferocious anger of these monsters."

"No human creature," said my uncle, suddenly lowering his voice to a mysterious whisper, "you are mistaken, my dear Henry. Look! look yonder! It seems to me that I behold a human being—a being like ourselves—a man!"

I looked, shrugging my shoulders, decided to push incredulity to its very last limits. But whatever might have been my wish, I was compelled to yield to the weight of ocular demonstration. Yes—not more than a quarter of a mile off, leaning against the trunk of an enormous tree, was a human being—a Proteus of these subterranean regions, a new son of Neptune keeping this innumerable herd of mastodons. *Immanis, pecoris custos, immanis ipse!* (The keeper of gigantic cattle, himself a giant!) Yes—it was no longer a fossil whose corpse we had raised from the ground in the great cemetery, but a giant capable of guiding and driving these prodigious monsters. His height was above twelve feet. His head, as big as the head of a buffalo, was lost in a mane of matted hair. It was indeed a huge mane, like those which belonged to the elephants of the earlier ages of the world. In his hand was a branch of a tree, which served as a crook for this antediluvian shepherd.

We remained profoundly still, speechless with surprise. But we might at any moment be seen by him. Nothing remained for us but instant flight. "Come, come!" I cried, dragging my uncle along; and, for the first time, he made no resistance to my wishes.

A quarter of an hour later we were far away from that terrible monster! Now that I think of the matter calmly, and that I reflect upon it dispassionately; now that months, years, have passed since this strange and unnatural adventure befell us,—what am I to think, what am I to believe?

No, it is utterly impossible! Our ears must have deceived us, and our eyes have cheated us! we have not seen what we believed we had seen. No human being could by any possibility have existed in that subterranean world! No generation of men could inhabit the lower caverns of the globe without taking note of those who peopled the surface, without communication with them. It was folly, folly, folly! nothing else!

I am rather inclined to admit the existence of some animal resembling in structure the human race—of some monkey of the first geological epochs, like that discovered by M. Lartet in the ossiferous deposits of Sansan. But this animal, or being, whichsoever it was, surpassed in height all things known to modern science. Never mind. However unlikely it may be, it might have been a monkey —but a man, a living man, and with him a whole generation of gigantic animals, buried in the entrails of the earth —it was too monstrous to be believed!

CHAPTER XXXVII
THE MYSTERIOUS DAGGER

During this time, we had left the bright and transparent forest far behind us. We were mute with astonishment, overcome by a kind of feeling which was next door to apathy. We kept running in spite of ourselves. It was a perfect flight, which resembled one of those horrible sensations we sometimes meet with in our dreams.

Instinctively we made our way towards the Central Sea, and I cannot now tell what wild thoughts passed through my mind, nor of what follies I might have been guilty, but for a very serious pre-occupation which brought me back to practical life. Though I was aware that we were treading on a soil quite new to us, I, every now and then noticed certain aggregations of rock, the shape of which forcibly reminded me of those near Port Gretchen.

This confirmed, moreover, the indications of the compass and our extraordinary and unlooked-for, as well as involuntary, return to the north of this great Central Sea. It was so like our starting point, that I could scarcely doubt the reality of our position. Streams and cascades, fell in hundreds over the numerous projections of the rocks. I actually thought I could see our faithful and monotonous Hans and the wonderful grotto in which I had come back to life after my tremendous fall.

Then, as we advanced still farther, the position of the cliffs, the appearance of a stream, the unexpected profile of a rock, would throw me again into a state of bewildering doubt. After some time, I explained my state of mental indecision to my uncle. He confessed to a similar feeling of hesitation. He was totally unable to make up his mind in the midst of this extraordinary but uniform panorama.

" There can be no doubt," I insisted, " that we have not landed exactly at the place whence we first took our departure; but the tempest has brought us above our starting point. I think, therefore, that if we follow the coast we shall once more find Port Gretchen."

" In that case," cried my uncle, " it is useless to continue our exploration. The very best thing we can do is to make our way back to the raft. Are you quite sure, Harry, that you are not mistaken ? "

" It is difficult," was my reply, " to come to any decision, for all these rocks are exactly alike. There is no marked difference between them. At the same time, the impression on my mind is, that I recognize the promontory at the foot of which our worthy Hans constructed the raft. We are, I am nearly convinced, near the little port; if this be not it," I added, carefully examining a creek which appeared singularly familiar to my mind.

" My dear Harry—if this were the case, we should find traces of our own footsteps, some signs of our passage; and I can really see nothing to indicate our having passed this way."

" But I see something," I cried, in an impetuous tone of voice, as I rushed forward and eagerly picked up something which shone in the sand under my feet.

" What is it ? " cried the astonished and bewildered Professor.

" This," was my reply. And I handed to my startled relative a rusty dagger, of singular shape.

" What made you bring with you so useless a weapon? "
he exclaimed. " It was needlessly hampering yourself."

" I bring it?—it is quite new to me. I never saw it before—are you sure it is not out of your collection? "

" Not that I know of," said the Professor, puzzled.
" I have no recollection of the circumstance. It was never
my property."

" This is very extraordinary," I said, musing over the
novel and singular incident.

" Not at all. There is a very simple explanation, Harry.
The Icelanders are known to keep up the use of these an-
tiquated weapons, and this must have belonged to Hans,
who has let it fall without knowing it."

I shook my head. That dagger had never been in the
possession of the pacific and taciturn Hans. I knew him
and his habits too well. " What can it be—unless it be
the weapon of some antediluvian warrior," I continued,
" of some living man, a contemporary of that mighty
shepherd from whom we have just escaped? But no—
mystery upon mystery—this is no weapon of the stone
epoch, nor even of the bronze period. It is made of excellent steel——"

Ere I could finish my sentence, my uncle stopped me
short from entering upon a whole train of theories, and
spoke in his most cold and decided tone of voice. " Calm
yourself, my dear boy, and endeavor to use your reason.
This weapon, upon which we have fallen so unexpectedly,
is a true *dague,* one of those worn by gentlemen in their
belts during the sixteenth century. Its use was to give
the *coup de grâce,* the final blow, to the foe who would not
surrender. It is clearly of Spanish workmanship. It belongs neither to you, nor to me, nor the eiderdown hunter,
nor to any of the living beings who may still exist so
marvelously in the interior of the earth."

" What can you mean, uncle? " I said, now lost in a
host of surmises.

" Look closely at it," he continued; " these jagged edges
were never made by the resistance of human blood and
bone. The blade is covered with a regular coating of
iron-mould and rust, which is not a day old, not a year old
not a century old, but much more——"

The Professor began to get quite excited, according to

custom, and was allowing himself to be carried away by his fertile imagination. I could have said something. He stopped me. "Harry," he cried, "we are now on the verge of a great discovery. This blade of a dagger you have so marvelously discovered, after being abandoned upon the sand for more than a hundred, two hundred, even three hundred years, has been indented by someone endeavoring to carve an inscription on these rocks."

"But this poignard never got here of itself," I exclaimed, "it could not have twisted itself. Someone, therefore, must have preceded us upon the shores of this extraordinary sea."

"Yes, a man."

"But what man has been sufficiently desperate to do such a thing."

"A man who has somewhere written his name with this very dagger—a man who has endeavored once more to indicate the right road to the interior of the earth. Let us look around, my boy. You know not the importance of your singular and happy discovery."

Prodigiously interested, we walked along the wall of rock, examining the smallest fissures, which might finally expand into the much wished for gully or shaft. We at last reached a spot where the shore became extremely narrow. The sea almost bathed the foot of the rocks, which were here very lofty and steep. There was scarcely a path wider than two yards at any point. At last, under a huge overhanging rock, we discovered the entrance of a dark and gloomy tunnel.

There, on a square tablet of granite, which had been smoothed by rubbing it with another stone, we could see two mysterious, and much worn letters, the two initials of the bold and extraordinary traveler who had preceded us on our adventurous journey.

$$\cdot \; \textformat{A} \cdot \textformat{S} \cdot$$

"A. S.," cried my uncle; "you see I was right. Arne Saknussemm, always Arne Saknussemm!"

CHAPTER XXXVIII
NO OUTLET—BLASTING THE ROCK

EVER since the commencement of our marvelous journey, I had experienced many surprises, had suffered from many illusions. I thought that I was case-hardened against all surprises and could neither see nor hear anything to amaze me again. When, however, I saw these two letters, which had been engraven three hundred years before, I stood fixed in an attitude of mute surprise.

Not only was there the signature of the learned and enterprising alchemist written in the rock, but I held in my hand the identical instrument with which he had laboriously engraved it. It was impossible, without showing an amount of incredulity scarcely becoming a sane man, to deny the existence of the traveler, and the reality of that voyage which I believed all along to have been a myth—the mystification of some fertile brain.

While these reflections were passing through my mind, my uncle, the Professor, gave way to an access of feverish and poetical excitement. " Wonderful and glorious Genius, great Saknussemm," he cried, " you have left no resource omitted to show to other mortals the way into the interior of our mighty globe, and your fellow-creatures can find the trail left by your illustrious footsteps, three hundred years ago. You have been careful to secure for others the contemplation of these wonders and marvels of creation. Your name engraved at every important stage of your glorious journey, leads the hopeful traveler direct to the mighty discovery to which you devoted such energy and courage. The audacious traveler, who shall follow your footsteps to the last, will doubtless find your initials engraved with your own hand upon the center of the earth. *I* will be that audacious traveler—*I*, too, will sign my name upon the very same spot, upon the central granite stone of this wondrous work of the Creator. But in justice to your devotion, and to your being the first to indicate the road, let this Cape, seen by you upon the shores of this sea discovered by you, be called of all time, Cape Saknussemm."

This is what I heard, and I began to be roused to the pitch of enthusiasm indicated by those words. A fierce excitement roused me. I forgot everything. The dangers of the voyage, and the perils of the return journey, were now as nothing! What another man had done in ages past, could I felt be done again; I was determined to do it myself, and now nothing that man had accomplished appeared to me impossible. "Forward—forward," I cried in a burst of genuine and hearty enthusiasm.

I had already started in the direction of the somber and gloomy gallery, when the Professor stopped me; he, the man so rash and hasty, he, the man so easily roused to the highest pitch of enthusiasm, checked me, and asked me to be patient and show more calm. "Let us return to our good friend, Hans," he said; "we will then bring the raft down to this place."

I must say that though I at once yielded to my uncle's request, it was not without dissatisfaction, and I hastened along the rocks of that wonderful coast. "Do you know, my dear uncle," I said, as we walked along, "that we have been singularly helped by a concurrence of circumstances, right up to this very moment."

"So you begin to see it, do you, Harry?" said the Professor, with a smile.

"Doubtless," I responded, "and strangely enough, even the tempest has been the means of putting us on the right road. Blessings on the tempest! It brought us safely back to the very spot from which fine weather would have driven us forever. Supposing we had succeeded in reaching the southern and distant shores of this extraordinary sea, what would have become of us? The name of Saknussemm would never have appeared to us, and at this moment we should have been cast away upon an inhospitable coast, probably without an outlet."

"Yes, Harry, my boy, there is certainly something providential in that wandering at the mercy of wind and waves towards the south: we have come back exactly north; and what is better still, we fall upon this great discovery. There is something in it which is far beyond my comprehension. The coincidence is unheard-of, marvelous!"

"What matter! It is not our duty to explain facts, but to make the best possible use of them."

"Doubtless, my boy; but if you will allow me——" said the really-delighted Professor.

"Excuse me, sir, but I see exactly how it will be; we shall take the northern route; we shall pass under the north-

ern regions of Europe, under Sweden, under Russia, under
Siberia, and who knows where—instead of burying ourselves under the burning plains and deserts of Africa, or
beneath the mighty waves of the ocean; and that is all, at
this stage of our journey, that I care to know. Let us advance, and Heaven will be our guide!"

"Yes, Harry, you are right, quite right; all is for the
best. Let us abandon this horizontal sea, which could
never have led to anything satisfactory. We shall descend,
descend, and everlastingly descend. Do you know, my
dear boy, that to reach the interior of the earth we have
only five thousand miles to travel!"

"Bah!" I cried, carried away by a burst of enthusiasm,
"the distance is scarcely worth speaking about. The
thing is to make a start."

My wild, mad, and incoherent speeches continued until
we rejoined our patient and phlegmatic guide. All was,
we found, prepared for an immediate departure. There
was not a single parcel but what was in its proper place.
We all took up our posts on the raft, and the sail being
hoisted, Hans received his directions, and guided the frail
barque towards Cape Saknussemm, as we had definitely
named it.

The wind was very unfavorable to a craft that was unable to sail close to the wind. We were continually reduced to pushing ourselves forward by means of poles.
On several occasions the rocks ran far out into deep water
and we were compelled to make a long round. At last,
after three long and weary hours of navigation, that is to
say, about six o'clock in the evening, we found a place at
which we could land.

I jumped on shore first. In my present state of excitement and enthusiasm, I was always first. My uncle and
the Icelander followed. The voyage from the port to
this point of the sea had by no means calmed me. It had
rather produced the opposite effect. I even proposed to
burn our vessel, that is to destroy our raft, in order to completely cut off our retreat. But my uncle sternly opposed
this wild project. I began to think him particularly lukewarm and unenthusiastic. "At any rate, my dear uncle,"
I said, "let us start without delay."

"Yes, my boy, I am quite as eager to do so as you can

be. But, in the first place, let us examine this mysterious gallery, in order to find if we shall need to prepare and mend our ladders."

My uncle now began to see to the efficiency of our Ruhmkorff's coil, which would doubtless soon be needed; the raft, securely fastened to a rock, was left alone. The opening into the new gallery was not twenty paces distant from the spot. Our little troop, with myself at the head, advanced.

The orifice, which was almost circular, presented a diameter of about five feet; the somber tunnel was cut in the living rock, and coated on the inside by the different material which had once passed through it in a state of fusion. The lower part was about level with the water, so that we were able to penetrate to the interior without difficulty. We followed an almost horizontal direction; when, at the end of about a dozen paces, our further advance was checked by the interposition of an enormous block of granite rock.

"Accursed stone!" I cried, furiously, on perceiving that we were stopped by what seemed an insurmountable obstacle.

In vain we looked to the right, in vain we looked to the left; in vain examined it above and below. There existed no passage, no sign of any other tunnel. I experienced the most bitter and painful disappointment. So enraged was I that I would not admit the reality of any obstacle. I stooped to my knees; I looked under the mass of stone. No hole, no interstice. I then looked above. The same barrier of granite! Hans, with the lamp, examined the sides of the tunnel in every direction. But all in vain! It was necessary to renounce all hope of passing through.

I had seated myself upon the ground. My uncle walked angrily and hopelessly up and down. He was evidently desperate. "But," I cried, after some moments' thought, "what about Arne Saknussemm?"

"You are right," replied my uncle, "he can never have been checked by a lump of rock."

"No—ten thousand times no," I cried, with extreme vivacity. "This huge lump of rock, in consequence of some concussion, has in some unexpected way closed up the passage. Many and many years have passed away since the return of Saknussemm, and the fall of this huge block of granite. Is it not quite evident that this gallery was formerly the outlet for the pent-up lava in the interior of the earth, and that these eruptive matters then circulated freely? Look at these recent fissures in the granite roof; it is evidently formed of pieces of enormous stone, placed here as if by the hand of a giant, who had worked to make a strong and substantial arch. One day, after an unusually heavy shock, the vast rock which stands in our way, fell through to a level with the soil and has barred our further progress. We are right, then, in thinking that this is an unexpected obstacle, with which Saknussemm did not meet; and if we do not upset it in some way, we are unworthy of following in the footsteps of the great discoverer, and incapable of finding our way to the Center of the Earth!"

In this wild way I addressed my uncle. The zeal of the Professor, his earnest longing for success, had become part and parcel of my being. I wholly forgot the past; I utterly despised the future. Nothing existed for me upon the surface of this spheroid in the bosom of which I was engulfed, no towns, no country, no Hamburg, no König-strasse, not even my poor Gretchen, who by this time would believe me utterly lost in the interior of the earth!

"Well," cried my uncle, roused to enthusiasm by my words, "let us go to work with pick-axes, with crowbars, with anything that comes to hand—but down with these terrible walls."

"It is far too tough and too big to be destroyed by a pick-ax or crowbar," I replied.

"What then?"

"As I said, it is useless to think of overcoming such a difficulty by means of ordinary tools."

"What then?"

"What else but gunpowder, a subterranean mine? Let us blow up the obstacle that stands in our way."

"Gunpowder!"

"Yes; all we have to do is to get rid of this paltry obstacle."

"To work, Hans, to work!" cried the Professor. The Icelander went back to the raft, and soon returned with a huge crowbar, with which he began to dig a hole in the rock, which was to serve as a mine. It was by no means a slight task. It was necessary for our purpose to make a cavity large enough to hold fifty pounds of fulminating gun cotton, the expansive power of which is four times as great as that of ordinary gunpowder.

I had now roused myself to an almost miraculous state of excitement. While Hans was at work, I actively assisted my uncle to prepare a long wick, made from damp gunpowder, the mass of which we finally enclosed in a bag of linen. "We are bound to go through," I cried enthusiastically.

"We are bound to go through," responded the Professor, tapping me on the back.

At midnight, our work as miners was completely finished; the charge of fulminating cotton was thrust into the hollow, and the match, which we had made of considerable length, was ready. A spark was now sufficient to ignite this formidable engine, and to blow the rock to atoms!

"We will now rest until to-morrow."

It was absolutely necessary to resign myself to my fate, and to consent to wait for the explosion for six weary hours!

CHAPTER XXXIX
THE EXPLOSION AND ITS RESULTS

THE next day, which was the twenty-seventh of August, was a date celebrated in our wondrous, subterranean journey.

I never think of it even now, but I shudder with horror. My heart beats wildly at the very memory of that awful day. From this time forward, our reason, our judgment, our human ingenuity, had nothing to do with the course of events. We were about to become the plaything of the great phenomena of the earth!

At six o'clock we were all up and ready. The dreaded moment was arriving when we were about to seek an opening into the interior of the earth by means of gunpowder. What would be the consequences of breaking through the crust of the earth.

I begged that it might be my duty to set fire to the mine. I looked upon it as an honor. This task once performed, I could rejoin my friends upon the raft, which had not been unloaded. As soon as we were all ready, we were to sail away to some distance to avoid the consequences of the explosion, the effects of which would certainly not be concentrated in the interior of the earth. The slow match we calculated to burn for about ten minutes, more or less, before it reached the chamber in which the great body of powder was confined. I should therefore have plenty of time to reach the raft and put off to a safe distance.

After a hearty repast, my uncle and the hunter-guide embarked on board the raft, while I remained alone upon the desolate shore. I was provided with a lantern which was to enable me to set fire to the wick of the infernal machine. " Go, my boy," said my uncle, " and Heaven be with you. But come back as soon as you can. I shall be all impatience."

" Be easy on that matter," I replied, " there is no fear of my delaying on the road." Having said this, I advanced toward the opening of the somber gallery. My heart beat wildly. I opened my lantern and seized the extremity of the wick.

The Professor, who was looking on, held his chronometer in his hand. " Are you ready? " cried he.

" Quite ready."

" Well, then, fire away!" I hastened to put the light to the wick, which crackled and sparkled, hissing and spitting like a serpent; then, running as fast as I could, I returned to the shore.

" Get on board my lad, and you, Hans, shove off!" cried my uncle. By a vigorous application of his pole Hans sent us flying over the water. The raft was quite twenty fathoms distant.

It was a moment of palpitating interest, of deep anxiety. My uncle, the Professor, never took his eyes off the chronometer. " Only five minutes more," he said in a low tone, " only four, only three."

My pulse went a hundred to the minute. I could hear my heart beating.

" Only two, one! Now, then, mountains of granite, crumble beneath the power of man! "

What happened after that? As to the terrific roar of the explosion, I do not think I heard it. But the form of the rocks completely changed in my eyes—they seemed to be drawn aside like a curtain. I saw a fathomless, a bottomless abyss, which yawned beneath the turgid waves. The sea, which seemed suddenly to have gone mad, then became one great mountainous mass, upon the top of which the raft rose perpendicularly.

We were all thrown down. The light gave place to the most profound obscurity. Then I felt all solid support give way not to my feet, but to the raft itself. I thought it was going bodily down a tremendous well. I tried to speak, to question my uncle. Nothing could be heard but the roaring of the mighty waves. We clung together in utter silence.

Despite the awful darkness, despite the noise, the surprise, the emotion, I thoroughly understood what had happened. Beyond the rock which had been blown up, there existed a mighty abyss. The explosion had caused a kind of earthquake in this soil, broken by fissures and rents. The gulf, thus suddenly thrown open, was about to swallow the inland sea, which, transformed into a mighty torrent, was dragging us with it. One only idea filled my mind. We were utterly and completely lost!

One hour, two hours—what more I cannot say, passed in this manner. We sat close together, elbow touching elbow, knee touching knee! We held one another's hands not to be thrown off the raft. We were subjected to the most violent shocks, whenever our sole dependence, a frail wooden raft, struck against the rocky sides of the channel. Fortunately for us, these concussions became less and less frequent, which made me fancy that the gallery was getting wider and wider. There could be now no doubt that we had chanced upon the road once followed by Saknussemm, but instead of going down in a proper manner, we had, through our own imprudence, drawn a whole sea with us!

These ideas presented themselves to my mind in a very vague and obscure manner. I felt rather than reasoned. I put my ideas together only confusedly, while spinning along like a man going down a waterfall. To judge by the air which, as it were, whipped my face, we must have been rushing at a perfectly lightning rate.

To attempt under these circumstances to light a torch was simply impossible, and the last remains of our electric machine, of our Ruhmkorf's coil, had been destroyed during the fearful explosion. I was therefore very much confused to see at last a bright light shining close to me. The calm countenance of the guide seemed to gleam upon me. The clever and patient hunter had succeeded in lighting the lantern; and though, in the keen and thorough draught, the flame flickered and vacillated and was very nearly put out, it served partially to dissipate the awful obscurity.

The gallery into which we had entered was very wide. I was, therefore, quite right in that part of my conjecture. The insufficient light did not allow us to see both of the walls at the same time. The slope of waters, which was carrying us away, was far greater than that of the most rapid river. The whole surface of the stream seemed to be composed of liquid arrows, darted forward with extreme violence and power. I can give no idea of the impression it made upon me.

The raft, at times, caught in certain whirlpools, and rushed forward, yet turned on itself all the time. How it did not upset I shall never be able to understand. When it approached the sides of the gallery, I took care to throw upon them the light of the lantern, and I was able to judge of the rapidity of motion by looking at the projecting masses of rock, which as soon as seen were again invisible. I believe we were going at a rate of not less than a hundred miles an hour.

My uncle and I looked at one another with wild and haggard eyes; we clung convulsively to the stump of the mast, which, at the moment when the catastrophe took place, had snapped short off. We turned our backs as much as possible to the wind, in order not to be stifled by a rapidity of motion which nothing human could face and live.

And still the long monotonous hours went on. The situation did not change in the least, though a discovery I suddenly made seemed to complicate it very much. When we had slightly recovered our equilibrium, I proceeded to examine our cargo. I then made the unsatisfactory discovery that the greater part of it had utterly disappeared. I became alarmed, and determined to discover what were our resources. My heart beat at the idea, but it was absolutely necessary to know on what we had to depend. With this in view, I took the lantern and looked around.

Of all our former collection of nautical and philosophical instruments there remained only the chronometer and the compass. The ladders and ropes were reduced to a small piece of rope fastened to the stump of the mast. Not a pickax, not a crowbar, not a hammer, and, far worse than all, no food—not enough for one day!

This discovery was a prelude to a certain and horrible death. Seated gloomily on the raft, clasping the stump of the mast mechanically, I thought of all I had read as to sufferings from starvation. I remembered everything that history had taught me on the subject, and I shuddered at the remembrance of the agonies to be endured. Maddened at the prospect, I persuaded myself that I must be mistaken. I examined the cracks in the raft; I poked between the joints and beams; I examined every possible hole and corner. The result was—simply nothing! Our stock of provisions consisted of nothing but a piece of dry meat and some soaked and half-mouldy biscuits.

I gazed around me scared and frightened. I could not understand the awful truth. And yet of what consequence was it in regard to any new danger? Supposing that we had had provisions for months, and even for years, how could we ever get out of the awful abyss into which we were being hurled by the irresistible torrent we had let loose? Why should we trouble ourselves about the sufferings and tortures to be endured from hunger, when death stared us in the face under so many other swifter and perhaps even more horrid forms?

I had the greatest mind to reveal all to my uncle, to explain to him the extraordinary and wretched position to which we were reduced, in order that, between the two, we might make a calculation as to the exact space of time which remained for us to live. It was, it appeared to me, the only thing to be done. But I had the courage to hold my tongue, to gnaw at my entrails like the Spartan boy. I wished to leave him all his coolness.

At this moment, the light of the lantern slowly fell, and at last went out! The wick had wholly burnt to an end. The obscurity became absolute. It was no longer possible

to see through the impenetrable darkness! There was one
torch left, but it was impossible to keep it alight. Then,
like a child, I shut my eyes, that I might not see the darkness.

After a great lapse of time, the rapidity of our journey
increased. I could feel it by the rush of air upon my face.
The slope of the waters was excessive. I began to feel
that we were no longer going down a slope; we were falling. I felt as one does in a dream, going down bodily—
falling; falling; falling!

I felt that the hands of my uncle and Hans were vigorously clasping my arms. Suddenly, after a lapse of time
scarcely appreciable, I felt something like a shock. The
raft had not struck a hard body, but had suddenly been
checked in its course. A waterspout, a liquid column of
water, fell upon us. I felt suffocating. I was being
drowned. Still the sudden inundation did not last. In a
few seconds I felt myself once more able to breathe. My
uncle and Hans pressed my arms, and the raft carried us
all three away.

CHAPTER XL
THE APE GIGANS

It is difficult for me to determine what was the real
time, but I should suppose, by after calculation, that it
must have been ten at night.

I lay in a stupor, a half dream, during which I saw visions of astounding character. Monsters of the deep were
side by side with the mighty elephantine shepherd. Gigantic fish and animals formed strange conjunctions. It
seemed in my vision that the raft took a sudden turn,
whirled round; entered another tunnel; this time illumined
in a most singular manner. The roof was formed of
porous stalactite, through which a moon-lit vapor appeared
to pass, casting its brilliant light upon our gaunt and hag- .
gard figures. The light increased as we advanced, while
the roof ascended; until at last, we were once more in a
kind of water cavern, the lofty dome of which disappeared
in a luminous cloud! My uncle and the guide moved as
men in a dream. I was afraid to waken them, knowing

the danger of such a sudden start. I seated myself beside them to watch.

As I did so, I became aware of something moving in the distance, which at once fascinated my eyes. It was floating, apparently, upon the surface of the water, advancing by means of what at first appeared paddles. I looked with glaring eyes. One glance told me that it was something monstrous.

But what? It was the great *Shark Crocodile* of the early writers on geology. About the size of an ordinary whale, with hideous jaws and two gigantic eyes, it advanced. Its eyes fixed on me with terrible sternness. Some indefinite warning told me that it had marked me for its own.

I attempted to rise—to escape, no matter where, but my knees shook under me; my limbs trembled violently; I almost lost my senses. And still the mighty monster advanced. My uncle and the guide made no effort to save themselves. With a strange noise, like none other I had ever heard, the beast came on. His jaws were at least seven feet apart, and his distended mouth looked large enough to have swallowed a boatful of men.

We were about ten feet distant, when I discovered that much as his body resembled that of a crocodile, his mouth was wholly that of a shark. His twofold nature now became apparent. To snatch us up at a mouthful it was necessary for him to turn on his back, which motion necessarily caused his legs to kick up helplessly in the air. I actually laughed even in the very jaws of death!

But next minute, with a wild cry, I darted away into the interior of the cavern, leaving my unhappy comrades to their fate! This cavern was deep and dreary. After about a hundred yards, I paused and looked around. The whole floor, composed of sand and malachite, was strewn with bones, freshly-gnawed bones of reptiles and fish, with a mixture of mammalia. My very soul grew sick as my body shuddered with horror. I had truly, according to the old proverb, fallen out of the frying-pan into the fire. Some beast larger and more ferocious even than the Shark-Crocodile inhabited this den.

What could I do? The mouth of the cave was guarded by one ferocious monster, the interior was inhabited by something too hideous to contemplate. Flight was impossible! Suddenly a groaning, as of fifty bears in a fight, fell upon my ears—hisses, spitting, moaning, hideous to hear—and then I saw—

Never, were ages to pass over my head, shall I forget the horrible apparition. It was the Ape Gigans, the antediluvian Gorilla! Fourteen feet high, covered with coarse hair, of a blackish brown, it advanced. Its arms were as long as its body, while its legs were prodigious. It had thick, long, and sharply-pointed teeth—like a mammoth saw. It struck its breast as it came on smelling and sniffing, reminding me of the stories we read in our early childhood of giants who ate the flesh of men and little boys!

Suddenly it stopped. My heart beat wildly, for I was conscious that, somehow or other, the fearful monster had smelt me out and was peering about with his hideous eyes to try and discover my whereabouts. I gave myself up for lost. No hope of safety or escape seemed to remain.

At this moment, just as my eyes appeared to close in death, there came a strange noise from the entrance of the cave; and turning, the Gorilla evidently recognized some enemy more worthy his prodigious size and strength. It was the huge Shark-Crocodile, which perhaps having disposed of my friends, was coming in search of further prey.

The Gorilla placed himself on the defensive, and clutching a bone some seven or eight feet in length, a perfect club, aimed a deadly blow at the hideous beast, which reared upwards and fell with all its weight upon its adversary. A terrible combat ensued. The struggle was awful and ferocious. I, however, did not wait to witness the result. Regarding myself as the object of contention, I determined to remove from the presence of the victor. I slid down from my hiding-place, reached the ground, and gliding against the wall, strove to gain the open mouth of the cavern. But I had not taken many steps when the fearful clamor ceased, to be followed by a mumbling and groaning which appeared to be indicative of victory.

I looked back and saw the huge ape, gory with blood, coming after me with glaring eyes, with dilated nostrils that gave forth two columns of heated vapor. I could feel his hot and fetid breath on my neck; and with a horrid jump—awoke from my nightmare sleep.

Yes—it was all a dream. I was still on the raft with my uncle and the guide.

The relief was not instantaneous, for under the influence of the hideous nightmare my senses had become numbed. After a while, however, my feelings were tranquilized. The first of my perceptions which returned in full force was that of hearing. I listened with acute and attentive ears. All was still as death. All I comprehended was silence. To the roaring of the waters, which had filled the gallery with awful reverberations, succeeded perfect peace.

After some little time my uncle spoke, in a low and scarcely audible tone—"Harry, boy, where are you?"

"I am here," was my faint rejoinder.

"Well, don't you see what has happened? We are going upwards."

"My dear uncle, what can you mean?" was my half delirious reply.

"Yes, I tell you we are ascending rapidly. Our downward journey is quite checked."

I held out my hand, and, after some little difficulty, succeeded in touching the wall. My hand was in an instant covered with blood. The skin was torn from the flesh. We were ascending with extraordinary rapidity.

"The torch—the torch!" cried the Professor, wildly; "it must be lighted." Hans, the guide, after many vain efforts, at last succeeded in lighting it, and the flame, having now nothing to prevent its burning, shed a tolerably clear light. We were enabled to form an approximate idea of the truth.

"It is just as I thought," said my uncle, after a moment or two of silent attention. "We are in a narrow well about four fathoms square. The waters of the great inland sea, having reached the bottom of the gulf, are now forcing themselves up the mighty shaft. As a natural consequence, we are being cast up on the summit of the waters."

"That I can see," was my lugubrious reply; "but where will this shaft end, and to what fall are we likely to be exposed?"

"Of that I am as ignorant as yourself. All I know is, that we should be prepared for the worst. We are going up at a fearfully rapid rate. As far as I can judge, we are ascending at the rate of two fathoms a second, of a hundred and twenty fathoms a minute, or rather more than three and a half leagues an hour. At this rate, our fate will soon be a matter of certainty."

"No doubt of it," was my reply. "The great concern I have now, however, is to know whether this shaft has any issue. It may end in a granite roof—in which case we shall be suffocated by compressed air, or dashed to atoms against the top. I fancy, already, that the air is beginning to be close and condensed. I have a difficulty in breathing." This might be fancy, or it might be the effect of our rapid motion, but I certainly felt a great oppression of the chest.

"Henry," said the Professor, "I do believe that the situation is to a certain extent desperate. There remain, however, many chances of ultimate safety, and I have, in my own mind, been revolving them over, during your heavy but agitated sleep. I have come to this logical conclusion—whereas we may at any moment perish, so at any moment we may be saved! We need, therefore, to prepare ourselves for whatever may turn up in the great chapter of accidents."

"But what would you have us do?" I cried; "are we not utterly helpless?"

"No! While there is life there is hope. At all events, there is one thing we can do—eat, and thus obtain strength to face victory or death."

As he spoke, I looked at my uncle with a haggard glance. I had put off the fatal communication as long as possible. It was now forced upon me, and I must tell him the truth. Still I hesitated. "Eat," I said, in a deprecating tone as if there were no hurry.

"Yes, and at once. I feel like a starving prisoner," he said, rubbing his yellow and shivering hands together. And, turning round to the guide, he spoke some hearty, cheering words, as I judged from his tone, in Danish. Hans shook his head in a terribly significant manner. I tried to look unconcerned.

"What!" cried the Professor, "you do not mean to say that all our provisions are lost?"

"Yes," was my lowly spoken reply, as I held out something in my hand, "this morsel of dried meat is all that remains for us three."

My uncle gazed at me as if he could not fully appreciate the meaning of my words. The blow seemed to stun him by its severity. I allowed him to reflect for some moments.

"Well," said I, after a short pause, "what do you think now? Is there any chance of our escaping from our horrible subterranean dangers? Are we not doomed to perish in the great hollows of the Center of the Earth?"

But my pertinent questions brought no answer. My uncle either heard me not, or appeared not to do so. And in this way a whole hour passed. Neither of us cared to speak. For myself, I began to feel the most fearful and devouring hunger. My companions, doubtless, felt the same horrible tortures, but neither of them would touch the wretched morsel of meat that remained. It lay there a last remnant of all our great preparations for the mad and senseless journey!

I looked back, with wonderment, to my own folly. Fully was I aware that, despite his enthusiasm, and the ever-to-be-hated scroll of Saknussemm, my uncle should never have started on his perilous voyage. What memories of the happy past, what previsions of the horrible future, now filled my brain!

CHAPTER XLI
HUNGER

HUNGER, prolonged, is temporary madness! The brain is at work without its required food, and the most fantastic notions fill the mind. Hitherto I had never known what hunger realy meant. I was likely to understand it now only too well.

After dreaming for some time, and thinking of this and other matters, I once more looked around me. We were still ascending with fearful rapidity. Every now and then the air appeared to check our respiration as it does that of aëronauts when the ascension of the balloon is too rapid. But if they feel a degree of cold in proportion to the elevation they attain in the atmosphere, we experienced quite a contrary effect. The heat began to increase in a most threatening and exceptional manner. I cannot tell exactly the mean, but I think it must have reached 122 degrees of Fahrenheit.

What was the meaning of this extraordinary change in the temperature? As far as we had hitherto gone, facts had proved the theories of Davy and of Lidenbrock to be correct. Until now, all the peculiar conditions of refractory rocks, of electricity of magnetism, had modified the general laws of nature, and had created for us a moderate temperature; for the theory of the central fire, remained, in my eyes, the only explainable one.

Were we, then, going to reach a position in which these phenomena were to be carried out in all their rigor, and in which the heat would reduce the rocks to a state of fusion? Such was my not unnatural fear, and I did not conceal the fact from my uncle. My way of doing so might be cold and heartless, but I could not help it. "If we are not drowned, or smashed into pancakes, and if we do not die of starvation, we have the satisfaction of knowing that we must be burned alive."

My uncle, in presence of this brusque attack, simply shrugged his shoulders, and resumed his reflections—whatever they might be.

An hour passed away, and except that there was a slight increase in the temperature no incident modified the situation. My uncle at last, of his own accord, broke silence. "Well, Henry, my boy," he said, in a cheerful way, "we must make up our minds."

"Make up our minds to what?" I asked, in considerable surprise.

"Well—to something. We must at whatever risk recruit our physical strength. If we make the fatal mistake of husbanding our little remnant of food, we may probably prolong our wretched existence a few hours—but we shall remain weak to the end."

"Yes," I growled, "to the end. That, however, will not keep us long waiting."

"Well, only let a chance of safety present itself,—only allow that a moment of action be necessary,—where shall we find the means of action if we allow ourselves to be reduced to physical weakness by inanition?"

" When this piece of meat is devoured, uncle, what hope will there remain unto us? "

" None, my dear Henry, none. But will it do you any good to devour it with your eyes? You appear to me to reason like one without will or decision, like a being without energy."

" Then," cried I, exasperated to a degree which is scarcely to be explained, " you do not mean to tell me—that you— that you—have not lost all hope."

" Certainly not," replied the Professor, with consummate coolness.

" You mean to tell me, uncle, that we shall get out of this monstrous subterranean shaft? "

" While there is life there is hope. I beg to assert, Henry, that as long as a man's heart beats, as long as a man's flesh quivers, I do not allow that a being gifted with thought and will can allow himself to despair."

What a resolution! The man placed in a position like that we occupied must have been very brave to speak like this. " Well," I cried, " what do you mean to do? "

" Eat what remains of the food we have in our hands; let us swallow the last crumb. It will be, heaven willing, our last repast. Well, never mind—instead of being exhausted skeletons, we shall be men."

" True," muttered I in a despairing tone, " let us take our fill."

" We must," replied my uncle, with a deep sigh—" call it what you will." My uncle took a piece of the meat that remained, and some crusts of biscuit which had escaped the wreck. He divided the whole into three parts. Each had one pound of food to last him as long as he remained in the interior of the earth.

Each now acted in accordance with his own private character. My uncle, the Professor, ate greedily, but evidently without appetite, eating simply from some mechanical motion. I put the food inside my lips, and hungry as I was, chewed my morsel without pleasure, and without satisfaction. Hans the guide, just as if he had been eider-down hunting, swallowed every mouthful, as though it were a usual affair. He looked like a man equally prepared to enjoy superfluity or total want. Hans, in all probability, was no more used to starvation than ourselves, but his hardy

Icelandic nature had prepared him for many sufferings. As long as he received his three rix-dollars every Saturday night, he was prepared for anything. The fact was, Hans never troubled himself about much except his money. He had undertaken to serve a certain man at so much per week, and no matter what evils befell his employer or himself, he never found fault or grumbled, so long as his wages were duly paid.

Suddenly my uncle roused himself. He had seen a smile on the face of our guide. I could not make it out. "What is the matter?" said my uncle.

"Schiedam," said the guide, producing a bottle of this precious fluid.

We drank. My uncle and myself will own to our dying day that hence we derived strength to exist until the last bitter moment. That precious bottle of Hollands was in reality only half-full; but, under the circumstances, it was nectar. The worthy Professor swallowed about half a pint and did not seem able to drink any more. "*Fortrafflig*," said Hans, swallowing nearly all that was left.

"Excellent—very good," said my uncle, with as much gusto as if he had just left the steps of the club at Hamburg.

I had begun to feel as if there had been one gleam of hope. Now all thought of the future vanished! We had consumed our last ounce of food, and it was five o'clock in the morning!

CHAPTER XLII
THE VOLCANIC SHAFT

MAN's constitution is so peculiar, that his health is purely a negative matter. No sooner is the rage of hunger appeased, than it becomes difficult to comprehend the meaning of starvation. It is only when you suffer that you really understand. As to anyone who has not endured privation having any notion of the matter, it is simply absurd. With us, after a long fast, some mouthfuls of bread and meat, a little mouldy biscuit and salt beef triumphed over all our previous saturnine thoughts.

Nevertheless, after this repast each gave way to his own

reflections. I wondered what were those of Hans—the man of the extreme north, who was yet gifted with the fatalistic resignation of Oriental character. But the utmost stretch of the imagination would not allow me to realize the truth. As for my individual self, my thoughts had ceased to be anything but memories of the past, and were all connected with that upper world which I never should have left. I saw it all now, the beautiful house in the Königstrasse, my poor Gretchen, the good Martha; they all passed before my mind like visions of the past. Every time any of the lugubrious groanings which were to be distinguished in the hollows around fell upon my ears, I fancied I heard the distant murmur of the great cities above my head.

As for my uncle, always thinking of his science, he examined the nature of the shaft by means of a torch. He closely examined the different strata one above the other, in order to recognize his situation by geological theory. This calculation, or rather this estimation, could by no means be anything but approximate. But a learned man, a philosopher, is nothing if not a philosopher, when he keeps his ideas calm and collected; and certainly the Professor possessed this quality to perfection.

I heard him, as I sat in silence, murmuring words of geological science. As I understood his object and his meaning, I could not but interest myself despite my preoccupation in that terrible hour. "Eruptive granite," he said to himself, "we are still in the primitive epoch. But we are going up—going up, still going up. But who knows? Who knows?"

Then he still hoped. He felt along the vertical sides of the shaft with his hand, and some few minutes later, he would go on again in the following style—"This is gniess. This is mocashites—silicious mineral. Good again; this is the epoch of transition, at all events, we are close to them —and then, and then——"

What could the Professer mean? Could he, by any conceivable means, measure the thickness of the crust of the earth suspended above our heads? Did he possess any possible means of making any approximation to this calculation? No. The manometer was wanting, and no summary estimation could take the place of it.

As we progressed, the temperature increased in the most extraordinary degree, and I began to feel as if I were bathed in a hot and burning atmosphere. Never before had I felt anything like it. I could only compare it to the hot vapor from an iron foundry, when the liquid iron is in a state of ebullition and runs over. By degrees, and one after the other, Hans, my uncle, and myself had taken off our coats and waistcoats. They were unbearable. Even the slightest garment was the cause of extreme suffering.

"Are we ascending to a living fire?" I cried; when, to my horror and astonishment, the heat became greater than before.

"No, no," said my uncle, "it is simply impossible, quite impossible."

"And yet," said I, touching the side of the shaft with my naked hand, "this wall is literally burning."

At this moment, feeling as I did that the sides of this extraordinary wall were red hot, I plunged my hands into the water to cool them. I drew them back with a cry of despair. "The water is boiling!" I cried.

My uncle, the Professor, made no reply other than a gesture of rage and despair. Something very like the truth had probably struck his imagination.

An invincible dread took possession of my brain and soul. I could only look forward to an immediate catastrophe, such a catastrophe as not even the most vivid imagination could have thought of. An idea, at first vague and uncertain, was gradually being changed into certainty. It was so terrible an idea that I scarcely dared to whisper it to myself. Yet all the while certain, and as it were, involuntary observations determined my convictions. By the doubtful glare of the torch, I could make out some singular changes in the granitic strata; a strange and terrible phenomenon was about to be produced, in which electricity played a part. Then this boiling water, this terrible and excessive heat? I determined as a last resource to examine the compass.

The compass had gone mad! Yes, wholly stark, staring mad. The needle jumped from pole to pole with sudden and surprising jerks, ran round, or as it is said, boxed the compass, and then ran suddenly back again as if it had the vertigo.

Terrible detonations, like heaven's artillery, began to multiply themselves with fearful intensity. I could only compare them with the noise made by hundreds of heavily-laden chariots being madly driven over a stone pavement. It was a continuous roll of heavy thunder.

And then the mad compass, shaken by the wild electric phenomena, confirmed me in my rapidly-formed opinion. The mineral crust was about to burst, the heavy granite masses were about to rejoin, the fissure was about to close, the void was about to be filled up, and we poor atoms to be crushed in its awful embrace! "Uncle, uncle!" I cried, "we are wholly, irretrievably lost!"

"What, then my young friend, is your new cause of terror and alarm?" he said, in his calmest manner. "What fear you now?"

"What do I fear now!" I cried, in fierce and angry tones. "Do you not see that the walls of the shaft are in motion? do you not see that the solid granite masses are cracking? do you not feel the terrible, torrid heat? do you not observe the awful boiling water on which we float? do you not remark this mad needle? every sign and portent of an awful earthquake?"

My uncle coolly shook his head. "An earthquake?" he questioned in the most calm and provoking tone.

"Yes."

"My nephew, I tell you that you are utterly mistaken," he continued.

"Do you not, can you not, recognize all the well-known symptoms——"

"Of an earthquake? by no means. I am expecting something far more important."

"My brain is strained beyond endurance—what, what do you mean?" I cried.

"An eruption, Harry."

"An eruption," I gasped. "We are, then, in the volcanic shaft of a crater in full action and vigor."

"I have every reason to think so," said the Professor in a smiling tone, "and I beg to tell you that it is the most fortunate thing that could happen to us."

The most fortunate thing! Had my uncle really and truly gone mad? What did he mean by these awful words —what did he mean by this terrible calm, this solemn smile?

"What!" cried I, in the height of my exasperation, "we are on the way to an eruption, are we? Fatality has cast us into a well of burning and boiling lava, of rocks on fire, of boiling water, in a word, filled with every kind of eruptive matter? We are about to be expelled, thrown up, vomited, spit out of the interior of the earth, in common with huge blocks of granite, with showers of cinders and scoriæ, in a wild whirlwind of flame, and you say—the most fortunate thing which could happen to us."

"Yes," replied the Professor, looking at me calmly from under his spectacles, "it is the only chance which remains to us of ever escaping from the interior of the earth to the light of day."

It is quite impossible that I can put on paper the thousand strange, wild thoughts which followed this extraordinary announcement. But my uncle was right, quite right, and never had he appeared to me so audacious and so convinced as when he looked me calmly in the face and spoke of the chances of an eruption—of our being cast upon mother earth once more through the gaping crater of a volcano!

While we were speaking we were still ascending; we passed the whole night going up, or to speak more scientifically, in an ascensional motion. The fearful noise redoubled; I was ready to suffocate. I seriously believed that my last hour was approaching, and yet, so strange is imagination, all I thought of was some childish hypothesis or other. In such circumstances you do not choose your own thoughts. They overcome you.

It was quite evident that we were being cast upwards by eruptive matter; under the raft there was a mass of boiling water, and under this was a heaving mass of lava, and an aggregate of rocks which on reaching the summit of the water would be dispersed in every direction. That we were inside the chimney of a volcano there could no longer be the shadow of a doubt. Nothing more terrible could be conceived!

But on this occasion, instead of Sneffels, an old and extinct volcano, we were inside a mountain of fire in full activity. Several times I found myself asking, what mountain was it, and on what part of the world we should be shot out. As if it were of any consequence! In the northern regions, there could be no reasonable doubt about that. Before it went decidedly mad, the compass had never made the slightest mistake. From the cape of Saknussemm, we had been swept away to the northward many hundreds of leagues. Now the question was, were we once more under Iceland—should we be belched forth on to the earth through the crater of Mount Hecla, or should we reappear through one of the other seven fire-funnels of the island? Taking in my mental vision a radius of five hundred leagues to the westward, I could see under this parallel only the little-known volcanoes of the northwest coasts of America. To the east one only existed somewhere about the eightieth degree of latitude, the Esk, upon the island of Jean Mayen, not far from the frozen regions of Spitzbergen. It was not craters that were wanting, and many of them were big enough to vomit a whole army; all I wished to know was the particular one towards which we were making with such fearful velocity. I often think now of my folly; as if I should have expected to escape!

Towards morning, the ascending motion became greater and greater. If the degree of heat increased instead of decreasing, as we approached the surface of the earth, it was simply because the causes were local and wholly due to volcanic influence. Our very style of locomotion left in my mind no doubt upon the subject. An enormous force, a force of some hundred of combined atmospheres produced by vapors accumulated and long compressed in the interior of the earth, were hoisting us upwards with irresistible power.

But though we were approaching the light of day, to what fearful dangers were we about to be exposed? Instant death appeared the only fate which we could expect or contemplate.

Soon a dim, sepulchral light penetrated the vertical gallery, which became wider and wider. I could make out to the right and left long dark corridors like immense tunnels, from which awful and horrid vapors poured out. Tongues of fire, sparkling and crackling, appeared about to lick us up. The hour had come!

"Look, uncle, look!" I cried.

"Well, what you see are the great sulphurous flames. Nothing more common in connection with an eruption."

" But if they lap us round! " I angrily replied.

" They will not lap us round," was his quiet and serene answer.

" But it will be all the same in the end if they stifle us," I cried.

" We shall not be stifled. The gallery is rapidly becoming wider and wider, and if it be necessary, we will presently leave the raft and take refuge in some fissure in the rock."

" But the water, the water, which is continually ascending? " I despairingly replied.

" There is no longer any water, Harry," he answered, " but a kind of lava paste, which is heaving us up, in company with itself, to the mouth of the crater."

In truth, the liquid column of water had wholly disappeared to give place to dense masses of boiling eruptive matter. The temperature was becoming utterly insupportable, and a thermometer exposed to this atmosphere would have marked between 189 and 190 degrees Fahrenheit. Perspiration rushed from every pore. But for the extraordinary rapidity of our ascent we should have been stifled.

Nevertheless, the Professor did not carry out his proposition of abandoning the raft; and he did quite wisely. Those few ill-joined beams offered, any way, a solid surface—a support which elsewhere must have utterly failed us.

Towards eight o'clock in the morning a new incident startled us. The ascensional movement suddenly ceased. The raft became still and motionless. " What is the matter now? " I said, querulously, very much startled by this change.

" A simple halt," replied my uncle.

" Is the eruption about to fail? " I asked.

" I hope not."

Without making any reply, I rose. I tried to look around me. Perhaps the raft, checked by some projecting rock, opposed a momentary resistance to the eruptive mass. In this case, it was absolutely necessary to release it as quickly as possible.

Nothing of the kind had occurred. The column of cinders, of scoriæ, of broken rocks and earth, had wholly ceased to ascend. " I tell you, uncle, that the eruption has stopped," was my oracular decision.

" Ah," said my uncle, " you think so, my boy. You are wrong. Do not be in the least alarmed; this sudden moment of calm will not last long, be assured. It has already endured five minutes, and before we are many minutes older we shall be continuing our journey to the mouth of the crater."

All the time he was speaking the Professor continued to consult his chronometer, and he was probably right in his prognostics. Soon the raft resumed its motion, in a very rapid and disorderly way, which lasted two minutes or thereabout; and then again it stopped as suddenly as before. " Good," said my uncle, observing the hour, " in ten minutes we shall start again."

" In ten minutes? "

" Yes—precisely. We have to do with a volcano, the eruption of which is intermittent. We are compelled to breathe just as it does."

Nothing could be more true. At the exact minute he had indicated, we were again launched on high with extreme rapidity. Not to be cast off the raft, it was necessary to hold on to the beams. Then the hoist again ceased. Many times since have I thought of this singular phenomenon without being able to find for it any satisfactory explanation. Nevertheless, it appeared quite clear to me, that we were not in the principal chimney of the volcano, but in an accessory conduit, where we felt the counter shock of the great and principal tunnel filled by burning lava.

It is impossible for me to say how many times this maneuver was repeated. All that I can remember is, that on every ascensional motion, we were hoisted up with ever-increasing velocity, as if we had been launched from a huge projectile. During the sudden halts we were nearly stifled; during the moments of projection the hot air took away our breath.

I thought for a moment of the voluptuous joy of suddenly finding myself in the hyperborean regions with the cold 30 degrees below zero! My exalted imagination pictured to itself the vast snowy plains of the arctic regions, and I was impatient to roll myself on the icy carpet of the north pole. By degrees my head, utterly overcome by a series of violent emotions, began to give way to hallucination. I was delirious. Had it not been for the powerful arms of Hans the guide, I should have broken my head against the granite masses of the shaft.

I have, in consequence, kept no account of what followed for many hours. I have a vague and confused remembrance of continual detonations, of the shaking of the huge granitic mass, and of the raft going round like a spinning top. It floated on the stream of hot lava, amidst a falling cloud of cinders. The huge flames roaring, wrapped us around.

A storm of wind which appeared to be cast forth from an immense ventilator roused up the interior fires of the earth. It was a hot incandescent blast!

At last I saw the figure of Hans as if enveloped in the huge halo of burning blaze, and no other sense remained to me but that sinister dread which the condemned victim may be supposed to feel when led to the mouth of a cannon, at the supreme moment when the shot is fired and his limbs are dispersed into empty space.

CHAPTER XLIII
DAYLIGHT AT LAST

WHEN I opened my eyes I felt the hand of the guide clutching me firmly by the belt. With his other hand he supported my uncle. I was not grievously wounded, but bruised all over in the most remarkable manner. After a moment I looked around, and found that I was lying down on the slope of a mountain not two yards from a yawning gulf into which I should have fallen had I made the slightest false step. Hans had saved me from death, while I rolled insensible on the flanks of the crater.

" Where are we? " dreamily asked my uncle, who literally appeared to be disgusted at having returned to earth. The eider-down hunter simply shrugged his shoulders as a mark of total ignorance.

" In Iceland? " I replied, not positively but interrogatively.

"*Nej*," said Hans.

" How do you mean? " cried the Professor; " no—what are your reasons? "

" Hans is wrong," said I, rising.

After all the innumerable surprises of this journey, a yet more singular one was reserved to us. I expected to see a cone covered by snow, by extensive and wide-spread glaciers, in the midst of the arid deserts of the extreme northern regions, beneath the full rays of a polar sky, beyond the highest latitudes. But contrary to all our expectations, I, my uncle, and the Icelander, were cast upon the slope of a mountain calcined by the burning rays of a sun which was literally baking us with its fires. I could not believe my eyes, but the actual heat which affected my body allowed me no chance of doubting. We came out of the crater half naked, and the radiant star from which we had asked nothing for two months, was good enough to be prodigal to us of light and warmth—a light and warmth we could easily have dispensed with.

When our eyes were accustomed to the light we had lost sight of so long, I used them to rectify the errors of my imagination. Whatever happened, we should have been at Spitzbergen, and I was in no humor to yield to anything but the most absolute proof.

After some delay, the Professor spoke. " Hem! " he said, in a hesitating kind of way, " it really does not look like Iceland."

" But supposing it were the island of Jean Mayen? " I ventured to observe.

" Not in the least, my boy. This is not one of the volcanoes of the north, with its hills of granite and its crown of snow."

" Nevertheless——"

" Look, look, my boy," said the Professor, as dogmatically as usual. Right above our heads, at a great height, opened the crater of a volcano from which escaped, from one quarter of an hour to the other, with a very loud explosion, a lofty jet of flame mingled with pumice stone, cinders, and lava. I could feel the convulsions of nature in the mountain, which breathed like a huge whale, throwing up from time to time fire and air through its enormous vents.

Below, and floating along a slope of considerable angularity, the stream of eruptive matter spread away to a depth which did not give the volcano a height of three hundred fathoms. Its base disappeared in a perfect forest of green trees, among which I perceived olives, fig trees, and vines loaded with rich grapes. Certainly this was not the ordinary aspect of the Arctic regions. About that there could not be the slightest doubt.

When the eye was satisfied at its glimpse of this verdant expanse it fell upon the waters of a lovely sea or beautiful lake, which made of this enchanted land an island of not many leagues in extent. Towards the setting sun, some distant shores were to be made out on the edge of the horizon. In one place appeared a prodigiously lofty cone, above the summit of which hung dark and heavy clouds.

"Where can we be?" I asked, speaking in a low and solemn voice.

Hans shut his eyes with an air of indifference, and my uncle looked on without clearly understanding. "Whatever this mountain may be," he said, at last, "I must confess it is rather warm. The explosions do not leave off, and I do not think it is worth while to have left the interior of a volcano and remain here to receive a huge piece of rock upon one's head. Let us carefully descend the mountain and discover the real state of the case. To confess the truth, I am dying of hunger and thirst."

Decidedly the Professor had ceased to be a truly reflective character. For myself, forgetting all my necessities, ignoring my fatigues and sufferings, I should have remained still for several hours longer—but it was necessary to follow my companions.

The slope of the volcano was very steep and slippery; we slid over piles of ashes, avoiding the streams of hot lava which glided about like fiery serpents. Still, while we were advancing, I spoke with extreme volubility, for my imagination was too full not to explode in words. "We are in Asia!" I exclaimed; "we are on the coast of India, in the great Malay islands, in the center of Oceana. We have crossed the one half of the globe to come out right at the antipodes of Europe!"

"But the compass!" exclaimed my uncle; "explain that to me!"

"Yes—the compass," I said, with considerable hesitation. "I grant that is a difficulty. According to it, we have always been going northward."

"Then it lied."

"Hem—to say it lied is rather a harsh word," was my answer.

"Then we are at the north pole——"

"The pole—no—well—well, I give it up," was my reply. The plain truth was, that there was no explanation possible. I could make nothing of it.

All the while we were approaching this beautiful verdure, hunger and thirst tormented me fearfully. Happily, after two long hours' march, a beautiful country spread out before us, covered by olives, pomegranates, and vines, which appeared to belong to anybody and everybody. In the state of destitution into which we had fallen, we were not particular to a grape.

What delight it was to press these delicious fruits to our lips, and to bite at grapes and pomegranates fresh from the vine. Not far off, near some fresh and mossy grass, under the delicious shade of some trees, I discovered a spring of fresh water, into which we voluptuously laved our faces, hands, and feet.

While we were all giving way to the delights of newfound pleasures, a little child appeared between two tufted olive trees. "Ah," cried I, "an inhabitant of this happy country."

The little fellow was poorly dressed, weak and suffering, and appeared terribly alarmed at our appearance. Halfnaked, with tangled, matted and ragged beards, we did look supremely ill-favored; and unless the country was a bandit land, we were not unlikely to alarm the inhabitants!

Just as the boy was about to take to his heels, Hans ran after him, and brought him back, despite his cries and kicks. My uncle tried to look as gentle as possible, and then spoke in German. "What is the name of this mountain, my friend?"

The child made no reply.

"Good," said my uncle, with a very positive air of conviction, "we are not in Germany." He then made the same demand in English, of which language he was an excellent scholar.

The child shook its head and made no reply.

" Is he dumb? " cried the Professor, who was rather proud of his polyglot knowledge of languages, and making the same demand in French. The boy only stared in his face.

" I must perforce try him in Italian," said my uncle, with a shrug. *" Dove noi siamo? "*

" Yes, tell me where we are? " I added, impatiently and eagerly.

Again the boy remained silent.

" My fine fellow, do you or do you not mean to speak? " cried my uncle, who began to get angry. He shook him and spoke another dialect of the Italian language. *" Come si noma questa isola? "*—what is the name of this island?

" Stromboli," replied the rickety little shepherd, dashing away from Hans and disappearing in the olive groves.

Stromboli! What effect on the imagination did these few words produce! We were in the center of the Mediterranean; amid the Eastern archipelago of mythological memory; in the ancient Strongylos, where Æolus kept the wind and the tempest chained up. And those blue mountains, which rose towards the rising of the sun, were the mountains of Calabria. And that mighty volcano which rose on the southern horizon was Etna, the fierce and celebrated Etna!

" Stromboli! Stromboli! " I repeated to myself. My uncle played a regular accompaniment to my gestures and words. We were singing together like an ancient chorus. Ah—what a journey—what a marvelous and extraordinary journey! Here we had entered the earth by one volcano, and we had come out by another. And this other was situated more than twelve hundred leagues from Sneffels, from that drear country of Iceland cast away on the confines of the earth. The wondrous chances of this expedition had transported us to the most harmonious and beautiful of earthly lands.

After a delicious repast of fruits and fresh water, we again continued our journey in order to reach the port of Stromboli. To say how we had reached the island would scarcely have been prudent. The superstitious character of the Italians would have been at work, and we should have been called demons vomited from the infernal regions. It was therefore necessary to pass for humble and unfor-

tunate shipwrecked travelers. It was certainly less striking and romantic, but it was decidedly safer.

As we advanced, I could hear my worthy uncle muttering to himself—"But the compass. The compass most
certainly marked north. This is a fact I cannot explain
in any way."

"Well, the fact is," said I, with an air of disdain, "we
must not explain anything. It will be much more easy."

"I should like to see a professor of the Johanneum Institution, who is unable to explain a cosmic phenomenon—it
would indeed be strange." And speaking thus; my uncle,
half-naked, his leathern purse round his loins, and his spectacles upon his nose, became once more the terrible Professor of Mineralogy.

An hour after leaving the wood of olives, we reached
the fort of San Vicenza, where Hans demanded the price
of his thirteenth week of service. My uncle paid him, with
many warm shakes of the hand.

At that moment, if he did not indeed quite share our
natural emotion, he allowed his feelings so far to give way
as to indulge in an extraordinary expression for him.
With the tips of two fingers he gently pressed our hands
and smiled.

CHAPTER XLIV
THE JOURNEY ENDED

THIS is the final conclusion of a narrative which will be
probably disbelieved even by people who are astonished at
nothing. I am, however, armed at all points against human incredulity.

We were kindly received by the Strombolite fishermen,
who treated us as shipwrecked travelers. They gave us
clothes and food. After a delay of forty-eight hours, on
the 31st of September a little vessel took us to Messina,
where a few days of delightful and complete repose restored us to ourselves.

On Friday, the 4th of October, we embarked in the *Vol-
turus*, one of the postal packets of the Imperial Messagerie
of France; and three days later we landed at Marseilles,
having no other care on our minds but that of our precious

but erratic compass. This inexplicable circumstance tormented me terribly. On the 9th of October, in the evening, we reached Hamburg.

What was the astonishment of Martha, what the joy of Gretchen! I will not attempt to define it. " Now, then, Harry, that you really are a hero," she said, " there is no reason why you should ever leave me again." I looked at her. She was weeping tears of joy.

I leave it to be imagined if the return of Professor Hardwigg made or did not make a sensation in Hamburg. Thanks to the indiscretion of Martha, the news of his departure for the Interior of the Earth had been spread over the whole world.

No one would believe it—and when they saw him come back in safety they believed it all the less. But the presence of Hans and many stray scraps of information by degrees modified public opinion. Then my uncle became a great man, and I the nephew of a great man; which, at all events, is something. Hamburg gave a festival in our honor. A public meeting of the Johanneum Institution was held, at which the Professor related the whole story of his adventures, omitting only the facts in connection with the compass.

That same day he deposited in the archives of the town the document he had found, written by Saknussemm, and he expressed his great regret that circumstances, stronger than his will, did not allow him to follow the Icelandic traveler's track into the very Center of the Earth. He was modest in his glory, but his reputation only increased.

So much honor necessarily created for him many envious enemies. Of course they existed, and as his theories, supported by certain facts, contradicted the system of science upon the question of central heat, he maintained his own views both with pen and speech against the learned of every country. Although I still believe in the theory of central heat, I confess that certain circumstances, hitherto very ill defined, may modify the laws of such natural phenomena.

At the moment when these questions were being discussed with interest, my uncle received a rude shock—one that he felt very much. Hans, despite everything he could say to the contrary, quitted Hamburg; the man to whom

THE DWELLER IN THE CENTER
Page 171

we owed so much would not allow us to pay our deep debt of gratitude. He was taken with nostalgia; a love for his Icelandic home. "*Farvel,*" said he, one day, and with this one short word of adieu, he started for Reykjawik, which he soon reached in safety.

We were deeply attached to our brave eider-duck hunter. His absence will never cause him to be forgotten by those whose lives he saved, and I hope, at some not distant day, to see him again.

To conclude, I may say that our Journey into the Interior of the Earth created an enormous sensation throughout the civilized world. It was translated and printed in many languages. All the leading journals published extracts from it, which were commentated, discussed, attacked, and supported with equal animation by those who believed in its episodes, and by those who were utterly incredulous. Wonderful! My uncle enjoyed during his lifetime all the glory he deserved; and he was even offered a large sum of money, by Mr. Barnum, to exhibit himself in the United States; while I am credibly informed by a traveler that he is to be seen in waxwork at Madame Tussaud's!

But one care preyed upon his mind, a care which rendered him very unhappy. One fact remained inexplicable —that of the compass. For a learned man to be baffled by such an inexplicable phenomenon was very aggravating. But heaven was merciful, and in the end my uncle was happy. One day, while he put some minerals belonging to his collection in order, I fell upon the famous compass and examined it keenly. For six months it had lain unnoticed and untouched. I looked at it with curiosity, which soon became surprise. I gave a loud cry. The Professor, who was at hand, soon joined me.

" What is the matter? " he cried.

" The compass! "

" What then? "

" Why, its needle points to the south and not to the north."

" My dear boy, you must be dreaming."

" I am not dreaming. See the poles are changed."

" Changed! "

My uncle put on his spectacles, examined the instrument, and leaped with joy, shaking the whole house. A clear light fell upon our minds.

" Here it is! " he cried, as soon as he had recovered the use of his speech. " Our error is now easily explained. But to what phenomenon do we owe this alteration in the needle! "

" Nothing more simple."

" Explain yourself, my boy. I am on thorns."

" During the storm, upon the Central Sea, the ball of fire which made a magnet of the iron in our raft, turned our compass topsy-turvy."

" Ah! " cried the Professor, with a loud and ringing laugh, " it was a trick of that inexplicable electricity."

From that hour my uncle was the happiest of learned men, and I the happiest of ordinary mortals. For my pretty Virland girl, abdicating her position as ward, took her place in the house in Königstrasse in the double quality of niece and wife. We need scarcely mention that her uncle was the illustrious Professor Hardwigg, corresponding member of all the scientific, geographical, mineralogical and geological societies of the five quarters of the globe.

THE END

Adventures of Captain Hatteras

BOOK I

The English at the North Pole

The English at the North Pole

CHAPTER I
THE " FORWARD "

O-MORROW, at ebb tide, the brig *Forward* will sail from the New Prince's Docks, captain K. Z.; chief officer, Richard Shandon; destination unknown."

Such was the announcement which appeared in the *Liverpool Herald* of April 5, 1860.

The departure of a brig is not a very important event for one of the largest trading ports in England. Indeed, who would notice it among the crowd of ships, of every tonnage and every nation, which the long miles of floating docks can scarcely contain; and yet from an early hour on the morning of April 9th, numbers of people began to assemble on the wharf. The whole maritime population of Liverpool seemed to agree to congregate there, and not only the sailors, but all classes, came flocking thither. The dock laborers left their work, the city clerks their dingy counting-houses, and the shopkeepers their deserted shops. Omnibus after omnibus set down its load of passengers outside the dock walls, till the entire city appeared to have turned out to see the *Forward* sail.

The *Forward* was a brig of 170 tons, fitted up with a screw propeller and an engine of 120-horse-power. She might easily have been confounded with other brigs in port by the ordinary onlooker, and yet to the practiced eye of a sailor there were certain peculiarities about her which made her unmistakable, as appeared from the conversation of a group of men assembled on the deck of the *Nautilus*, a vessel lying close by. They were eagerly discussing the probable destination of the *Forward*, and each one had his own conjecture.

"What do you think of her masts?" said one. "It certainly ain't usual for steamships to have such large sails."

"Depend upon it," said a broad, red-faced quartermaster, "that yon craft reckons more on her masts than her engine. She hasn't all that topsail for nothing. To me it is clear enough the *Forward* is bound for the Arctic or Antarctic Seas, where great ice mountains shut out the wind rather more than suits a strong, brave ship."

"You must be right, Master Cornhill," said a third sailor; "and have you noticed the bow, what a straight line it makes to the sea?"

"Ay! and more than that, it is sheathed with cast-steel as sharp as a razor, which would cut a three-decker in two if the *Forward* fell foul of it sideways at full speed," replied Cornhill.

"That it would," added a Mersey pilot, "for she can make fourteen knots an hour easily with her screw. It was wonderful to see how she cut through the water on her trial trip. Take my word for it, she's a good runner, and no mistake."

"Besides," said Cornhill, "do you see the size of the helm-post?"

"Yes; but what does that prove?"

"That proves, my boys," said Cornhill, in a disdainful, self-satisfied manner, "that you can neither see nor think; that proves that it was a great matter to give full play to the rudder, a very necessary thing in the frozen seas of the north."

"Right, right," said the sailors.

"And, what's more," continued one of them, "the loading of the ship confirms your opinion. I had it from Clifton, who is one of her men, that she is taking provisions for five years, and coals too. That is all the cargo; nothing but coals and provisions, and great bales of woolen clothing and seal-skins."

"That settles it, of course," replied Cornhill. "But you say you know Clifton—hasn't he told you where they are going?"

"He doesn't know himself; he is in perfect ignorance. All the crew have been engaged like that. Where he's going, he'll hardly know himself before he's there."

" It looks to me very much as if they were all going to Old Nick," said an incredulous listener.

" And did you ever hear of such wages? " continued Clifton's friend. " Five times more than the common pay! Ay, if it hadn't been for that, Dick Shandon wouldn't have found a man to sign the articles. To make a voyage in such a queer-looking ship, bound for nobody knows where, and coming back nobody knows when—I must confess it wouldn't suit me."

" It doesn't matter much whether it would or not, old fellow, for you couldn't go; they wouldn't have you on board the *Forward*," said Cornhill.

" Pray, why not? "

" Because you can't meet one of the conditions required. I am told that all married men are ineligible, so you are shut out."

" There's so much bounce about the brig altogether," Cornhill went on, " even down to the very name, the *Forward*. Forward where to? And then there is no captain! "

" Yes, there is," said a frank, boyish-looking young sailor.

" What! a captain has turned up? "

" Yes, a captain."

" You are fancying, youngster, that Shandon is the captain," said Cornhill.

" But I tell you," returned the lad, " that——"

" And I tell you," interrupted Cornhill, " that Shandon is the mate and nothing more. He is a brave hardy sailor, an old hand in whaling expeditions, and a thorough good fellow, quite fit to be captain, but captain he is not, any more than you or I. He doesn't even know who is to take the command. At the right time the real captain is to make his appearance, but when that is to be, or in what part of the world, no one knows, for Shandon has not said, nor is he allowed to reveal the ship's destination."

" All that may be, Master Cornhill," replied the young sailor, " But I assure you that at this very moment there is someone on board, someone whose arrival was announced in the very letter which contained the offer to Mr. Shandon of chief officer's berth! "

" What! " retorted Cornhill, frowning angrily at the

audacious youngster. " Do you dare to stand out that there is a captain on board? "

" Yes, certainly, Master Cornhill."

" You say that to my face ! "

" Of course I do; I had it from Johnson, one of the officers on board."

" From Mr. Johnson? "

" Yes, he told me himself."

" Johnson told you, did he? "

" He not only told me, but showed me the captain."

" Showed you the captain ! " repeated Cornhill in blank amaze.

" Yes ! he showed me the captain."

" And you really saw him? "

" Yes ! with my own eyes."

" And who is it, pray? "

" It is a dog."

" A dog? "

" A dog with four feet? "

" Yes ! "

The sailors of the *Nautilus* seemed stupefied. Under any other circumstances, such a declaration would have provoked shouts of laughter. The idea of a dog being captain of a brig of 170 tons. It was too ludicrous. But there was something altogether so extraordinary about this *Forward* that one need think twice before denying or even ridiculing the boy's assertion, and instead of laughing, Cornhill said gravely:

" So it was Johnson who introduced you to this novel sort of a captain, and you actually saw him? "

" As plain as I see you."

" Well, Cornhill, what do you think of that? " asked the sailors, eagerly.

" I think nothing," replied Cornhill, roughly, " except that the *Forward* either belongs to the devil, or to some fools let loose from Bedlam ! "

The crew continued silently gazing at the wonderful brig, watching the final preparations for departure, but not one among them dared to say, or even so much as pretended to believe, that Johnson had been only making a fool of the boy, and imposing on his credulity.

The story of the dog had already got abroad, and more

than one among the crowds that thronged the quays sought to catch a glimpse of this dog-captain, half-believing him supernatural.

Besides, for many months past the *Forward* had been attracting public attention. The peculiarities about her build, the mystery hanging over her, the incognito preserved by the captain, the strange way in which Shandon had received his appointment, the special care taken in selecting the crew, and the unknown destination—all combined to invest her with a singular charm of romance.

The *Forward* had been constructed at Birkenhead by Messrs. Scott & Co., one of the most famous shipbuilders in England. The firm had received from Richard Shandon a minute plan, detailing every particular as to tonnage and dimensions, and also a sketch drawn with the greatest care, and evidently the production of a practiced seaman. As considerable sums were forthcoming, the work was commenced at once, and proceeded with as rapidly as possible.

The brig was characterized by the utmost solidity. She was evidently intended to resist enormous pressure, for the frame was not only made of teak-wood—a sort of oak which grows in India, and is remarkable for its extreme hardness—but was firmly bound together by strong iron bars. It was indeed a matter of surprise among the seafaring population that frequented the building yard, why the entire hull was not sheet iron like most steamers, and many inquiries were put to the shipwrights, but all the answer received was that they were obeying orders.

By slow degrees the brig began to take shape on the stocks, and connoisseurs were struck by the elegance and strength of her proportions. As the crew of the *Nautilus* had remarked, the stem made a right angle with the keel. It had no breakhead, but a sharp edge of cast steel made in the foundries of R. Hawthorn, at Newcastle. This metal prow glittering in the sun, gave a peculiar look to the ship, though there was nothing absolutely warlike about it. However, there was a cannon of 16 lbs. caliber mounted on the forecastle, on a pivot, to allow of its being easily pointed in all directions; and yet, in spite of both stem and cannon, the vessel was not the least like a ship intended for battle.

On the 5th of February the *Forward* was ready, and made a successful launch in the presence of an immense crowd of spectators.

The day after the launch, the engine arrived from Newcastle, from the works of Messrs. Hawthorn. This engine, of 120-horsepower, and provided with oscillating cylinders, was of considerable size for a brig of 170 tons, but did not take up much room. As soon as it was placed on board, the work of provisioning began, and no easy matter it was to stow away food for six years. The stores consisted principally of salted and smoked meat, dried fish, biscuit and flour, mountains of coffee and tea were thrown into the hold in a perfect avalanche. Richard Shandon superintended personally the storage of this precious cargo, arranging it like a man who understood his business. Everything was numbered and labeled and disposed in the most orderly manner. A large quantity of pemmican was also taken on board, an Indian preparation, which contains much nourishment in small bulk.

The nature of the provisions left no doubt as to the length of the cruise; and to an observing eye, there was none as to the ship's destination, at the sight of those barrels of lime-juice, and lumps of chalk, and packets of mustard, and sorrel, and cochlearia seed; in other words, the abundance of anti-scorbutic preparations proved that the *Forward* was bound for the Polar Seas. Shandon had no doubt received special orders about this part of the cargo, for he paid studious attention to it, and also fitted up the medicine chest with the most scrupulous care.

The stock of firearms was not great, a reassuring fact to timid people, but on the other hand, the powder-magazine was full to overflowing. What was it intended for? There was far more than one solitary cannon could possibly use. Then there were also enormous saws, and other powerful instruments, such as levers, hand-saws, heaps of bullets, immense hatchets, not to speak of a goodly number of blasting cylinders, the explosion of which would have blown the Custom House at Liverpool into the air. It was all very strange, if not alarming, even without taking into account the fusees, and signals, and fireworks of all descriptions.

The boats too were objects of great curiosity to the gaping crowd that hung about the New Prince's Docks. There was a canoe made of tinned iron, covered with gutta-percha, a long mahogany whaling-boat, and a number of halkett-boats or india-rubber cloaks, which could be converted into canoes by inflating the lining.

The *Forward* was certainly altogether a most mysterious, puzzling vessel, and people grew quite excited about her, now that the hour for sailing had come.

CHAPTER II
THE UNEXPECTED LETTER

EIGHT months prior to the time when our story commences, Richard Shandon had received the following letter:

"ABERDEEN, *Aug. 2nd*, 1859.

"Sir,—This letter is to inform you that a sum of £16,000 sterling has been placed in the hands of Messrs. Marcuart & Co., bankers, Liverpool. I also enclose checks signed by me, which you can draw on the said bankers up to the above-mentioned amount.

"You do not know me. It matters not. I know you. That is the most important thing.

"I offer you the place of chief officer on board the brig *Forward,* bound for an expedition which may be long and perilous.

"If you refuse, that is all about it; if you accept, your salary will be £500, to be raised one-tenth each year you are away.

"The brig *Forward* has at present no existence. You will have to get her built, and ready to go to sea by the beginning of April at the latest.

"I subjoin a detailed plan and a draft, to which you will scrupulously adhere. The ship is to be constructed by Messrs. Scott & Co., who will arrange matters with you.

"I beg you will pay special attention to the selection of the crew of the *Forward*. This will consist of the captain, myself, the chief officer, yourself, a second mate, a boatswain, two engineers, an ice-master, eight sailors, and two stokers—eighteen men altogether, including Dr. Clawbonny, of your city, who will introduce himself to you at the right time.

"It is necessary that all the men chosen for the expedition of the *Forward* shall be English, unencumbered by family ties, unmarried, sober, as neither beer nor spirits are allowed on board, and ready for any enterprise and any suffering. Give the preference to those of sanguine temperament, who possess a great amount of animal heat.

"You will offer them five times as much as the ordinary wages, with an increase of one-tenth each year of service. At the close of the expedition £500 is guaranteed to each man and £2,000 to yourself. These deposits will be left with Messrs. Marcuart & Co., the aforesaid bankers.

"The campaign will be long and arduous, but honorable. You need have no hesitation about it, Mr. Shandon.

"Reply to me by letter, addressed to *K. Z., Poste restante, Gotteborg, Sweden.*

"P. S.—On the 15th of February next you will be forwarded a large Danish stag-hound with loose hanging lips, very dark in color, and striped with black. You will take him on board, and order him to be fed with barley bread mixed with boiled greaves. You will notify his safe arrival to me at Leghorn, Italy, addressed to the same initials.

"The captain of the *Forward* will present himself, and make himself known when he is required. You will receive further instructions just before you sail.

"K. Z., Captain of the *Forward.*
"To Mr. Richard Shandon, Liverpool."

CHAPTER III
DR. CLAWBONNY

RICHARD SHANDON was a good sailor and a man of established reputation. He had been in command of whalers for years, and was familiar with the Arctic Seas. A letter like the foregoing did not consequently astonish him so much as might have been expected. Astonished he certainly was, but in a cool, composed sort of fashion, like a man who has received similar communications before. He was in a position, too, to meet the required conditions. He had neither wife, nor child, nor relatives; he was free, in all respects. So having no one to consult, he went straight off to the bankers, Messrs. Marcuart & Co., for "if the money is there," he said to himself, "the rest is all right."

The money was there sure enough, for Shandon was received by the firm with all respect due to a man who has £16,000 quietly waiting for him in their strong chest; so without loss of time he called for pen and ink, and wrote a letter in a large sailor-like hand, to the address given, signifying his acceptance of the offered trust.

That very same day he put himself in communication with the shipbuilders at Birkenhead, and twenty-four hours after, the keel of the *Forward* was planted on the stocks in their building-yard.

Richard Shandon was about forty years of age, a robust, brave, energetic fellow—three qualifications necessary to a sailor, for they impart self-reliance, vigor, and sangfroid. He got the character of being jealous and difficult to get on with, one who had made his men fear him, but never gained their love. This did not interfere, however, with his getting a crew, for he was too well known as a skillful leader to have any trouble in finding men to follow him.

Shandon was rather afraid, though, that the mysterious nature of the enterprise would cripple his movements, and determined to noise it abroad as little as possible. "That's my best plan," he said to himself, "for those old ferrets would be down on me, who must know the why and the wherefore of everything, and as I am quite ignorant myself, I should be rather at a loss for an answer. This K. Z. is a queer old fellow, and no mistake, but, after all, what does that matter? He knows me, and reckons on me, and that is enough. As to the ship, she will turn out a beauty, and my name is not Richard Shandon, if she is not meant for the frozen seas. But I'll keep that secret to myself and my officers."

Shandon's next business was to pick out his men in accordance with the rules laid down by the captain. He knew a fine active young fellow, called Wall, who was thirty years of age, a capital sailor, and who had been more than one voyage to the North Seas. He offered him the post of second mate, and James Wall accepted it blindfold, for all he cared for was being on the ocean, and the destination mattered little. Shandon told him the whole story, however, from beginning to end, both to him and to a sailor named Johnson, whom he chose as boatswain.

"Not much luck to be had there," said James Wall; "But still perhaps as much there as anywhere else. Even if it is to find the North-West passage, people come back alive, right enough."

"Not always," said Johnson; "but that's no reason for not going."

"Besides, supposing we are right in our conjectures," added Shandon, "we must allow we could hardly make a voyage under more favorable circumstances. The *Forward* will be a first-rate ship, and her steam-engine will be a great help. All we want is eighteen men."

"Eighteen men?" replied Johnson; "that is the same number the American Dr. Kane had on board when he made his famous journey towards the Pole."

"It is singular enough, certainly," said Wall, "what can induce a private individual to cross the sea again, from Davis's Straits to Behring's Straits. The Franklin Expeditions have cost England more than £760,000, without producing any practical result. Who can be fool enough to throw away his own fortune into the bargain like this?"

"Don't forget, James, though," replied Shandon, "that we are reasoning on a mere supposition. Whether we are actually going to the North or the South Seas, I know no more than you. Perhaps, indeed, it is on some new quest altogether. Moreover, there is a Dr. Clawbonny to make his appearance some of these days, who will no doubt be commissioned to give us fuller information. We shall see all in good time."

"Ay! we must just wait," said Johnson, "And, meantime, I am going to make it my business to look after right men to go with us; and as to their having plenty of animal heat in them, I'll guarantee that before hand. You may safely leave that to me."

This Johnson was a valuable man, well acquainted with the northern latitudes. He had been quartermaster on board the *Phoenix*, one of the vessels despatched in search of Franklin in 1853. The brave fellow had accompanied Lieutenant Bellot in his journey across the ice, and been eye-witness of his death. Johnson knew the whole sea-faring population of Liverpool, and set to work immediately to select his crew

He was so effectually aided by Shandon and Wall, that by the beginning of December the number was complete. But the task had not been easy; many had been attracted by the tempting pay offer, but had not courage to risk the unknown expedition, while more than one who had bravely pledged himself to go, came and retracted his word and gave back his advance note, having been dissuaded by his friends from so hazardous an undertaking. All, of course, wished to penetrate the mystery, and so pressed Shandon with questions that he was obliged to refer them to Johnson, who gave the same unvarying answers to each.

" What is it you want me to tell you, old boy? " he would say. " I know no more than you do. Anyhow, you'll be in good company, with jolly fellows who know what they're about. That's something, isn't it? So be quick and make up your mind—take it or leave it! "

Sometimes he would add, " My only difficulty is which to choose, for such high wages as you are offered you will find plenty to jump at them. Not a man among you ever heard of such pay being given before."

" Well, it certainly is a great temptation; we should get enough to live on all the rest of our days," said the sailors.

" I don't conceal from you," continued Johnson, " that the expedition will be a long one, and full of hardship and danger. That is formally told us in our instructions, so let us have a clear understanding, that each man may know what he undertakes; he commits himself, in all probability to attempt all that is, humanly speaking, possible, and perhaps even more. If you haven't a brave heart, then, and an iron constitution, or if you can't look the certainty in the face that there are twenty chances to one against your ever returning, you had better be off, and leave the berth for somebody less chicken-hearted."

" But at least tell us who the captain is," was the rejoinder.

" The captain is Richard Shandon, his friend, till he introduces you another."

Now, to speak the truth, Richard thought this himself, and quietly indulged the hope that, at the last moment, he would receive definite instructions about the voyage, and have entire command placed in his hands.

Shandon and Johnson had implicitly obeyed the injunctions given for choosing the crew. They were all fresh and florid looking, full of energy and pluck, and having caloric enough in them to heat the engine almost; in fact, the very men to stand extreme cold. In outward appearance, certainly, they were not all equally strong; and two or three among them, especially two sailors called Gripper and Garry, and Simpson the harpooner, Shandon almost hesitated to take, for they belonged to " Pharaoh's lean kine," but they were well-built, and their circulation was good, so their names were entered.

The whole crew were Protestants, belonging to the same religious denomination. It was a matter of some importance that the men should think alike, as far as creed was concerned, to prevent party strife; for it has been always found in long voyages that assembling the men for reading the Scriptures and common prayer is a powerful means of promoting harmony, and of cheering them in hours of despondency. Shandon knew by experience the excellent moral effect of such practices, as they are invariably adopted on board all vessels that winter in 'Arctic regions.

The next business of Shandon and his officers was the provisioning of the ship. In doing this they strictly followed the instructions of the captain—instructions so clear, precise, and minute, that the quantity and quality were given of even the smallest article. Ready money was paid for everything, and a discount of eight per cent, received, which Richard carefully put to the credit of K. Z.

Crew, provisions, and cargo were all ready by January, 1860. The *Forward* was rapidly assuming proportions, and Shandon never let a day pass without a visit to Birkenhead, to see how things went on. On the 23rd of that same month, he was going across as usual in one of the large steamers that ferry passengers over the Mersey. It was one of those foggy mornings when you can scarcely see your hand before you; but, in spite of the obscurity, Shandon could make out the figure of some stranger advancing

V. II Venre

towards him, and as he got nearer, saw it was a little stout man, with a bright jovial face and kindly eye, who came up, and seizing both his hands, shook them so heartily in his own, in such an impulsive, familiar, free-and-easy style, that a Frenchman would have said he came from the sunny south.

But though the new comer was not a Southerner, he made a narrow escape of it, for he was full of talk and gesticulation, and seemed as if he would explode unless he came out with all he thought. His small intellectual eyes and large mobile mouth were safety-valves to let out the steam, and he talked and talked so incessantly that Shandon was fairly overpowered. He made a shrewd guess, however, who this voluble little man was, and, taking advantage of a momentary pause, managed to say, " Doctor Clawbonny, I presume? "

" Himself in person, my good sir. Here I have been seeking you for a whole quarter of an hour, and asking everybody for you everywhere. Only imagine my impatience! Five minutes more, and I should have lost my wits. It is really then Richard Shandon I see. You actually exist? you're not a myth? Your hand, your hand, that I may grasp it in mine. Yes, it is a genuine flesh and blood hand, and there is a veritable Richard Shandon. Well, come, if there's a chief officer, there must be a brig called the *Forward* that he commands; and if he commands she is going to sail, and if she's going to sail she will take Dr. Clawbonny on board."

" Yes, Doctor, surely. There is a brig called the *Forward,* and she is going to sail, and I am Richard Shandon."

" That's logic," said the Doctor, drawing a long breath, " that's logic, and I am overjoyed to hear it, for now I have reached the summit of my ambition. I have waited long, and wished to go a voyage; and now with you to command——"

" Allow me," interrupted Shandon.

But Clawbonny took no notice, and went on, " With you; we are sure of pushing onward, and never yielding an inch of our ground."

" But, sir," began Shandon again.

" You are a tried man, sir; you have seen service. You have a right to be proud."

" If you will please allow me to——"

" No, I will not allow your skill, and bravery, and hardi-
hood to be underrated even by you.   The captain who has
chosen you for his chief officer knows his man, I'll be
bound."

" But that's not the question," said Shandon, impatiently.

" Well, and what is the question, then?   Don't keep me
in suspense, pray."

" You won't let me speak.   Please to tell me, Doctor,
how you came to join in the expedition of the *Forward*."

" Well, it was through a letter which I have here from
the brave captain, a very laconic one, though it says all
that is necessary."

And drawing the said letter out of his pocket, he handed
it to Shandon, who read as follows:—

INVERNESS, *Jan. 22nd,* 1860.

" If Dr. Clawbonny is willing to embark in the brig
Forward, let him present himself to the chief officer, Richard Shandon, who has received orders concerning him."

" The Captain of the *Forward,* K. Z.

" To Dr. Clawbonny, Liverpool."

" The letter came this morning, and here I am ready to
go on board."

" But, at any rate," said Shandon, " you know where we
are going, I suppose?"

" Not I; but what does it matter to me, so long as I go
somewhere?   People call me a learned man, but they are
much mistaken.   I know nothing, and if I happen to have
published some few books which sell pretty well, they are
not worth anything, and it is very good of the people to
buy them.   I know nothing, I tell you, except that I am
an ignoramus.   Now I have a chance of completing, or
rather recommencing, my studies in medicine, in surgery,
in history, in geography, in botany, in mineralogy, in
conchology, in geodesy, in chemistry, in natural philosophy,
in mechanics, in hydrography.   Well, I accept the offer,
and don't need much pressing, I assure you."

" Then you know nothing about the destination of the
Forward?" said Richard, in a disappointed tone.

" I know this much, Mr. Shandon, that she is going
where there will be much to learn and discover, and much

to instruct us, for we shall come across other nations with different customs from our own; she is going, in short, where I have never been."

" But you know nothing more definite than that? " exclaimed Shandon.

" I have heard some talk of her going to the North Seas. So much the better if we are bound for the Arctic."

" But don't you know the captain? " asked Shandon again.

" Not at all; but he is a brave fellow, you may be sure."

By this time the steamer had arrived at Birkenhead, and Clawbonny and Shandon landed on the pier, and at once repaired to the shipbuilding-yard. The sight of the brig almost made the little doctor beside himself with joy, and he went subsequently every day to look at her on the stocks.

He made his abode with Shandon, and undertook the arrangement of the medicine-chest, for he was a duly qualified doctor and a clever man, though rather unpractical. At twenty-five years of age he was just an ordinary surgeon, but at forty he was a learned man, well known throughout the whole city, and a leading member of the Literary and Philosophical Institute of Liverpool. He possessed a small private fortune, which enabled him to practice gratuitously in a great many cases, and his extreme amiability made him universally beloved. He never did an injury to a single human being, not even to himself. Lively and rattling as he was, and an incessant talker, he had an open heart and hand for everybody.

As soon as the news of his appointment to the *Forward* spread through the city, his friends besieged him with solicitations to remain at home. But their arguments and entreaties only made him more determined to go, and when the little man once got a crotchet in his brain no one could turn him from it.

On the 5th of February the *Forward* was launched, and two months later she was ready to go to sea.

Punctually to the time, on the very day fixed for his coming by the captain's letter, a large Danish dog made his appearance, sent by rail from Edinburgh to Richard Shandon's address. He was an ill-favored, snappish, unsociable animal, with a peculiar expression in his eye. A brass collar round his neck bore the name of the ship, and he was installed on board the same day, and a letter despatched to Leghorn to inform the captain of his safe arrival.

The crew of the *Forward* was now complete, with the exception of the captain. It numbered the following individuals: 1. The Captain, K. Z. 2. The Chief Officer. 3. The Second Officer, James Wall. 4. Doctor Clawbonny. 5. Johnson, the boatswain. 6. Simpson, the harpooner. 7. Bell, the carpenter. 8. Brunton, the chief engineer. 9. Plover, the second engineer. 10. Strong, a colored man, the cook. 11. Foker, the ice-master. 12. Wolsten, the gunsmith. 13. Bolton, sailor. 14. Garry, sailor. 15. Clifton, sailor 16. Gripper, sailor. 17. Pen, sailor. 18. Warren, stoker.

CHAPTER IV
THE DOG-CAPTAIN

THE 5th of April brought the sailing day. Dr. Clawbonny's coming on board somewhat reassured people's minds, for where the learned Doctor went it must be safe to follow; but still the sailors seemed so restless and uneasy, that Shandon longed to be fairly out at sea, for he did not feel sure of any of them till they had lost sight of land.

Dr. Clawbonny's cabin was on the poop, which took up all the stern of the vessel. The captain's cabin and the chief officer's were on either side, overlooking the deck. The captain's remained hermetically closed after being furnished according to his written directions, and the key, as he ordered, was sent to him at Lubeck, so that no one could enter but himself.

This was a great vexation to Shandon, as it damped his ambitious hopes of getting sole command. In fitting up his own cabin, he took for granted they were going to the Arctic, and knowing, as he did, so thoroughly all that was required, he left nothing wanting.

The cabin of the second mate was in the forecastle, where the men slept—a large, roomy place, with a stove in the center, and every accomodation, for the sailors were treated as precious cargo on this vessel, and well provided for.

Dr. Clawbonny looked after himself, and he had had plenty of time, as he had taken possession of his cabin since the 5th of February, the day the *Forward* was launched.

"The happiest of the animals," he said, "would be a snail, who could make a shell to his own liking, and I mean to be an intelligent snail."

And truly his shell did him credit, for the Doctor took a perfect delight in arranging his scientific treasures. His books, and herbals, and cases, and mathematical instruments; his thermometer, and barometers, and hygrometers, and udometers; his glasses, and compasses, and sextants; and maps and charts; and phials, and powders, and medicine-bottles—all were arranged and classified with an amount of order that might have shamed the British Museum. Inestimable riches were stored up in that small space of six feet square, and it must be owned the good Doctor was not a little proud of his sanctum, though three of his least corpulent friends would have sufficed to crowd it uncomfortably.

To complete the description of the *Forward* it need only further be said that the dog's-kennel was built right below the window of the mysterious cabin, but its savage inmate preferred wandering between decks and in the hold. It seemed impossible to make him sociable, nobody could do anything with him, and in the night his piteous howls would resound through the whole vessel.

What was the reason? Could it be grief for his absent master? or was it instinctive fear of the voyage? or did it bode approaching danger. This last was the common opinion among the sailors, and many a one joked over it who verily believed the poor dog was an imp of the devil.

Pen, a coarse brutal fellow at all times, rushed so furiously at the beast one day that he fell right against the capstan, and split his head open frightfully. Of course this accident was laid to the "uncanny dog's account."

Clifton was the most superstitious of all the crew, and he made the singular discovery, that whenever the animal was promenading the deck he went to the side the wind was, changing his position as the ship tacked, just as if he had been the captain.

Dr. Clawbonny was so gentle and winning that he would have tamed a tiger, but all his attempts to get into this dog's good graces were in vain.

Besides, the animal would answer to none of the names borne by his canine brethren, so in the end he got called "Captain," for he appeared perfectly familiar with ship life. This was certainly not his first voyage, and more than one of the sailors fully expected to see him some day suddenly assume the human form, and begin giving orders in a stentorian voice.

Richard Shandon had no apprehensions on that score, though he had anxieties enough of another nature, and the night before sailing he had a long confidential talk on the subject with the Doctor and his two officers.

The four sat comfortably together in the saloon indulging themselves with a glass of grog—a farewell glass, for, in accordance with the instructions received from Aberdeen, every man on board, from the captain down to the stoker, must be a total abstainer; that is to say, neither wine, nor beer, nor spirits would be allowed on board, except in case of illness, or when ordered by the doctor.

For more than an hour they had been talking over the departure of the ship next day, for if the captain's words were verified, the morning would bring a letter containing final instructions.

"I hope," said Shandon, "that if this letter doesn't give us the name of the captain, it will tell us at least the destination of the ship, or how shall we know which way to steer?"

"Goodness me!" exclaimed the impatient doctor, "were I in your place I should be off even if no letter came; it will find its way to us by hook or by crook, I'll warrant."

"You stick at nothing, Doctor. But pray, how should we direct our course then?"

"Towards the North Pole, most assuredly. That's a matter of course; it doesn't admit of a doubt."

"Not admit of a doubt!" said Wall; "and why not towards the South Pole?".

"The South Pole! Never! Would the captain ever dream of exposing a brig to all the difficulties of crossing the broad Atlantic?" said the Doctor.

"You say go to the North," continued Shandon, "but

that's a wide word. Is it to be to Spitzbergen, or Green-land, or Labrador, or Hudson's Bay? It is true enough that all these routes lead to the same impassable fields of ice; but that doesn't remove the necessity of choosing one or other, and I should be greatly puzzled to decide upon which. Can you help me, Doctor?"

"No," replied the loquacious little man, vexed at having no answer ready. "But the question is just this, if you don't get a letter, what will you do?"

"I shall do nothing; I shall wait."

"You won't sail!" cried Clawbonny, aghast at the pos-sibility.

"No, not I."

"That's the wisest way," said Johnson, quickly, while the Doctor rose, and began pacing the floor, for he was too agitated to sit still. "Yes, that's the wisest way, and yet too great delay might be attended with bad conse-quences. In the first place, this is a good time of the year; and if North it is to be, we ought to take advantage of the breaking up of the ice to get past Davis's Straits. Then, again, the men are getting more restless every day; their friends and old shipmates are constantly urging them to leave the *Forward;* and if we wait much longer we may find ourselves in a pretty fix."

"That's quite true," added James Wall; "and if once a panic got amongst the crew, they would desert to a man, and I very much doubt if you would succeed in getting fresh hands."

"But what's to be done, then?" asked Shandon.

"Just what you said," replied the Doctor, "wait; but wait till to-morrow before you begin to despair. Every one of the captain's promises have been kept hitherto, and there is no ground for believing that we shall not be told where we're going when the right time comes. For my own part, I have not the slightest doubt that we'll be in full sail to-morrow in the Irish Sea, so I vote that we have one more glass of grog, and drink to our safe voyage. It certainly has a rather mysterious beginning, but, with such sailors as you, a thousand chances to one but we'll have a prosperous ending."

"And now, sir, if I may give you my advice," said Johnson, "I would give orders to be ready to sail to-morrow, that the crew may not imagine there is any uncertainty. To-morrow, whether a letter comes or not, I would weigh anchor. Don't light the fires, for the wind bids fair to keep steady, and we shall be able to get out easily with the tide. Let the pilot come on board and we'll get over to Birkenhead, and cast anchor off the point. This will cut us off from communication with the shore, and yet be near enough to allow of this wonderful letter reaching us, should it arrive after all."

"That's well spoken, my good Johnson," said the Doctor, holding out his hand to the old tar.

"Well, so be it, then," said Shandon, "and now goodnight." They each retired to their respective cabins, but were too excited to sleep much, and were up again by sunrise.

The morning letters had all been delivered, but not one came for Richard Shandon. Still he went on with his preparations for sailing, and, as we have seen, the news had spread over Liverpool and brought together an unusual concourse of spectators. Many came on board to give a farewell embrace to a friend, or a last entreaty not to go, and some to gratify their curiosity by looking over the vessel, and trying once more to discover its real destination. But they found the chief officer more taciturn and reserved than ever, and went off grumbling.

Ten o'clock struck, and eleven; at one o'clock the tide would turn. Shandon stood on the poop gazing with uneasy troubled looks at the crowd.

It was a cloudy day and the waves were dashing high outside the basin, for there was a pretty strong south-east wind blowing, but this could not prevent them getting easily out of the Mersey.

Twelve o'clock struck and no letter. Dr. Clawbonny began to walk impatiently up and down, staring about through his eye-glass, and gesticulating in the most excited manner. Shandon bit his lips silently till the blood came.

Presently Johnson came up to him and said, "If we are to sail with this tide, sir, we have no time to lose; for it will take us a full hour to get out of the docks."

Shandon threw a last look round, consulted his watch, and said briefly, "Go."

This monosyllabic reply was enough for Johnson. He gave immediate orders for all visitors to go ashore, and the sailors began to haul in the ropes. There was a simultaneous rush towards the side of the vessel. The general confusion which ensued was greatly increased by the furious yelling of the dog, and reached a climax when the animal made one sudden bound from the forecastle right into the midst of the crowd, who fled before him right and left. He gave a loud deep bark, and jumped on the poop, carrying a letter between his teeth. Incredible as the fact may appear, it could be confirmed by at least a thousand eye-witnesses.

"A letter!" exclaimed Shandon. "Then *he* is on board."

"*He* has been, there is no doubt, but he is not now," replied Johnson, pointing to the deck, which was quite clear of all strangers.

"Captain! Captain!" called the Doctor, trying to take the letter out of his mouth; but the dog resisted stoutly, and was evidently determined to give the message to none but the right party.

"Here, Captain!" shouted Shandon; and at once the beast sprang forward and passively allowed him to withdraw the anxiously-expected missive, giving three loud, clear barks, which were distinctly heard amid the profound silence on the ship and on the quay.

Shandon held the letter in his hand without opennig it, till the Doctor exclaimed, impatiently, "Do, pray, read it."

The letter bore no postmark, and was simply addressed, "To the Chief Officer, Richard Shandon, on board the brig *Forward*." Shandon opened it, and read as follows:—

"You will steer your course towards Cape Farewell. You will reach it on the 20th of April. If the captain does not come on board, you will go through Davis's Straits, and up Baffin's Bay to Melville Bay.

"The captain of the *Forward*.

"K. Z."

Shandon carefully folded up this laconic epistle, put it in his pocket, and gave orders to sail.

The *Forward* was soon out of the basin, and, guided by a Liverpool pilot, got into the Mersey, the crowd hurrying along the Victoria Docks to have a last glimpse as she passed by. The fore and mainsails were soon hoisted, and the brig, with a speed worthy of her name, rounded Birkenhead Point, and glided swiftly away into the Irish Sea.

CHAPTER V
OUT AT SEA

THE wind was favorable, though very variable, and full of sudden squalls, and the *Forward* cut her way rapidly through the waves. At five o'clock the pilot gave up his charge into Shandon's hands, jumped into the boat, and was soon out of sight.

Johnson was right. Once fairly out at sea, there was no more trouble with the sailors. They fell into regular ways at once, and in their admiration of the ship's good qualities, forgot the mystery hanging round her.

The little Doctor almost lived on deck, gulping down the sea air as if he could never be satisfied. He would walk up and down in the stormiest weather, and, for a man of learning, his *sea legs* were pretty fair. "The sea is a beautiful thing to look at," he said to Johnson, coming on deck after breakfast. "I am rather late in beginning my acquaintance with it, but I'll soon make up for it."

"You are right, Dr. Clawbonny. I wouldn't give one fag-end of sea for all the continents in the world. People say that sailors soon grow tired of their calling, but here have I been, forty years at sea, and I enjoy it as much as the first day."

"And what a pleasure there is in feeling a good ship under your feet; and, if I'm any judge, the *Forward* is a regular ' brick.' "

"You are quite right there," said Shandon, coming up at that moment; "it is a well-built ship, and I must confess I have never seen one better provisioned and equipped for an Arctic expedition. That reminds me that, thirty years ago, Captain Ross, going in search of the North-West passage——"

"Went in the *Victory*," interrupted the Doctor, "a brig of nearly the same tonnage as ours, and with a steam-engine, too?"

"What! Do you know all about it?"

"Don't I!" said the Doctor. "Steam was then in its infancy, and the engine on the *Victory* caused much injurious delay. Captain Ross, after vainly trying to repair it, ended by doing away with it altogether, and left it behind in his first winter quarters."

"Why, Doctor," exclaimed Shandon, "I see you are quite familiar with all the facts."

"I ought to be," replied the Doctor, "for I have read the narratives of Parry, and Ross, and Franklin, and the reports of McClure and Kennedy, and Kane, and McClintock; and then one thing I recollect—this same McClintock's vessel, called the *Fox*, was a screw brig, like ours, and he succeeded in gaining his object in a more direct and easy manner than any of his predecessors."

"That is perfectly true," said Shandon. "This McClintock was a brave sailor. I have seen him at work; and you may add that, like him, we shall be in Davis's Straits before April is out; and if we can manage to get past the ice, it will greatly shorten our voyage."

"At all events," returned the Doctor, "I hope we'll be better off than the *Fox* was in 1857, for she got blocked in among the ice to the north of Baffin's Bay, the very first year, and had to stay there all the winter."

"We'll hope for better luck, Mr. Shandon," said Johnson; "and, certainly, if we can't get on with a ship like the *Forward*, we had better give up trying for good and all."

"Besides," said the Doctor, "if the captain is on board, he will know what's to be done better than we do in our complete ignorance, for this wonderfully laconic letter of his gives us no clue to the object of the voyage."

"We know what route to take, at any rate," said Shandon, rather sharply, "and that is a good deal. We can manage now, I should think, to do without supernatural interventions and instructions for a full month at least. Besides, you know my own opinion of this mysterious captain."

The Doctor laughed, and said, "I thought with you, once, that he would put you in command of the ship, and never come on board; but now——"

"But what?" said Shandon in a snappish tone.

"But since the arrival of this second letter my views on the subject are somewhat modified."

" And pray why, Doctor ? "

" Because, though the letter tells you what course to take, it does not tell you the destination of the *Forward*. Now, he must know where we are going, and I should like to know how a third letter can be sent to you when we are out in the middle of the sea. On the shores of Greenland the postman would certainly be a *rara avis*. What I think, Shandon, is, that our gallant captain is waiting for us at some Danish settlement at Holsteinberg or Upernavik. He will have gone there to complete his cargo of seal-skins, and to buy his sledges and dogs—in fact, to get everything ready that is required for a voyage to the Arctic Seas. I shall not be at all surprised to see him walk out of his cabin some fine morning, and give orders to the crew in the most ordinary matter-of-fact fashion imaginable."

" Possibly," said Shandon, drily; " but meantime the wind is freshening, and it is not very prudent to risk a topmast in a stiff breeze." This broke off the conversation, and he walked away immediately, and bade the men reef sails.

" He sticks to his notion," said the Doctor to Johnson.

" Ay, and more's the pity," said the boatswain, " for you may be right, Mr. Clawbonny."

Towards evening on Saturday, the wind changed to a hurricane, and almost drove the ship against the Irish coast. The waves were very high, and the brig rolled and pitched so heavily, that if the Doctor had felt inclined to be seasick, he would have had every excuse. At seven they lost sight of Cape Malinhead on the south. This was the last glimpse of Europe, and more than one of the brave crew of the *Forward,* destined never more to return, stood gazing with long, lingering look. The gale ceased towards nine at night, and the brig continued her course towards the northwest.

During the hurricane Richard Shandon had closely studied his men, analyzing each individual, as every captain ought to do, that he may know what characters he has to work with, and be on his guard. James Wall was a most devoted officer but he was deficient in the initiative faculty; he could understand and obey, but that was all: he was only fit for a third-rate position. Johnson, an experienced old Arctic sailor, had nothing to learn in the way of *sang froid*

and boldness. Simpson, the harpooner, and Bell, the carpenter, were reliable men, slaves of duty and discipline.

The ice-master, Foker, a sailor brought up in Johnson's
school, would be a valuable man.

Of the other sailors, Garry and Bolton appeared the best.
Bolton was a lively, chattering fellow. Garry was about
thirty-five years of age, an energetic-looking young man,
but rather pale and sad.

The three sailors, Clifton, Gripper, and Pen, were less
enthusiastic and resolute. They were rather fond of
grumbling; and Gripper would have given up his engagement, even at the last moment, if he had not been ashamed.
So long as things went well, and there was not much work
to do, and no danger to risk, he might reckon on these three
well enough; but they needed to be well fed. They took
very badly to the teetotal regimen, though they knew it was
to be enforced beforehand, and whenever the meal-time
came round they were always regretting their brandy or
gin, though they made up for it by drinking huge bowls of
tea and coffee, which might be had almost *ad libitum* on
board.

As for the two engineers, Brunton and Plover, and the
stoker Warren, they had sat with folded arms hitherto:
their work had not begun.

Shandon knew now how much each man could be depended on.

On the 14th of April the *Forward* crossed the great current called the Gulf Stream, which runs along the eastern
shore of the American continent as far as the Banks of
Newfoundland, and then curves southeast to the coast of
Norway. They found they were in latitude 51° 37′, and
longitude 20° 58′, about 200 miles from Greenland. The
weather had become cold, and the thermometer had fallen
to 32°—that is, to freezing point.

The Doctor had not yet donned his winter costume, but
he had followed the example of the sailors and officers,
and put on an oil-skin jacket and trousers, and a big " sou'-
wester," and high boots, into which he dropped all of a
lump; and really, to see him on deck when the rain was
falling in torrents, and the waves dashing over the vessel,
he might have been taken for some marine animal, though
the comparison would not flatter his vanity.

For two days the weather was extremely unfavorable, the wind was southwest, and the *Forward* could make no way. From the 14th to the 16th the sea continued rough and stormy; but on the Monday a violent shower came, the result of which was an almost immediate calm. Shandon pointed out this peculiar phenomenon to the Doctor, who replied:

"It quite confirms the curious observations made by Scoresby, a Fellow of the Royal Society of Edinburgh, of which I have the honor to be a corresponding member. You see that during rain the waves are less susceptible to the action of the wind, even when violent. On the contrary, in dry weather, the sea is easily agitated by a comparatively slight breeze."

"But how do you account for this?"

"That is easily answered. I don't account for it at all," said the Doctor.

Just at that moment the ice-master, who was on watch at the mast-head, signaled a floating mass on the starboard side, about fifteen miles to leeward.

"An iceberg in these latitudes!" exclaimed the Doctor.

Shandon pointed his glass in the given direction, and confirmed the announcement of the pilot.

"That's strange!" said the Doctor.

"Does that astonish you?" asked the chief officer, smiling. "What! we are actually fortunate enough to find something that astonishes you!"

"Well, it astonishes me, and yet it doesn't," replied the Doctor, smiling, "for, in 1813, the brig *Anne*, of Poole, got blocked in among ice-fields in the forty-fourth degree of north latitude, and Dayement, her captain, counted icebergs by hundreds."

"Capital!" said Shandon; "you can still find something to tell us about it that we don't know."

"Oh! not very much," was the modest reply of the amiable little man, "except that icebergs have been met with in still lower latitudes."

"I know that, my dear Doctor, without your telling me, for when I was a cabin-boy aboard the *Fly*, a sloop-of-war——"

"In 1818," interrupted the Doctor, "at the end of March or we might say April, you passed between two great islands of floating ice in the forty-second degree of latitude.

"Really, you're too bad, Doctor!" exclaimed Shandon.

"But it is true. I have no reason to be astonished, then, at finding a floating iceberg in front of our ship, seeing we are ten degrees farther north."

"I declare, Doctor, you're a perfect well; you have only to let down the bucket."

"All right. I shall dry up sooner than you think; and now, all I want to make me the happiest of doctors is, to see this curious phenomenon a little nearer."

"Precisely," said Shandon. "Johnson," he added, calling to his boatswain, "it seems to me the wind is getting up."

"Yes, sir," said Johnson, "we are losing speed, and the currents from the Straits of Davis will soon begin to affect us."

"You are right, Johnson; and if we want to be at Cape Farewell by the 20th of April, we must put on steam, or we shall be dashed against the coast of Labrador. Mr. Wall, will you give orders for the fires to be lighted immediately?"

His orders were executed forthwith, and in another hour the steam had acquired sufficient power to propel the screw, and the *Forward* was racing along against the wind with close-reefed sails at full speed.

CHAPTER VI
THE GREAT POLAR CURRENT

BEFORE long, the numerous flights of birds—puffins, petrels, and others peculiar to these desolate shores—indicated that they were approaching Greenland. The *Forward* was steaming rapidly north, leaving leeward a long cloud of black smoke.

On Tuesday, the 17th of April, the ice-master signaled the *blink* of ice about twenty miles ahead, at least. A radiant band of dazzling whiteness lighted up all the surrounding atmosphere, in spite of somewhat heavy clouds. Experienced Arctic sailors cannot mistake this appearance; and the old hands on board at once pronounced it to be the luminous reflection from a field of ice about thirty miles in the distance.

Towards evening the wind fell south, and became so favorable that Shandon was able to dispense with steam, and depend once more on the sails.

On the 18th, at three o'clock, an ice-stream was discovered in the far horizon, making a broad shining white line between sea and sky. It was evidently drifting more from the east coast of Greenland than from Davis's Straits; and about an hour afterwards the brig encountered it, and sailed right through the loose floating masses.

On the morrow, at daybreak, a ship was descried, which proved to be the *Valkyrien,* a Danish corvette, going to Newfoundland. The current from the Straits began to be sensibly felt, and Shandon was obliged to crowd sail to get on at all.

He was standing on the poop with his two officers and the Doctor, examining the force and the direction of the current, when the Doctor asked if it was true that this same current was uniformly found in Baffin's Bay.

"Undoubtedly that's the case," replied Shandon; "and sailing vessels have great difficulty in making head against it."

"All the more," said James Wall, "as they fall in with it, both on the east side of America, and on the west side of Greenland."

"Well, then," said the Doctor, "that is quite an argument in favor of a North-West passage. This current travels at the rate of about five miles an hour, and one can hardly suppose it has its origin in the bottom of the bay."

"Here is another fact to confirm your reasoning. This current goes from north to south; but in Behring's Straits there is a contrary current going from south to north, which must be the origin of this."

"That certainly proves that America is completely detached from the Polar regions, and that the waters of the Pacific flow round its coast, and fall into the Atlantic. Besides, the superior elevation of the Pacific makes it all the more likely that the European seas would be fed by its waters."

"But, surely," said Shandon, "there must be same facts

to support this theory. Hasn't our learned Doctor any to tell us?" he added, half ironically.

"Oh, yes!" said Clawbonny, with a good-humored air of complacency, "I could tell you this, which may interest you, that whales which have been wounded in Davis's Straits have been captured subsequently on the coast of Tartary with the European harpoon still sticking in their sides."

"And since they have neither doubled Cape Horn nor the Cape of Good Hope, they must have got round North America. That is proof positive, Doctor."

"If you're not convinced yet, my good Shandon, I can bring forward other facts, such as the drift-wood which so abounds in Davis's Straits—larches, and aspens, and tropical substances. Now, we know that this South current would prevent this drift-wood from entering; if it comes out there, it must have got in by Behring's Straits, for there is no other way."

"I am quite satisfied, Doctor; one couldn't be long incredulous with you."

"Look out!" exclaimed Johnson; "here comes something quite à propos to our conversation. I see a jolly-sized log of wood floating there, and I propose we fish it up, with our chief officer's leave, and ask what country it comes from."

Shandon agreed, and soon after the log was hauled up on board, though with considerable difficulty. It was a trunk of mahogany, worm-eaten to the very center, which accounted for its floating.

"Here's a triumphant proof," exclaimed the Doctor, enthusiastically. "Since it cannot have been carried into Davis's Straits by the Atlantic currents, and since it cannot have been driven into the Polar basin by any of the North American rivers, seeing that it grew just below the Equator, it is evident it comes in a direct line from Behring's Straits. Besides, look at the worms. They belong to a species peculiar to the tropics. Listen, I'll tell you the whole history of this log. It was carried into the Pacific Ocean by some river, from the Isthmus of Panama or Guatemala. From thence it was borne along by the current into Behring's Straits, and driven out into the Polar Sea. I should assign rather a recent date to its departure, for it is neither old enough nor soaked enough to have been long on the road. After getting through Baffin's Bay, past that long succession of straits, it was violently caught up by the Polar current, and brought through Davis's Straits, to take its place on board the *Forward,* for the special delectation of Dr. Clawbonny, who now craves permission to keep a piece of it as a specimen."

" By all means," said Shandon; " but allow me to tell you that you are not the only possessor of a waif like this. The Danish governor of the Isle of Disko, on the coast of Greenland——"

" I know," said the Doctor. " He has a table made of a trunk picked up in similar circumstances. I know all about it, Shandon; but I don't envy him his table for there is enough there to make me a whole bed-room suite, if it were worth the trouble."

During the night the wind blew with extreme violence, and the drift-wood became more frequently visible. It was a time of the year when any aproach to the shore would be dangerous, as the icebergs are very numerous. Shandon therefore gave orders to lessen sail, and take in all that was not absolutely necessary.

The next business was to give out warm clothing for the crew, as the thermometer went down below freezing point. Each man received a woolen jacket and trousers, a flannel shirt, and wadmel stockings, like those worn by the Norwegian peasants. Each man was also provided with a pair of perfectly waterproof sea-boots.

As for " Captain," he was quite contented with his natural covering. He did not seem to feel the change of temperature, and, likely enough, had been accustomed to it before. Moreover, a born Dane can hardly complain of cold; and " Captain " was wise enough not to expose himself much; he was seldom visible, generally stowing himself away in the darkest recesses of the ship.

Towards evening, through a rift in the fog, the coast of Greenland was indistinctly visible—the Doctor just caught a glimpse through the glass, of peaks and glaciers, and then the fog closed over it again, like the curtain falling at the theater at the most interesting part of the play.

On the 20th of April the *Forward* sighted a fallen iceberg, a hundred and fifty feet high. It had been in the same place from time immemorial, and had become firmly fixed below; as, for every foot above water, an iceberg has nearly two below, which reckoning would give this a depth of about eighty fathoms. No thaw seemed to have affected it, or touched its strange outlines. It was seen by Snow; by James Ross, in 1829, who made an exact drawing of it; and by Lieutenant Bellot, in 1851. The Doctor, of course, was anxious to carry away some souvenir of an ice mountain so celebrated, and succeeded in sketching it very successfully.

At last Cape Farewell came in sight, and the *Forward* arrived on the day fixed, amidst snow and fog, with the temperature at 12°. If the unknown captain should chance to turn up here, he certainly could not complain.

"Here we are, then," said the Doctor, "at this famous cape! Well named it is, for many have reached it like us who never saw it more. Do we, indeed, say farewell to our friends in Europe? Frobisher, Knight, Barlow, Vaughan, Scroggs, Barentz, Hudson, Blosseville, Franklin, Crozier, Bellot—all passed this way, never to return! For them it was indeed a Cape Farewell."

All the past history of Greenland rose up to memory, as the Doctor stood gazing dreamily over the side of the ship, watching the deep furrow she made in plowing the waves, and imagination peopled the icy, desolate shore with pale shadows of the many bold adventurers who had found a grave and winding sheet in the snow.

CHAPTER VII
DAVIS'S STRAITS

DURING the day the *Forward* bored her way easily through the loose ice. The wind was favorable, but the temperature very low, owing to the passage of the air currents over the ice-fields.

The night was the most trying time, requiring the utmost vigilance. The icebergs so crowded the narrow strait that upwards of a hundred could often be counted on the horizon at one time. They were constantly being shed off by the glaciers on the coast, through the combined action of the waves and the April weather, and either melted away or became engulfed in the depths of the ocean. It was necessary, also, to guard against coming into collision with the drift-wood, which was floating about in continuous heavy masses, so the " crow's-nest " had to be attached to the topgallant mast-head. This was a cask with a movable bottom, in which the ice-master took up his position, to keep a sharp look-out over the sea. Here he was partially sheltered from the wind, and could both give notice of any ice that came in sight and direct the course of the vessel through it when necessary.

The nights were short. The sun had reappeared since the close of January, and inclined more and more to show himself above the horizon; but the snow came between, and though not exactly causing darkness, made navigation a work of difficulty.

On the 21st of April Cape Desolation came in sight through the fog. The men were worn out with fatigue, for they had not a minute's rest since they got in among the ice. It was found necessary to have recourse to steam to bore a way through the close, heavy packs.

The Doctor and the boatswain were standing at the stern, having a chat, while Shandon was in his cabin, trying to get a few hours' sleep. Clawbonny was very fond of having a talk with the old sailor, for he had made so many voyages, and seen and heard so much, that his conversation was always sensible and interesting. The Doctor took quite a fancy to him, and Johnson heartily reciprocated his liking.

" How different this country is from all others," said Johnson. " It is called Greenland, but certainly it is only during a very few weeks in the year that it justifies its name."

" But who knows, my good fellow, whether in the tenth century it might not have been justly called so? More than one total change like that has taken place on our globe; and perhaps I shall astonish you considerably when I tell you that, according to Icelandic chroniclers, there were two hundred flourishing villages on this continent eight or nine hundred years ago."

" You astonish me so much, Mr. Clawbonny, that I couldn't believe it, for it is a miserable country."

" Miserable it may be, but for all that it affords enough

to satisfy the inhabitants, and even civilized Europeans, too."

"True enough. Both at Disko and Upernavik we shall find men who have taken up their abode in this inhospitable climate; but, for my own part, it has always seemed to me that their stay there must be a matter of necessity rather than of choice."

"I can quite think that, yet a man can get used to anything; and the Greenlanders don't appear to me so much to be pitied as the laboring classes in our great cities. They may be badly off, but one thing is certain, they are not unhappy. I say badly off; but that does not quite express my meaning. What I would say is, they lack many comforts to be found in the temperate zones, and yet their constitutions are so adapted to this rude climate, that they find a measure of enjoyment in it which we cannot even imagine."

"I suppose it is so, Mr. Clawbonny, since Heaven cannot be unjust; but I have been here many a time, and yet I never can see these dreary solitudes without a feeling of sadness coming over me. And then what names they have given to these capes, and bays, and headlands! Surely they might have found something more inviting than Cape Farewell and Desolation. They have not a very cheering sound to navigators."

"I have thought the same thing myself," replied the Doctor; "and yet these names have a geographical interest attaching to them which we must not overlook. They record the adventures of those who gave them. If I find Cape Desolation among such names as Davis, Baffin, Hudson, Ross, Parry, Franklin, and Bellot, I find soon afterwards Mercy Bay. Cape Providence is good company for Port Anxiety; Repulse Bay leads me to Cape Eden; and Turnagain Point to Refuge Bay. Here I have before me the whole succession of dangers and disappointments, obstacles, and successes, despairing failures, and accomplished results, linked with illustrious names of my countrymen; and as if on a series of ancient medals, I read in this nomenclature the whole history of these seas."

"You have certainly made out a very good case for it, Mr. Clawbonny. I only hope, in our voyage, we may oftener come to Success Bay than Cape Despair."

"I hope that, too, Johnson; but, tell me, have the crew got over their fears at all?"

"They have partly, sir; and yet, to speak frankly, since we entered the strait, their heads are full again of this eccentric captain of ours. More than one of them expected him to make his appearance the moment we reached Greenland, and there's no sign of him yet. Between ourselves, Mr. Clawbonny, are you not surprised?"

"I certainly am, Johnson."

"Do you believe in the actual existence of this captain?"

"Most assuredly."

"But what can possibly induce him to act in this manner?"

"Well, if I say what I really think, it is this—the captain wished to get the sailors too far on to be able to back out of the undertaking; and if he had shown himself on board ship when we were going to sail, I don't know how he would have managed at all, with everybody clamoring to know the destination."

"Why not?"

"My stars! if he is going to attempt some superhuman enterprise, and try to push his way where human feet have never trod, do you suppose he would have found a crew at all to go with him? But by going to work like this, he has dragged the men on so far, that going farther becomes a necessity."

"That's very possible, Mr. Clawbonny. I have known more than one bold adventurer, whose mere name would have been enough to prevent anyone from joining any expedition led on by them."

"Anyone except me," said the Doctor.

"And me, after you, Doctor," replied Johnson. "No doubt, then, our captain belongs to these daring adventurers. Well, we shall see, I suppose. When we reach Upernavik, or Melville Bay, I daresay our brave incognito will quietly install himself on board, and inform us where he has a fancy to drag the ship."

"I think that is very likely; but the difficulty is to get to Melville Bay. Just look at the ice all round us. There is hardly room for the ice to get through. See that immense plain stretching out yonder!"

"In our Arctic language, Mr. Clawbonny, we call that

an *ice-field*—that is to say, a surface of ice which extends beyond the reach of sight."

"And what do you call this broken ice on the other side —those long pieces which keep so closely together?"

"That's a *pack*. If the loose masses assume a circular form, we call it *palch;* and if elongated, a *stream*."

"And all that floating ice, there—has that any particular name?"

"That is called *drift ice*. If it rose higher out of the water it would be *icebergs* or *ice-hills*. It is dangerous for ships to come into contact with them, and they have to be carefully avoided. Look! do you see that protuberance, or sort of ridge of broken ice on the surface of the field? That is called a *hummock,* and is formed by the collision of *fields*. If its base was submerged, it would be called a *calf*."

"Well, it is certainly a curious spectacle," said the Doctor, "and one that acts powerfully on the imagination."

"Yes, indeed," replied Johnson, "for the ice often assumes the most fantastic forms."

"For instance, Johnson," interrupted the Doctor, "look at that assemblage of huge blocks. Couldn't you fancy it was some eastern city, with its minarets and mosques glittering in the pale moonlight? And then a little way off is a long succession of Gothic arches, which remind one of Henry the Seventh's Chapel at Westminster, or the Houses of Parliament."

"Ay, Mr. Clawbonny, each man shapes those to his own fancy; but I can tell you both churches and towers are dangerous places to live in, or even to get too near. There are some of those minarets tottering at their base, and the smallest of them would crush our brig to pieces."

"And yet men have dared to venture here without having steam to fall back upon. It is difficult to imagine a common sailing ship being able to pick her way through those moving rocks."

"It has been done, however, Mr. Clawbonny. When the wind became contrary, which happened to myself more than once, we anchored our ship to one of those blocks, and waited patiently, drifting along with it more or less, till a favoring breeze allowed us to resume our course again. I must confess, however, it was a very slow fashion of sailing. We did not get on farther in a whole month than we should have done in a day, if we had at all a fair wind."

"It strikes me," said the Doctor, "that the temperature keeps getting lower."

"That would be vexing," said Johnson, "for we need a thaw to loosen these packs, and make them drift into the Atlantic. The reason they are so numerous in Davis's Straits is the narrowness of the space between Cape Walsingham and Holsteinberg; but after we get beyond the 67th degree, we shall find the sea more navigable during May and June months."

"Yes; but how to reach it is the question."

"That's it, Mr. Clawbonny. In June and July we should have found the passage open, as the whalers do; but our orders were positive—we were to arrive here in April. That makes me think that our captain is some thorough 'go-ahead' fellow who has got an idea in his head, and is determined to carry it out. He would not have started so soon if he had not meant to go a long way. Well, if we live we shall see."

The Doctor was right about the temperature. The thermometer was only 6° at mid-day, and a breeze was blowing from the southwest, which, though it cleared the sky, considerably impeded the course of the ship, as the strong current it produced drove the loose, heavy masses of ice right across her bows. Nor did all these masses move in the same direction. Some—and those the largest among them —floated in an exactly opposite direction, obeying a countercurrent below.

It is easy to understand what difficulty this caused in navigation. The engineers had not a single moment's rest. Sometimes a lead or opening was discovered in an ice-field, and the brig had to strain her utmost to get into it. Sometimes she had to race with an iceberg to prevent the only visible outlet from being blocked up; while again some towering mass would suddenly overturn, and the ship must be backed in an instant to avoid being crushed. Should frost set in, all the accumulation of floe-pieces driven into the narrow pass by the north wind, would consolidate firmly, and oppose an insurmountable barrier to the progress of the *Forward*.

The petrels and other sea-birds were innumerable. They were flying about in all directions, filling the air with their discordant cries. Amongst them was also a great number of sea-gulls, with large heads, short necks, and compressed beaks, spreading their long wings, and disporting themselves in the loose snow. These feathered gentry quite enlivened the landscape.

The drift-wood was still abundant, and the logs came dashing against each other with great noise. Several cachelots, or sperm whales, with enormous, swollen heads, approached the vessel; but it was out of the question to think of giving them chase, though Simpson the harpooner's fingers itched to try to spear them. Towards evening, seals were also seen swimming about between the floes, the tips of their snouts just above water.

On the 22d, the temperature became still lower. The steam had to be at high pressure to enable the *Forward* to gain any favorable lead whatever. The wind kept steadily northwest, and the sails were close-reefed.

Being Sunday, the sailors had less work. After morning service, which was read by Shandon, the crew occupied themselves in shooting guillemots, a species of sea turtledoves. They caught a great number, which were dressed according to Clawbonny's receipt, and furnished an agreeable addition to the ordinary fare of both officers and men.

At three o'clock in the afternoon the *Forward* reached the Kin of Zaal, and the Sukkertop, or Sugarloaf—a wild, lonely peak, rising 3000 feet above the shore. There was a heavy swell in the sea, and from time to time a dense fog would suddenly overspread the gray sky. However, at noon the observations had been taken, and it was found that the latitude was $65° 20'$, and longitude $54° 22'$. Two degrees higher had therefore to be made before a more open sea could be reached.

For the three following days it was one continuous struggle with the floes. It was a fatiguing business to work the engine: the steam was stopped or driven back every minute, and escaped hissing from the valves.

While the fog lasted, the approach of icebergs could only be known by the hollow detonations produced by the avalanches. The brig had then to turn aside at once, for there was danger of coming into collision with fresh-water blocks, as hard as rock, and remarkable for their crystal transparency. Shandon took care to replenish his supply of water by shipping several tons of these every day.

The Doctor could never get accustomed to the optical illusions caused by refraction. For instance, an iceberg twelve miles off looked like a little white mass quite close; and his eye needed long training to enable him to judge objects correctly in a region where a phenomenon like this was of frequent occurrence.

At length, what with towing the brig along in fields, and driving back threatening blocks with long poles, the crew were completely worn out, and yet on Friday, the 27th of April, the *Forward* was still outside the Polar circle.

CHAPTER VIII
WHAT THE CREW THOUGHT ABOUT IT

By watching the chance, however, and taking advantage of every favorable lead, the *Forward* managed to gain a little ground, but instead of avoiding the enemy, it was evident that direct attack would soon be necessary, for ice-fields, many miles in extent, were approaching, and as these masses when in motion represent a pressure of more than ten millions of tons, great care was requisite to avoid nippings, that is, getting crushed in among them on both sides of the ship. The saws were ordered to be brought up and placed in readiness for immediate use.

It was hard work now for the crew, and some began to grumble loudly, though they did not refuse to obey, while others took things as they came with philosophic indifference.

"I couldn't tell for my life what brings it into my head just this moment," said Bolton, gayly, "but I can't help thinking of a jolly little grog-shop in Water Street, where a fellow can make himself very comfortable with a glass of gin and a bottle of porter. You can see it too, quite plain, can't you, Gripper?"

"Speak for yourself," said Gripper, in the surly tone he generally adopted. "I can see nothing of the sort."

"It's only a way of speaking, Gripper; of course I didn't suppose that those ice-cities which Mr. Clawbonny

so admires have even one solitary little public-house in
them, where a brave Jack Tar can get a tumbler or two of
brandy."

"You may be quite sure of that, Bolton; and for that
matter you might add, there is nothing even to be had on
board to keep a poor fellow's heart up. A queer idea,
certainly, to forbid spirits to Arctic sailors!"

"I can't see that," said Garry, "for you remember what
the Doctor said, that it was absolutely necessary to avoid
all stimulants if a man wished to go far north, and keep
well and free from the scurvy."

"But I have no wish to go far north, Garry. I think
it is all lost labor, even coming this length. I can't see the
good of being so bent and determined on pushing through
where the Fates are dead against us."

"Ah, well, we shan't push through, anyway," said Pen.
"When I think I have even forgotten the taste of gin!"

"You must comfort yourself, my boy," said Bolton,
"with what the Doctor said."

"Oh, it's all very fine to talk," said Pen, in his coarse,
brutal voice, "but it remains to be seen whether all this
stuff about health isn't a mere sham to save the rum."

"Pen may be right, perhaps, after all," said Gripper.

"Pen right!" exclaimed Bolton. "His nose is too red
for that, and if this new regimen is beginning to bring it
back to its natural color a bit, he may thank his stars instead of complaining."

"What harm has my nose done to you, I should like to
know?" said Pen, angrily, for this was an attack on his
weak point. "My nose can take care of itself; it doesn't
want your advice. Mind your own business."

"Come, Pen, don't get rusty. I didn't think your nose
was so sensitive. Why, man, I like a good glass of whisky
as well as other people, especially in such a climate as this,
but if it does one really more harm than good, I am quite
willing to go without it."

"You do without it?" said Warren, the stoker, "but
I am not so sure that everyone else on board does without it."

"What do you mean, Warren?" said Garry, looking
fixedly at him.

"I mean this, that for some reason or other there are

spirits on board, and I don't believe some folks in the cabin don't make themselves jolly."

" Pray, how did you know that?" asked Garry.

Warren could not answer; he was only talking for talking sake, as the saying is.

" Never mind him, Garry," said Bolton. " You see he knows nothing about it."

" Well," said Pen, " we'll go and ask for a ration of gin from the chief officer. We've earned it well, I'm sure, and we'll see if he refuses."

" I advise you to do nothing of the sort," rejoined Garry, seriously.

" Why not?" asked Pen and Gripper.

" Because you'll only get ' No ' for an answer. You knew the regulation when you signed the articles. You should have thought about it sooner."

" Besides," replied Bolton, who always sided with Garry, " Richard Shandon is not the master; he has to obey like all the rest of us."

" Obey whom, I should like to know?"

" The captain."

" Confound the captain," exclaimed Pen. " Can't you see through all this make-believe. There is no more any real captain than there is any tavern among those ice-blocks. It's only a polite fashion of refusing us what we have a right to demand."

" But there is a captain," replied Bolton, " and I would wager two months' wages that we shall see him before long."

" So much the better," said Pen. " I, for one, should like to say a few words to him."

" Who's talking about the captain?" said a fresh interlocutor.

It was Clifton who spoke—an anxious, superstitious man.

" Any more news about the captain?" he asked.

" None," was the unanimous reply.

" Well, some fine morning I quite expect to find him in his cabin, without anyone knowing how he got there, or where he came from."

" Be off with you," said Bolton. " You seem to think the captain is a sort of Brownie, like those that the Scotch Highlanders talk about."

"Laugh as much as you like, Bolton, but that won't change my opinion. Every day, when I pass his cabin, I take a look through the key-hole, and you see if I don't come and tell you some day what he looks like, and how he's made."

"Plague take him," said Pen; "I suppose his timbers are no different from other people; and if he's going to try and force us where we don't want to go, he'll soon show us what stuff he is made of."

"That's pretty good," said Bolton. "Here's Pen, who doesn't even know the man, wanting to pick a quarrel with him directly."

"Doesn't know him?" returned Clifton; "that remains to be proved."

"What do you mean?" asked Gripper.

"I know what I'm saying."

"But we don't," was the common exclamation.

"Why, hasn't Pen quarreled with him already?"

"With the captain?"

"Yes, with the dog-captain, for it comes to the same thing."

The sailors gazed dubiously at each other, hardly knowing what to say or think.

At last Pen muttered between his teeth, "Man or dog, as sure as I'm alive, I'll settle accounts with him one of these days."

"Clifton," asked Bolton, seriously, "do you actually profess to believe that the dog is the real captain? Johnson was only fooling you."

"I firmly believe it," said Clifton, with an air of perfect conviction, "and if you were to watch him as I have done, you would have seen his strange behavior for yourself."

"What strange behavior? Tell us about him."

"Haven't you seen the way he marches up and down the deck, and looks at the sails, as if he were on watch?"

"Yes, that's quite true; and one evening I positively caught him, with his fore-paws up, leaning against the wheel."

"Impossible!" said Bolton.

"And doesn't he leave the ship now every night, and go walking about among the ice, without caring either for the bears or the cold?"

" That is true, too," said Bolton.

" Besides, is the animal like any other honest dog, fond of human society? Does he follow the cook about, and watch all his movements when he brings in the dishes to the cabin? Don't you hear him at night, when he is two or three miles from the ship, howling till he makes your flesh creep, which, by the way, isn't a very difficult matter in such a temperature. And, to crown all, have you ever seen him eat any food? He will take nothing from anybody. His cake is never touched, and unless someone feeds him secretly, I may safely say he is an animal that lives without eating. Now, you may call me a fool if you like, if that isn't peculiar enough."

" Upon my word," said Bell, the carpenter, who had listened to all Clifton's arguments, " it is not impossible you may be right."

The other sailors were silent, till Bolton changed the subject by asking where the *Forward* was going.

" I don't know," said Bell. " At a given moment, Shandon is to receive his final instructions."

" But how? "

" How? "

" Yes, how? that's the question," repeated Bolton.

" Come, Bell, give us an answer," urged the others.

" I don't know how," said the carpenter. " I can tell no more than you can."

" Oh! by the dog-captain, of course," exclaimed Clifton. " He has written once already; I daresay he can manage a second letter. Oh, if I but knew half that dog does, I should feel fit to be First Lord of the Admiralty."

" So, then, the short and long of it is, that you stick to your opinion, Clifton," said Bolton.

" I've told you that already."

" Well," said Pen, in a deep, hollow voice, " all I know is, if that beast don't want to die in a dog's skin, he had better be quick, and turn into a man, for I'll do for him as sure as my name is Pen."

" And what for? " said Garry.

" Because I choose," was the rude reply. " I am not bound to give an account of my doings to anyone."

" Come, boys, you have had talk enough," said Johnson, interrupting the conversation to prevent a quarrel. " Get to work; it is time the saws were all up, for we must get beyond the ice."

"So be it, and on a Friday, too. We shan't get beyond quite so easily," said Clifton, shrugging his shoulders.

From what cause it was impossible to say, but all the efforts of the crew were in vain. That day the *Forward* made no way whatever, though she dashed against the ice-fields with all her steam up. She could not separate them, and was forced to come to anchor for the night.

Next day the wind was east, and the temperature still lower. The weather was fine, and, as far as the eye could reach ice-plains stretched away in the distance, glittering in the sun's rays with dazzling whiteness. At seven in the morning, the thermometer stood eight degrees below zero.

The Doctor felt much inclined to stay quietly in his cabin, and devote himself to the reperusal of his volumes of Arctic voyages; but his custom was always to do whatever was most disagreeable to himself at the time being, and as it was certainly anything but pleasant to go on deck in such bitter weather and lend a helping hand to the men, he adhered to his rule of conduct, and left his snug warm quarters below, and went upstairs to do his share of work in towing the vessel along. He wore green spectacles to protect his eyes; but from this time he began to make use of snow-spectacles, to avoid the ophthalmia so frequent in Arctic latitudes.

By evening the *Forward* had gained many miles, thanks to the activity of the men and the skill of Shandon. At midnight they cleared the sixty-sixth parallel, and on sounding, the depth was found to be twenty-three fathoms. Land was about thirty miles to the east.

Suddenly the mass of ice, which had hitherto been motionless, broke in pieces, and began to move. Icebergs seemed to surge from all points of the horizon, and the brig found herself wedged in among a crowd of moving bergs, which might crush her at any moment. The task of steering became so difficult that Garry, who was the best hand at the wheel, could never leave it. Ice-mountains were re-forming behind the ship, and there was no alternative but to bore a way forward through the loose floes.

The crew were divided into two companies, and ranged on the starboard and larboard; each man armed with a long pole pointed with iron, to push back the most threatening packs. Before long, the brig entered a narrow pass between two high blocks, so narrow, that the tops of the sails touched the rock, like walls on either side. This led into a winding valley, full of whirling, blinding snow, where masses of drift ice were dashing furiously against each other, and breaking up into fragments with loud crackings.

But it was soon but too evident that there was no outlet to this gorge; an enormous block was right in front of the ship, and drifting rapidly down on her. There appeared no way of escape, for going back was impossible.

Shandon and Johnson stood together on the forepart of the vessel, surveying her perilous position; Shandon giving orders with one hand to the steersman and with the other to James Wall, who transmitted them to the chief engineer.

" How is this going to end, Johnson? "

" As Heaven pleases," was the boatswain's reply.

The ice-block, an enormous berg a hundred feet high, was now within a cable's length of the *Forward,* threatening her with instant destruction.

It was a moment of intense agonizing suspense, and became so unbearable that the men flung down their poles in spite of Shandon's commands, and hurried to the stern.

Suddenly a tremendous noise was heard, and a perfect waterspout broke over the deck. An enormous wave upheaved the ship, and the men cried out in terror, all but Garry, who stood up quietly at the helm, and kept the vessel in the right course.

But when the men recovered themselves a little, and ventured to look the gigantic foe again in the face, it was gone! The whole berg had completely disappeared, the pass was free, and there was a long channel beyond, lighted up by the oblique rays of the sun, which offered an uninterrupted passage to the *Forward.*

" Well, Mr. Clawbonny," said Johnson; " how do you explain this phenomenon? "

" It is one that often occurs, and is very simple, my good friend," replied the Doctor. " When these floating icebergs become detached at the time of the thaw, they sail separately along and preserve their equilibrium perfectly, but as they gradually drift farther south, where the water is relatively warmer, they begin to melt and get under-

V. II **Venre**

mined at the base, and the moment comes when their center of gravity is displaced, and down they go. If this had happened, however, but two minutes later, it would have fallen on the ship and crushed her to atoms."

CHAPTER IX
A LETTER

THE Polar circle was entered at last. The *Forward* passed Holsteinberg at twelve o'clock on the 30th of April. Picturesque mountain scenery appeared on the eastern horizon, and the sea was open and free from icebergs, or rather any icebergs that were visible could easily be avoided. The wind was in the S. E., and bore along the brig in full sail up Baffin's Bay.

The day would have passed unmarked by any unusual incident but for the following occurrence, which, strange as it may appear, actually took place. At six in the morning, when Richard Shandon's watch was over, and he came back to his cabin, he found a letter lying on his table directed thus:

" To the chief officer, Richard Shandon,
" On board the *Forward*,
" Baffin's Bay."

Shandon could not believe his own eyes, and would not even take the letter in his hands till he had called the Doctor and James Wall and the boatswain to look at it.

" It is certainly very strange," said Johnson.

" I think it is charming!" exclaimed the Doctor.

" At any rate," replied Shandon, " we shall know the secret now, I suppose."

He tore open the envelope hastily and read as follows:

" The captain of the *Forward* is pleased with the coolness, skill, and courage displayed in recent trying circumstances by the crew and officers, and yourself. He begs you to convey his thanks to the men.

" You will please direct your course north to Melville Bay, and from thence attempt to make Smith's Sound.
" The Captain of the *Forward*,
" K. Z."

" Monday, April 30th, off Cape Walsingham."

"And that's all!" exclaimed the Doctor.

"That's all," was Shandon's reply.

"Well!" said Wall, "this Quixotic captain doesn't even so much as speak of coming on board now. I infer from this he doesn't intend to come at all."

"But this letter," said Johnson, "how did it get on board the vessel?"

Shandon was silent.

"Mr. Wall is right," replied the Doctor, picking up the letter which had fallen on the floor, and giving it back to Shandon.

"The captain won't come on board for a very good reason."

"And what is it?" inquired Shandon, eagerly.

"Because he is there already!" said the Doctor flatly.

"Already! What do you mean?"

"If he is not, how do you explain the arrival of the letter?"

Johnson nodded his head approvingly.

"It is not possible!" exclaimed Shandon. "I know every one of the crew; and, if your idea were correct, the captain must have been on board ever since the ship sailed. It is perfectly impossible, I say; for there is not a man among them I haven't seen more than a hundred times in Liverpool during the last two years. No, no, Doctor; your theory is altogether inadmissible."

"Well, then, how do you account for it?"

"Any way but that. I grant you that the captain, or someone employed by him, may have taken advantage of the fog and darkness to slip on board unperceived. We are not far from land, and the Esquimaux kayaks glide alone noiselessly between the icebergs. He might easily have managed to climb up the ship and deposit the letter. The fog has been quite dense enough for that."

"Yes, and dense enough, too, to keep anyone from seeing the brig; for if we could not notice an intruder coming on deck, it is not very likely he would be able to discover the vessel."

"I think that too," said Johnson. "What do you say, Mr. Shandon?"

"Anything you like, except that he is one of the crew," said Shandon, in an excited manner.

"Perhaps it is one of the sailors who has been commissioned by him," suggested Wall.

"That may be," said the Doctor.

"But which of them?" asked Shandon. "I tell you, all the men have been personally known to me this long time."

"At any rate, the captain will be welcome whenever he chooses to come, be he man or fiend," said Johnson. "But there is one piece of information in the letter at all events. We are not only going to Melville Bay but to Smith's Straits."

"Smith's Straits," repeated Shandon, mechanically.

"It is evident," continued Johnson, "that the object of the *Forward* is not to seek the North-West passage, since we must leave Lancaster Sound, the only entrance to it, on the left. This supposes very difficult navigation for us in unknown seas."

"Yes," said Shandon, "Smith's Sound was the course taken by the American Dr. Kane in 1853; and what dangers he encountered! He was given up for lost for a long time. However, if we are to go, we go. But where? To the Pole?"

"Why not?" asked the Doctor.

Johnson shrugged his shoulders at the bare possibility of such a mad attempt.

"Well, then," said Wall, "to come back to the captain; if he exists, I hardly see any place in Greenland where he can be waiting for us except Disko, or Upernavik, so in a few days at most we shall know better how the case stands."

"But, Shandon," asked the Doctor, "are you not going to tell the men about this letter?"

"With your leave, sir," said Johnson, addressing Shandon, "I say not."

"And why not?"

"Because anything so unheard-of and so mysterious dispirits the men. They are very uneasy as it is about the issue of this strange expedition, but if anything supernatural should occur, it might have the worst possible effect on them, and we could never rely on them when most wanted."

"What is your opinion, Doctor?" asked Shandon.

"Johnson's reasoning seems convincing, I think," was the reply.

"And what say you, James?"

"I incline to Johnson, sir."

After a few moments' reflection, Shandon read the letter carefully again, and then said:

"Your opinion is very sensible, but excuse me, gentlemen, I cannot adopt it."

"Why not, Shandon?"

"Because my instructions are plain and precise. I am told to convey a message from the captain to the crew. All I have to do is to obey orders, however they may have come to me, and I cannot——"

"But, sir," interrupted Johnson, mainly concerned at the disastrous effect of any such communication on the sailors.

"My good fellow," said Shandon, "I can understand your opposition, but I put it to yourself, whether I have any option in the matter. Read the letter. 'He begs you to convey his thanks to the crew.'"

"Well, then," said Johnson, when his love of discipline was thus appealed to, "shall I assemble the men on deck?"

"Do so," replied Shandon.

The news of a communication from the captain soon spread, and the sailor needed no second summons to hear the mysterious letter. They listened to it in gloomy silence, but gave way to all sorts of wild conjectures, as they dispersed to their work. The superstitious Clifton ascribed everything, as usual, to the dog-captain, and said triumphantly: "Didn't I say that animal could write?"

From this day forward he always took care to touch his cap whenever he chanced to meet him about the ship.

One thing was patent to the observation of anyone—the captain, or his ghost, was always watching over their doings, and prudent individuals began to think it advisable to keep quiet, and say as little about him as possible.

By observations taken at noon on the 1st of May, the longitude was found to be 32° and the latitude 68°. The temperature had risen, and the thermometer stood at 26° above zero.

The Doctor was on deck, amusing himself with the gambols of a white bear and her cubs, on a pack of ice frozen fast to the shore. He tried to capture her, with the assistance of Wall and Simpson; but the brute was evidently of a peaceable disposition, for she never showed fight at all, but scampered off with her progeny at full speed.

Cape Chidley was doubled during the night with a favoring breeze, and suddenly the high mountains of Disko rose to view. The Bay of Godavhn, where the Governor-General of the Danish settlements resided, was left on the right.

Isle Disko is also called Whale Island. It was from this place that Sir John Franklin wrote his last letter to the Admiralty, on the 12th of July, 1845, and it was there that McClintock touched on his return, on the 27th of August, 1859, bringing incontestable proofs of the loss of the expedition.

The shore was one continuation of icebergs, of the most peculiar fantastic shapes, so firmly cemented to the coast that the most powerful thaws had been unable to detach them.

Next day, about three o'clock, they sighted Sanderson Hope, to the N.E. Land was on the starboard side, about fifteen miles off, the mountains looking brownish-red in the distance. In the course of the evening, several whales of the species called *finners,* which have their fins on the back, were seen disporting themselves among the ice, blowing out large volumes of air and water through the apertures in the head.

During the night of the 5th of May, the Doctor observed the luminous disc of the sun, for the first time, appear completely above the horizon, though from the 31st of January there had been constant daylight.

To those who are not accustomed to it, there is something in this continual day which excites wonderment at first, but soon gives place to weariness. One would hardly believe how necessary the darkness of night is for the preservation of the sight. The Doctor felt the constant glare positively painful, intensified as it was by the dazzling reflection of the ice.

On the 5th of May the *Forward* passed the seventy-second parallel. Two months later, she would have fallen in with numerous whalers about to commence their fishing, but at present the Straits were not free enough to allow their vessels to get into Baffin's Bay.

The next day the brig arrived in sight of Upernavik, the most northerly of the Danish settlements on the coast.

CHAPTER X

PERILOUS NAVIGATION

SHANDON, Dr. Clawbonny, and Johnson, accompanied by Foker and Strong, the cook, got into the whaling-boat, and went on shore.

The Governor, with his wife and five children, came courteously to meet their visitors. Dr. Clawbonny knew enough Danish to establish friendly relations between them, and Foker, the ice-master, who was also interpreter, knew about twenty words of the Esquimaux tongue, and a good deal can be done with twenty words if one is not very ambitious.

The Governor was born in Isle Disko, and had never been out of it in his life. He did the honors of his town, composed of three wooden houses for himself and the three Lutheran ministers, a school, and a few shops, which were stocked by shipwrecked vessels. The rest of the town consisted of snow-huts, with one single opening, into which the Esquimaux crawled on all-fours.

A great part of the inhabitants had gone out to meet the *Forward,* and more than one advanced as far as the middle of the bay in his kayak.

The Doctor knew that the word *esquimaux* means *eater of raw fish,* but he also knew that this name is considered an insult by the natives; and he therefore took care to call them " Greenlanders."

And yet their oily sealskin clothes and boots, and the greasy, fœtid smell of both men and women—for one sex is hardly distinguishable from the other—told plainly enough the description of food on which they lived, as well as the disease of leprosy which prevailed to some extent among them, as it does among most ichthyophagous races, though it did not affect their health.

The Lutheran clergyman and his wife, with whom the Doctor was anticipating some pleasant intercourse, were on a visitation in the south, below Upernavik, so he was obliged to make the best of the Governor. This worthy functionary was not very lettered; a little less intelligence would have made him an ass; a little more, and he would have known how to read.

The Doctor also wished to make a personal inspection of an Esquimaux hut, but, fortunately for him, the entrance was too small to allow of his admission. It was a happy escape, for nothing can be more repulsive than the interior of a Greenland hut, with its heap of dead and living things, seal-flesh, and Esquimaux rotten fish, and stinking garments; not even a solitary window to purify the air; nothing but a hole at the top, which allows the smoke to escape, but not the fœtid smell.

Shandon, meanwhile, was obeying the instructions of his unknown commander, and procuring means of transport over the ice. He had to pay £4 for a sledge and six dogs, and even then the natives wished to get out of their bargain. He also sought to engage the services of Hans Christian to manage the dogs, the same young man that accompanied the McClintock expedition, but found he had gone to the south of Greenland.

But the most important part of Shandon's business was to try and discover whether there was any European at Upernavik waiting for the arrival of the *Forward*. Was the Governor acquainted with any stranger, an Englishman most probably, who had taken up his abode in this region? When had he last had any intercourse with whalers or other vessels?

To these questions the Governor replied that not a single stranger had landed on the coast for more than ten months. It was evidently a hopeless mystery, and Shandon could not help crowing a little over the disappointment of the sanguine Doctor.

" You must own it is quite inexplicable," he said; " nothing at Cape Farewell, nothing at Isle Disko, nothing at Upernavik."

" Wait a few days, and if it turns out there is nothing at Cape Melville either, I shall hail you as the only captain of the *Forward*."

Towards evening, the whale-boat came back to the ship, bringing Strong, the cook, with some dozens of eider-ducks' eggs, twice the size of common hens' eggs, and of a greenish color. His forage for fresh provisions had not been successful, but still the eggs were a very welcome addition to the salt junk.

The wind was favorable next day, but Shandon still delayed weighing anchor. He determined to wait till morning to give time for anyone to come on board that wished, and fired a salute from the cannon every hour to make known the presence of the vessel. It made a tremendous noise among the icebergs, but had no effect beyond frightening the mollymokes and rotches, who came flying out in clouds. Squibs and rockets in abundance were sent up during the night, but equally without result. There was no alternative but to proceed.

By six o'clock next morning the *Forward* had lost sight of Upernavik and its ugly posts all along the shore, with strips of seal intestines and paunches of deer hanging to dry. The wind was S.E., and the temperature had risen to 32°. The sun appeared through the fog, and the icebergs began to give way a little beneath his melting beams.

The white, dazzling reflections of his rays, however, had a disastrous effect on the men. Wolsten the gunner, Gripper, Clifton, and Bell, were attacked with snow blindness, a very common disease in spring, and often terminating among the Esquimaux in total loss of sight. The Doctor advised everyone, and especially those suffering from the complaint, to wear a green gauze veil, and he was the first to follow his own prescription.

The dogs Shandon had purchased at Upernavik turned out rather wild at first, but they soon became used to the ship, and Captain got on very well with his new associates. He seemed no stranger to their ways, and, as Clifton was not slow to remark, he had evidently been among his Greenland brethren before.

After leaving Upernavik the appearance of the coast quite changed. Immense glaciers stood out against the gray sky, and in the west, beyond the opening of Lancaster Sound, vast ice-fields extended, ridged with hummocks at regular intervals. There was great danger of the brig becoming nipped, as each instant the leads got more impracticable. Shandon had the furnaces lighted, and till the 11th managed to pursue a winding course among the loose floes, but on the morning of the 12th the *Forward* found herself beset on all sides. Steam proved powerless, and there was no alternative but to cut a way through the ice-fields. This involved great fatigue, and a mutinous spirit began to manifest itself in some of the crew, such as Pen, Gripper, Warren, and Wolsten. Certainly it was hard labor to saw through huge masses six and seven feet thick, and when this was accomplished it was almost as hard to tow the vessel along by means of the capstan and anchors fixed in the ice in holes made with a center-bit. The broken ice, too, had to be constantly pushed back under the floes with long poles tipped with iron, to keep a free passage, and all this physical toil, amid blinding snow, or dense fog, combined with the low temperature, the ophthalmia, and the superstitious fears of Clifton, contributed to weaken the mental and bodily energy of the men.

When the sailors have to deal with a bold, intrepid, decided leader, who knows his own mind and what he intends to do, confidence is felt in spite of themselves; they are one in heart with their captain, strong in his strength and calm in his calmness. But the crew of the *Forward* were conscious of Shandon's irresolution and hesitancy, for, notwithstanding his natural energy of character, he betrayed his weakness by his frequent countermand of orders, by imprudent remarks, and in a thousand little things that did not escape the notice of his men.

The simple fact, besides, that Shandon was not the captain, was enough to make his orders matters of discussion, and from discussion to rebellion is an easy step.

Before long, the malcontents had won over the head engineer to their side, a man who had been hitherto a very slave of duty.

On the 16th of May, six days from the time the *Forward* had reached the ice-fields, Shandon had not made two miles farther north. This was a very serious aspect of affairs, for they were in imminent danger of being locked in till the next season.

About eight in the evening, Shandon and the Doctor, accompanied by Garry, went out on a voyage of discovery over the vast outstretching plains of ice. They took care not to go too far from the ship, for it would have been difficult to find the way back. The Doctor was quite amazed at the peculiar effects of refraction. He came to a place where he thought he had only to make a little jump, and found to his surprise he had five or six feet to leap over, or *vice versa*, a fall being the result in both cases, which, though not dangerous, was painful on such a hard sharp surface.

Shandon and his companions were in search of leads, or navigable openings, and in pursuance of this object, about three miles from the ship, they climbed, though with considerable difficulty, to the top of an iceberg, above three hundred feet high. From this they had an extended view over a widespread heap of desolation. It was like gazing at the ruins of some mighty city, with its fallen obelisks and overturned towers and palaces. It was a veritable chaos, and far as the eye could see, not a single lead was visible.

" How shall we get through? " asked the Doctor.

" I don't know," replied Shandon, " but get through we must, even if we have to blast those mountains with powder. I certainly have no intention of being imprisoned in the ice till next spring."

" As the *Fox* was, just about this very same part," said the Doctor. " Bah! we shall get out, never fear, with a little philosophy. I would back that against all the engines in the world."

" One must confess things don't look very favorable this year."

" That is true enough. The aspect of the regions is much the same as it was in 1817."

" Do you suppose, then, Doctor, it is not always alike— the same to-day as it has always been? "

" Unquestionably I do, Shandon. From time to time sudden breakings up occur, which scientific men have never been able to explain. Till 1817 this sea was constantly blocked up, but in that year an immense cataclysm took place, which hurled the icebergs into the ocean, and many of them fell on the Bank of Newfoundland. From that time Baffin's Bay has been nearly free, and has become the rendezvous of numerous whalers."

" It is easier now, then, for ships to go north? " asked Shandon.

" Immensely so," said the Doctor; " but it has been a subject of remark, that for some years past there has been a tendency in the Bay to refill and close again, an additional reason why we should push on with all our might; though, I must confess, we are much like a party of strangers going through unknown galleries, when each door closes behind as they pass through, and cannot be reopened."

" Do you advise me to go back? " asked Shandon, looking at the Doctor, as if he would read his inmost soul.

" *I* advise you to go back! No, I have never yet learned

to put one foot behind the other, and I say *go on,* even should we never return; only, what I wish to impress on you is this, that if we set to work imprudently, we know the risks we incur."

"'And you, Garry," asked Shandon, "what is your opinion?'"

"I should go right on, certainly, sir. I agree with Mr. Clawbonny. However, it rests with you entirely. Give your orders, we will obey."

"All don't say so, Garry," was Shandon's reply. "All are not in the mood to obey. Suppose they refuse? What then?"

"I have told you my mind," replied Garry, coldly, "because you asked me, but you are not obliged to follow my advice."

Shandon made no response; but after carefully scanning the horizon once more, climbed down the iceberg again, followed by his two companions.

CHAPTER XI
THE DEVIL'S THUMB

DURING Shandon's absence the crew had been busily engaged in various attempts to lessen the pressure of the ice. This task was entrusted to Pen, Clifton, Bolton, Gripper, and Simpson, in addition to the two engineers and the stokers, who had to take their share of work as sailors, now that their services were not required at the engine.

"I tell you what," exclaimed Pen, angrily, "I have had enough of this, and I swear that if the ice does not break up within three days, I'll fold my arms, and not do another hand's turn!"

"Fold your arms!" said Gripper; "you had far better use them to get back. Do you suppose we are inclined to stay here all the winter till next spring?"

"Truly it would be a dismal place to winter in," said Plover, "for the vessel is exposed on all sides."

"And who knows," asked Brunton the engineer, "whether the sea will be a bit more open next spring than it is to-day?"

"It isn't a question of next spring," replied Pen; "this is

Thursday, and if the passage is not open by Sunday morning we turn round and go south"

"That's a sensible speech," said Clifton.

"Do you go in for that?" inquired Pen.

"Yes," was the unanimous reply.

"And it is only just," said Warren; "for if we are obliged to work in this fashion, and tow the ship along by main force, my opinion is that our labor would be better spent in dragging it back."

"We shall see that on Sunday," said Wolsten.

"Let me get orders," said Brunton, "and I'll soon light the furnaces."

"As for that," returned Clifton, "we can light them ourselves."

"If any one of the officers," continued Pen, "has a fancy to winter here, he is quite at liberty. He'll find no difficulty in making a snow-hut for himself, where he can live like a regular Esquimaux."

"That's out of the question, Pen," said Brunton, "we cannot leave anyone behind; and, what's more, I don't think the chief officer will be difficult to persuade. He seems very uneasy now, and if we propose the thing quietly to him——"

"That remains to be seen," said Plover. "Richard Shandon can be a hard, obstinate man when he likes; we must feel our way carefully."

"Only to think," said Bolton, eagerly, "that in a month's time we might be back in Liverpool. We shall easily get over the ice-belt down south. Davis's Straits will be open at the beginning of June, and we have only to get right out into the Atlantic."

"We have this to take into account besides," said the prudent Clifton, "that, in getting Shandon to come back with us, we act on his responsibility, and our shares and bounty money are sure; whereas, if we return alone, it is at least doubtful if we get them."

"But suppose the officers will not go back?" resumed Pen, bent on pushing the question to the extreme.

There was no reply for a moment, and then Bolton said: "We shall see when the time comes; all we have to do now is to win over Richard Shandon to our side, and I don't think that will be difficult."

" There is one on board, at all events, I'll leave behind,"
said Pen, with a frightful oath, " though he should eat my
arm off."

" That dog? " said Plover.

" Yes, that dog; and I mean to do for him before I am
much older."

" The sooner the better," replied Clifton, never weary
of his favorite subject. " He is the cause of all our misfortunes."

" I believe he dragged us into the ice," said Gripper.

" Ay, and gathered it up like this in front of us, for such
compact masses are never seen at this time of the year,"
added Wolsten.

" It is through him my eyes are so bad," said Brunton,
wearily.

" And through him we have neither gin nor brandy," said
Pen.

So the men went on, each one having his own grievance
against the dog

" Worst of all," said Clifton, " he is the captain! "

" A curse of a captain he is too! " exclaimed Pen, in a
paroxysm of senseless rage   " Well, he determined to come
here, and here he shall stay."

" But how shall we got hold of him? " said Plover.

" Now's our chance," replied Clifton; " Shandon is not
on board; Wall is alseep in his berth; and the fog is so thick
that Johnson will never see us."

" But the dog? " interrupted Pen.

" Captain is lying asleep this moment close beside the coal-
bunker," replied Clifton; " if anyone chooses to——"

" I'll undertake to get him," cried Pen in a fury.

" Take care, Pen; he has grinders that can break iron
bars."

" If he stirs I'll rip him up," declared Pen, taking up a
knife, as he rushed down between decks, followed by Warren, who wished to have a hand in the business.

Both came back presently, carrying the dog in their arms,
muzzled and tied up. They had surprised him in his sleep,
and escape was impossible.

" Hurrah for Pen! " exclaimed Plover.

" And now what's to be done with him? " inquired
Clifton.

"Drown him, and see if he ever makes his appearance again," replied Pen, with a grim smile of satisfaction.

About two hundred paces from the ship was a seal-hole, a circular crevasse made by the animals, out of which they come to breathe at certain intervals, basking on the surface of the ice, retreating below when danger approaches.

Pen and Warren directed their course to this hole, and, in spite of the poor dog's vigorous struggles, succeeded in plunging him into the sea, pitilessly placing an immense block of ice afterwards over the opening, to deprive him completely of all hope of release from his liquid prison.

"A good voyage to you!" shouted the cruel Pen as he returned to the vessel with Warren, unperceived by Johnson, for in addition to the thick fog the snow had commenced to fall heavily.

About an hour afterwards Shandon and his two companions came back. Shandon had discovered a single lead to the north-east, and determined to take advantage of it. The crew obeyed his orders with alacrity, for three days still remained; and, moreover, they wished to prove the impracticability of proceeding farther north.

Sawing the ice and tracking went on busily during a part of that night and all next day, and the *Forward* had gained two miles.

On the 18th they sighted land, and came within five or six cables' length of a singular peak, called, from its strange shape, the Devil's Thumb.

At the very same place the *Prince Albert,* in 1851 and the *Advance,* with Dr. Kane, in 1853, were caught in the ice and detained for several weeks.

It was a dismal spot. The weird, fantastic form of the towering peak, the dreary, desolate surroundings, the ominous crackings of the glaciers, echoing and re-echoing over the distant plains, and the vast encircling icebergs, some of them three hundred feet high, invested the whole region with peculiar gloom, and Shandon felt no time must be lost in getting out of it. By dint of strenuous efforts, in twenty-four hours he had pushed on about two miles; but this was not enough. Yet what was to be done? He felt as if his energies were paralysed by the false position in which he was placed, and a sort of shrinking fear began to creep over him, for he knew that he could not carry out the instructions of his unknown captain, without exposing the ship to great danger. The men were worn out. It took them more than three hours to cut a passage twenty feet long through floes four or five feet thick, and their health was already seriously impaired. Shandon was also uneasy at the silence of the crew and their unusual zeal; he dreaded it might be the calm which precedes a storm.

Imagine, then, the painful surprise and disappointment, even the despair, which he felt to find, through an insensible movement of the ice-fields, the *Forward* lost in one night the ground she had gained at the cost of so much fatigue. On the morning of Saturday, the 18th, they were right in front of the Devil's Thumb again, in a more critical position than before, for the icebergs had increased, and passed like phantoms through the fog.

Shandon was completely unnerved. His intrepid heart failed him, and he, like his men, quaked for fear. He had heard of the disappearance of the dog, but did not dare make any inquiry, lest a mutiny should break out.

It was terrible weather that day. A whirlwind of snow and thick mist wrapped the brig in an impenetrable veil. Occasionally the violent tempest would dispel the fog for an instant and disclose to the terrified gazer the gaunt, spectral form of the Devil's Thumb. Nothing could be done or even attempted except to anchor on an immense floe, for the darkness momentarily increased, and the man at the wheel could not even see the officer on watch at the bows.

Shandon retired to his cabin, a prey to the most tormenting anxieties. The Doctor employed himself in arranging his notes, and the sailors lounged about the deck, or betook themselves to the forecastle. The hurricane increased, and, through a sudden rift in the fog, the Devil's Thumb appeared slowly rising higher and higher.

" Good Heavens ! " exclaimed Simpson, starting back in dismay.

" What's the matter ? " asked Foker.

He needed no answer; for terrified outcries were heard on all sides—one exclaiming, " It is going to crush us ! " and another, " We are lost ! " and a third called loudly for Mr. Wall and Shandon, who speedily obeyed the summons. The Doctor followed, and for a minute all three stood in silent amaze.

It was a most alarming spectacle. Through a partial opening in the fog, the Devil's Thumb seemed quite close to the ship; its size increased to colossal magnitude, and on the summit a second cone appeared, point downwards, as if pivoted on the first, oscillating to and fro, and apparently about to fall on the brig and crush her beneath its enormous weight. Instinctively, everyone drew back, and several of the sailors jumped down on the ice and left the ship.

"Every man to his post," shouted Shandon, in stern tones. "No one is to leave the ship."

"Don't be afraid, my friends," said the Doctor. "There is no danger. It is simply the effect of the mirage, Mr. Shandon and Mr. Wall."

"You are right, Mr. Clawbonny," said Johnson. "These silly fellows are terrified at a shadow!"

Most of the sailors came back at the Doctor's reassuring words, and fear gave place to admiration, as they stood gazing at the marvellous phenomenon, which only lasted a few minutes longer.

"They call that a mirage," said Clifton, "but take my word for it, some fiend has to do with it."

"That's sure and certain," said Gripper. But the rift in the fog had revealed to Shandon's eyes a favorable lead, and he determined to profit by it without delay.. He placed the men on each side of the opening. The hawsers were thrown out to them, and the work of tracking commenced.

They went on for many long hours, and Shandon had the furnaces lighted to use all available means of getting rapidly on.

"It is a providential chance," he said to Johnson, "and if we can only make a few miles farther, we may be out of difficulties. The men are in a mind to work, for they are glad to get clear of the Devil's Thumb, so we will take advantage of their mood as long as it lasts."

All of a sudden the brig ceased moving.

"What's wrong, Wall?" asked Shandon. "Any of the ropes broken?"

"No, sir," said Wall, looking over the side, "but the sailors are all running helter-skelter towards the ship, and here some of them are climbing up the side as if they were out of their wits with fright."

V. II Venre

"What's the matter?" called Shandon, coming towards the bows.

"Let us on board! Let us on board!" exclaimed the sailors in panic-stricken tones.

Shandon looked towards the north and shuddered.

A strange-looking animal, with smoking tongue hanging out of enormous wide open jaws, was bounding towards the ship, and had come within a cable's length of her. He seemed more than twenty feet high; his hair stood on end, and his formidable tail, full ten feet long, swept the snow and sent it flying in thick clouds. He was evidently in pursuit of the sailors, and the apparition of such a monster was enough to scare the bravest.

"It is a bear!" said one.

"It is a dragon!" exclaimed another.

"It is the lion in the Revelation!" suggested a third, while Shandon ran to his cabin and seized a loaded pistol. The Doctor armed himself with a revolver, and stood ready to fire at the huge animal, who seemed, from his enormous size, to belong to the antediluvian world.

The beast came nearer, making tremendus leaps and Shandon and the Doctor discharged their weapons simultaneously. An unlooked-for result followed. The sudden explosion shook the atmosphere and changed the entire aspect of things

The Doctor burst out laughing, and said, "Refraction again!"

"Refraction!" exclaimed Shandon.

But the crew shouted "The dog! the dog-captain!" and Pen thundered out, "Ah! it is the dog, always that cursed dog!"

And the dog it really was, who had snapped his cords and managed to get out on the ice again at another seal-hole.

Refraction, which is common enough in Arctic latitudes, had made him assume these formidable dimensions, while the vibration in the atmosphere had restored him to his original proportions. But this occurrence had a bad effect on the sailors, who were by no means disposed to accept a purely physical explanation of it. The strange phenomenon at the Devil's Thumb, and the reappearance of the dog under such peculiar circumstances, brought things to a climax, and loud murmurings were heard on all sides.

CHAPTER XII
CAPTAIN HATTERAS

THE *Forward* steamed rapidly along through the open channel. Johnson took the wheel himself, and Shandon kept a vigilant look-out on the horizon. His joy was of short duration, for he soon saw that the channel terminated in a circle of mountains.

However, he determined to go on and take his chance, rather than turn back.

The dog ran beside the brig on the ice, but kept a good distance off. Strangely enough, however, if he got too far behind, a peculiar whistle was heard, which recalled him immediatly.

The first time this whistle was noticed, the sailors were all on deck. They looked about, but no stranger could be seen far or near, and yet the whistle was distinctly repeated several times.

Clifton was the first to sound an alarm.

"Do you hear that?" he asked; "and, look, how the animal bounds along when he is called."

"It is quite incredible," replied Gripper.

"This finishes it," exclaimed Pen. "I'll go no farther."

"Pen is right," said Brunton. "It is tempting Heaven."

"Tempting the fiend!" replied Clifton. "I'd rather lose my share than go another step."

"We shall never return," said Bolton, in a dejected tone.

It was clear the crew were ripe for mutiny.

"Not another step! Are we all agreed on that?"

"Yes!" was the unanimous reply.

"Well, then," said Bolton, "let us go to Shandon; I'll be spokesman."

Off they went in a body to the poop.

The *Forward* was just entering at that moment a vast amphitheatre, perhaps about eight hundred feet in diameter, without a single outlet save the passage by which they had reached it.

Shandon felt he had imprisoned his ship and himself, but what was to be done? A heavy responsibility rested on his shoulders.

The Doctor folded his arms and silently gazed at the surrounding ice-walls, the average height of which was three hundred feet.

At that moment Bolton came up with his friends, and said in a voice trembling with excitement:

"Mr. Shandon, we cannot go farther."

"You say that to me?" exclaimed Shandon, his cheek crimsoning with passion.

"We say this, we have done enough for our invisible captain, and we have made up our minds to go no farther."

"You have made up your minds? You speak like that, Bolton? Take care."

"Your threats won't hinder us," said Pen, rudely.

Shandon had made a few steps towards this rebellious crew, when Johnson came up to him and said in a low voice:

"If we wish to get out of this there is not an instant to lose. An iceberg is fast nearing the channel, which may completely block it up, and keep us here prisoners."

After a brief survey, Shandon turned towards the men and said:

"You shall give an account of this conduct to me by-and-by. Meantime, turn about the ship."

The sailors rushed to their posts. The *Forward* shifted rapidly. Fresh fuel was supplied to the furnaces, and the engine worked at high pressure, for everything depended on speed. It was a race between the brig and the iceberg.

"Put on more steam!" shouted Shandon, and the engineer obeyed at all risks, almost endangering the safety of the brig; but his efforts were in vain. The iceberg had been caught by some deep-sea current, and was bearing down fast towards the passage. The brig was still more than three cables' length off when the berg entered, and, adhering firmly to the ice on either side, shut up the outlet entirely.

"We are lost!" exclaimed Shandon, imprudently.

"Lost!" re-echoed from the crew.

"Let each take care of himself!" said one.

"Try the boats!" said another.

"Let's go to the stores!" said Pen. "If we are to be drowned, we may as well drown ourselves in gin."

The general disorder had reached its highest pitch, and broken all bounds. Shandon felt himself powerless. His tongue seemed palsied, and the power of speech forsook him. The Doctor paced up and down in an agitated manner, while Johnson folded his arms, and maintained a stoical silence.

Suddenly a loud, commanding, impressive voice thundered out the words:

" Every man to his post   Stop the ship!"

Johnson instinctively obeyed, and it was high time, for the *Forward* was steaming along at such a rate, that, before another minute, it must have dashed against the rocky walls.

But Johnson was the only man that obeyed.   Shandon, Clawbonny, and the entire crew, even the stoker and the cook, assembled on deck, and they all saw a man coming out of the captain's cabin, the mysterious cabin, so closely locked hitherto, the key of which was in the captain's sole possession.   This man was none other than the sailor Garry.

" Sir," said Shandon, turning pale.   " Garry, you— what right have you to command?"

" Duk!" called Garry, giving the same identical whistle which had so perplexed the crew.

At the sound of his right name the dog gave one bound on to the poop, and stretched himself quietly at his master's feet.   Not one of the crew said a word.   The possession of the key, the dog sent by him, which now proved, as it were, his identity, together with the tone of command, which it was impossible to mistake, had a great effect on the minds of the men, and sufficed to establish Garry's authority.

Besides, Garry was hardly recognizable.   He had shaved off his big whiskers, and his face appeared more impassive than before, and more energetic and imperious.   He was dressed now as befitted his rank, and had the air of one used to command.

The crew were quite taken by storm, and, with sailor-like mobility of character, burst out in loud cheers for the captain, who desired Shandon to muster them in order, as he wished to inspect them.   When they were all drawn up in file, he passed along in front of them and had a suitable word to say to each, treating them according to their past conduct.

Then he mounted the poop, and in a calm voice said:

" Officers and sailors, I am an Englishman like yourselves, and my motto is that of Admiral Nelson, ' England expects every man to do his duty.'

" As an Englishman I am unwilling, we are unwilling, that any should be braver than ourselves, and venture where we have not been. 'As an Englishman it vexes me, it vexes us, that others should have the glory of penetrating the Artic regions farther than ourselves. If ever human foot shall tread on polar ground, it must be the foot of an Englishman. See, yonder waves your country's flag! I have fitted out this ship, I have consecrated my fortune to this enterprise, I will consecrate my life and yours to it, but that flag shall float over the North Pole. Have no fear. For each degree north you make from this day you shall receive £1000 sterling. We have only reached the 72nd yet, and there are 90. My name will guarantee my good faith. I am Captain Hatteras!"

"Captain Hatteras!" exclaimed Shandon.

This name had an ominous sound, for he was well known among sailors as a man who stuck at nothing to gain his end, and had little regard for his own or any other man's life

"And now," resumed Hatteras, " let the brig be anchored to icebergs, and order the furnaces to be put out. Each man resume his usual occupation; and, Shandon, I wish to speak with you in my cabin. I must talk matters over with you and the Doctor, and Johnson and Wall. Boatswain, dismiss the men."

And who was this Hatteras? He was the only son of a brewer in London, who left an immense fortune. He went to sea in early youth, notwithstanding his brilliant prospects. Not that he had any love for the merchant service; but he had a burning longing after geographical discoveries. Lean and wiry in body, like most men of sanguine temperament, of average height, well-knit frame, and muscles like iron; with a calm, rigid face, and thin, compressed lips, and cold though fine eyes, he looked the very personification of a man who would stick at nothing. He was one who would never draw back from what he had begun, and who would stake other men's lives as deliberately as his own. People had need think twice before committing themselves to any of his projects.

John Hatteras had all the pride of an Englishman to excess. It was he that said one day to a Frenchman, who, with true national courtesy, tried to pay him a compliment, by declaring that if he had not been a Frenchman he should have wished to be an Englishman: "And I, sir, if I had not been an Englishman, should have wished to be an Englishman."

The speech showed the man. His most ardent desire was that his country should have the monopoly in geographical discoveries, and it was a great grief to him that in the fifteenth and sixteenth centuries England had no place in the glorious phalanx of navigators. True, in modern times she can boast her roll of illustrious names; but that was not enough to satisfy Hatteras; he must needs invent a country to have the honor of finding it. He had remarked the fact, that though the English were far behind in respect of discovery, there was one corner of the globe where their efforts seemed concentrated—the Arctic regions. He was not content with the successful search for the North-West Passage; the Pole itself must be reached, and he had twice made the attempt in vessels equipped at his own expense. To accomplish this was the one purpose of his life.

After several prosperous voyages in the southern seas, Hatteras made his first venture north by Baffin's Bay, in his sloop, the *Halifax,* but did not succeed in getting higher than the 74th degree of latitude. The sufferings of his crew were frightful, and his foolhardy daring was carried to such a pitch that the sailors had little inclination for another voyage under such a captain.

However, in 1850, Hatteras equipped a schooner, the *Farewell,* and managed to enlist twenty gallant fellows in his service, but only by throwing out the tempting bait of high wages. It was at that time that Dr. Clawbonny wrote to him, requesting to take part in the expedition; but the post of surgeon was already filled up, and fortunate it was for the Doctor.

The *Farwell* pushed as far north as the 76th degree, but there she was forced to winter. The crew were exposed to so many hardships, and the cold was so intense, that not a man survived but John Hatteras himself, and he was rescued by a Danish whaler, after a march across the ice of two hundred miles

His return alone produced a great sensation in Liverpool. Who would ever dare to accompany Hatteras again in his mad attempts? Yet he himself never despaired, and his father just then died, leaving him a nabob's fortune.

In the interim, a brig, the *Advance,* manned by seventeen

men, and commanded by Dr. Kane, was sent out by Grinnell, an American merchant, to the discovery of Franklin. It got as far, by Baffin's Bay and Smith's Straits, as the 82nd degree—nearer the Pole than any previous adventurers.

The vessel was American, Grinnell was American, Kane was American. This fact was a great grief to Hatteras, and the mortification of being outstripped by the Yankees rankled in his heart. He resolved that, come what might, he would distance them all and reach the Pole.

For two years he had been living in Liverpool, preserving a strict incognito. He passed for a sailor; he discovered the man he wanted in Richard Shandon, and made proposals both to him and Dr. Clawbonny by anonymous letters. The *Forward* was built, manned, and equipped. Hatteras took care to keep his name a secret, for he would not have found a single sailor to follow him. He determined not to take command of the brig unless compelled by imperative necessity, and not till the crew had gone too far to recede. He had also, as we have seen, kept such tempting offerings as glittering gold in reserve, that the poor fellows could not have refused to follow him to the world's end.

And to the world's end, indeed, it was that he vowed to go.

Now that affairs had come to a crisis, John Hatteras hesitated no longer to proclaim himself openly. His dog, the faithful Duk, who had been the companion of his voyages, was the first to acknowledge him, and happily for the brave, and unhappily for the timid, it was settled beyond dispute that the captain of the *Forward* was John Hatteras.

CHAPTER XIII
CAPTAIN HATTERAS DISCLOSES HIS PLANS

THE unexpected appearance of this bold personage did not produce the same effect on all the crew. Some rallied round him, completely attracted by his daring or by the love of money. Others were willing to join in the adventure, while reserving to themselves the right of protest at some future time. Besides, it would be no easy matter to resist such a man. The 20th was on a Sunday, and was kept as a day of rest for all on board.

'A' council of officers was held by the captain in his cabin, comprising Shandon, Wall, Johnson, and the Doctor. "Gentlemen," said Hatteras, in the gentle yet commanding tone peculiar to him, "you are aware of my project to reach the North Pole. I desire to know your opinion about it. What do you think, Shandon?"

"My business, captain, is not to think, but obey," said Shandon, coldly.

Hatteras showed no surprise at such a retort, but replied equally coldly: "Richard Shandon, I request your opinion as to our chance of success."

"Well, captain," was the answer, "facts will speak for me. Every attempt of the kind has hitherto failed; I hope we may be more fortunate."

"We shall be," said the captain. "And you, gentlemen, what do you think of it?"

"For my part," returned the Doctor, "I think your plan is practicable, and as it is evident that some day or other the Pole will be reached by navigators, I don't see why it should not be us as well as others."

"And there are also reasons why it should be so," resumed Hatteras; "all our measures have been adopted with a view to that end, and we shall profit by the experience of our predecessors. By the way, Shandon, thank you for your painstaking care in the equipment of the ship. There are, to be sure, a few black sheep among the crew that I must take in hand; but, on the whole, I have nothing but praise to bestow."

Shandon bowed stiffly. He felt his false position acutely. Hatteras understood his silence, and did not press him further.

"As for you, gentlemen," he continued, addressing Wall and Johnson, "I could not have the co-operation of braver or more experienced officers."

"Anyhow, captain, I'm your man," replied Johnson; "and though I must say I think your enterprise a little hazardous, you may rely on me, come what may."

"And equally on me," said James Wall.

"And for you, Doctor, all I can say is, I know your worth."

"Well, that is more than I do," replied the little man, smiling

"But now, gentlemen," resumed Hatteras, "It is well that you should know on what indisputable facts I base my expectation of reaching the Pole. In 1817, the *Neptune,* of Aberdeen, went north from Spitzberg, as far as the 82nd degree. In 1826, the celebrated Parry, after his third voyage in the 'Artic Seas, went also north from Spitzberg a hundred and fifty miles. In 1852, Captain Inglefield sailed up Smith's Sound as far as the 78th degree. All these vessels were English, and commanded by Englishmen, our fellow-countrymen."

Hatteras paused here, and went on in a sort of constrained voice, as if the words could hardly find utterance. "I ought to add that, in 1854, the American, Dr. Kane, in command of the brig *Advance,* got still higher; and that Morton, his lieutenant, crossed the ice-fields and hoisted the flag of the Union beyond the 82nd degree. Having said this, I shall not revert again to the subject. What I wish to tell you is, that the captains of all these vessels agree in stating that, extending from these high latitudes, there is a polar basin entirely free from ice."

"Free from ice!" exclaimed Shandon; "that's impossible."

The captain's eyes flashed for an instant, but he replied calmly: "You will please to notice, Shandon, that I am giving you facts and names——"

"But, captain," interrupted Shandon again, "the facts are so contradictory!"

"Wrong, Shandon, wrong," said Dr Clawbonny; "science goes to support these facts, not to disprove them, as I should like to show you, if the captain will allow me."

"Say on, Doctor," said Hatteras.

"Well, Shandon, listen, then. It is clear, from geographical facts and from the study of the isothermal lines, that the coldest point of the globe is not at the Pole, but several degrees from it. Hence Brewster and Bergham, and others conclude that there are two points of greatest cold, one in 'Asia, in 79° 30' of north latitude and 120° of east longtitude; the other in America, in 78° of north latitude and 97° of west longitude. It is this latter which concerns us; and, you see, Shandon, it is situated about 12° below the Pole. Now, then, I ask you, why should not the sea at the Pole be as free from ice as it is in the summer in the 66th parallel, that is to say, to the south of Baffin's Bay?"

"Mere chimeras and suppositions! Sheer conjecture!" replied Shandon, obstinately.

"Well, Shandon, let us consider the case both ways. Either there is a clear, open sea, or there is not. If there is, the *Forward* will sail along without difficulty, if it is all frozen over we shall use our sledges, and so whichever it may turn out, there is nothing to hinder us gaining the Pole. You will allow it is not impracticable; when once the brig gets as far as the 83°, we have only six hundred miles farther to go."

"And what is that!" exclaimed the enthusiastic Doctor, "when we know that a Cossack, Alexis Markoff, traveled along the northern coast of the Russian Empire over the Frozen Sea, in sledges drawn by dogs, a distance of eight hundred miles, in twenty-four days?"

"You hear that, Shandon?" returned Hatteras; "and now tell me if Englishmen cannot do as much as the Cossacks?"

"I should think so!" exclaimed Johnson and the Doctor; but Shandon made no reply till Hatteras said: "Come, Shandon, tell me."

Then all he said was in a freezing tone.

"Captain, I can only repeat what I have already told you—I will obey."

"Well," continued Hatteras, "let us look now at our actual situation. We are caught among the ice, and it seems to me impossible to get into Smith's Sound this year. This is what we had better do, then."

He unfolded a map and spread it out on the table, and tracing the route with his finger, said:

"Please to follow me. Though Smith's Sound is closed against us, Lancaster Sound is not, on the west side of Baffin's Bay. My opinion is, that we should enter this and go up as far as Barrow's Straits, and from thence on to Beechey Isle. Sailing vessels have taken this course a hundred times, and certainly with our screw it could not be more difficult, at any rate. Once at Beechey Isle, we will get as far north as possible up Wellington Channel, and come out just at the very point from which the open water was visible. This is only the 20th of May; under favorable circumstances we shall be there in a month, and make it our starting point for the Pole. What is your opinion, gentlemen? "

" It is clearly our only course," said Johnson.

" Well, we shall adopt it then, and start to-morrow. Let us make this Sunday a day of rest, and be sure that you attend, Shandon, to the regular reading of the Scriptures with the men. These religious observances have a most salutary effect on the human spirit, and a sailor especially needs to put his trust in God."

" I will see to it," replied Shandon, as he went away with Johnson and Wall.

" Doctor," said the captain, when they were left alone, " that man, Shandon, can't get over his mortification! He is eaten up with pride; I can no longer depend on him."

Next morning the boat was lowered, and Hatteras went round in it to examine all the icebergs in the basin. He noticed during his survey that its dimensions were constantly narrowing, owing to the slow, steady pressure of moving ice, and that consequently the brig would be crushed inevitably before long, unless an immediate breach was made The energy of the man was shown by the plan he took to effect this.

His first business was to have steps cut in one of the icebergs, and climb to the top of it. From this elevation he saw there would not be much difficulty in clearing a passage to the south-west. He ordered a mine to be dug almost to the heart of the mountain, and in the chamber of this he deposited 1000 lbs. of gunpowder. The blasting cylinders were only adapted for breaking ice-fields; they would have been useless against the towering masses by which the brig was encircled. A gutta-percha tube containing a wick was carried from the chamber to the outside, and the passage communicating was filled up with snow and blocks of ice, which the ensuing night, combined with the action of the east wind, would make as solid as granite

All this preparation was Monday's work, and next morning by seven o'clock the *Forward* was under steam, ready to seize the first opening to make her exit. Johnson was entrusted with the lighting of the taper, which was reckoned to burn for half an hour before coming in contact with the powder This was ample time to ensure his safe return to the vessel, and, in fact, he was back in ten minutes.

The crew were all on deck, and the weather was fine and tolerably clear, for the snow had ceased to fall. Hatteras stood on the poop with Shandon and the Doctor, counting the minutes by his chronometer.

At thirty-five minutes to eight a dull explosion was heard, far less astounding than might have been expected. The outline of the mountains suddenly changed as in an earthquake, a thick white smoke rose towards the sky, and long crevasses striped the sides of the iceberg, the summit of which seemed hurled from a distance, and fell in shattered fragments round the *Forward*.

But the pass was not yet open Enormous blocks of ice remained suspended in the air, propped up by the adjacent mountains, and their fall would only block up the basin still further

Hatteras took in the situation at a glance, and calling to the gunner, desired him to triple load the cannon.

"What! are we going to attack the mountain with cannon-balls?" asked the Doctor.

"Not exactly," said Hatteras, "that would be useless. No ball, Wolsten, but only a triple charge of powder. Be quick!"

All was ready in a few minutes.

"What will he do without ball?" muttered Shandon.

"We'll see," said the Doctor.

But the brig was too far from the iceberg, and Hatteras ordered the engineer to put the screw in motion A few turns was sufficient, and the command was given—Fire! A considerable explosion followed, which caused such an atmospheric commotion that the blocks were suddenly precipitated into the sea.

"Put on all steam possible, Brunton!" shouted the captain; "and get right out, Johnson, into the pass?"

Johnson seized the helm, the *Forward* dashed through the foaming waves, and next minute was free It was a sharp run for her, and she had scarcely cleared the opening before the prison closed again behind her.

It was a moment of intense excitement, and there was but one heart on board that beat quietly. This was the captain's, and the crew, unable to restrain their feelings of admiration for him, burst out into cheers, and shouted, "Hurrah for John Hatteras!"

On Wednesday, the 23rd May, the *Forward* resumed her adventurous navigation, skillfully tacking so as to keep clear of packs and bergs, thanks to her steam, that obedient power that has been so often wanting in Arctic ships.

The temperature was rising. At 6 A. M. the thermometer stood at 26 deg., at 6 P. M. at 29, and at midnight 25. A light breeze was blowing from the south-east.

About three o'clock on Thursday morning the *Forward* came in sight of Possession Bay, on the coast of America, and soon afterwards caught a glimpse of Cape Burney. Several Esquimaux were making hard for the ship, but Hatteras had no time to waste waiting for them. The puffins, and ducks, and white gulls were very numerous; and in the distance the snowy hoods of the Catherine and Elizabeth mountains were visible above the clouds.

On Friday, at six o'clock, Cape Warender was passed on the right, and Admiralty Inlet on the left. There was a strong sea, and heavy waves frequently dashed over the bridge.

Hatteras would have liked to keep along the northern coast for the sake of reaching Beechey Isle sooner, but an impenetrable barrier of ice barred his further progress in that direction, and he was, to his great vexation, forced to go by the south.

This was the reason why the *Forward* found herself on the 26th at Cape York, easily recognized by a lofty and almost perpendicular mountain which overlooks it. The latitude was found on observation to be 74° 4", and the longitude 84° 23".

Hatteras opened the map, and pointed out to the Doctor the routes they had been taking and meant to take.

"We are in cross roads, I may call it," he said, "open to the wind on all sides. Here is Lancaster Sound, Regent Inlet, Wellington Channel, and Barrow's Straits."

"It is a wonder to me how navigators know which route to take, when they have all four to choose from."

"Believe me there is little choice in the matter Sometimes Barrow's Straits are closed one year and open the next, and sometimes there is no passage at all but through Regent's Inlet."

"How the wind blows!" said the Doctor, drawing his hood closer over his ears."

" Yes, the north wind especially; it is so strong as to drive us out of our course."

" Well, but if it does that it surely ought to drive the ice south, and clear the way."

" It ought, but the wind doesn't always do what it ought. Look at that ice-field ahead; it looks perfectly impenetrable, and yet we must try to find some opening, for get to Beechey Isle I must at any rate, to replenish our stock of coal."

" Can you get coal there? " asked the Doctor, in astonishment.

" Most certainly. By order of the Admiralty, great stores were deposited there for the benefit of future expeditions; and though McClintock may have availed himself of them in 1859, there will be some left for us, I assure you."

" The Admiralty always kept five or six ships out here, I believe, till it was proved beyond a doubt that the whole of Franklin's ill-fated expedition had perished."

" Yes, they did. For fifteen years these regions were being explored, and one good result has followed anyway—that is our knowledge of the Polar Seas has greatly increased."

" It could hardly be otherwise, seeing the number of expeditions since 1848, when the first alarm was raised about the missing ships. Since McClintock returned in the *Fox*, however, not another vessel has ventured to try her fortune in those dangerous seas."

" Well, we'll try ours," said Hatteras, " come what may."

CHAPTER XIV
THE " FORWARD " DRIVEN SOUTH

THE weather cleared towards evening, and the shore became visible between Cape Sepping and Cape Clarence. The sea was open towards Regent Inlet, but as if the Fates had conspired against the *Forward's* progress north, there was still an impassable barrier of ice, which shut them out from Port Leopold.

Hatteras, who was extremely annoyed, though he did not show it outwardly in the least degree, had to fall back on his powder again to force an entrance, but he succeeded in getting in by mid-day on Sunday, the 27th of May, and safely moored his brig to great icebergs hard and solid as rocks.

A few minutes afterwards he jumped down on the ice and went ashore, followed by the Doctor and Johnson, and the faithful Duk, who was almost frantic with joy at being on land again. He had grown much more sociable and gentle since his master was acknowledged captain, reserving his animosity for certain folks among the crew, who were no greater favorites with him than they were with Hatteras.

The port inside was unusually free from ice, and the steep perpendicular cliffs were gracefully wreathed with snow. The house and beacon constructed by James Ross were still in a tolerable state of preservation, but the provisions had been ransacked by the foxes and bears, and showed marks of recent visits from them. Likely enough, two-footed marauders had been there too, for ruins of Esquimaux huts were visible about the bay.

The six graves, marked by little hillocks, where six of the crews of the *Enterprise* and *Investigator* lay buried, remained intact, respected alike by man and beast.

It is impossible to set foot for the first time on Artic ground without a feeling of peculiar emotion, as one relic and another is discovered, and the excitable little Doctor was almost overcome.

"Look!" he said to his companions; "there is the house that James Ross called 'The Camp of refuge!' If Franklin's Expedition had reached this spot it would have been saved. There is the very engine Ross left behind, too, and the stove where the crew of the *Albert* warmed themselves in 1851, looking just as if Kennedy, the captain, had but just quitted the place yesterday! And there is the sloop that sheltered him and his party for several days when they got separated from the ship, and must have perished but for Lieutenant Bellott, who set out to seek them, even though it was October."

"I knew Bellott," said Johnson, "and a brave, noble officer he was."

While the Doctor was pursuing his investigations with all the enthusiasm of an antiquary, Hatteras was busily exploring in all directions for food and fuel, though he met with small success. The next day was employed in carrying what he had found to the ship. The Doctor meantime continued his rambles, taking care not to get too far away. He sketched a good many of the principal objects of interest, and managed to make a pretty fair collection of the different varieties of Arctic birds.   He also saw several large seals, lying by their breathing-holes on the ice, but could not shoot any of them.   In one of his excursions he discovered a large stone with this inscription on it:

[E. I.]
1849.

These were the initials of the *Enterprise* and *Investigator*, a memento left behind of their voyage   He went on as far as Cape Clarence, where John and James Ross waited, in 1833, so impatiently, for the breaking up of the ice.   The ground was strewn over with bones and the skulls of animals, and traces were seen of Esquimaux huts.

The Doctor was thinking of setting up a cairn at Port Leopold, with a written statement in it of the arrival of the *Forward,* and the object of the expedition, but Hatteras was so decidedly opposed to leaving any indications whatever of their progress, lest some rival should take advantage of them, that the Doctor had to abandon his project.   Shandon greatly blamed the captain's infatuation, as in the event of any misfortune happening to the *Forward* no vessel could go to her rescue.

But Hatteras would listen to no reason, and the moment loading was completed he recommenced his efforts to break through the ice.   After many dangerous attempts, however, he was forced to give it up, and go back the way he came, through Regent's Inlet, for he would not winter in Port Leopold for anything.   It was open meantime, certainly, but a sudden dislodgment of the ice-fields might close them in any moment.

Hatteras was almost distracted with anxiety, though there was no outward manifestation of it.   He had no alternative but to turn his ship and go south, come what might.

Regent's Channel is about the same width the whole extent from Port Leopold to Adelaide Bay.   The *Forward* was more fortunate than most ships, for she made an uninterrupted passage through, thanks to her steam, instead of beating about for a month or more, often driven back by contrary winds.

Most of the crew were well content to turn their backs

on the north. They had no sympathy with the captain's project of reaching the Pole—indeed, they were almost terrified at him, dreading what next he might attempt, for they knew how little he cared for consequences.

It was evening when the brig came in sight of Edwin Bay, easily recognized by its high perpendicular rocks; and the next morning she saw Batty Bay in the distance, where the *Prince Albert* spent her long dreary winter.

The Doctor and Johnson, perhaps, were the only individuals on board who took any interest in the country. Hatteras was always poring over his charts, and hardly spoke a word. The farther south they went, the more taciturn he become, often sitting on the poop for hours together, with folded arms, gazing gloomily on the horizon, and any orders he gave were in the fewest words possible and in sharp, stern tones. Shandon kept himself aloof as much as he could, and gradually withdrew from all intercourse with Hatteras beyond what actual business required. James Wall was still devoted to Shandon, and faithfully copied his example. The rest of the crew were watching the course of events, ready to take the side that would be best for their own interests. There was no longer on the ship that unity of purpose and interchange of sentiment which is so necessary for the accomplishment of great things. Hatteras knew this well.

Two whales were seen during the day, and a white bear, but time was too precious to waste in pursuit of them, though a few ineffectual shots were fired.

On Wednesday morning the extremity of the inlet was reached, and the brig pursued her course, keeping along the west coast round a point, which, on referring to the chart, the Doctor found was Somerset House, or Fury Point.

"This, then," he said to Johnson, "is the very point where the *Fury* was so broken by the ice in 1815 that she had to be abandoned, and her crew went on board her consort, the *Hecla,* and returned home to England."

"That is the advantage of having a second ship, you see," replied Johnson; "but Captain Hatteras is not the man to be fettered with a companion!"

"Do you think that it is imprudent of him, Johnson?" asked Clawbonny.

"I? I think nothing about it, Mr. Clawbonny. Stop!

Do you see those stakes on the shore, with tattered rags hanging on them, as if a tent had once been there?"

"Yes, Johnson; it was there that Parry disembarked his ship's stores; and, if my memory is correct, the roof of the house he built was made of a topsail, covered over with the running rigging of the *Fury*."

"But that was in 1825. It must be very much changed since then."

"Not altogether though, Johnson. In 1829, John Ross found that little frail hut life and health to his crew. In 1851, when Prince Albert sent out an expedition, it was still standing. Captain Kennedy had it repaired, and that was nine years ago. It would be an interesting memorial to go ashore and examine, but Hatteras is not in the mood to stop!"

"And there is no doubt he is right, Mr Clawbonny. If time is money in England, out here it is salvation; and to stop a day—ay, even an hour—might ruin a voyage. Let him act as he thinks right."

On Thursday, the 1st of June, the weather became milder, the thermometer rising to thirty-two degrees. Summer made its influence felt even in those Artic regions, and the men were glad to lay aside some of their winter coverings.

Towards evening, the *Forward* doubled Cape Garry, about a quarter of a mile from shore, and went on to Brentford Bay, keeping as close to the coast as possible, for the fog had increased with the heat, and a close watch was necessary for the discovery of Bellot's Strait. It was somewhere in this latitude, but, if closed by ice, so perfectly undistinguishable from the land, that Sir John Ross never suspected its existence even in 1828, and, though he noted down and named the smallest irregularities with the greatest care on his charts, he made this one continuous coast.

It was Captain Kennedy who really discovered the Straits in 1852, and called them after the French officer, as a just tribute of gratitude for the important services he had rendered the expedition.

CHAPTER XV
THE MAGNETIC POLE

THE nearer Hatteras approached the Strait, the more his anxiety increased. He felt the fate of his voyage was about to be decided, for though he had outstripped all his predecessors up to this time, as even McClintock, the most fortunate of them, had taken fifteen months to reach the same place, it mattered little, indeed nothing, if he could not succeed in getting through Bellot's Strait.

He would trust the look-out to no one, but went up to the "crow's-nest" himself, and stayed there the greater part of Saturday morning.

The crew understood perfectly their critical position, and preserved an unbroken silence. The engine had slackened speed, and the brig kept to the shore as closely as possible; but it needed a practiced eye to discover the least opening among those close packs.

Hatteras was comparing his charts and the coast. The sun broke out for a brief instant before noon, and Shandon and Wall managed to take a pretty correct observation, which they reported aloud to Hatteras.

It was a trying morning for all; but at last, about two o'clock, a cry resounded from the mast-head:

"To the west, and put on steam!"

The brig instantly obeyed. She turned her prow in the given direction, and rushed forward between two ice-streams.

The entrance was found, and Hatteras gave up his post to the ice-master, and came down on the poop.

"Well, captain," said the Doctor, "we have actually entered this famous strait at last."

"Yes," replied Hatteras, lowering his voice, "but it is not enough to enter, we have to get out again."

Without another word he turned, and walked off to his cabin.

"He is right," said the Doctor, "for we are in a mouse-trap, without much room to do anything; and if we are blocked in for the winter, well, we are not the first that have got into this same fix, and they got out, so I suppose we shall!"

The Doctor was right. It was in that very place that McClintock wintered in 1858, and the little dock was then in sight where he found shelter, and which he called Port Kennedy.

Bellot's Strait is about a mile wide and seventeen long, with a current running from six to seven knots. It is encased in mountains calculated at 1600 feet high. The *Forward* had to proceed cautiously, but still she made progress. Storms are frequent in such a narrow space, and the brig did not escape heavy seas and strong squalls of wind. In spite of every precaution taken by the captain in reefing and lowering masts and sails, it was a fatiguing strain on the ship. It was impossible almost to stand on deck, and most of the men studied their own comfort, and went off, leaving Hatteras with Shandon and Johnson. The little Doctor did not feel any more inclination than the sailors to brave the snow and rain, but, acting on his old rule, always to do that which is most disagreeable to him, he went up to bear the others company; and since he could not hear himself speak, and even barely see himself, he was obliged to keep his reflections for his own benefit.

He found Hatteras trying to pierce through the curtain of fog before him, for, according to his reckoning, they ought to have come to the end of the strait by six o'clock; but no outlet was visible, and the only thing that could be done was to anchor the ship fast to an iceberg, and wait till morning.

It was fearful weather; every instant it seemed as if the *Forward* would snap her chains, and there was great danger of the iceberg itself giving way beneath the violence of the west wind, and drifting along, ship and all. The officers were on the *qui vive* the whole night, and felt the gravest apprehensions. There was not only a perfect waterspout of snow, but showers of hail lashed up by the hurricane from the ice-fields; the whole atmosphere was, as it were, bristling with sharp arrows.

Strangely enough, there was a great rise in the temperature during this fearful night. The thermometer stood at 57°, and the Doctor, to his great surprise, thought he saw several flashes of lightning in the south, followed by very distant thunder.

About five in the morning, the weather changed again with astonishing rapidity, and the thermometer fell to freezing point. The wind veered north, and became calm. The western opening of the strait was now visible enough, but it looked entirely blocked up. Hatteras almost doubted whether it had ever been the opening.

However, the brig got under way again, and glided slowly along between the ice-streams, crushing the edges of the packs against her side timbers. The packs were still six to eight feet thick, and the utmost care was necessary to avoid coming into collision with any of them.

At noon, and for the first time, a magnificent solar phenomenon was observed, a halo with two parhelia. The Doctor took the exact dimensions: the outer corona was only visible for about 30° on each side of the horizontal diameter. The two images of the sun were remarkably distinct. The colors of both the arches were red nearest the sun, and then yellow, green, and very pale blue, fading into white outside.

Old sailors in the Arctic seas generally consider this phenomenon the presage of a heavy snowfall. Should their opinion prove correct, it would place the *Forward* in a still more awkward position. Hatteras felt that everything depended on getting forward without delay. He spent the remainder of the day and the whole of the night following on deck, without allowing himself a moment's rest, seeking for some practicable lead.

But next morning, when the Doctor joined him on the poop, he beckoned him right away to the after part of the ship, where they were quite out of ear-shot, and said:

"We are caught! It is impossible to get any farther."

"Impossible?" asked the Doctor.

"Yes, impossible! All the powder in the *Forward* would not gain a quarter of a mile for us."

"What's to be done, then?"

"Who knows? Confound this weather. It is an ill-omened year."

"Well, captain, if we must winter here, we must— that's all! As well here as anywhere else."

"True enough!" said Hatteras, in a low voice; "but we must not winter, especially in the month of June. Wintering at all is full of moral and physical danger. A crew soon becomes enervated by inactivity, combined with positive suffering, and I had made up my mind not to winter till we were in a much more northerly latitude."

"But Fate decreed that Baffin's Bay should be closed."

"Ay! and it could open for others—for that American!" exclaimed Hatteras, angrily.

"Come, Hatteras," said the Doctor; "this is only the 5th of June. Don't let us despair. A sudden opening may occur. You know the tendency of the ice to separate, even in calm weather. Perhaps in less than an hour there may be a free outlet."

"I wish it may be so, we would soon get through it, and once outside this strait we may be able to go north again by Peel's Strait, or the McClintock Channel. Then we——"

"Captain," said James Wall, interrupting him suddenly, "our rudder runs the risk of being torn away by the packs."

"Well, it must take its chance; I cannot have it removed. I wish to be ready at any hour, both day and night. See that it is protected as much as possible, Mr. Wall, by avoiding coming into contact with the ice; but let it remain in its place, remember."

"But——" said Wall.

"I wish for no remarks, sir!" said Hatteras, sternly. "Go."

Wall returned to his post, and Hatteras exclaimed passionately:

"Oh! I would give five years of my life to find myself at the north. I know no passage that is more dangerous than this, and to increase the difficulty, now that we are getting near the magnetic pole, the compass there is not acting properly, the needle seems getting lazy or foolish, for it is constantly shifting its direction."

"I must confess it is perilous navigation now; but after all, everyone who joined the expedition knew the dangers he had to expect, so he needn't be surprised."

"Ah, Doctor, my crew are very much changed, and, as you have just heard, the officers begin to set up their opinion. The pecuniary advantages offered to the sailors made them engage in the service; but the worst of it is, when men join like that, all they care for is to get home again, and be paid as quickly as possible. Then, too, I am not seconded by my officers as I ought to be, Doctor. If I fail in my undertaking it will not be the fault of such and such a sailor, but through the ill-will of certain officers. Ah, won't I make them pay dearly for it!"

"Hatteras, you are exaggerating."

"I am not exaggerating in the least. Do you believe the sailors are sorry we cannot get north? On the contrary, they rejoice in my difficulties, thinking I shall be forced to relinquish my project. That is the secret of our hearing no grumbling just now. As long as the *Forward* has her beak head to the south, they are all ready enough to work. The fools! They fancy they are always nearer England! But if I succeed in getting north, you will see things change. However, I swear that not a single human being will make me go out of my track. Let me only find the smallest opening to get my brig through, and in she'll go, even if she has to leave her copper bottom behind her."

The captain was destined to get his wishes partially realized, for in the course of the evening, as the Doctor had said, there was a sudden change The ice-fields cracked and opened, and the *Forward* boldly dashed in between them, crushing the loose ice with her metal prow. She went without stopping all night, and next morning, about six o'clock, got outside the strait.

But what was the captain's secret vexation to find the way to the north still obstinately shut against him. He had sufficient self-command to conceal his despair, and as if the only route open had been the very one he preferred, he sailed down Franklin's Strait; not being able to get north by Peel's Strait, he determined to go round the point and up the McClintock Channel. But he felt that Shandon and Wall were not deceived; they well understood his bitter disappointment.

For thirty-six hours the *Forward* followed the windings of the Coast of Boothia, without getting near Prince of Wales Island. Hatteras raised the steam, burning away the coals in prodigal fashion, always hoping to replenish his store at Isle Beechey. On Thursday he reached the extremity of Franklin's Strait, and again found the route to the north barred against him.

His situation was hopeless now. He could not even go back, for the heavy packs were pushing him continually forward, and what had been open water but an hour before when the brig passed through, was now solid ice.

It was a terrible predicament for the *Forward*, for she could not get north, and yet dared not stop for fear of a crush. All that she could do was to flee as if before a storm.

On Friday, the 8th June, he arrived at the mouth of James Ross's Strait, one which he must avoid at any cost, for it had no outlet except to the west, right on the American coast. The longitude here was found to be 90° 46′ 45″, and the latitude 70° 5′ 17″. On referring to the map the Doctor discovered they had reached the magnetic pole, for this was the very part where it had been discovered by James Ross.

The shore near the coast was flat, rising in the background about a mile from the sea to a height of about sixty feet.

Finding that the boiler needed to be cleaned, the captain anchored his brig to the ice, and allowed the Doctor and Johnson to go ashore. As for himself, he felt no interest in anything that was not immediately connected with his projects, and only cared to shut himself up in his cabin and pore over his charts.

The Doctor and his companion were soon on land, carrying a compass with them for their experiments. The Doctor wished to test for himself the accuracy of James Ross's observations. He easily discerned the heap of chalk stones he had set up, and on hastening towards it, perceived through an opening the identical tin case in which he had deposited a minute account of his discovery. Not a single human being seemed to have visited this dreary coast for thirty long years!

If a magnetized needle is suspended here as delicately as possible, it will immediately assume an almost vertical position under the magnetic influence. The center of attraction then, if not exactly below the needle, must be but a very short distance off.

The Doctor made his experiments with the utmost care, and was more successful than even James Ross, who could never get a higher declination for his vertical needle than 89° 59′, owing to the imperfection of his instruments, while Dr. Clawbonny had the extreme satisfaction of seeing his needle indicate a declination of exactly 90°.

"This, then," he said, tapping the ground with his foot, "is the actual magnetic pole of our globe."

"Is it just here?" asked Johnson.

"In this precise spot."

"I suppose then it is all nonsense to talk about a magnetic mountain, or a mass of lodestone!"

"Yes, my good fellow, it is all 'old wives' fables.' As you see for yourself, there is not a sign of a mountain endowed with the power of attracting ships, and tearing away their iron, down to anchors and nails. Even your boots do not feel any heavier, as if they were dragging you down, do they? You can walk as easily here as anywhere else."

"But how can it be explained?"

"It can't be explained. We are not learned enough for that yet. But this one thing is an ascertained mathematical fact—the magnetic pole is here, in this very place."

"Ah! Mr. Clawbonny, what would the captain give if he could say as much of the North Pole?"

"He will say it some day, Johnson, that he will."

"I fervently hope he may."

Just at this moment the signal was made for their return, and after hastily erecting a cairn to mark the exact spot, they hurried back to the brig.

CHAPTER XVI
THE STORY OF SIR JOHN FRANKLIN

THE *Forward* succeeded in cutting right across the James Ross's Strait, but it was only done by dint of saws and petards, and at the cost of great fatigue to the crew. Fortunately the temperature was bearable, 30° higher than James Ross had found it at the same time of the year. The thermometer stood at 34°.

On Saturday, Cape Felix was doubled, at the extreme point of King William's Island. The sight of this island made a deep impression on the minds of the men, and they gazed with mournful interest at the coast as they sailed along. This was the theater of one of the most terrible tragedies the world has ever seen, for, only a few miles to the west, the *Erebus* and *Terror* were lost.

Johnson and the Doctor were going over the particulars of the sad catastrophe as the vessel fled swiftly on, and bays and promontories passed before the eye like some vast panorama. Several of the sailors, overhearing the subject of conversation, drew nearer to listen, and before long the Doctor had the whole crew round him. Seeing their eager curiosity, and knowing what an impression the recital would make in such circumstances, the Doctor recommenced his narrative

"You know, I suppose, my good fellows," he said, "the early history of Franklin. He was a cabin-boy, like Cook and Nelson, and, after serving during his youth in several great expeditions, he determined, in 1845, to prosecute a search for the North-West Passage. He was in command of the *Erebus* and *Terror,* two ships that had been previously employed in an Arctic expedition undertaken by James Ross. The *Erebus* carried seventy sailors, including the officers, with Fitz-James as captain; Gore and Vesconte as lieutenants; Des Vœux, Sargent, and Couch as quartermasters; and Stanley as surgeon. The *Terror* numbered sixty-eight men. Her captain was Crozier; the lieutenants, Little, Hodgson, and Irving; quartermasters, Horesby and Thomas; and surgeon, Peddie. Not one of these ill-fated individuals ever returned to their native land, but you may read nearly all their names on the different bays, and capes, and straits, and points, and channels, and islands that are met with in this region. There were 138 men altogether. The last letters received from Franklin were dated July 12th, 1845, and written from Isle Disko. 'I hope,' he wrote, 'to weight anchor to-night for Lancaster Sound.' What has happened since his departure from Disko? The last time the ships were seen was in Melville Bay, by the captains of the *Prince of Wales* and the *Enterprise,* two whalers; and since then there has been no word of them. We are able to follow Franklin, however, in some of his subsequent movements. He went to the west, and up Barrow's Strait and Lancaster Sound, as far as Isle Beechey, where he spent the winter of 1845."

"But how was that ascertained?" asked Bell, the carpenter.

"By three graves discovered by the Austin expedition in 1850, in which three of Franklin's sailors were interred; and also by a document found by Lieutenant Hobson, of the *Fox,* which is dated 1848. From this we learn that, at the close of the winter, the *Erebus* and *Terror* went up Wellington Channel as far as the 77th parallel; but, instead of con-

tinuing their route to the north, which was doubtless found
to be impracticable, they returned south."

" And it was their ruin," said a grave voice. " Salvation
was in the north.

Everyone turned to see who was the speaker. It was
Hatteras, leaning against the railing of the poop, who made
his home-thrust at the crew.

" There is no doubt," continued the Doctor, " that Franklin's intention was to reach the American coast; but he was
overtaken by furious tempests, and both ships got caught in
the ice a few miles from this, and were dragged N. N. E. of
Point Victory. But the ships were not abandoned till the
22nd April, 1848. What happened during those nineteen
months, who knows? What did the poor fellows do with
themselves all that time? No doubt they explored the country, and tried their utmost to reach a place of safety, for
Franklin was a man of great energy, and if his measures
were unsuccessful——"

" It was, perhaps, his crew who proved false to him? "
again interrupted Hatteras, in a hollow voice.

No one dared to look up, for the cap fitted. The Doctor
resumed his narrative, and said:

" The document I have mentioned gives the additional
information of the death of Sir John Franklin. He sank
under his fatigues on the 11th of June, 1847. Honor to his
memory," he added, baring his head respectfully.

All the men silently followed his example. After a pause,
Doctor Clawbonny went on to say:

" What became of the men after their admiral's death?
Ten months elapsed before they forsook the ship, and the
survivors then numbered one hundred and five men. Thir-
ty-three were dead! A cairn was erected on Point Victory
by order of the captains, Crozier and Fitz-James, and in it
this their last document was deposited. See, we are just
passing the very place. You can still see the remains of this
cairn on the very extremity of the point. And there is Cape
Jane Franklin, and there is Point Franklin, and there is
Point le Vesconte, and there is Erebus Bay, where they
found the sloop made out of pieces of one of the ships and
laid on a sledge. They also discovered silver spoons there,
and tea and chocolate, besides religious books and provisions
in abundance. For the hundred and five survivors, under

the guidance of Captain Crozier, set out for the great Fish River. How far did they get? Did they reach Hudson's Bay? Do any of them still survive? Who can say what has become of them all now?"

"I can say what has become of them," replied John Hatteras, in loud, ringing tones. "Yes, they did reach Hudson's Bay, and divided into several parties. Yes, they took the route south, and in 1850 a letter of Dr. Rae mentioned the fact that on this very island before us, the Esquimaux fell in with a detachment of forty men hunting seals over the ice, dragging a boat with them, and looking pale and haggard, worn out with suffering and fatigue. And subsequently thirty corpses were found on the mainland, and five on an adjacent isle, some half buried, and some lying quite exposed; others under a boat turned upside down, and others still under the remains of a tent; here an officer, with his telescope on his shoulder and his loaded gun beside him, and not far off cauldrons with the fragments of a ghastly sickening meal.

"On the receipt of this intelligence, the Admiralty requested the Hudson's Bay Company to dispatch experienced men to search the entire region. They explored the whole of the Black River to its mouth. They visited the islands of Montreal, Maconochie, and Point Ogle. But it was all in vain! Everyone of the hapless company was dead! Dead from starvation, and pain and misery, after making a horrible attempt to prolong their wretched lives by cannibalism! This is what has become of them. The route south is strewed with their mangled remains! Do you still desire to walk in their footsteps?"

The thrilling voice and impassioned gestures and earnest face of Hatteras produced an indescribable effect on the men, and, carried away by their emotion, they shouted with one accord:

"To the North! To the North!"

"To the North, then, we'll go, my men! Safety and glory lie there! Heaven is on our side; the wind has shifted! The channel is open, turn about the ship!"

The sailors rushed to their posts, the *Forward* was soon making at full speed for the McClintock Channel.

Hatteras was right, the ice had given way, and the ship found her passage almost unobstructed. On the 14th of

June she had gone beyond Osborn Bay, and farther than any of the expeditions of 1851. The ice-packs were still numerous, but she never lacked water below her keel.

CHAPTER XVII
THE ROUTE TO THE NORTH

THE crew had apparently returned to their good habits of discipline and obedience. Their work was not fatiguing now, and they had abundance of leisure. The temperature still remained above freezing point.

Duk, who had grown quite friendly and sociable, struck up the closest friendship with Dr. Clawbonny. They were on the best possible terms, though it must be confessed Duk was quite master, and made the little Doctor do whatever he pleased. Towards the crew, too, and officers generally, Duk was amiable enough, except towards Shandon, and from him he always ran away as fast as he could, doubtless impelled by some secret instinct. He also kept a sharp tooth For Penn and Warren; and what a tooth it was! He growled whenever they came near, though they never again attempted to lay a finger on him. No one dared to touch the captain's dog, his " familiar spirit," as Clifton called him.

On the whole, however, the confidence of the men seemed restored, and they were behaving well.

" It looks as if the crew had laid the captain's words to heart," remarked Wall to Shandon one day. " They don't appear now to have any misgivings about success."

" They are wrong," said Shandon; " if they were only to reflect and examine their situation, they would see we are going from one imprudent step to another."

" And yet," returned Wall, " the sea is certainly more open, and we are going on no untried route. Are you not exaggerating, Shandon? "

" No, Wall, I am not; the hatred or jealousy, if you choose to call it so, which I feel towards Hatteras, has not blinded my eyes. Tell me, have you been down to see how the coals stand? "

" No," replied Wall.

" Well, just you go, and you will see how fast our stock

is diminishing. The rule with us should have been to rely on our sails mainly, reserving the screw for special occasions when the wind was contrary, or there were strong opposing currents; our combustibles ought to be husbanded with the most rigid economy, for who knows where we may be driven, or how long we may be frozen up in these seas? But Hatteras, in his frenzied ambition to push north and reach the inaccessible Pole, never troubles himself about such small matters. Whether the wind is for or against us, he must have all the steam up, and if he goes on much longer in the same fashion, we stand a chance of finding ourselves in a pretty fix some day, and even of our total loss."

" If what you say is true, Shandon, the case is serious," replied Wall.

" Yes, Wall, very serious; not merely for the engine, which would be utterly useless without coal, just perhaps when we most needed it; but for ourselves, too, when we think of having to winter here, which we certainly must do, soon or late One needs to think of cold a little in a country where the quicksilver even freezes in the thermometer."

" But, if I am not mistaken, Shandon, the captain is reckoning on replenishing his stock at Isle Beechey. He can get an abundance of fuel there."

" Can people go just where they choose, Wall, in these seas? Can we ever reckon on finding the straits open? And supposing he should miss the isle, or be unable to get to it, what will become of us? "

" You are right, Shandon. It is certainly imprudent of Captain Hatteras, but why don't you talk to him on the subject."

" No, Wall," said Shandon, with ill-concealed bitterness, " I have made up my mind to be silent. I have no responsibility now; I shall watch the course of events and do whatever I am told without expressing an opinion."

" Let me tell you, Shandon, you are wrong. This is a question of our common interest, and imprudence on the captain's part may cost us all dear."

" And would he listen, Wall, if I were to speak? "

Wall could not reply in the affirmative. He evaded the question by asking whether the representations of the crew would have more effect.

"The crew!" repeated Shandon, shrugging his shoulders. "Why, Wall, you surely cannot have noticed the men. They are not caring the least about their safety just now. All they know is, that they are getting near the 72nd parallel, and that each degree beyond that will bring them a thousand pounds!"

"You are right, Shandon," replied Wall. "The captain knows the best way to keep his men."

"For the present, at any rate, it is the best," replied Shandon.

"What do you mean?"

"I mean that while there is no danger and no hard work, things will go on very well. Hatteras has caught them with a golden bait, but what's only done for money is never much worth. Wait till we get into difficult and trying circumstances; wait till sickness, and cold, and misery, and despondency come upon us, and all the calamities towards which we are madly rushing, and you'll see how few of them will think much of the prize to be won."

"Then you don't think Shandon, that Hatteras will succeed in his attempt?"

"No, Wall, he will not succeed. An enterprise like this requires perfect harmony of thought and feeling among the leaders, and this is wanting among us. More than that, Hatteras is a madman. All his past history proves it. Well, we shall see. A time may come when he will be compelled to give up the command of the ship to a less venturesome man."

"I don't know about that," said Wall, with a doubtful shake of the head. "He will always have some to stand by him; he will have——"

"He will have Dr. Clawbonny," said Shandon, interrupting him, "a learned man who cares for nothing but learning; Johnson, a sailor, who is a slave to discipline, and who never takes the trouble to examine a question; and perhaps one or two others, such as Bell, the carpenter, not more than four at the outside—four out of eighteen of us. No, Wall; Hatteras has not the confidence of the crew, and he knows that well enough. He bribes them with money. He managed to work on their excitable natures very cleverly with the Franklin story; but that won't last, I tell you, and if he don't succeed in reaching Isle Beechey he is ruined."

" If the crew only suspected that——"

" I beg you say nothing to them whatever on the subject. They will soon make their own remarks. Moreover, we could not do better meantime than continue our present course. Perhaps, after all, what Hatteras thinks going north may prove going back. McClintock Channel opens into Melville Bay, but that succession of straits that leads to Baffin's Bay, begins there too; Hatteras had better take care! The road to the east is easier than that to the north."

Shandon's words revealed his secret sentiments. No wonder Hatteras felt he was a traitor.

As far as the crew went, however, his opinion of them was quite right. Their contentment was entirely owing to the prospect of soon reaching the 72nd parallel. The love of money had taken complete possession of them, and Clifton had calculated accurately the sum that would fall to each. There were sixteen men altogether on board, not counting the captain and the Doctor, who, of course, were not to share in the prize. The amount promised was £1,000; that gave £62 10s to each individual. Should they ever reach the Pole, the eighteen degrees more would enrich them still further with a sum of £1,125—quite a fortune. This would cost the captain £18,000, but he was rich enough to be able to pay it.

On the 16th of June the *Forward* coasted past Cape Aworth. The white peaks of Mount Rawlinson seemed to pierce the very heavens, the snow and fog making its height appear colossal. The temperature was still some degrees above freezing point. Cascades and cataracts were rushing down the sides of the mountains, and the loud noise of falling avalanches struck upon the ear like the continuous discharge of heavy artillery, reverberating over the glaciers for an immense distance. It was a splendid spectacle, and the ship hugged the coast so closely that objects were distinctly visible. Rare heaths were discovered growing on sheltered rocks, with their pink flowers timidly peeping above the snow. A few miserable looking lichens of a reddish color were also seen, and a dwarf willow, which crept along the ground.

At last, on the 19th of June, the 72nd parallel was crossed, and the brig entered Melville Bay—the " Silver Bay," as Bolton christened it. On the 25th, in spite of a strong breeze from the N. E., she passed the 74th degree, and found herself in Melville Sound, one of the largest in those regions. It was Captain Parry who first traversed it in his great expedition of 1819, and it was for this his crew gained the prize of £5,000 offered by Government.

CHAPTER XVIII
A WHALE CHASE

MELVILLE SOUND, though perfectly navigable, was not free from ice. Extensive ice-fields stretched beyond as far as the eye could reach, with solitary icebergs appearing here and there, standing motionless, as if anchored firmly to the glaciers.

But the *Forward* found good leads everywhere, and steamed rapidly along, in spite of the variable wind, which kept shifting from one point of the compass to another.

The sudden changes of the wind are most remarkable in these Arctic Seas. Often, but a few minutes will separate a dead calm from a strong tempest, as Hatteras found to his cost on the 23rd of June, just as he reached the middle of the immense bay.

The most constant winds are those which blow from the polar ice-belt towards the open water, and these are extremely cold. On this day the thermometer sank several degrees, and the wind suddenly veered south. Thick snow began to fall, and such violent gusts of wind arose, that Hatteras ordered all the sails to be close-reefed; but, before his commands could be executed, one of the smaller yards was already torn away.

Hatteras never left the deck while the gale lasted, though the fury of the blast compelled him to change his position. There he stood, issuing his orders with the most imperturbable calmness, though the sea was lashed mountains high by the raging tempest, and his brig was tossed up and down on the waves like a child's toy—now borne aloft perpendicularly on the crest of some gigantic billow, her steel prow gleaming for an instant in the light; and then precipitated into an abyss amidst clouds of smoke, her stern and screw rising completely out of the water; rain and snow all the time falling in torrents.

The Doctor, of course, could not lose the opportunity of getting drenched to the skin. He stayed on deck with the rest, in silent admiration of the grandeur of the spectacle; and he found his endurance well repaid by the sight of a peculiar phenomenon, which is only observable in polar latitudes.

The storm raged within certain limits, not extending farther than three or four miles. This arises from the fact that, in passing over the ice-fields, the wind is robbed of much of its power, and its fury is soon exhausted. Every now and then, in a fall of the swell the Doctor caught glimpses of a clear sky and a calm sea beyond the ice. The brig had only to go right forward to get into smooth sailing; but she ran the risk of being dashed to pieces in the transit. However, after some hours, Hatteras succeeded in getting beyond the storm, though only by a few cable-lengths, leaving it still raging in the distance.

The appearance of the bay was totally altered. A great number of bergs had become detached from the coast ice by the double influence of wind and waves; and these were scudding along towards the north, crossing and clashing against each other in every direction. They could be counted by hundreds, but the Sound was so wide that the *Forward* found little difficulty in steering clear of them. It was a magnificent sight; for the moving masses, being endowed with unequal degrees of velocity, seemed like so many runners on a vast race-course.

The Doctor was surveying the scene with enthusiastic admiration, when Simpson, the harpooner, came up, and drew his attention to the changing tints of the sea, from bright blue to olive green.

Long bands stretched from north to south, with the edges so sharply marked, that the line of demarcation could be traced as far as the eye could reach. Sometimes, again, they came to sheets of clear, transparent water, close to others which were perfectly opaque.

"Well, Mr. Clawbonny," said Simpson, "what do you say to this? Isn't it very peculiar?"

"I adopt the theory of Scoresby, the whaler," replied the Doctor. "He thought that the blue waters had been deprived of the myriads of animalculæ and medusæ—a class of zoöphytes with which the green waters are loaded. He had made many experiments on the subject, and I quite believe he is right."

"Ay, sir; but there is more than that to be learnt from the color of the water."

"Is there, really?"

"Yes, Mr. Clawbonny, you may take a harpooner's word for it; if the *Forward* were only a whaler, we should have good sport."

"And yet," said the Doctor, "I don't see the smallest whale anywhere."

"All right! Take my word for it, I say, we'll see some before long. It is a lucky chance for a whaler to come across those green stripes in this latitude."

"And why so?" asked the Doctor, always eager to gain information from those who had a practical knowledge of the subject in hand.

"Because it is in those green waters that most of the whales are caught," replied Simpson.

"How is that?"

"Because the whales find most there to eat."

"Is that a positive fact?"

"Oh, I have tested it a hundred times in Baffin's Bay, and I don't see why it should not hold equally good in Melville Sound."

"I daresay you are right, Simpson."

"Stop a bit!" said the harpooner, leaning over the side of the vessel. "Do you see that, Mr. Clawbonny?"

"It looks like the wake of a ship."

"Well, that is the fatty substance the whale leaves behind in its track. Trust me, the animal that left it can't be far off."

There was certainly a peculiar smell in the atmosphere, and the Doctor watched carefully to see if Simpson's predictions would be verified.

He had not to watch long, for the man at the masthead called out:

"A whale! To leeward of us!"

All eyes turned in the given direction; and, sure enough, about a mile from the ship, jets of water thrown up to a considerable height were plainly visible.

"There she is!" exclaimed Simpson. "That's her and no mistake, blowing away!"

"She has disappeared!" said the Doctor.

"She could soon be found, if we wanted," replied Simpson, in a tone of regret.

But, to his amazement—for no one would have dared to propose such a thing—Hatteras gave orders to equip the whaling-boat. He was not sorry to be able to afford his men a little diversion, and perhaps secure a few barrels of oil. His permission to capture the whale gave great satisfaction to all on board; and, forthwith, four sailors jumped into the boat. Johnson was to steer, and Simpson took his place in the front, harpoon in hand. The Doctor could not be kept from joining the party. The sea was pretty calm, and in ten minutes the boat was at the spot.

The whale had just plunged below again, but soon reappeared, discharging a volume of mucous matter and vapor combined, from the blow-holes in the head.

"There! there!" cried Simpson, pointing to a spot about eight hundred yards from the boat.

The enormous monster rose and sank in the waves incessantly, her huge black back looking like a rock in midocean. Whales are slow swimmers, and this one seemed in no hurry, certainly.

The boat cautiously approached unperceived by the enemy, owing to the opaqueness of the green water. To see a frail bark attack these leviathans is always a thrilling spectacle, and this whale must have measured nearly 100 feet. Larger ones are frequently met with between the 72nd and 80th degrees, and ancient writers speak of some specimens more than 700 feet long; but such descriptions are evidently entirely fabulous.

As soon as the boat got close to the whale, Simpson stopped the rowers, and, brandishing his harpoon, hurled it so dexterously at the foe that the sharp barbs buried themselves deep in the thick layer of fat on her back. The wounded monster dived below, and immediately the four oars were set up on end, and the line let out which was attached to the harpoon. It was lying in a coil at the front of the boat, and the rapidity with which it unwound itself was prodigious.

For more than half an hour the boat was dragged along after the whale in the direction of the moving icebergs, and always farther away from the brig. The motion was so rapid that it was necessary to wet the rope to prevent its taking fire from the excessive friction. When the whale at last slackened speed, the line was carefully drawn up by degrees, and coiled up again. Presently the animal rose to the surface once more, lashing the sea with her ponderous tail, and making a perfect waterspout, which fell on the boat like a violent shower of rain.

The men began to row vigorously forward, and Simpson seized a lance, and stood ready for combat. But, next moment, their coveted prey darted in between two gigantic ice-mountains, where it would have been dangerous to follow.

"Confound it!" exclaimed Johnson.

"Go on! Go on!" shouted Simpson, wild with excitement. "We are sure of her now."

"But we cannot go after her between those icebergs!" said Johnson.

"Yes, yes, we can," cried Simpson.

While they were still discussing whether to venture or not, the question was settled for them, for the passage began rapidly to close; and Johnson had only barely time to cut the rope with a hatchet when the rocky walls met, crushing the unfortunate animal between them with irresistible force.

"Lost!" exclaimed Simpson.

"Saved!" was Johnson's reply; while the Doctor, who had never shown the white feather throughout, coolly said, "My word! but that was a sight worth seeing."

The crushing power of these mountains is prodigious. The whale had met with no unusual death; for Scoresby mentions the fact that, in one summer, thirty whales perished in Baffin's Bay in a similar manner. He also saw a ship with three masts smashed flat, and two other ships were pierced through, as if by a lance, by fallen icebergs more than a hundred feet long, with sharp spiked ends, which met together across the decks.

A few minutes later, the boat regained the brig, and was drawn up to its accustomed place on deck.

"It is a lesson," said Shandon, aloud, "for rash people who will venture into narrow channels."

CHAPTER XIX
ISLE BEECHEY

On the 25th of June the *Forward* sighted Cape Dundas, the north-easterly point of Prince of Wales' Island. The difficulty of navigation increased as the packs became more numerous. The distance that, in ordinary circumstances, the brig would have made in a day, took her from the 25th to the 30th of June.

Hatteras knew as well as Shandon how the coals stood: but relying on finding stores at Isle Beechey, he would not lose a moment for the sake of economy. The *distance* south, short as it was, had greatly delayed him; and though he had taken the precaution to start in April, he was not a whit farther on now than preceding expeditions had been at a similar period.

On the 30th of June, Cape Walker came in sight, and soon afterwards Cape Bellot, so named from the brave young French officer who perished in the English expedition. Three cheers were given to his memory as the brig passed, pushing her way through the loose floes across Barrow's Straits.

Hatteras was so afraid of missing the island that he hardly quitted his post on the deck for an instant. All that skill and *sang froid,* and even nautical genius, could do, he did. Fortune certainly showed him no favor, for at this time of the year he ought to have found the straits nearly free from ice; but at length, by neither sparing his steam, nor his men, nor himself, he gained his end.

On the 3rd of July the ice-master signaled land ahead to the north, and after consulting the chart Hatteras came to the conclusion that this must be Isle Beechey. Johnson's heart beat quicker as they approached, for this was not his first visit, and memory was busy with the past. He had been quartermaster on board the *Phoenix,* the expedition in which Lieutenant Bellot had been engaged, and Hatteras looked to him for information as to the facilities for anchorage. The weather was magnificent, and the thermometer continued steadily at 57°.

" Well, Johnson, do you recognize the place? " said the captain, as they were getting rapidly near.

" Yes, sir, it is certainly the island; but we must bear a little more to the north, the coast is more accessible there."

"But what about the huts and the stores?" asked the captain.

"Oh, you cannot see those till you get on shore. They are behind those hillocks you see there.'"

"'And you say you landed considerable stores there?"

"'Ay! that we did, captain. It was here that the Admiralty sent me in 1853, under the command of Inglefield, with the *Phoenix* steamer and a transport loaded with provisions. We carried enough with us to revictual an entire expedition."

"But the commander of the *Fox* drew on them largely in 1855, did he not?" said Hatteras.

"Rest easy, captain, you'll see there is enough and to spare yet, and the cold has such a wonderful power of preserving food, that we shall find everything as good as the first day it was packed."

"I don't care about the provisions. I have plenty for several years. It is the fuel I am anxious about."

"Well, captain, we left more than one thousand tons of coals there, so you need not fear about that."

"We might land now, I think," said Hatteras, who had been closely watching the shore, glass in hand.

"You see yon point, sir," said Johnson. "When we have doubled that we are quite near our anchorage. Yes! it was from that very point we started on our way back to England with Lieutenant Cresswell and the twelve sick sailors belonging to the *Investigator*. Ah! well, we had back Lieutenant McClure safe. Poor young Bellot never saw his native land again. His is a sad story; but, captain, I think we may cast anchor now."

"Very well," said Hatteras, giving the order immediately.

The brig had just reached a little bay, sheltered by nature from the north, south, and east winds, and within a cable's length of the shore.

"Mr. Wall," said Hatteras, "get the boat ready, and six men to go with her to carry coals on board."

"Yes, sir," said Wall.

"I am going ashore in the pirogue with the Doctor and boatswain. Mr. Shandon, you will please to accompany us."

"At your service," replied Shandon.

A few minutes later all four landed on a low, rocky beach.

"You must be our guide, Johnson," said the captain. "Do you know the place again?"

"Perfectly, sir," was the reply; "but I see a monument there that is new to me."

"That!" exclaimed the Doctor; "I can give you the history of that. But let us go up to it, for I expect it will best explain itself."

They soon reached it, and the Doctor, taking off his cap reverently, said:

"This is a monument erected to Franklin and his companions."

And so it was. Lady Franklin sent a tablet of marble to Dr. Kane in 1855, and entrusted another to McClintock in 1858, to be set up in Isle Beechey. McClintock executed his commission religiously, and placed this tablet beside the funeral stone raised to the memory of Bellot by Sir John Barrow. It bore the following inscription:—

TO THE MEMORY OF

FRANKLIN, CROZIER, FITZ-JAMES

AND ALL THEIR BRAVE COMRADES,

*Officers, and faithful companions, who suffered and perished for the cause of Science and
the glory of their Country.*

This Stone is erected near the place where they spent their last Arctic winter, and from whence they set out to triumph over difficulties or die. It betokens the hallowed memory in which they are held by admiring fellow-countrymen and friends, and the anguish, subdued by faith, of her who has lost in the leader of the expedition the most devoted and affectionate of husbands.

It is thus that He led them to the heaven above where all rest in peace.

1855.

This stone on a lonely shore of these distant regions, spoke sorrowfully to the heart. All that remained of Franklin and his brave band, so full of life and hope, was this marble block. And yet in spite of such gloomy warning, the *Forward* was about to rush on in the very path of the *Erebus* and *Terror*.

Hatteras was the first to rouse himself from such dangerous contemplations. He climbed hastily up a little hill, from the top of which Johnson said the storehouses could be seen.

Shandon and the Doctor rejoined them immediately; but none of the party could discover anything but a far-stretching expanse, without a trace of human habitation.

" Well, that's strange! " said Johnson.

" What now? Where are the depots? " asked Hatteras, sharply.

" I don't know—I can't see," stammered Johnson.

" You have mistaken the road perhaps," suggested the Doctor, thoughtfully.

" Yet it seems to me," said Johnson, " that it was just here——"

" Well, be quick, pray, and tell us where to go," said the impatient captain.

" Let us go down again; for I may be wrong. It is seven years ago now since I was here, and my memory may be at fault."

" Especially in a country where such monotonous uniformity prevails."

" And yet——" muttered Johnson.

Shandon made no remark.

After waiting a few minutes longer, Johnson stopped all of a sudden, and said:

" No, I am right, after all! "

" Well," replied Hatteras, looking about, " and where are they? "

" Do you see how the ground seems to swell out there," said Johnson, " just where we are standing, and can you trace the shape of these big mounds in it? "

" Well, and what's that to do with the question? " inquired the Doctor.

" These are the graves of three of Franklin's sailors," was the reply. " I'm sure of it; and a hundred paces off was the principal depot. I am not mistaken now, and if the stores are not there, it must be owing to——"

He did not venture to say what he thought; but a terrible suspicion shot through Hatteras, and made him rush impetuously forward. But where were the stores on which he had so confidently reckoned? This was the right place;

but destruction, and pillage, and ruin had been at work, and not a vestige remained of the vast supplies laid up for the relief of hard bestead navigators. And who had committed these depredations?   Was it the wolves and bears?   No, for they would only have destroyed the provisions; but not so much as the tattered remnant of a tent was left, not a morsel of wood, nor a piece of iron; and, worse still, for the *Forward* at any rate, not an atom of coal!   It was evident that frequent intercourse with European ships had taught the Esquimaux the value of these things, for they must have been coming back and forward ever since the *Fox* had touched at the island, constantly pillaging, till all trace of a storehouse had disappeared in the snow.

Hatteras was dumfounded.   The Doctor shook his head and gazed silently.   Shandon said nothing; but a close observer might have seen a malicious smile on his lips.

Just at this moment the men came with the boat to fetch the coal.   They understood all at a glance.   Shandon went up to the captain and said:

" Mr. Hatteras, I don't see the use of giving way to despair.   Fortunately, we are at the entrance of Barrow's Strait, which will take us straight to Baffin's Bay."

" Mr. Shandon," replied Hatteras, " fortunately we are at the entrance to Wellington Channel, which will take us straight to the north! "

" And how are we to work the ship, sir? "

" By her sails.   We have still fuel for two months, and that is more than enough for our winter's sojourn."

" You will allow me to say——" began Shandon.

" I will allow you to follow me on board, sir! " interrupted Hatteras; and, turning on his heel, he walked off to the boat, and shut himself in his cabin as soon as they reached the brig.

CHAPTER XX
HEAVY WORK

On the 3rd and 4th of July the thermometer stood at 57°, and it never rose higher than this during the whole time of the expedition.   But on Thursday, the 5th, the wind shifted to S. E., and became very violent, accompanied by whirling eddies of snow. The temperature fell the night before 23°. Hatteras, without caring about the ill-humor of the crew, gave orders to weigh anchor. For thirteen days, that is to say, since leaving Cape Dundas, the *Forward* had not made one degree farther north. This did not satisfy the money-loving Clifton party at all; and, for the time being at least, they were quite as willing as the captain to try and push their way through Wellington Channel.

This channel was first fully explored in 1851, by Captain Penny, on the whalers *Lady Franklin* and *Sophia;* and it was one of his officers, Lieutenant Stewart, who succeeded in getting as far as Cape Beecher, in latitude 76° 20″, and made the discovery of an open sea. An open sea! This was the hope which inspired Hatteras.

"What Stewart found, I shall find too," he said to the Doctor; "and then we can sail easy enough to the Pole."

"But have you no misgivings about the crew?" asked the Doctor.

"My crew!" repeated Hatteras, bitterly; but he added presently, in a low voice, as if speaking to himself, "Poor fellows!" The Doctor was amazed, for it was the first time he had betrayed the least kindly feeling. But he had hardly time to recover his surprise before the old hardness came back, and Hatteras exclaimed vehemently: "No! they must and shall go with me!"

The *Forward* found no great difficulty in getting through the ice, for the ice-streams were pretty far apart; but still she made little progress, owing to contrary winds. It was not till the 10th that she passed at length the 75th parallel, to the great joy of Clifton.

They had now reached the very point where the *Advance* and the *Rescue,* two American vessels in Dr. Kane's expedition, had met with such terrible disasters. Shandon took care to rehearse the whole story of suffering and danger to the crew, with what dispiriting effect may be imagined.

The ice-packs were now very numerous, and navigation became exceedingly difficult. Hatteras endeavored vainly to get past Isle Hamilton, but the wind was contrary. Then he tried to glide the brig in between Isle Hamilton and Isle Cornwallis, and again he failed, after wasting five precious days in the attempt. The temperature was constantly getting lower, and on the 19th of July fell to 26°.

It rose somewhat the next day; but this premonition of an Arctic winter's approach was not lost on Hatteras. The wind was inclined to keep steadily in the west, dead against the ship, while he was all impatience to reach the latitude where Stewart had discovered the open sea. On the 19th he determined to go up the channel, come what might. By working the screw, the brig could fight her way against the rough gales of wind and driving snow; but, above all things, the scanty store of fuel must be husbanded. On the other hand, the channel was too wide to permit of "tracking," as it is called in Arctic language—that is, towing with ropes along a margin of ice. Hatteras, therefore, had recourse to a method sometimes adopted by whalers in similar circumstances. Without giving a moment's consideration to the fatigue of his crew, he ordered the boats to be lowered to the level of the water, so as just to touch the surface, though without detaching them from the sides of the ship, to which they were then firmly fastened fore and aft. In these boats the men had to seat themselves in turn, with oars in hand, and row vigorously to drag the vessel forward against the wind.

It was slow work, and one can imagine the labor it was for the crew. But at length, after four days' sailing in this fashion, the *Forward* emerged into Queen's Channel, and reached Baring's Island.

The wind was still adverse; but the crew could do no more. Their health was too much shaken, and the Doctor feared he could detect in several the first indications of scurvy. He lost no time in combating the terrible malady, for he had lime juice and lime pastilles, in abundance.

Hatteras knew well enough he could no longer count on his men. Mildness and persuasions were of no avail now: he resolved to conquer by severity, and even to show himself pitiless on occasion. Richard Shandon he especially mistrusted, and he had his doubts about James Wall too. Dr. Clawbonny, Johnson, Bell, and Simpson, he knew were devoted to him, body and soul. Pen, Gripper, Clifton, and Warren, he was quite aware were only waiting their time to break out in open mutiny, and drag the brig back to England; and the others were ready to take either side at any moment.

Meanwhile, what was to be done? The crew were not

only badly disposed, but so exhausted that they could not possibly continue such fatiguing efforts, and for twenty-four hours they had remained absolutely stationary in sight of Isle Baring. And yet the temperature was always getting lower, for it was far on now in July. On the 24th the thermometer fell to 22°. Young ice formed during the night of considerable thickness, and should snow come down, it would soon be firm enough to bear a man's weight. There was a gray, dirty look about the sea already which betokened the commencement of the process of crystallization.

There was no mistaking these alarming symptoms. Should the leads close, Hatteras would be obliged to winter here without having gained his object, or even caught a glimpse of the open basin which was so close at hand, if the reports of his predecessors had been correct. He determined to push forward at all risks, and as he could not use the oars in the present wornout state of his men, nor the sails, for the wind was contrary, he gave orders to kindle the furnaces.

CHAPTER XXI
BEGINNINGS OF MUTINY

This unexpected command occasioned great surprise on board the *Forward,* and loud exclamations were heard on all sides. Shandon looked fixedly at Wall, and the engineers stood perfectly stupefied.

" Did you hear me? " shouted the captain in an angry tone.

Brunton moved towards the hatchway, but stopped short again as a voice called out: " Don't go, Brunton! "

" Who spoke? " exclaimed Hatteras.

" It was I that spoke," said Pen, boldly, going up to the captain.

" And you said——"

" I said and I say," interrupted Pen with an oath, " that we have had enough of this work? that we are not going farther; that we neither intend to be killed with hard work, nor frozen to death in the winter; and that the furnaces shall not be lighted! "

"Mr. Shandon," replied Hatteras, coolly, "lay that man in irons."

"But, captain," objected Shandon, "what the man has said is——"

"Repeat what this man has said, and I'll have you locked in your cabin and guarded. Seize that man! Does no one hear me?"

Johnson, Bell, and Simpson went forward; but the infuriated Pen was beside himself. He caught up a handspike, and brandishing it above his head, cried out:

"Touch me who dare!"

Hatteras went right up to him with a loaded revolver, which he aimed at his head, and said quietly: "Lift your finger, and I blow your brains out."

A murmur of disapprobation was heard; but it died away immediately when Hatteras said: "Silence among you, or that is a dead man."

Pen made no further attempt at resistance, but allowed Johnson and Bell to disarm him and lead him away to the hold.

"Go, Brunton!" said Hatteras.

The engineer obeyed without further parley, and the captain went up to the poop, followed by the Doctor.

As soon as the steam had acquired sufficient pressure, the anchors were lifted, and the *Forward* stood off for Point Beecher, and went towards the east, cutting through the newly-formed ice with her sharp prow.

She had to wend her way through narrow channels between numerous small islands. The ice-streams were constantly threatening to unite, hummocks had formed here and there already, and it was easy to see that the first frost that set in would consolidate the whole into one impenetrable mass.

Yet every now and then the sun would reappear and chase away the whirling snow, the thermometer would rise several degrees, difficulties would vanish as if by enchantment, and a stretch of clear, open water would greet the eye.

On Thursday, the 26th of July, the brig sailed close past Isle Dundas, still keeping her prow steadily towards the north; but almost directly afterwards she came to an enormous bank of ice, eight to nine feet high, composed of small icebergs that had been detached from the coast.

There was no getting past it except by making a deep bend out of the course. At last a lead was discovered; but still the *Forward* made slow progress, for the fog came on, and this is a serious obstacle to a sailing vessel among ice. So long as the pilot can see a mile ahead, he can easily steer his way through the packs; but often it is so thick that he cannot see a cable's length before him, and the difficulty was increased by the blinding snow.

The birds were still very numerous, and their cries were deafening; the seals lolling indolently on the drifting floes, betrayed little fear, though they stretched out their long necks and gazed with wondering eyes as the vessel passed by.

At length, after six days' wearisome navigation, Point Beecher appeared to the north. Hatteras betook himself to the mast-head, and remained there for hours; for the open sea discovered by Stewart in May, 1851, could not be far off, and yet no sign of it as yet could be discovered. He came down again after his long watch without saying a word.

"Do you believe in this open sea?" asked Shandon, speaking to James Wall.

"I begin to have my doubts," was the reply.

"Was I not right, after all, in treating this pretended discovery as a mere chimera? And yet no one would listen to me, and even you, Wall, took the other side of the question."

"They will listen to you now, Shandon."

"Yes, when it is too late," he replied, and retired to his cabin, to which he had confined himself almost entirely since his discussion with the captain.

According to Penny, the sea ought to be quite clear now, for they had reached Point Barrow after taking ten days to go thirty miles. What was Hatteras to think? Was Penny's statement altogether apocryphal, or had winter already set in?

On the 15th of August the snow-covered head of Mount Percy appeared through the fog, and next day the sun set for the first time after incessant day for so long. However, the darkness which followed was by no means complete; though the sun had set, the refraction of his rays still gave sufficient light.

On the 19th of August, Cape Franklin was sighted to the east, and Cape Lady Franklin to the west; the one doubtless was the extreme point reached by the bold navigator; and the other was so called by his grateful countrymen, in honor of his devoted wife, as a touching symbol of the loving bond that united them so closely.

The Doctor, following Johnson's advice, was trying to inure himself to the cold as much as possible, by remaining nearly always on deck, in spite of wind and snow. His health was unimpaired, though he had grown a little thinner. He was quite prepared for fresh dangers, and gayly welcomed each precursor of winter.

"Look at that flock of birds migrating south!" he called out one day to Johnson. "How swift they fly, shrieking their last adieu as they go!"

"Yes, Mr. Clawbonny, something tells them it is time to go, and off they start."

"More than one among us, Johnson, I wager, would like to follow their example."

"Chicken-hearted fellows!" said Johnson. "Those poor flying things have not their food all ready to hand like us, and of course they must seek it elsewhere. But sailors, with a good ship under their feet, ought to go to the world's end."

"You hope then that Hatteras will succeed in his projects?"

"He will succeed, I'm sure of it, Mr. Clawbonny," answered Johnson.

"I agree with you, Johnson, and even if only one faithful friend remained to him——"

"We should make two."

"You are right, Johnson," said the Doctor, grasping the brave fellow's hand.

Prince Albert's Land, which the *Forward* was now alongside, is also called Grinnel's Land, and though Hatteras so hated the Yankees that he would never have given it that name, most people know it by the American designation. Both names were bestowed on it at the same time, though by different people—Penny in honor of Prince Albert, and Lieutenant de Haven, the commander of the *Rescue,* in honor of Grinnel, the American merchant, at whose expense the expedition had been sent out.

V. II Venre

After a succession of unheard-of difficulties, the *Forward* sighted Mount Britannia, though it was scarcely visible through the fog, and next day dropped anchor in Northumberland Bay, and found herself completely closed in on all sides.

CHAPTER XXII
ASSAULT OF THE ICEBERGS

AFTER seeing that the vessel was properly moored, Hatteras withdrew to his cabin and studied his chart attentively. He found he was in latitude 76° 57′, and longitude 92° 20′; in other words, almost close to the 77th parallel. This was where Sir Edward Belcher passed his first winter on the *Pioneer* and the *Assistance* and from this point he organized his exploring parties, and succeeded in reaching the 78th degree. Beyond this he found that the coast inclined to the S. E. towards Jones's Sound, which opens into Baffin's Bay, but on the N. W. he could discern nothing as far as the eye could see but clear, open water.

Hatteras gazed long and earnestly at the blank white space on the map which represented the unexplored regions round the Pole, and he said to himself:

" After all these testimonies from Stewart, Penny, Belcher, I cannot doubt. The open sea must be there. These bold, hardy men have seen it with their own eyes. Can it be that it was during some exceptional winter, and that now——? but no, that cannot be the case, for several years elapsed between the discoveries. The basin exists and I will find it, and see it for myself! "

He went again on the bridge, but the ship was wrapped in dense fog, and the mast-head was hardly visible from deck; yet Hatteras made the ice-master come down, and went himself to take his place in the " crow's-nest." He was anxious to watch for the least rift in the fog to examine the northwest horizon.

Shandon could not lose the chance to say to his friend:

" Well, Wall, where is this open sea? "

" You were right, Shandon, and we have not more than six weeks' coal left now."

" Oh! the Doctor will find some scientific method of warming ourselves without fire. I have heard people say that ice can be made with fire, so perhaps he can make us fire with ice."

Next morning the fog cleared off for a few minutes, and Hatteras could be seen eagerly scanning the horizon from his elevated position; but he came down without saying a word, and gave orders to sail forthwith. It was easy to tell that his last hope had failed him.

The *Forward* weighed anchor, and once more resumed her uncertain course towards the north. It was evident there would be a general frost before long, for the sea was covered with whitish patches, looking like spots of oil, and whenever the wind fell the whole surface was speedily covered with a sheet of ice, which broke up, however, and disappeared as soon as the breeze returned. Towards night the thermometer fell to 17°.

Often the leads seemed quite closed; but an unexpected movement of the ice-streams would open the way in some new direction, and the brave vessel would dash in at once and follow it up boldly; but the cold was so intense that during these forced stoppages, the steam that escaped from the valves would condense immediately and fall in snow on the deck. Sometimes there was another cause of delay. The loose ice would get entangled among the machinery, and adhere so firmly that the engine was powerless. The sailors had to bring levers and handspikes, and break it away, before the screw could work.

Thirteen days passed thus, during which the *Forward* was dragging wearily through Penny's Straits. The crew grumbled, but obeyed, for they saw that going back was impossible. To go forth would be attended with less peril now than to return south: it was time to think of winter quarters.

The men had long talks among themselves about their present situation, and even ventured to discuss it with Shandon, knowing quite well he was on their side.

"You say then, Mr. Shandon," said Gripper, "that we cannot go back?"

"It is too late now," replied Shandon.

"I suppose, then," said another sailor, "all we can do is to make ourselves comfortable for the winter?"

"It is our only resource. I was not believed when I——"

"Next time you will be," said Pen, who had returned to his duty.

"As I shall not be master on board——" replied Shandon.

"Who knows?" said Pen. "John Hatteras is at liberty to go as far north as he thinks proper, but we are not obliged to follow him."

"He need only remember his first voyage to Baffin's Bay, and what came of it," replied Gripper.

"Ay! and his voyage in the *Farewell*," said Clifton, "when he lost his ship in the Spitzberg seas!"

"And came home alone," added Gripper.

"Alone with his dog," replied Clifton.

"We have no desire to sacrifice ourselves for such a man's good pleasure," put in Pen.

"No, nor to lose our hard-earned prize-money," rejoined the avaricious Clifton. "When we have passed the 78th parallel," he went on, "and we are not far off now, that will be just £375 for each of us!"

"But shan't we forfeit it," asked Gripper, "if we return without the captain?"

"No," answered Clifton; "if it is proved that our return was absolutely necessary."

"But the captain might——"

"Rest easy, Gripper," replied Pen. "We shall have a captain, and a good one, that Mr. Shandon knows. When a commander goes mad, he is displaced, and the power given to another. Isn't it so, Mr. Shandon?"

"My friends," replied Shandon, evasively, "you will always find in me a devoted heart to you; but let us wait the course of events."

It was evident the storm was gathering over the head of Hatteras. But he went boldly on, firm and unshaken as ever, full of energy and confidence. He saw that he would be forced to winter in these regions; but what of it? Had not Sir John Ross and McClure passed three winters in succession here? What they had done, others could do.

On the 31st of August the thermometer stood at 13°. The end of the navigable season had arrived.

Leaving Exmouth Isle on the right, the *Forward* passed Table Isle, into the middle of the Belcher Channel. There was scarcely an inch depth of water now under her keel;

and, far as the eye could reach, nothing was to be seen but ice-fields.

Fortunately, it was possible to get a few minutes farther north yet, by breaking the young ice with enormous rollers and petards. The great thing to be dreaded in low temperatures is a calm atmosphere, as ice forms so rapidly in the absence of wind. Even contrary winds were joyfully welcomed, but they did not continue long; a calm night came, and all was frozen.

The *Forward* could not winter in such a situation, however, exposed to winds and icebergs, and the currents of the channel; and Hatteras sought to get beyond Point Albert, where there was a sheltered bay which would afford a safe refuge.

But, on the 8th of September, they came to a high, impassable wall of ice, which rose between them and the north. The temperature fell to 10°, and Hatteras was almost at his wits' end. He risked his ship a hundred times in impracticable leads, and displayed prodigies of skill in extricating her again. Thoughtless and imprudent, and even blind as he was, no one could deny that he was a good sailor—indeed, one of the very ablest.

The *Forward* was now in a really perilous situation. All was ice behind, and ice of such thickness, that the men could run on it securely and tow the brig along.

Since there was no getting round this wall, Hatteras determined to attack it with his blasting-cylinders. It took the whole of one day to make holes in the ice of sufficient depth, but he hoped all would be ready next morning for the explosion.

However, during the night the wind began to rage furiously. The sea rose under the ice as if shaken by some submarine disturbance; and the terrified voice of the pilot was heard shouting, "Look out at the stern! Look out at the stern!"

Hatteras looked in the direction indicated, and certainly it was an alarming sight that met his gaze. An enormous iceberg, towering aloft like a mountain, was coming rushing towards the ship with the speed of an avalanche.

"All hands on deck!" sang out Hatteras.

The huge moving mass was not more than half a mile distant. On it came, tearing up the floes, crushing and overturning, and sweeping the packs along like grains of sand before the hurricane-blast.

"This is the worst danger that has ever threatened us yet," said Johnson to Dr. Clawbonny.

"Yes, it looks appalling enough, certainly," replied the Doctor.

"It is a regular assault, and we must prepare to meet it," said Johnson.

"I declare, one could fancy it was a whole pack of ante-diluvian monsters, such as might be supposed to live about the North Pole. They all seem pushing each other, and hurrying on to see which will arrive first."

"Aye, and some are armed with sharp lances, which I advise you to steer clear of, Dr. Clawbonny."

"It is going to be a regular siege," exclaimed the Doctor. "Come and let us be up on the ramparts."

Away he rushed to the stern, where all the crew were stationed with poles, and iron bars, and hand spikes, ready to repulse the formidable enemy.

The avalanche arrived, increasing in height as it came, owing to the accumulation of smaller icebergs it caught up in its train. Cannon-balls were fired, by the captain's orders, to break the threatening line of attack; but it advanced nearer and nearer, and at length dashed against the brig with a tremendous crash, breaking part of the bulwarks.

"Keep to your posts, and look out for the bergs," shouted Hatteras.

There was much need, for they were boarding the vessel with irresistible force: already packs weighing several hundredweight had scaled the sides, while the smaller ones, which had been dashed up in the onset as high as the masts, fell down in a shower of pointed arrows, breaking the shrouds and cutting the rigging. Some of the sailors were sorely wounded by these bristling barbs as they stood, pole in hand, each doing his utmost to repulse their assailants, though almost overpowered by their numbers. Among others, Bolton had his left shoulder completely ripped up. The noise was terrible, and to add to it, Duk barked his loudest with rage. The darkness of night greatly increased the horrors of the situation, without hiding from view the angry packs glistening in their dazzling whiteness.

From time to time the voice of Hatteras was heard amid all the din and clamor of this strange, preternatural, impossible contest between men and icebergs. The brig, yielding to the enormous pressure, leaned over on her larboard till her mainmast touched the ice-fields.

Hatteras understood the danger: it was a moment of terrible anxiety, for each instant the brig might turn over completely, or her masts be torn away.

Presently an enormous mass began to rise at the side of the ship, extending right along her hull. It seemed forced upward by some irresistible power, higher and higher, till at last it was on a level with the poop. Should it fall on the *Forward,* all was over. It turned and stood on end, higher than the tallest mast, and tottered on its base. A cry of terror escaped all lips, and there was a general rush to the other side.

Suddenly the vessel was entirely lifted up, and for a brief space seemed to float in the air. Then she came down again and fell back on the ice, to be caught up next minute in a tremendous roller, which made her timbers shiver, and swept her right over to the other side of the insurmountable barrier, on to an ice-field, into which she sank at once by her own weight, and regained her proper element.

" We are over the icebergs! " exclaimed Johnson.

" Praise God! " said Hatteras.

But though the ice barrier was surmounted, the brig was motionless, fast locked in on all sides, and though the keel was in the water, yet unable to stir.

It was soon evident, however, that if the brig was motionless, the field was not, and Johnson called out to the captain:

" We are driving, sir."

" Well, we must just drive! " replied Hatteras.

And, indeed, what else could they do? Resistance was impossible.

The day came, and it was quite clear that, owing to the action of some submarine current, the ice-field was moving rapidly north.

To provide for any possible catastrophe, for the brig might be dashed on some coast or crushed with the pressure of the ice, Hatteras had a great quantity of provisions brought up on deck, together with the tents and all the requisites for encamping, and the clothing and blankets of the crew. Following the example of McClure in similar circumstances, he also encircled the ship with a girdle of hammocks inflated with air, so as to ward off great seas, and the ice so accumulated on these that there was soon a high wall all around, and nothing of the ship was visible except the mainmast.

For seven days they sailed along in this strange fashion. On the 10th of September they caught a glimpse of Point Albert, the western extremity of New Cornwall. But they soon lost sight of it, as the ice-field began now to move in an easterly direction. Where could it go, and where would it stop? Who could say.

The crew waited with folded arms. At last, on the 15th of September, about three in the afternoon, the ice-field came into collision, no doubt, with another field, for it stopped suddenly short, and a violent shock shook the vessel to her center. Hatteras, who had taken his bearings during the day, consulted his chart. He found himself in the north, with no land in sight, in longitude 95° 35', and latitude 78° 15', in the heart of that unknown sea, where geographers have placed the point of greatest cold.

CHAPTER XXIII
PREPARATIONS FOR WINTERING

THE average temperature of the regions in which Hatteras found himself was 15° lower than any other part of the world. He was two hundred and fifty miles, by his reckoning, distant from the last point of known land—that is, from New Cornwall—and his ship was fast locked in ice, as if embedded in granite.

It was a terrible situation to be in, and he knew what a fearful winter he would have to go through, with a brig in such a position and a half-mutinous crew. But his courage rose to meet the danger, and he lost no time in commencing preparations for winter quarters, aided by the long experience of Johnson.

Far as the eye could see, there was nothing but ice; not a drop of water was visible in all the region. But the surface of the ice-fields was by no means smooth and uniform.

Numerous icebergs raised their towering heads round the ship, forming such a belt, that on three sides she was completely sheltered from the wind, and only the southeast could blow on her. If one could only suppose rocks instead of icebergs and verdure instead of snow, and the sea in its normal condition, the *Forward* would have been lying in a pretty sheltered bay. But what desolation reigned around! What a dismal prospect met the gaze!

The first business of the crew was to anchor the brig securely, for, motionless as she was, there might be a sudden break up of the ice-field, or some submarine current might affect it. The sails were not taken down, but closely furled, and before long the ice had encased them completely. Only the running rigging was removed.

The pressure of the ice was so great, that it became necessary to cut it away all round the ship. The packs had accumulated on her sides, and weighed her down beyond her usual floating line. It was a tedious, difficult progress, occupying several days; but when at length the keel was released, the brig rose at once nine inches. Hatteras thought it advisable to take the opportunity of examining it thoroughly, while it was exposed. Thanks to the solidity of its construction, it was found to be quite uninjured, though the copper sheathing was almost entirely torn off.

The next business was to slope away the ice right along the hull, following the outline of the ship. By doing this, the ice-field united again under the keel and prevented all further pressure.

The Doctor lent a helping hand in all these operations, infecting the men with his own good-humor, and getting and giving information. He heartily approved of this adjustment of the ship, and thought it an excellent precaution.

"There is no other way of resisting the pressure, sir," said Johnson; "now we can build a wall of snow all round as high as the gunwale, and make it ten feet thick, if we like, for we have no lack of material."

"Capital!" said Dr. Clawbonny; "for snow is a non-conductor of caloric. It reflects instead of absorbs, and will prevent the internal heat from escaping."

"Yes, sir, and we not only fortify ourselves against the cold, but against four-footed enemies, should they take a fancy to pay us a visit. We'll make a famous job of it, and so you'll say when our work is finished."

"There will be two flights of steps outside the ship— one fore and one aft. As soon as the steps are cut, we shall pour water over them, and this will make them as hard as a rock, and we shall have stairs fit for a king."

Before long the whole vessel had disappeared beneath a thick coating of ice. A roof made of tarred canvas was spread over the deck the entire length of the ship and hanging down the sides. This was covered with snow, to prevent any external cold from penetrating. The deck was thus converted into a promenade, also covered with snow two and a half feet thick, well beaten and trodden down to make it as hard as possible. Over this a layer of sand was sprinkled, which became speedily incrusted, and gave the deck the appearance of a macadamized road.

"I shall soon fancy myself in Hyde Park," said the Doctor; "or in the hanging-gardens of Babylon."

At a convenient distance from the ship a fire-hole was made; that is to say, a well was dug in the ice, to provide a constant supply of water, a very necessary measure both for the frequent baths ordered the crew and in case of fire breaking out on board. This well was dug as deep as possible, as the water is not so cold as near the surface.

The interior of the vessel was arranged with a view to ward off the double danger of the Arctic regions—cold and damp. The first brings the second—a foe still more to be dreaded.

The *Forward* being constructed especially for the expedition, was admirably adapted for the purpose. The forecastle was wisely planned, and war had been successfully waged in the corners where damp first crept in. It would have been better if the men's room had been circular, but still with a good fire in the stove, it was very comfortable. The walls were hung with deers' skins, instead of anything woollen, as wool catches every vapor, and by their condensation, impregnates the atmosphere with humidity.

The partitions were taken down in the poop, and the officers had one common room larger and more airy than the forecastle, and also heated by a stove. Both it and the men's room had a sort of ante-chamber, which cut off all direct communication with the exterior. This prevented the heat from escaping, and made a gradual passage from one temperature to another. All wet clothes were put off in these vestibules, and snow scraped from the boots.

A proper provision was made for the admission of air into the stoves, and the fires were carefully regulated. The temperature was kept up at 50°, and the smallest possible amount of coal used, as Hatteras found, on inspecting the bunkers, that, with the severest, most rigid economy, he had only enough for two months longer.

A drying-place was contrived for such clothing as had to be frequently washed, for nothing could be dried in the open air.

The delicate parts of the engine were carefully removed, and the engine-room hermetically closed.

The regulation of the ship life was a matter of serious consideration to Hatteras. At six the men rose, and three times a week their hammocks were carried out into the fresh air. Every morning the planks of the two living rooms were rubbed with hot sand. Boiling tea was served up at each meal, and as much variety as was practicable introduced in the daily bill of fare. The dietary scale included bread, flour, suet, and raisins for puddings; sugar, cocoa, rice, lemon-juice, preserved meat, salt pork and beef, pickled cabbage, and mixed pickles. The kitchen was outside the living rooms; it would have been an addition to the heat to have placed it inside, but the cooking of food is a constant source of evaporation and moisture, so that it would have been a doubtful benefit.

Health is greatly dependent on food, and in high latitudes as much as possible of animal substances requires to be consumed.

"We must take example by the Esquimaux," said the Doctor; "they have been taught by nature, and are apt scholars. Arabs and Africans can live on a few dates and a handful of rice, but here it is important to eat much. An Esquimaux absorbs daily from ten to fifteen pounds of oil. If his fare would not meet your taste, you must replace it by substances which abound in oil and sugar; in a word, you must have carbon and make carbon. It is all well enough to put coals in the stove, but we must not forget we have a stove inside us which needs always replenishing."

The most scrupulous cleanliness was also rigidly enforced. Each man was obliged to take a bath of the icy water every other day as a matter of health, and also as an excellent means of preserving natural heat. The Doctor himself set the example; it was rather a trying operation at first, but in the end he found it positively agreeable.

The men had to be on their guard not to get frostbitten when they were out of doors shooting, or working or exploring. In the event of this happening, however, the frozen part was briskly rubbed with snow till circulation was restored. The clothing of the men was also carefully attended to; they were all wrapped in flannel, and wore deerskin capes and sealskin trousers.

The making of these several arrangements occupied three weeks, and the first of October arrived without any particular occurrence to record.

CHAPTER XXIV
AN OLD FOX OF THE JAMES ROSS EXPEDITION

THE thermometer fell daily lower. There was little or no wind, and the weather was tolerably fine. Hatteras took advantage of the clear atmosphere to go out and reconnoiter. He climbed the highest iceberg he could find, but, as far as he could see, and aided by the glass, nothing was visible but mountains and plains of ice. All was dreary chaos, and he went back on board to try and reckon the probable length of his captivity.

The hunting party, including the Doctor, James Wall, Simpson, Johnson, and Bell, kept the ship in fresh meat. All the birds had disappeared except the ptarmigans, but these were in such abundance and so easily shot that there was no fear of the supply being exhausted.

Hares, foxes, wolves, ermines, and bears were also to be found, but they were so ferocious that it was not easy to get near them; and, besides, when they had put on their winter coats it was hard to distinguish them from the snow, as they then possess its spotless whiteness, the fur becoming completely changed as winter draws on.

Seals of every variety were also frequently met with. It was a great object to kill these, not only for their skins, but

their fat, which is an excellent combustible. Their liver
is also good food, if nothing better can be had.   Sometimes
they could be counted by hundreds, and two or three miles
away from the ship the ice was bored all over with their
breathing holes; yet they were very difficult to secure, and
many were wounded that succeeded afterwards in making
their escape below the ice.

However, on the 19th, Simpson managed to get hold of
one not far from the ship.   He had taken the precaution
to stop up its hole, so that it was at the mercy of the hunters.
After a long struggle the animal was dispatched; it measured nine feet, and was a magnificent specimen.   The doctor, wishing to preserve the head for his museum of natural
history and the skin for future needs, prepared both, by a
cheap and easy method.   He plunged the body in the fire-
hole, and allowed the myriads of shrimps and prawns to
eat away the flesh.   In half a day the operation was complete, and no tanner in Liverpool could have done it better.

As soon as the sun had passed the autumnal equinox,
the Arctic winter may be said to begin.   From the 23rd
of September the sun begins to descend below the horizon,
and on the 25th of October disappears altogether, not to
return till the month of February.

We must not imagine, however, that the darkness is total
during the sun's long absence.   The moon does her best
to replace him, and the stars shine their brightest.   The
planets are peculiarly resplendent, and the *Aurora Borealis*
is a frequent phenomenon, so that there is a sort of twilight for several hours every day, except when fog and snow
wrap the whole region in gloomy night.

Meantime, however, the weather was favorable.   No
one had any reason to complain of it, except the ptarmigans and the hares, and the hunters positively allowed them
no rest.   They also set fox-traps, but the wary animals
would not allow themselves to be caught.   They often even
scratched up the snow under the trap and devoured the
bait, and came off scot free.

On the 25th of October a hurricane of extreme violence
broke loose; thick snow filled the air, and made pitch darkness about the *Forward*.   For some hours great anxiety
was felt on board about Bell and Simpson, who were out
hunting.   They did not reach the ship till next day, after

being buried in snow five feet thick for twelve hours. They had wrapped themselves in their deerskins and lain down, letting the hurricane sweep over their heads till they were almost frozen, and could hardly get back to their quarters. The Doctor had great difficulty in restoring the circulation.

The storm raged for eight days without ceasing; no one stirred out.

During this compulsory leisure each man lived apart, as it were, some sleeping, others smoking, and certain individuals talking together in a low voice, but breaking off the conversation if Johnson or the Doctor came near; there was no bond of union among them. They never assembled together for anything but evening prayers, and on the Sundays for divine service.

Clifton was perfectly aware of the fact, that now that the 78th parallel was passed, his share of the prize-money had risen to £375. This was quite enough to satisfy his ambition. The others thought so too, and contented themselves now with indulging in day-dreams of enjoying the fortune won at such a price.

Hatteras remained almost invisible; he neither took part in hunting nor walking; he showed no interest in any of the meteorological phenomena which so excited the wondering admiration of the Doctor. He lived for one single idea; three words will tell it—the North Pole. He was only thinking of the time when the *Forward* would be released from her imprisonment, and able to resume her adventurous voyage.

The Doctor employed himself in arranging his notes, of which this narrative is the reproduction. He was never idle, and his even temper never failed him; but for all that he was glad enough when the storm was over, and he could resume hunting as usual.

On the 3rd of November he set out with Johnson and Bell about six in the morning. The ice-fields were smooth, and the snow, which lay so thick on them, was firm and hard beneath their tread. The weather was cold and dry; the moon shone with incomparable brilliancy, irradiating every object with wondrous luster.

The Doctor had brought his friend Duk with him; he was much more serviceable in hunting than the Greenland dogs, who seem to posess none of the sacred fire of the race inhabiting temperate zones.   But, in spite of all his cleverness in scenting game and running it down, the hunters had not found so much as a hare after two hours' walking.

"I suppose all the game has fled south," said the Doctor, stopping at the foot of a hummock.

"It certainly looks like it," rejoined Bell.

"I don't think that's it," said Johnson; "hares, and foxes, and bears are made for this climate.   In my opinion it is the hurricane that has caused their disappearance, but the south winds will soon bring them back.   If you were speaking of reindeer or muskdeer, it would be quite a different thing."

"And yet on Melville Island there are troops of those very animals," said the Doctor.   "Certainly it lies a little further south, but when Parry wintered there he found them in abundance always."

"We are not quite so well off," said Bell; "yet if we could only lay in a store of bear's flesh, we should not have much to complain of."

"Bell talks of bear's flesh," said Johnson, "but we want his fat far more just now than even his flesh or fur."

"You are right, Johnson; you are always thinking about the stores," replied Bell.

"No wonder," returned Johnson, "when the bunkers will be empty in at least three weeks, even with the utmost economy."

"Yes, that's our greatest danger, for this is only the beginning of November, and February is to come yet, the coldest month in the year in this zone.   Well, if we can't get bear's grease, we can always get seal's fat, at any rate."

"Not for long, Mr. Clawbonny," replied Johnson; "these animals will soon cease to show themselves above the ice, either owing to fear or to the increasing cold."

"Then, after all," said the Doctor, "we shall have to fall back on the bear, and certainly he is the most useful of all the Arctic animals, for we can get food and clothing, and light and fire out of him.   Listen, Duk," he continued, patting the dog, "we want a bear, old boy!   Go and fetch him; there's a good old fellow!"

Duk, who had been scenting along the ice all the time, darted off like an arrow, barking vociferously.   The hunters followed, but, though they could hear him still distinctly, they had to go a full mile before they came up to him. They found him standing on a little hill, on the top of which some enormous creature was moving about.

"We've got our wish for the asking," said the Doctor, loading his gun.

"Aye, it is a bear, and no mistake, and a jolly big one, too," said Bell, imitating the Doctor's example.

"I don't know, it is a strange sort of bear," added Johnson, preparing to fire after his companions.

Duk was barking furiously. Bell advanced within twenty feet and fired; but the ball took no effect.

Johnson's turn came last, but his ball was powerless like the others.

"I see how it is!" exclaimed the Doctor; "it is that confounded refraction again, one never gets used to it. Why, that bear is more than a thousand paces off."

"Let us go nearer then," replied Bell.

Away rushed all three towards the animal, who did not appear the least disturbed by their shots.

As soon as they were at the right distance they fired again, and the bear gave one tremendous spring and fell at the foot of the hill mortally wounded, there was no doubt.

Duk rushed upon him tooth and nail, holding him fast till the hunters came up.

"Well, it hasn't been much trouble to kill that bear, anyhow," said the Doctor.

"Three shots and he is done for," exclaimed Bell, contemptuously.

"It is very strange!" said Johnson.

"Unless we have chanced to come just at the very moment he was dying of old age," suggested the Doctor, laughing.

"My word, it is little matter whether he is young or old. It is a lucky prize for us."

But what was their blank amazement on reaching their victim to find that it was a white fox instead of a bear!

"Well, I declare," said Bell, "if that's not too bad!"

"Yes, I think so," replied the Doctor. "To kill a bear, and then pick up a fox."

Johnson stood stupefied, not knowing what to say.

At last the Doctor burst out laughing again, and said:

"It is just the refraction, that everlasting refraction!"

"What do you mean, Mr. Clawbonny?" asked the carpenter.

"Why, that we were deceived in the size as well as in the distance. Refraction made us fancy we saw a bear when it was only a fox. It is a mistake that has happened more than once to hunters in the Arctic regions."

"Well, we'll eat him anyhow, whether it is a bear or fox. Let us carry him off."

But just as Johnson was about to throw him over his shoulders, he stopped short and said:

"Here's something stranger still!"

"What's that?" asked the Doctor.

"Look here, Mr. Clawbonny. The beast has a collar round his neck."

"A collar!" exclaimed the Doctor, bending down to examine the animal.

Sure enough there was a brass collar half worn away round his neck, peeping through his white fur. The Doctor fancied he could perceive an inscription on it, and pulled it off to make a closer inspection.

"What does it say?" asked Johnson.

"It says that this fox is at least twelve years old, a fox caught by James Ross in 1848."

"Is it possible!" exclaimed Bell.

"There is not the least doubt of it. I am only sorry we killed the poor beast. While James Ross was wintering here, he snared a great quantity of white foxes, and had brass collars riveted on their necks, with the name and whereabouts of his two ships, the *Enterprise* and *Investigator*, inscribed on it, and also where the provision depots were to be found. These animals roam great distances in quest of food, and Ross's idea was that some of them might fall into the hands of Franklin's party. And now, instead of that, we have shot him with our balls, when he might have saved the lives of two ships' crews."

"We won't eat him, at any rate," said Johnson; "and besides, he is twelve years old. We'll keep his skin though, as a memento of this curious adventure."

Throwing the dead fox across his shoulder, and followed by his two companions, Johnson began to retrace his steps towards the vessel, guided by the stars. Their expedition had not been altogether unsuccessful, for they managed dur-

ing the homeward route to bring down several brace of
ptarmigan.

Just about an hour before they reached the ship, a phenomenon occurred, which filled the Doctor with amazement.

It was a regular shower of shooting-stars. They fell in
myriads, completely eclipsing the light of the moon. This
grand meteoric display lasted several hours. A similar
shower was observed in Greenland by the Moravian
Brethren in 1799. The Doctor sat up all night to gaze at
this wonderful phenomenon, which continued till seven
o'clock the next morning.

CHAPTER XXV
THE LAST BIT OF COAL

THE bears appeared absolutely impregnable; not one was
taken. Indeed, nothing was killed except a few seals, and
then the wind changed and the snowfalls became so violent
that it was impossible to leave the ship.

On the 15th of November the thermometer fell to 24°
below zero. This was the lowest temperature they had
hitherto experienced, yet with a calm atmosphere the cold
would have been bearable, but the stormy wind that blew
seemed to fill the air with sharp lancets.

Even had it been possible to venture out, the least exercise
would soon have made a man pant for breath. Not a fourth
part of the usual work could be done by the crew, and woe
to the hapless individual who was incautious enough to touch
anything made of iron. He felt as if he had been suddenly
burnt, and the skin was torn off his hand, and remained
sticking to the article he had so imprudently grasped.

The only relief to the close confinement was a daily walk
of two hours on the covered-in deck, and the permission to
smoke, which was not allowed down below.

The stoves had to be carefully attended to, for if the fires
got the least low, the walls became covered with ice, and not
only the walls, but every peg, and nail, and inch of metal.

The instantaneousness of this phenomenon astonished the
Doctor. The breath of the men seemed to condense in a
second, and leap, as it were, from fluid to solid, falling in
snow all round them. Only a few feet away from the fire

the cold was felt in all its intensity, and it was little wonder
that the poor shivering fellows huddled round the stove in
a close group, scarcely ever changing their position.

Yet the Doctor counseled them wisely to try and get
inured to the temperature by gradually exposing themselves
to its influence.   But his advice was in vain, though he
practiced what he preached.   The men were nearly all too
lazy or too benumbed to leave their post, and preferred
sleeping away their time in the warm unwholesome atmosphere.

As for Hatteras, he seemed not to feel the change in the
temperature in the least.   He walked about as usual in perfect silence, and would be absent from the ship for hours,
and return, to the astonishment of his crew, without a sign
of cold on his face.   What was the secret of this?   Was he
so wrapped in one idea that he was actually not susceptible
of outward impressions?

"He is a strange man!" said the Doctor to Johnson.
"He amazes even me; he has a blazing fire inside him!"

"It is a positive fact," replied Johnson; "that he goes
about in the open air with not a stitch more clothing than he
wore in the month of June!"

"Oh! as far as clothes are concerned, that is nothing;
what's the good of wrapping up a man who has got no heat
in himself?   You may as well try and warm ice by putting
it in a blanket.   Hatteras does not need that; he is so con-
stituted that really I should not be astonished to see things
catch alight that come near him, as if they had touched glow-
ing coal!"

On the 28th the thermometer fell to 32° below zero.
There was only enough coal to last ten days longer.

Hatteras dispensed now with the fire in the poop, and
shared the common room of the men with Shandon and
the Doctor.   This brought him into more direct contact
with his crew, who bestowed on him sullen, scowling
glances.   He heard their reproaches and recriminations,
and even threats, without daring to punish.   Indeed, he
seemed deaf to all that was spoken, and sat in a corner
away from the fire, with his arms folded, in perfect silence.

In spite of the Doctor's advice, Pen and his friends refused to take the least exercise.   They spent whole days

crouching over the stove, or in their hammocks rolled up in the blankets, and the consequence was that their health gave way, and scurvy, that terrible disease, made its appearance on board.

The Doctor had been dealing out lemon-juice and lime pastilles every morning for a considerable time, but these usually efficacious remedies had no apparent effect. The malady ran its course, and soon assumed the most frightful forms.

What a sight the unhappy sufferers presented! Their legs swollen to an enormous size, and covered with large dark-blue spots; their gums bleeding, and lips so tumid, that articulation was almost impossible.

Clifton was first attacked by the cruel malady, and he was soon followed by Gripper, Brunton, and Strong. Those who escaped were forced to witness the sufferings of the others, for there was but one living room, and this had to be forthwith turned into a hospital, as within a few days thirteen out of the eighteen men, which composed the crew of the *Forward,* were confined to their hammocks. Pen was not attacked, thanks to his vigorous constitution. Shandon exhibited a few premonitory symptoms, but he succeeded in warding these off by exercise and regimen, and remained tolerably well.

The Doctor attended his patients with unremitting care, and his heart was often wrung with the sight of pain he could not relieve. He did all he could to raise the spirits of the dejected men, and by conversation and sympathy, and ingenious devices, to lighten the monotony of their long, weary days. He read aloud, and drew largely on the stores of his wonderful memory for their amusement; but often and often his stories would be interrupted by a groan or moaning cry from one or other, and he would have to break off, and try anew all the resources of his healing art.

Meantime, his own health remained unimpaired. He became no thinner, and his corpulence was better than the warmest clothing. He often congratulated himself on being like the seal and the whale, so encased in good thick fat that he could easily bear the rigors of an Arctic winter.

Hatteras, for his part, felt nothing, either mentally or physically. The sufferings of his men seemed not to touch him in the least, though, perhaps, he would not allow his emotion to appear, and a close observer might have discovered a humane heart beating under that iron exterior.

The thermometer fell still lower; the deck was quite deserted except by the Esquimaux dogs, who kept howling piteously. The 8th of December arrived, and the Doctor went out as usual to look at the thermometer. The mercury was frozen—completely frozen!

"Forty-four degrees below zero!" he exclaimed, in dismay. Yes! and on this very day the last atom of coal was thrown into the stove.

CHAPTER XXVI
CHRISTMAS

FOR a moment despair gained the upper hand, and death seemed staring the unhappy crew in the face—death from cold. The fire got lower each moment, and the effect was soon felt on the temperature of the room. Johnson went to fetch some of his new combustible, and filled the stove with it, adding tow impregnated with frozen oil, which speedily gave out abundant heat. True, the stench was unbearable, and the boatswain was sufficiently convinced that his substitute for coal would find no favor in the middle-class houses of Liverpool. But what was to be done? It was this fat or nothing.

"And yet," said Johnson, "this stinking stuff may bring us some good after all."

"How's that?" asked the carpenter.

"It will be sure to attract the bears. They will think it a most savory odor."

"Well, but I don't see what we want with bears," replied Bell.

"Friend Bell," returned Johnson, "we can't reckon on any more seals; they have taken their departure for a long time, and if the bears don't furnish their share of combustible material, I don't see what is to become of us."

"You are right, Johnson. We are in a perilous situation —it is frightful to think of it. Only suppose our stock of this fat coming to an end! I see no way, I must confess!"

"Except one."

"And what is that?" asked Bell.

"Except one, Bell, but the captain would never consent to it; and yet it may come to that," added Johnson, shaking his head, for he knew he had only fat enough to last a week.

The old sailor was right. Several bears were seen to leeward, and the few men that remained well gave them chase. But these animals are endowed with such remarkable swiftness and such cunning, that they completely baffle their pursuers. It was found impossible to get near them, and not a single ball took effect, even fired by the best shots.

The crew of the brig were certainly in a serious plight. Forty-eight hours without fire in such a temperature would seal their doom.

At last, on the 20th of December, about 3 P. M., things came to a crisis. The fire burnt out, and the sailors stood around the stove gazing at each other with wild, haggard faces. Hatteras remained motionless in his corner. The Doctor paced up and down in an agitated manner, at his wits' end to devise some expedient, not knowing what to say or do.

But others acted for him now. Shandon, cool and determined, and Pen with flashing angry eyes, and two or three of their comrades who were still able to drag themselves along, went towards Hatteras.

"Captain," said Shandon.

But Hatteras, buried in thought, did not hear him.

"Captain!" he said again, touching his hand.

"Sir!" said Hatteras, starting up.

"Captain, we have no fire."

"Well," replied Hatteras.

"If it is your intention to let us perish with cold," said Shandon with terrible irony, "perhaps you will be kind enough to inform us."

"My intention," replied Hatteras in a grave tone, "is that each man shall do his duty to the end."

"There is something higher than duty, captain—the right of self-preservation. I tell you again we have no fire, and if we don't get one, not a man among us will be alive in two days' time."

"I have no wood," said Hatteras in a hollow voice.

"Very well," exclaimed Pen, passionately; "when people have no wood, they must go and cut it down where it grows."

Hatteras paled with rage, and said:

" Where may that be? "

" On deck," was the insolent reply.

" On deck! " repeated the captain, clenching his fist, his eyes sparkling with indignation.

" Certainly," returned Pen; " when the ship can't sail, burn her."

Hatteras lifted a hatchet when Pen began to speak, and swinging it over his head, would have killed him on the spot, had not the Doctor rushed forward and pulled him aside by main force. The hatchet fell on the ground, sticking fast in the planks.

Johnson, Bell, and Simpson gathered round Hatteras, determined to support his authority, but plaintive moans rose from the sick-beds, and feeble voices were heard imploring fire.

Hatteras had a struggle to command himself sufficiently to speak, but after a few minutes' silence, he said, in a calm tone:

" If we destroyed the ship, how could we get back to England? "

" Perhaps, sir, we might burn those parts that are not absolutely necessary, such as the gunwale," suggested Johnson. " We should always have the boats to fall back upon," said Shandon; " and, moreover, what is there to hinder us from building a smaller ship out of the remains of the old one? "

" Never! " replied Hatteras.

" But, sir——" began several voices at once.

" We have a great quantity of spirits of wine on board," said Hatteras. " Burn it all to the last drop."

" Well, go and fetch the spirits of wine, my men," said Johnson.

By steeping large wicks in this inflammable liquid a pale flame was soon visible in the stove, and the temperature of the room was raised a little.

During the next few days the wind was south, and the thermometer rose a few degree. Some of the sailors ventured out again for a few hours, but ophthalmia and scurvy kept the greater part on board still close prisoners.

But the respite was of short duration, and on the 25th the mercury was again frozen in the tube.

By means of spirits of wine, however, the Doctor managed to thaw it, and discovered to his horror that the temperature was 66° below zero. He had not thought it possible that life could be sustained in such conditions.

The ice lay glittering on the flooring, and a thick fog filled the room, mingled with the snow caused by the condensation of the breath of the inmates. The men could hardly see one another; hands and feet had become almost dead and quite blue. The first symptoms of delirium appeared, and the tongue lost the power of articulation.

From the day that Pen had threatened to burn the ship, Hatteras had almost lived on deck, remaining on the bridge for long hours mounting guard over his treasure: for this wood was like his own flesh, and he would as soon have thought of cutting off a limb as cutting off an inch of it. There he stood, completely armed, and wholly insensible to cold and snow, though the frost had stiffened his clothes, and encased him in an icy covering. Duk always accompanied him, barking and howling.

On the 25th of December, however, he went below for a while, and the Doctor, summoning all his remaining strength, went up to him directly and said:

"Hatteras, we are dying for want of fire."

"Never!" said Hatteras, understanding the unuttered request that lay in his words.

"It must be done," replied the Doctor, gently.

"Never!" repeated Captain Hatteras even more vehemently; "never will I consent. Let them disobey if they choose!"

Johnson and Bell needed no further permission, but rushed on deck, hatchets in hand. Hatteras heard the wood falling beneath their strokes, and wept.

And this was Christmas Day, so dear to English hearts! the day of family gatherings, when children and children's children cluster so joyously about the fireside. What a bitter contrast this to those festive hours, ringing with the glad laugh of merry children round their Christmas tree! to those tables groaning with the abundance of roast beef and plum-pudding, and mince pies, and all the rich Christmas viands! Nothing here on all sides but pain, and misery, and despair; nothing of Christmas, save the "Yule log," and this—part of a lost ship, lost amid the ice and snow of the frigid zone.

However, the fire soon made its reanimating influence felt, and steaming bowls of tea and coffee lent their aid in restoring the benumbed men to some degree of physical comfort, and even revived the dying hope in their hearts.

The 1st of January was marked by an unexpected discovery. The weather was mild, and the Doctor had resumed his usual studies. He was reading Sir Edward Belcher's " Narrative of his Polar Expedition," when he came across a passage he had never noticed before. He read it over and over again, to satisfy himself it was no mistake.

Sir Edward stated that after reaching the end of the Queen's Channel, he met with traces of human habitation on the shore.

" ' We found the remains,' he said, ' of dwellings far superior to any of those which would be inhabited by the wandering tribes of Esquimaux. The walls had good foundations, and there was a paved space, covered with fine gravel. We saw a great quantity of bones of reindeer, and walrus, and seals. *We found coal there.*' "

As the Doctor read these concluding words, an idea crossed his mind, which he determined to communicate to Hatteras forthwith, so, book in hand, he went in search of him.

" Coal, did you say ! " exclaimed the captain, when he told him of his discovery.

" Yes, Hatteras, coal ! that's to say, our means of salvation."

" But coal on this barren coast," returned Hatteras. " No, that's not possible ! "

" Why doubt it, Hatteras ? Belcher would never have stated the fact if he had not seen it with his own eyes ! "

" Well, granting it to be true, what then, Doctor ? "

" We are not more than a hundred miles from the place where Belcher saw this coal ; and what's an excursion of a hundred miles ? Nothing. Much longer journeys have often been made over the ice in quite as cold weather as this. Let us set off, captain."

" We will ! " exclaimed Hatteras, clutching eagerly at the forlorn hope.

Johnson was speedily informed of the project, which met his hearty approval. He communicated the news to the rest.

" Let them go," whispered Shandon, mysteriously.

But before ever commencing preparations for departure, Hatteras took the utmost pains to calculate the exact position of the *Forward*. This was a matter of the utmost importance, for otherwise it would be impossible to find the ship again after once leaving her. After much difficulty he succeeded in making an accurate reckoning, and went down again to compare it with his chart.

For a minute he looked as if stupefied, and then asked the Doctor if he knew the exact latitude when they had taken up winter quarters.

"Of course I do," was the reply. "It was 78° 15″ latitude, and 95° 35″ longitude."

"Well, then," returned Hatteras, in a low voice, "our ice-field is drifting, we are two degrees farther north, and more to the west, and three hundred miles at least from your coal depot."

"And these poor fellows are not aware of it!" exclaimed the Doctor.

"Hush!" said Hatteras, laying his finger on his lips.

CHAPTER XXVII
PREPARATIONS FOR DEPARTURE

CAPTAIN HATTERAS would not acquaint his men with the discovery he had made, and he was right, for there was no knowing into what excesses despair might have led them, had they felt themselves thus irresistibly dragged farther north.

To himself, however, the knowledge of the fact afforded the greatest joy. This was the first happy moment he had known for many long months; but not even to the Doctor did he speak of it, and he had such perfect self-control that his friend never suspected his hidden sentiments, though he sometimes wondered to himself what could make his eye so unusually bright.

By getting nearer the Pole, the *Forward* had got farther away from the coal-bed mentioned by Sir Edward Belcher, and instead of a hundred miles, it would be necessary to go back at least two hundred and fifty miles. However, after a short consultation with Clawbonny and Johnson, it was resolved to adhere to the project.

They reckoned that the journey would take forty days at the outside, and Johnson undertook to provide all that was necessary.

His first care was the sledge. It was of Greenland make, thirty-five inches wide and twenty-four feet long, made of long planks bent up back and front, and stretched in the form of a bow by strong ropes to give it elasticity. This sledge would run easily over hard ice, but in snowy weather a wooden framework was added, which lifted it a little above the ground. To make it glide along still more smoothly, the bottom was rubbed over, in Esquimaux style, with a mixture of sulphur and snow.

Six dogs were selected as steeds for this equipage—strong, hardy animals, in spite of their lean, skinny appearance, and able to drag 2,000 pounds weight without being over fatigued. The harness was in good condition, and altogether the sledge was a reliable affair.

For camping, a tent was provided, in the event of being unable to construct a snow hut; also a large Mackintosh sheet to spread over the snow, to prevent it from melting by contact with the body; several woolen blankets and buffalo skins, and the Halkett-boat.

The stores consisted of five cases of pemmican, weighing about 450 pounds; twelve gallons of spirits of wine, tea, and biscuit; together with a little " portable kitchen," and a quantity of wicks and tow; besides powder and shot, and two double-barreled guns. Each man, following Captain Parry's example, was provided with an india-rubber belt, in which tea, coffee, and water could be carried, and kept in a liquid state by the heat of the body, accelerated by the motion of walking.

Johnson bestowed special pains on the manufacture of the snow-shoes. These were fixed on wood, and strapped with leather. They served the purpose of skates, but, where the ground was very hard and slippery, deer moccasins were better, and each member of the party was therefore furnished with two pairs of both.

These important preparations occupied four whole days. Every morning Captain Hatteras reckoned his exact position, and found that the ice-fields had ceased moving. It was absolutely necessary to ascertain this for the sake of returning.

Whom to choose for the expedition was the next consideration.   This was a matter of deep thought to Hatteras, for many of the men were useless to take; and yet would it be wise to leave them behind?   However, since the lives of all depended on the success of the enterprise, he finally decided to take none with him but tried and trusty followers.

Shandon consequently was excluded, but he showed no regrets on that score.   James Wall was out of the question, for he could not rise from his hammock.

None of the sick men were getting worse, happily, and as their treatment consisted mainly in constant friction and large doses of lemon-juice, the Doctor's presence was not required.   He therefore resolved to head the party, and no one made the faintest protest against his decision.

Johnson was most desirous to accompany the captain in his perilous undertaking; but Hatteras took him aside, and in an affectionate, almost agitated manner, said:

" Johnson, I have no confidence in anyone but yourself; you are the only officer to whom I can entrust my ship.   I must know you are here to watch Shandon and the others. Winter has them fast in iron chains, but who knows what wickedness they may be capable of?   You shall be furnished with formal instructions to assume command if necessary. You will be my second self.   Our absence will extend to four or five weeks at most, and I shall be easy in having you here while I am obliged to be away.   You must have wood, Johnson, I know, but as much as possible spare my poor ship. You understand me, Johnson? "

" Yes, captain," said the old sailor, " and I will remain here since it is your wish."

" Thanks! " said Hatteras, grasping his hand warmly. Then he added: " If you do not see us come back, Johnson, wait till the ice breaks up, and try to push farther towards the Pole; but should the others oppose this, don't think of us at all, but take the ship back to England."

" Is this truly your will, captain? "

" My absolute will," replied Hatteras.

" Your commands shall be obeyed," said Johnson simply.

The Doctor felt the loss of his old friend, but he knew Hatteras had decided for the best.

The two others chosen were Bell and Simpson.   Bell was in good health, and a brave, devoted fellow, and would be most useful in putting up the tent, and making snow-houses. Simpson was a man of softer mould, but he was willing, and might be serviceable in hunting and fishing.

Thus, then, the detachment consisted of Hatteras, Clawbonny, Bell, Simpson, and the faithful Duk—four men and seven dogs.

During the first few days of January, the temperature remained on the average of 33° below zero. Hatteras eagerly watched for a change of weather, and often consulted the barometer: but in these high latitudes no reliance can be placed on any barometer. When it is high, it often brings snow and rain, and when it is low, fine weather.

At last, on the 5th of January, an east wind brought a temporary rise in the temperature of 15°, and Hatteras resolved to start next day. He was impatient to be off, for he could not bear to see the brig cut to pieces before his eyes. The entire poop had already gone to feed the stove.

On the 6th, therefore, the order to set out was given. The Doctor gave his last injunctions to his patients, and Bell and Simpson shook hands silently with their comrades. Hatteras was about to bid his men " good-by " aloud, but black scowling looks met him on all sides, and he fancied a mocking smile lurked on Shandon's lips. He was silent, and perhaps for an instant hesitated about leaving; but it was too late now to alter his plan. The sledge was packed and harnessed, and Bell had already gone on. The rest of the party followed, and Johnson accompanied them for about a quarter of a mile. Hatteras would not allow him to go farther, so he bade them farewell with many a lingering look, and returned to the brig.

CHAPTER XXVIII
ACROSS THE ICE-FIELDS

THE little band of adventurers went on towards the southeast. Simpson managed the sledge, aided zealously by Duk. Hatteras and the Doctor brought up the rear, and Bell was the scout in advance.

The rising of the thermometer announced an approaching snow storm, which soon began and greatly increased the difficulties of the way. The surface of the ice was very uneven and rugged, and the dogs were constantly stumbling, at great risk of overturning the sledge.

Hatteras and his companions wrapped themselves closely in their skin clothing, of rude Greenland make, and certainly somewhat unshapely, but admirably adapted to the necessities of the climate. The hoods were drawn right over head and face, and nothing left exposed but eyes, nose, and mouth.

They walked along over the monotonous plain almost in silence, for it was torture to open the mouth: sharp crystals formed immediately between the lips, which even the warm breath was powerless to melt.

Numerous traces of bears and foxes were met with, but not a solitary animal was perceived during the whole of the first day. It did not matter much, for it would have been both useless and dangerous to hunt them, since the sledge was heavily enough loaded already.

It is customary generally with exploring parties to lighten the sledges by depositing stores on the way at intervals, which are taken up on returning; but this was impracticable on ice-fields, which might drift off at any moment.

At mid-day Hatteras made a halt for breakfast, which consisted of pemmican and hot tea, and glad enough were the poor travelers of the reviving beverage.

After resting an hour, the march was resumed, and by night they had gone about twenty miles. Men and dogs were tired out: but in spite of fatigue, a snow-hut must be built before they could lie down to sleep. This was an hour and a half's work. Bell showed great skill in cutting the blocks and laying one above another in a circular dome-like form. The snow served for mortar to fill up all interstices, and became so hard that the whole hut soon appeared as if made of one solid piece. The only entrance was a narrow opening, into which they had to crawl on all-fours. The Doctor squeezed in somehow, though it was rather a tight fit, and the others followed. The portable kitchen was lighted, and supper speedily prepared.

When the repast was over, the mackintosh was spread on the ground, and shoes and socks put to dry by the little spirit stove, and then three of the party wrapped themselves in their warm blankets and went to sleep, leaving the fourth man to keep watch and prevent the opening from getting stopped up. This was necessary for the safety of the rest, and each man had charge in his turn.

Duk shared his master's quarters. His brethren were outside, and found a bed for themselves among the snow.

Sleep soon came to the weary men, and at 3 A. M. the Doctor rose to mount guard. He could hear the storm raging without, but within the hut the temperature was tolerably comfortable.

Next morning at six o'clock the monotonous march began once more. It was easier walking, however, for the snow had hardened. They often came across what looked like cairns, or possibly Esquimaux hiding-places, and the Doctor could not rest easy till he had demolished one; but, to his disappointment, he found it was nothing but a block of ice.

" What did you hope to find, Mr. Clawbonny? " asked Hatteras. " Are we not the first that have ever trod this ice? "

" Likely enough, and yet who knows! "

" Don't let us waste time in useless searches," returned the captain. " I am in haste to get back to my ship, even without the coal we so need! "

" Doctor," said Hatteras, often, " I was wrong to leave the brig. It was a mistake. A captain's place is on board, and nowhere else."

" Johnson is there."

" I know that, but let us make haste."

The sledge went swiftly on, and owing to some peculiar phosphorence in the snow, seemed traversing red-hot ground, raising a cloud of sparks as it ran along. The Doctor hurried forward to examine this phenomenon more closely, but all of a sudden, in trying to jump over a hummock, he disappeared. Bell ran towards the spot immediately, but the Doctor was nowhere to be seen, and though he shouted his name, there was no reply till the captain, who came up just then with Simpson, called out:

" Doctor! where are you? "

" Down here, in a hole," was the reassuring answer. " Throw me the end of a rope, and let me get to the earth's surface again."

The hole into which he had fallen was full ten feet deep, but his three companions succeeded in drawing him safely up, though not without difficulty.

" Are you hurt? " asked Hatteras.

" Never a bit! there is no fear of me," he replied, shaking the snow off his good-tempered face.

" But how did it happen? "

" Oh! it is all owing to refraction—always that stupid refraction," he said, laughing. " I thought I was going to jump over a gap not more than a foot broad, and I found myself in a hole ten feet deep. Take a lesson from me, and don't venture a step till you have tried the ground with your staff. There is no trusting to one's senses in this region, for both ears and eyes deceive one."

" Can we go on? " said Hatteras.

" Oh, go on, by all means. This little tumble will do me more good than harm."

Once more they set off, and by the time they halted for the night had gone a distance of five-and-twenty miles.

While the hut was being constructed for their night quarters, nothing would serve the Doctor but he must climb to the top of an iceberg and look about him.

The moon was almost full, and shining in the clear sky with extraordinary brilliancy. The stars, too, were wondrously beautiful, and as he gazed over the plain below, the surpassing grandeur of the spectacle amply repaid for the fatigue of the ascent. It resembled some vast cemetery full of monuments of every description, in which twenty generations lay slumbering; and in spite of cold and weariness, the Doctor could not tear himself from the scene. He was so absorbed and entranced that his companions could scarcely persuade him to come down. But the hut was ready, and it was high time to think of sleep, so he crept in after the others, and was soon in the arms of Morpheus.

The next few days passed without any particular incidents, sometimes making quicker and sometimes slower progress, till they reached the 15th of January.

The moon was now in her last quarter, and only visible for a short time. The sun, though never appearing above the horizon, made a sort of dim twilight for about six hours in the day. But it was too faint to show the road, and the travelers had to steer the way by the compass. Bell went first, and set up a landmark for the rest to follow, so as to keep in a straight course as far as possible.

On the 15th of February, which was on a Sunday, Hatteras calculated that they had made a hundred miles. He devoted the morning to repairing sundry articles and to religious worship, and started again about noon.

The temperature was cold, only 32° above zero, and the air very clear.

Suddenly, without any warning and without any apparent reason, a sort of vapor began to rise from the ground, and condensed into minute frozen particles, instantly filling the atmosphere like dense fog, and rising to the height of about ninety feet, where it remained stationary. It was impossible to see a foot before one, and long prismatic crystals hung from everybody's clothes.

This was the frost rime that had surprised the travelers, and its first effect was to make them wish to keep close together. Each began feeling and fumbling for the other, and calling out his name. But in this dense fog there was not only no seeing, but no hearing, for sounds cannot pass through it.

The same thought apparently struck each to fire a gun as a signal. But the confusion that followed was indescribable, for the noise was echoed far and wide, in one continuous roll.

Each man was left to his own instinct, and each acted in a characteristic manner. Hatteras stopped short, and stood with his arms folded to wait patiently. Simpson managed to keep fast by the sledge. Bell felt for foot-marks on the ground, and the Doctor went tumbling about among the great blocks of ice, now going to the left and then to the right, and the losing himself completely.

After stumbling along in this fashion for five minutes or so, he said to himself:

"This can't last! Strange climate; rather too freaky for my taste. There is no reckoning on it. Hallo, captain, where are you?" he shouted again.

But there was no response, and he resolved to reload his gun and fire a second time.

While doing this, he fancied he could discern the outlines of some dark object close by, and he called out:

"At last! Hatteras, Bell, Simpson, who is it? Speak!"

A low growl was the only reply.

"Ha! what can this be?" thought the good little man.

The moving mass came nearer, its proportions being increased by the fog rather than diminished. A terrible suspicion crossed the Doctor's mind.

"It is a bear!" he said to himself. And a bear it actually was, of huge dimensions. Bruin had lost his way in the fog like his neighbors, and was going hither and thither in all directions, almost knocking right against his enemies, though he little imagined their proximity.

"I'm in a pretty fix now," thought the Doctor, remaining quite still.

The animal sometimes came so close to him that he could feel his breath, and the next minute he disappeared in the frost rime. Sometimes he caught a glimpse of enormous paws beating the air, and more than once they touched him so near that his clothes were torn by the sharp claws, and he leaped back in affright.

But in leaping back the Doctor felt his foot struck rising ground, and by the help of his hand he succeeded in getting on the top of first one block of ice and then another and another, till he reached at last the summit of an iceberg nearly ninety feet high, and found himself in clear air, quite above the level of the fog.

"That's capital!" he said, and looking round, discovered his three companions also emerging from the frost rime.

"Hatteras!"

"Doctor Clawbonny!"

"Bell!"

"Simpson!"

These exclamations were almost simultaneous. The sky was illumined by a magnificent halo, which tinged the frost rime with its soft rays, and gave it the appearance of liquid silver, from which the peaks of the icebergs issued.

The travelers discovered they were in a sort of amphitheater about a hundred feet in diameter, and though they had each clambered up different icebergs, and were considerable distances apart, yet, thanks to the intense cold, and extreme purity of the atmosphere, they could hear one another's voice quite easily, and were able to carry on a conversation.

"Where's the sledge?" asked the captain.

"Down there, eighty feet below," replied Simpson.

"Is it all right?"

"First-rate."

"And what about the bear?" inquired the Doctor.

"What bear?"

"The bear I met, that almost made me break my neck."

"A bear!" exclaimed Hatteras; "we had better look after him."

"No, no!" said the Doctor; "we should only lose ourselves, and gain nothing by it."

"Well, but suppose he fell on our dogs?"

At that very moment Duk began barking furiously, and Hatteras exclaimed:

"That's Duk! I'm sure there's something up! I'm going down, at any rate."

"Stop, Hatteras, stop! I think the fog is clearing," said the Doctor.

It was not clearing, but it was gradually getting lower, like a pond getting empty. It seemed to sink into the earth from whence it had risen.

Soon the top of the sledge appeared, then the dogs; then about thirty other animals were seen, and large, shapeless moving masses. Duk was leaping and jumping about, appearing and disappearing in the fog.

"Foxes!" exclaimed Bell.

"Bears!" said the Doctor. "I can see one—three—five!"

"Let's see to the dogs and the provisions," shouted Simpson.

It was high time, for a whole pack of foxes and bears had attacked the sledge and were making fine havoc of the food. The dogs barked might and main, but their fury had no effect, and the work of pillage was fast going on.

"Fire!" cried Hatteras, discharging his gun.

His companions followed his example immediately, to the evident alarm of the four-footed robbers, for the whole troop scampered away at once, and speedily disappeared among the icebergs.

CHAPTER XXIX
THE CAIRN

THIS peculiar phenomenon of the Arctic regions lasted about three-quarters of an hour, so that the bears and foxes had time to regale themselves comfortably. The supply was most opportune for the poor starving animals, and they had not been backward in profiting by it, for the marks of their sharp claws were all over the sledge. Cases of pemmican were broken open and emptied, bags of biscuits devoured, tea strewn among the snow, and one keg of spirits of wine smashed to pieces, and all the contents lost; blankets, and skins, and coverings tossed here and there in all directions—nothing had been left untouched by the famished and voracious beasts.

"This is a bad job for us," said Bell, contemplating the scene of desolation.

"One that can't be remedied, I fear," added Simpson.

"We had better see what mischief has been done first, and then talk about it afterwards, I think," said the Doctor.

Hatteras made no remark, but busied himself silently in collecting the scattered bags and cases. The loss of any of the spirits of wine was most vexatious, for without it there would be an end to tea and coffee, or any warm beverage whatever. After picking what biscuits and pemmican were still eatable, the Doctor made an estimate of the damage done, and found that 200 pounds of pemmican and 150 pounds of biscuits had disappeared; so that if the journey was to be continued, they must be content with half the usual rations.

It became a question, therefore, whether to go on or return to the ship, and recommence the expedition. But to return would be to lose 150 miles already gained, and, moreover, to return without the coal would have a most disastrous effect on the crew!

All but Simpson decided in favor of going on, even at the price of the hardest privations. The poor fellow's health had begun to give away, and he was anxious to be back on board ship; but, finding he stood alone in his opinion, he yielded to the others, and resumed his place beside the sledge.

The monotonous journey went on much as usual, unmarked by any fresh event till the 17th of January, when the whole aspect of the region suddenly changed. A great number of sharp towering peaks, like pointed pyramids, appeared on the horizon, and the soil in certain places rose above the snow. It was composed apparently of gneiss, schist, and quartz, with some admixture of chalky rock. The travelers had reached firm land once more, and this land could be none other than New Cornwall.

The Doctor congratulated himself on being off the treacherous ice, and only a hundred miles from Cape Belcher; but, strangely enough, the difficulties of the journey increased rather than diminished, and they soon had cause to regret the smooth, almost unbroken ice over which the sledge could glide with comparative ease, for the road was rugged in the extreme, full of sharp rocks, and precipices, and crevices. They were obliged to make a circuitous course towards the interior, to get to the top of the steep cliffs on the coast, and across tremendous gorges, where the snow was piled up thirty or forty feet high.

It was hard work to drag the sledge along, for the dogs were exhausted, and the men had to harness themselves and help. Several times everything had to be taken out of it before they could get to the top of some steep hill, the glassy sides of which afforded no foothold for man or beast.

On the evening of the second day after their arrival on the coast of New Cornwall, the men were so completely exhausted that they were unable to erect their usual snow-hut. They passed the night under the tent, wrapped in their buffalo skins, and tried to dry their wet stockings by the heat of their own bodies. Before morning the thermometer fell to 44° and the mercury froze.

The inevitable consequences of such exposure followed. Simpson's health was shaken alarmingly; an obstinate cold clung to him, and violent rheumatic pains, which obliged him to lie all day on the sledge. Bell had to take his place in guiding the dogs, for though he was far from well, he was not unable to keep about. The Doctor also suffered considerably, but he never complained; he held out bravely, and went first to act as scout. Hatteras, impassible, impenetrable, and hard as ever, was as strong as the first day, and walked silently behind the sledge.

On the 20th of January the temperature was so low that the slightest exertion was followed by complete prostration; and yet the road was so rugged and difficult that the Doctor,

and Bell, and Hatteras, too, had to harness themselves
to the sledge with the dogs. Constantly jolting over the
uneven ground had broken the front part, and it was necessary to stop and repair it. Delays like these soon became
frequent.

The three men were jogging along through a deep ravine,
where the snow was up to their waists, and the perspiration
was streaming from every pore in spite of the intense cold,
when Bell, who was nearest the Doctor, looked at him in
alarm, and, without saying a word, caught up a handful of
snow, and began rubbing his worthy friend's face as vigorously as possible, to the great bewilderment of the Doctor,
who tried to push him off, exclaiming:

"What now, Bell?"

But Bell still went on rubbing, till the little man's eyes,
nose, and mouth were all full of snow, and he called out
again:

"I say, Bell, what's all this? Are you mad? What do
you mean?"

"I mean this, that you have me to thank for it if you still
have a nose."

"A nose?" replied the Doctor, putting up his hand to his
face.

"Yes, Mr. Clawbonny, you were completely frost-bitten.
Your nose was quite white when I looked at you, and without my rough treatment you would have lost an ornament
that is very necessary in life, though rather inconvenient in
traveling."

Bell was right. A few minutes longer, and the Doctor's
nose would have been gone, but, happily, friction had restored the circulation, and the danger was past.

"Thanks, Bell; I'll do as much for you some day, perhaps."

"I quite reckon on it, and Heaven grant we may have
no worse misfortunes to come!" replied the carpenter.

"Ah! you refer to Simpson; the poor fellow is in great
pain."

"Have you any fear for him?" asked Hatteras, quickly.

"I have captain."

"What is it you apprehend, Doctor?"

"A violent attack of scurvy. His legs are swelling already, and his gums are affected. There he lies wrapped up

in the blankets, half-frozen, and these constant jolts aggravate his sufferings. I pity him, Hatteras, but I can do nothing for him!"

"Poor Simpson!" murmured Bell.

"Perhaps we might rest a day or two," suggested the Doctor.

"Rest a day or two!" cried Hatteras, "when the lives of eighteen men hang on our return!"

"Still——" began the Doctor.

"Clawbonny, Bell, listen to me. We have only food enough for twenty days! Can we afford to waste an instant?"

Neither the Doctor nor Bell made any reply, and the sledge went on.

In the evening the little cavalcade stopped at the foot of an ice-hill, in which Bell soon cut out a cave to shelter them for the night.

The Doctor stayed up with Simpson, while the others slept, for the scurvy had made frightful ravages on the poor man's frame already, and he moaned piteously with pain.

"Ah! Mr. Clawbonny," he said.

"Come, cheer up, my lad!" replied the Doctor.

"I shall never go back! I feel it! I can go no farther; I would rather die."

The Doctor only replied by redoubling his attentions. Forgetting his own fatigue, he busied himself in preparing some soothing draught for his suffering patient, for lime-juice and friction were now powerless.

When morning came, the unfortunate man had to be replaced on the sledge, though he entreated to be left behind to die in peace. The weary march was resumed, amid increasing difficulties, for icy fogs pierced the travelers to the very marrow, and hail and snow lashed their faces with merciless severity.

Duk, like his master, seemed to feel nothing, and showed wonderful sagacity in finding out the best road.

On the morning of the 23rd, when it was nearly quite dark, as there was a new moon, Duk was suddenly missing. He had been out of sight for several hours, and Hatteras grew uneasy, for the tracks of bears were pretty numerous. He was just considering what was best to be done, when he caught the soud of loud, furious barking in the distance, and, urging the sledge forward, soon came up to his faithful beast at the bottom of a ravine.

Duk was standing motionless in front of a sort of cairn, and barking violently.

"This time it is a cairn, at all events," said the Doctor.

"What's that to us?" asked Hatteras.

"Hatteras, if it is a cairn, it may contain some valuable document for us, or perhaps it is a depot of provisions, and that is worth our while to look at."

"And what European can have been this way?" said the captain, shrugging his shoulders.

"But though no European has been, may not the Esquimaux have been here and made a hiding-place for the spoils of their hunting and fishing? It is quite in keeping with their habits."

"Well, well, Clawbonny, examine it if you choose, but I question if you get anything for your pains."

By the help of mattocks the cairn was soon demolished, and a box was discovered, inside which was a paper quite damp with moisture. The Doctor seized it with a beating heart, and handed it to Hatteras, who read as follows:——

"Altam——, *Porpoise* 13 Dec. 1860 12° longitude, S 55° lat."

"The *Porpoise!*" said the Doctor.

"The *Porpoise!*" repeated Hatteras. "I know no vessel of that name that has been in these seas."

"It is quite evident that whatever vessel she is, her crew, or possibly some of her shipwrecked men, passed this way less than two months ago," replied Clawbonny.

"That is quite certain," added Bell.

"What shall we do?" asked the Doctor.

"Continue our journey," replied Hatteras, coldly. "I know nothing of the *Porpoise,* but I know that the brig *Forward* is waiting our return."

CHAPTER XXX
THE DEATH OF SIMPSON

THE journey was resumed, each of the party absorbed in his own reflections about the unexpected discovery just made. Hatteras knit his brows uneasily, and said to himself:

" What vessel can this be? What is she doing so near the Pole? "

The Doctor and Bell only thought of going to the rescue of some poor fellows like themselves, or being rescued by them.

But before long they were engrossed enough with their own dangers and difficulties, for their situation became hourly more perilous.

Simpson was getting gradually worse, and the Doctor's practiced eye saw death rapidly approaching. He could do nothing for him; he was suffering acutely himself from ophthalmia, which might end in total blindness without care. The twilight was strong enough now to cause a glaring reflection on the snow which burnt the eyes. Spectacles would have been some protection, but it was impossible to wear them, as the glasses became encrusted with ice immediately, and consequently perfectly opaque, and yet it was necessary to keep a constant look-out to avoid accidents. This must be done at all risks, so Bell and the Doctor agreed to undertake the duty in turn, and bandage their eyes in the intervals.

On the 25th of January the road become even more dangerous and difficult, from the steep declivities they met with constantly, when one false step would have precipitated them into deep ravines.

Towards evening a violent tempest swept over the snowy ridges, and soon increased to such a hurricane, that they were forced to stop and lie down on the ground. But the temperature was so low that they would all inevitably have been frozen to death, had not Bell succeeded after much difficulty in making a snow hut, in which they took shelter and recruited themselves scantily with a few morsels of pemmican and some hot tea. There were only four gallons of spirits of wine now remaining, as it was not only used in making tea and coffee, but in getting water to drink, for it must not be imagined that snow can be employed to quench thirst without being melted. In temperate countries, where the thermometer is scarcely ever so low as freezing point, it might not be injurious, but beyond the polar circle it is quite a different matter. The snow there is so intensely cold, that one could no more lay hold of it with the naked hand than red-hot iron; consequently, there is such a difference of temperature between it and the stomach, that swal-

lowing any portion would actually cause suffocation.   The
Esquimaux would rather endure prolonged agonies of thirst
than attempt to relieve it with snow.

At three in the morning, when the storm outside was at
the worst, the Doctor was taking his turn at watch, and
sitting in a corner of the hut, leaning against the wall, when
a piteous moan from Simpson aroused his attention.   He
rose hastily to go to him, and struck his head against the
roof, but thinking nothing more of it, he stooped down beside Simpson, and began rubbing his blue swollen legs.   He
had continued the friction for about a quarter of an hour,
when he wanted to shift his position.   On trying to get up,
for he had been kneeling, he knocked his head against the
roof a second time.

" This is strange! " he said to himself, and put his hand
to feel above him.   The roof was sinking, there was no
mistake.

" Quick, quick, friends! " he exclaimed, rousing Bell and
Hatteras, who started up in alarm, and in their turn struck
their heads against the roof.

" We shall be crushed! " cried the Doctor.   " Out! out!
this minute."

It was pitch-dark inside, but they managed to drag Simpson through the opening, and just saved themselves in time,
for the next minute the entire hut fell in with a loud noise.

The unfortunate travelers were now exposed to the full
fury of the tempest, in addition to the extreme cold.   Hatteras hastened to put up the tent; but it would not stand
before the violence of the hurricane, and all they could do
was to shelter themselves beneath the canvas, which was
soon covered with a thick coating of snow, and preserved
the poor fellows from being frozen alive.

Towards morning the storm abated, and the little party
prepared to start afresh.   In harnessing the dogs, Bell discerned that the wretched, half-starved animals had begun
to gnaw their leather traces, and two of the beasts were evidently ill, and would not be able to go very far.

They set out again, however, for sixty miles more had
yet to be traversed before they reached the goal.

On the 26th, Bell, who was in advance, called out suddenly
to his companions.   On hastening towards him, he pointed
out a gun placed bolt upright against a mass of ice.

Hatteras lifted it up, and found it loaded and in good condition.

"The men belonging to the *Porpoise* cannot be far off!" exclaimed the Doctor.

On examination, the gun proved to be of American manufacture, and the very touch of it sent a thrill through the veins of the captain.

"Forward!" he said, in hollow tones, and the cavalcade marched on, down the steep sides of the mountains. Simpson appeared to be insensible; his strength was too far gone now to moan.

The storm had by no means ceased, and the sledge went slower and slower. Only a few miles' progress was made in twenty-four hours, and, notwithstanding the severest economy, the stock of provisions was fast decreasing; but as long as more than enough remained for the journey back, Hatteras pushed forward.

On the 27th, a sextant was found half buried in the snow, and then a gourd still containing some brandy, or rather a lump of ice, in the center of which all the spirit had taken refuge in the form of a ball of snow.

It was evident that Hatteras had unintentionally got on the track of some great disaster, for in pursuing the only practicable road, he was constantly finding evidences of a terrible shipwreck. The Doctor kept a sharp look-out for any fresh cairns, but had seen none hitherto.

He felt saddened by the thought, however, that even should any poor creature be discovered, he could do nothing to help them. His companions and himself were beginning to be in want of everything. Their clothes were torn, and their provisions getting very scant. Should the shipwrecked crew be numerous, they would all perish with hunger. Hatteras appeared anxious to hurry away from the chance of meeting them; but was he not right? Was he not responsible for the lives of his men? Ought he to compromise their safety by bringing strangers on board?

Yet these strangers were fellow-men, perhaps fellow-countrymen! Ought they to be abandoned without at least an effort to save them? The Doctor asked Bell his opinion about it, but could get no reply. Suffering had hardened his heart. Clawbonny did not dare to appeal to Hatteras—all he could do was to trust to Providence.

Towards evening Simpson grew worse, and his end seemed near. His limbs were rigid, and his face wore a terrible despairing look, which changed to one of fierce vindictive rage, whenever his glance fell on Hatteras. A whole volume of accusations and reproaches, perhaps not unmerited, might be read in the expression of his eye.

Hatteras did not go near him; he evidently shunned his presence, and was more tacitun, reserved, and incommunicative than ever.

It was a fearful night. The storm raged with redoubled violence, and three times the tent had been torn down, and the snow-drift had beat piteously on the unsheltered men, blinding their eyes, freezing them to the marrow, and cutting their faces with the sharp pieces of ice broken off the surrounding icebergs. The dogs howled lamentably, and poor Simpson lay dying. Bell succeeded once more in securing the tent, which, frail as it was, protected them from snow, if not from cold, but a sudden blast tore it up a fourth time, and whirled it completely away.

" Really this is beyond endurance! " exclaimed Bell.

"Courage! " said the Doctor, catching hold of his arm to keep himself from being blown down the ravine.

The death-rattle was heard in Simpson's throat. Suddenly he made one expiring effort, half raised himself, shook his clenched fist at Hatteras, who looked at him with fixed steady gaze, and fell back lifeless, with the unspoken execration on his lips.

" Dead! " exclaimed the Doctor.

" Dead! " echoed Bell.

Hatteras came forward to look, but was driven back by the wind. The dead man counted him his murderer, but he was not overwhelmed by the accusation, though a tear escaped his eye, and stiffened on his pale cheek.

This was the first of the crew that had fallen a victim— the first who would never return to England—the first who paid the penalty with his life of the captain's indomitable obstinacy.

The Doctor and Bell gazed at him with a sort of terror, as he stood motionless the livelong night, resting on his stick, as if defying the tempest that roared about him.

CHAPTER XXXI
THE RETURN TO THE " FORWARD "

ABOUT six in the morning, the wind suddenly shifted north, and became calm. The sky cleared, and the first glimmer of twilight silvered the horizon, to be succeeded in a few days by the golden rays of the sun.

Hatteras went up to his dejected companions, and said in a gentle, sad voice:

" My friends, we are more than sixty miles still from the spot mentioned by Belcher. We have just barely enough food to last us back to the ship. To go farther would be to expose ourselves to certain death, without profit to anyone. We will retrace our steps."

" You have come to a good resolution, Hatteras, I think," said the Doctor. " I would have followed you wherever you had chosen to go : but our strength is diminishing day by day, and we can scarcely drag one leg after the other. I heartily approve of your decision."

" And you are of the same mind, Bell? " asked Hatteras.

" Yes, captain I am," was the reply.

" Very well, then," return Hatteras, " we will give ourselves two days' rest. That is not too much. The sledge is in great need of repair. I think our best plan will be to make a snow-hut, to shelter us till we are ready to begin our journey back."

This point settled, all three set to work with ardor, and soon built up a hut at the bottom of the ravine where they had last halted.

It must have cost Hatteras a tremendous struggle to relinquish his project. All this toil and trouble wasted, and one man's life into the bargain! And how would he be received by the crew, returning thus empty handed? But Hatteras felt he could not hold out longer.

He gave all his attention now to the thorough repair of the sledge. It had not more than 200 lbs. weight to carry, and was soon brought into working trim. The worn-out, tattered garments were mended, and new snow shoes and moccasins replaced the old ones, which were no longer wearable. These necessary occupations took up one entire day and the morning of another, the poor fellows resting themselves at the same time after their sore fatigues, and trying to get up their strength for the weary march back.

Ever since they had been in the hut, the Doctor had re-marked Duk's strange behavior. The animal kept running in and out, and going round and round a heap of snow and ice, giving occasionally a low bark and wagging his tail impatiently, with an inquiring look at his master.

Clawbonny could not understand what ailed the dog, but at last came to the conclusion that his restlessness was caused by the sight of Simpson's corpse, which there had not been time yet to bury. He resolved to have it interred that very day, as they were to set off next morning as soon as it was light.

Bell undertook to assist, and the two, provided with mat-tocks, set off together to dig a deep hole in the bottom of the ravine. The heap round which Duk kept watch seemed the most favorable spot, and they proceed to lift off the ice and snow, which seemed lying in layers. After removing the snow, they attacked the ice; but at the third stroke the Doctor's mattock encountered some hard substance, which proved to be a fragment of a wine bottle. Bell, who was at work on the opposite side, turned up that same instant a crumpled-up bag, in which were some pieces of biscuit in a perfect state of preservation.

"Heigho!" exclaimed the Doctor. "What's this, I wonder?"

He called out to Hatteras, who came up immediately.

Duk still kept on barking, and scratching at the ice with his paws.

"Can we have come upon a depot of provisions?" asked the Doctor.

"Possibly," said Bell.

Hatteras advanced no opinion, but simply said:

"Go on digging."

More fragments of food soon appeared, and then a case of pemmican about a quarter full.

"If it is a depot, the bears have certainly been here before us, for see, nothing is whole!" said Hatteras.

"It is to be feared that is the case," replied Clawbonny, "for——"

He did not finish his sentence, for he was interrupted by an exclamation from Bell, and looking across, saw he had uncovered a human leg!

"A corpse!" cried the Doctor.

"It is no depot," said Hatteras; "it is a tomb."

When the corpse was entirely disinterred, it proved to be that of a young man of not more than thirty years of age. He wore the common dress of Arctic navigators, and the Doctor could not form an opinion as to the date of his death, for the body was in a state of perfect preservation.

Ere long, a second corpse was dug out, a man about fifty apparently, whose countenance bore traces of evident suffering.

"These men have never been buried!" exclaimed the Doctor. "They have met their death by just such an accident as almost befell ourselves."

"You are right, Mr. Clawbonny," replied Bell.

"Go on," said Hatteras.

Bell felt half afraid, for who could say how many more bodies might be under that heap of ice?

"Their snow hut has fallen in," said the Doctor. "Perhaps some poor fellow may be still living under the mass. Let us see."

The whole mass was speedily cleared away, and a third body dragged out; that of a man about forty. His appearance was not so cadaverous as the others, and on examining him closely, the Doctor thought he could perceive some faint tokens of life.

"He is not dead!" he exclaimed, lifting him up with Bell's assistance, and carrying him into the hut; while Hatteras stood motionless and unconcerned, contemplating the scene of the catastrophe.

The Doctor proceeded to strip the exhumed man entirely, and finding no trace of any wound about him, set to work, with Bell, to try the effect of vigorous friction with wisps of tow steeped in spirits of wine. By slow degrees they succeeded in restoring some animation, but the poor fellow was in such a state of utter exhaustion, that he was quite unable to articulate, and his tongue stuck to the roof of his mouth as if frozen.

Leaving Bell to continue the treatment, Dr. Clawbonny searched the pockets of his patient to see if he could find any letters or papers. But they were empty.

He went out to Hatteras, and found him standing with the half-burnt envelope of a letter in his hand, which he had found in the ruins of the hut. This much of the direction written on it was still legible :——

————tamont.

————orpoise.

————w York.

"Altamont!" exclaimed the Doctor. "Ship *Porpoise,* New York!"

"An American!" said Hatteras, with a start.

"I will save him," said the Doctor, "as sure as I'm alive, and we'll get to the bottom then of this mystery."

He returned to Altamont and redoubled his efforts, till he had the satisfaction of bringing the unfortunate man back to life, though not to consciousness. He could neither see, nor hear, nor speak. He was alive, and that was all.

Next morning Hatteras came up to the Doctor and said:

"We cannot delay our return. We must be off!"

"Let us be off by all means, Hatteras. The sledge is not loaded, we can lay this poor fellow on it, and take him with us."

"So be it," said Hatteras; "but let us bury these dead bodies first."

The unknown sailors were laid once more in their icy grave, and poor Simpson's form filled the place of Altamont. A brief prayer was spoken as a last adieu, and then the three men turned silently away, and commenced their journey towards the ship.

Two of the dogs being dead, Duk came and offered his services as plainly as a dumb beast could, and a most effective coadjutor he proved, working with the conscience and the will of a Greenlander.

The return march was unmarked by any particular incidents. February being the coldest month of the Arctic winter, the ice was uniformly hard and unbroken, and though the travelers suffered intensely from the low temperature, they had no fierce storms to contend with during its continuance.

The sun had reappeared since the 31st January, and each day rose higher above the horizon.

The Doctor and Bell were at the end of their strength, and nearly blind and lame. Poor Bell was forced to use crutches.

Altamont still breathed, but he was in a state of complete

insensibility, and sometimes the Doctor despaired, till unremitting care again revived the flickering spark of life.

Hatteras thought night and day of his brig, and full of anxious forebodings and questionings as to the state in which he might find her, he hurried impatiently forward, always in advance of the others.

On the 24th of February, in the early morning, he came to a sudden stop.

About three hundred paces distant he saw a bright red glare, from which an immense volume of black smoke rose up towards the sky.

"Look at that smoke!" he shouted. His heart beat violently, and again he shouted to his companions:

"Look! Down there! All that smoke! My ship is on fire."

"It can't be the *Forward*," said Bell. "We are more than three miles away."

"Yes, it is," replied the Doctor. "It is the mirage which makes her seem so near us."

"Let us run," said Hatteras, rushing forward. His companions followed with what speed they could, leaving Duk to guard the sledge.

An hour afterwards and they came in sight of the vessel. It was a terrible spectacle! The ship was blazing in the midst of the icebergs which surrounded her. Flames enveloped the keel, and Hatteras could catch the sound of her cracking timbers. A few paces distant a man was seen, flinging up his arms wildly, and gazing in mute despair.

This solitary man was old Johnson. Hatteras ran towards him, exclaiming in broken tones: "My ship! my ship!"

"You, captain! Is it you?" cried Johnson. "Stop! Not a step farther!"

"Tell me," said Hatteras, with a terrible look on his face.

"The villains!" replied Johnson. "They set the ship on fire and started off, forty-eight hours ago!"

"Curse them!" said Hatteras fiercely.

Just then a tremendous explosion was heard which shook the whole region, and laid the icebergs flat on the ice. The flames had reached the gunpowder and blown the ship to atoms. For a minute there was a dense cloud of smoke, and then the *Forward* disappeared in a gulf of fire.

Bell and the Doctor came up that same instant, and found the captain overwhelmed with despair. But suddenly he roused himself, and said, in a strong, cheery voice:

"Friends! the cowards have fled! Fortune favors the brave. Johnson and Bell, you have courage; Doctor you have science; I have faith. Yonder is the North Pole. Let's begin again."

Such manly, courageous words put new life into the hearts of his companions, and yet their situation was indeed terrible to contemplate. Four men, and one of them dying, forsaken and left to perish without resources in the very heart of the Polar regions.

THE ADVENTURES OF CAPTAIN HATTERAS ARE CONTINUED IN
"THE DESERT OF ICE."